Corporations
and
Society

**Recent Titles in
Contributions in American Studies
*Series Editor: Robert H. Walker***

CORPORATIONS AND SOCIETY

Power and Responsibility

EDITED BY

WARREN J. SAMUELS

AND

ARTHUR S. MILLER

Contributions in American Studies, Number 88

Greenwood Press

NEW YORK • WESTPORT, CONNECTICUT • LONDON

Library of Congress Cataloging-in-Publication Data

Corporations and society.

(Contributions in American studies, ISSN 0084-9227 ;
no. 88)
Bibliography: p.
Includes index.
1. Corporation law—United States.   2. Industry
and state—United States.   3. Industry—Social aspects—
United States.   I. Samuels, Warren J., 1933-   .
II. Miller, Arthur Selwyn, 1917-   .   III. Series.
KF1414.C675   1987   346.73'066   86-19451
                          347.30666
ISBN 0-313-25072-3 (lib. bdg. : alk. paper)

Library of Congress Catalog Card Number: 86-19451
ISBN: 0-313-25072-3
ISSN: 0084-9227

First published in 1987

Greenwood Press, Inc.
88 Post Road West, Westport, Connecticut 06881

Printed in the United States of America

The paper used in this book complies with the
Permanent Paper Standard issued by the National
Information Standards Organization (Z39.48-1984).

10 9 8 7 6 5 4 3 2 1

Copyright Acknowledgments

Chapter 3 is a summation of part of, including passages from, Martin J. Sklar, *The Corporate
Reconstruction of American Capitalism, 1890-1916: The Market, the Law, and Politics* (Cambridge University Press, forthcoming). The editors wish to thank Cambridge University Press for
permission to reproduce materials from the book.

The editors acknowledge with thanks the cooperation of the *West Virginia Law Review* in which
Morton J. Horwitz's article appeared in Volume 88, Issue 2, Winter 1985-86.

In honor of Adolf A. Berle, Jr.,
and
Gardiner C. Means

The court does not wish to hear argument on the
question whether the provision in the Fourteenth
Amendment to the Constitution, which forbids a State to
deny to any person within its jurisdiction the equal
protection of the laws, applies to these corporations.
We are all of the opinion that it does.

Chief Justice Waite,
Santa Clara Co. v. Southern Pacific Railroad,
118 U.S. 394, 396 (1886)

CONTENTS

PREFACE

This book is divided into four parts. The first treats the complex doctrinal history in which the *Santa Clara* declaration of corporate personhood figured. The second examines judicial linguistics: the definition of reality encapsulated in legal terms and the policy premises and consequences thereof for recreating legal-economic reality. The third examines the arguable specific policy consequences of the larger matrix of legal decisions of which the holding in *Santa Clara* is a part. The fourth offers some lines of reasoning and some specific suggestions for policy, based on the normative premise that the corporation as an institution of private government, thus of social control, should be democratized.

The study of the doctrinal origins of the personhood conception begins with Morton Horwitz's analysis of the several theories of the corporation that competed in the nineteenth century for status as the putative policy basis of legal decision: the natural entity theory, the grant or concession theory, and the artificial entity theory. Horwitz examines these doctrinal conflicts and the larger developments of which they were a manifestation, including the growth of limited liability, the rise of a national stock market, and tensions between liberal individualism and the rise of powerful collective institutions, such as the national corporation and especially of corporate giants. Horwitz also argues that the holding in *Santa Clara* was itself neither definitive nor conclusively dispositive of the critical policy issues; indeed, that the *Santa Clara* holding became a precedent into which eventually was absorbed the natural-entity reasoning formulated in cases over the next three decades.

In the next chapter Martin J. Sklar explores the later conflict between corporate-liberal and corporate-statist solutions to the problem of corporate power and the eventual adaptation of the legal order to corporate capitalism. Sklar argues that the Court widened the sphere of liberty attaching to corporate property and operations, setting limits on the reach of the law while extending the reach of the corporation and effectively extending limited liability of the stockholders to the limited liability of the corporation against the powers of government. The corporation was thus provided with a legal environment conducive to it, in contrast to the use of law supportive of limits upon the structure and behavior of the corporate sector. In terms of legal-economic fundamentals, insofar as the law was responsible for the division of power within the nominally private sector, law was used to reinforce corporate power, especially the power of the corporate giants, and law was kept from being used to protect the freedom and power of other groups against corporate power.

Michael Barzelay and Rogers M. Smith next treat what they call the neoclassical institutionalist view of the corporation (which they also show to be comprised of variegated if not disparate elements) as a model or group of models with little appreciation of historical reality and of the forces at work that have produced the modern corporation. They emphasize the critical role of ideology or political vision in the formation and evolution of legal rules. That role they see as part of the complex interpenetration between natural and social conditions, received legal rules, power structure, and ideology. They explore the changing conception of the corporation as both an effect and a cause in the U.S. political economy, especially the role of differential ideological tendencies regarding the divisions of power within the nominally private sphere and between the nominally private and public spheres. They indicate that the rationality nuances of the neoclassical institutionalist view conflict with the reality of often unintended consequences of policies adopted for other, perhaps more limited, purposes, due to the interactive nature of the total social processes involved. In part through its emphasis on the role of ideology in the formation of the rights governing the actually achieved efficient results, the chapter points to the conflict between the perceived requirement of a competitive market and the engineered belief in the status quo power structure, including corporate giantism, as efficient. This chapter continues the exploration of the preceding chapters into the complex doctrinal history of corporate personhood. It also ties in, through its emphasis on the role of ideology, with the discussion in the next part of judicial language, and, through its emphasis on the logical and substantive possibility of alternative formulations or institutionalizations of private enterprise systems, with the concluding part on democratizing the corporation.

The contributions in part II focus on the role of legal language as social control, specifically how legal terms and concepts, such as corporate personhood, function to define reality for legal purposes. On the basis of these legal definitions of reality, reality itself is made and remade. Warren Samuels begins by outlining certain fundamental considerations on an abstract theoretical level but applied to the concept of corporate personhood. Included are the following themes: legal definitions as the embodiment of social policy; legal meaning as a variable influencing perception and choice and influenced by perception and choice; the relation between belief and power in the construction of the economy as a normative artifact; the place of the personhood conception in the transformation of law in the nineteenth century and the consequent redefinition and reformulation of socioeconomic reality; the complexities of privateness and publicness applicable to the legal institution of the corporation; the differential nuances of individualist and managerialist conceptions of the corporation; and the relation of the personhood conception to both the system of private and public governance and perceptions of corporations as complex organizations of collective action and identity, as in economics.

This positivistic descriptive interpretation is followed by John J. Flynn's normative critique of what he considers to be the misuse of the personhood concept in law. Along with several other contributors, Flynn indicates the legal and constitutional asymmetries consequent to the use of the personhood concept, generally focusing on the selective combinations of empowerment, protection, and exposure, that is, of differential immunities from government action. Where corporations are given constitutional protection, others, exposed to the exercise of protected-unregulated corporate power, are prevented from enlisting the aid of government in the protection of their interests. Not all economic actors are equally protected or immunized from community control through government or from the actions of other economic actors. This is accomplished, in part, through the nondeliberative use of legal concepts as if they were axiomatic definitions with a predetermined and unchanging meaning to be mechanically applied to the "facts" routinely served up for decision. These concepts are treated as reified absolutes, whereas in reality they serve both to channel legal policy making and to obfuscate the making of policy, continuing the pretense that the law is a given—something to be discovered and not made. Legal terms, and the normative premises and preconceptions ensconced within them, thus are vehicles of policy but function or are used in such a way as to obscure rather than enhance the policy process—for example, permitting entry to certain considerations while preventing others from arising, thus selectively channeling but also masking the linking of facts to policy in the light of consequences.

The next chapter, by Aviam Soifer, pursues the nuances of the manipulation of legal language through an analysis of the implicit selectivity contained in the adoption by the courts of what is inexorably selective paternalism. Legal language, such as the personhood concept, functions to mask under the rubric of laissez-faire and similar notions and symbols or myths the exercise of legal (court) social control in such a manner as to reinforce the hegemony of business and its interests and values. In the process, there is inevitably both protection and disablement of interests and also selective perception of paternalism. Judicial language masks the exercise of legal social control (such as legal determination of the division of power within the nominally private sector) simultaneously with channeling that exercise in certain directions rather than others.

The contributions comprising part III explore the policy and performance consequences of such use of law. They focus on the structure, exercise, and consequences of corporate power in an economy dominated by giant corporations, in part in relation to permissive antitrust legislation and enforcement. David Dale Martin continues the identification of legal-constitutional asymmetries by identifying several double standards: how, in part through the use of the personhood concept, incorporation provides protection to the incorporating persons but not protection from them to others; how loosely knit combinations are prohibited from doing what closely knit combinations in corporate form are permitted to do (centralize decision making as to price, output, investment, and allocation of customers); and how a parent company and its wholly owned subsidiary are incapable of conspiring.

In the final chapter in this part, Walter Adams and James W. Brock use the automobile industry as a means of identifying the social consequences that follow from the matrix of legal policy facilitative of corporate power, including the results of the personhood concept. This matrix of policy has abetted the growth of particular structural and behavioral characteristics and certain social results of the exercise of corporate power in that industry. These include urban congestion, automotive air pollution, automotive safety, and the relation between fuel consumption and automobile size. Their analysis demonstrates the policy chain commencing with the differential empowerment consequent to the personhood concept and concluding with the social consequences of corporate policy and behavior as corporate management exercises what can or must be called private governance and social control—concluded only in one sense, because these social consequences have feedback effects on the further empowerment of corporate managements.

The final part begins with Arthur S. Miller's examination of the idea of the corporation as a person in the larger context formed by the convergence of the class system of power, private versus public government, and what he calls the secret or parallel constitution. Miller articulates a point of view that recognizes the political-economic game played by the powerful to use government to shape the economy to their own advantage and to prevent consolidations of social power adverse to their interests. He notes the asymmetry regarding corporate rights and corporate duties so far as government and other interests are concerned. He favors the constitutionalization of the corporation, by which he means redressing the imbalance between the protection offered the corporation and the protection offered others, especially in the light of the private governance nature of the corporation. Miller would thus recognize and control the already de facto constitutional status of the corporation in favor of economic pluralism and democracy.

In the next chapter, Samuel Loescher advances the concept of diverse competition as a supplement to such traditional notions as rivalrous competition, restraint of trade, and economies of scale for use in antitrust regulation. Loescher's focus is on diversity enabling opportunities for independent experimentation as well as socioeconomic pluralism. Such diversity he envisions as a necessary and desirable limit to industrial centralization, not the least so as to promote industrial productivity. He supports a number of measures intended to generate greater diversity of competition.

Daniel Bronstein and Martin Benjamin next question whether such values as honesty, integrity, sympathy, charity, autonomy, and respect for the moral and legal rights of others, which are often valued for their own sake by individuals qua individuals, have any intrinsic status for corporations or, for that matter, any other forms of organization. In a closely reasoned analysis, they argue that corporations are end or goal directed and cannot acknowledge acts as wrong in and of themselves. Thus corporations as goal-directed entities cannot be held to interpersonal standards. They cannot be treated as persons in the same sense as individuals and should not have extended to them the constitutional protections enjoyed by human persons. That this has been the policy of the law has resulted in unresolved problems generic to attempts to reconcile the fiction of legal persons with the logic of corporate behavior, various ideological rationalizations notwithstanding.

In the final chapter, William A. Lovett explores a form of the realization of individualism and economic democracy that, in part through the adoption of the personhood concept, has hitherto been kept from full materialization. He proposes the reformulation of the corporation along the lines of profit sharing and employee stock ownership plans. Interestingly, Lovett's analysis is congruent with that of Friedrich A. von Hayek, discussed by Warren Samuels in chapter 5. Hayek proposes that stockholders individually have the right to determine the distribution of profits between dividends and retained earnings and the elimination of voting rights accompanying corporate ownership of stock in another corporation.

The gravamen of these potential reforms is both simple and fundamental: the existing form of the corporation, abetted in part by judicial construction of the personhood concept, has helped form the market as we know it, but different structural features of the corporation can be adapted to help form different market structures. Whether seen as an economic institution, as private property, as private governance, or as social control, the corporation, whether or not perceived as a person, is not something predetermined. It has always been and it remains today an institution—a means of both the control and liberation of individual power and a set of human beliefs—capable of reformulation. The theme of this book is that the corporation is both less and more than it has hitherto frequently been made out to be. The corporation in its present form is not predeterminedly absolute, and yet it is an important institution of governance and social control. If this book is successful, it will have disabused readers of the finality of the chains of reasoning that have been used to legitimize the status quo corporate system, underscored the critical place of the corporation in the total system of social power, and suggested how complex are the forces at work that have produced the corporation both as it exists and as it may change and be changed. It will also have awakened readers to the fact that more is involved in Berle and Means's treatment of the modern corporation in relation to private property than the issue of ownership versus control, however important that may be. The crux of the matter is the total structure of social power and the complex interrelations between nominally economic (or market) and legal forces, which in our society importantly help drive the total system.

1

INTRODUCTION: CORPORATE
AMERICA

Our thesis is that the currently popular deterministic explanations are in-
accurate and misleading, that concentration is largely an artificial, institutional phenomenon which originates in, or derives sustenance from, the
actions and policies of the federal government. Our study indicates that some
of these policies, whether or not so intended, have had a profound effect
on the structure of the economy, that they have served to promote concentration and to restrict and weaken competition; in short, that the federal
government—although by tradition, popular regard, and legal mandate the
defender of competition—has by a process of function perversion become
one of the principal bulwarks of concentration and monopoly.

Walter Adams and Horace Gray[1]

The United States is the corporate society par excellence. Corporations are the
"dominant social invention" of the past century. "The corporation," economist
Robert Lekachman observes, "occupies a place as important in our time as that
of the Holy Roman Church in medieval Europe or of the monarch who ruled by
reason of divine right during the sixteenth and seventeenth century heyday of
mercantilism."[2] This book examines the power and social responsibility of modern corporations, particularly the giant firms, in a collection of original essays
that reveal the way in which the legal process employs legal concepts to fashion
the economy—whether one likes its doing so and without regard to whether one
likes the product of the choices so made. It is a contribution in the tradition of
institutional economics, of legal realism, and perhaps even of the nascent movement called critical legal studies. There is, furthermore, an inevitable political
dimension, either explicit or implicit, in these chapters.

During the formative years of the republic, corporations were few in number
and tiny as compared with the behemoths that characterize and dominate the
American economy today. It is true, to be sure, that some of the original thirteen
states—Virginia is a notable example—began as joint-stock companies, owned
by Englishmen who wished to profit from the untapped resources of the New

World. Only approximately 300 corporations, each comparatively small in size, were present as late as 1800. When, however, the gathering forces of the industrial revolution began to be felt, corporations began to proliferate. Large amounts of capital and cheap labor from Europe were major contributors to corporate growth aimed at exploitation of the seemingly inexhaustible riches of the new nation. The Supreme Court helped this development. Under Chief Justice John Marshall, the justices in effect "nationalized" the American economy.[3] Alexander Hamilton, perhaps the most influential of all of the founding fathers, was the philosopher for this development—in his famous *Report on Manufactures*, among other state documents.

After the Civil War, corporations multiplied, growing far larger than their predecessors. A century later, John Kenneth Galbraith was to attribute this rapid growth to certain "imperatives of technology."[4] Whether or not that is accurate, it still remained true, as Thomas C. Cochran observed, that "the ability to create by charter an abstract, indestructible, immortal, and to some degree irresponsible entity that could gather the savings of a community or a nation and pour them into immense works did . . . alter the character of the business system more than any other change of this period."[5] During the past century, the giant business firm—the supercorporation—has dominated both the U.S. economy and, as some of the chapters argue, the political order. The corporation therefore should be viewed from a number of perspectives: as an economic enterprise, a political organization, a sociological community, and a legal entity. In sum, it requires analysis as a constitutional phenomenon.

This is not now, nor was it historically, uniformly recognized. Until the Supreme Court, with an intuition known only to the justices, rather casually announced in 1886 that the corporation was a constitutional person,[6] the business firm was not perceived as such an extraordinary agglomeration. The change came in the Supreme Court's *Santa Clara* decision, an otherwise obscure case that, had it not been for Chief Justice Morrison Waite's announcement that the justices did not want to hear oral argument on the question of corporate personhood because they all believed that a corporation was a person within the meaning of the Fourteenth Amendment, would have long since been relegated to oblivion. The ruling has had far-reaching consequences, so it is fitting and proper that its centenary be observed. This book is less a celebration of the *Santa Clara* decision than an examination of its import.

Santa Clara changed the nature of the U.S. political economy. Not long after it was rendered, economists such as Henry Carter Adams[7] and political scientists such as Arthur Bentley[8] began to write about the social implications of corporate personhood. The first systematic study of the business corporation was John P. Davis's *Corporations: A Study of the Origin and Development of Great Business Combinations and of Their Relation to the Authority of the State.*[9] Completed in 1897 but not published until 1905, this massive work illuminates both the history and the nature of corporate activity. Corporations, Davis wrote, are social organizations "midway between the state and the individual, owing their existence to the latter's need of organization and the former's inability to supply it.''[10] It is fair to say that much of the subsequent writing about corporations as social institutions is exegesis on themes early struck by Davis. He may not be often cited, but his observations have set the tone for later analyses.

To Davis, corporations are the major part of the "mechanism of government.''[11] This is recognized today by some political scientists, notably Grant McConnell and Robert Dahl.[12] But the Davis insight has seldom been accepted by members of the legal and economics fraternities, who for the most part continue to insist that, as Gertrude Stein might have said, the corporation is a person is a person is a person and, therefore to be treated as any other natural individual. There are exceptions, of course, in both professions, but they merely prove the general rule of academic and professional myopia.

Of more direct present significance is Davis's view that corporations have changed in the past century from divisions of society to associations of individuals. His conclusions merit full quotation:

A great change that is still not without its effect on the law of corporations took place, or more properly, culminated in the sixteenth century. The standpoint from which all institutions were viewed was shifted from society as a whole to the individual. Social forces were conceived as moving from below and not from above. The destruction of tradition and the elevation of reason was one phase of the change. To be sure, the view was not to find full expression in philosophy until the eighteenth century, but the Reformation was a practical application of it. Private contract largely superseded status in the determination of social relations. Corporations were viewed not so much as *divisions of society* as *association of individuals*. They were now enlarged individuals, not reduced societies. The legal theory of artificial personality was in such complete harmony with the view of society and the individual from the shifted standpoint that it acquired great permanence in the course of the sixteenth century. (*Emphasis in original.*)[13]

This is not quite true insofar as the United States is concerned. Until the Supreme Court's fiat in the *Santa Clara* case, corporations, as Henry Carter Adams observed in 1896, were bodies "created by law for the purpose of attaining public ends through an appeal to private interests"; they thus were "arms of the state.''[14] Given the historical background Davis outlined, however, there should be small wonder that the Court ruled as it did in *Santa Clara* and even less wonder that the ruling has now become so accepted that few challenge it. The decision is both a classic example of judicial lawmaking and a reflection of the values of the governing coalition in the United States (law, however created, being more a posteriori than a priori).[15]

By the latter part of the nineteenth century, corporations had become the chosen instruments of U.S. economic policy. They were, and still are, the means by which the enormous natural riches of the United States were transmuted into consumer goods (to the profit of their owners and managers). With the spread during recent decades of business the planet over, corporations now garner the wealth of other nations for the same purposes. But they have remained private in legal and constitutional theory. By being private—by being a constitutional person—corporations are able to exercise power in the development and allocation of wealth. Decisions taken by corporate managers make the economy a "system of power."[16] Since, however, they are viewed as associations of individuals rather than divisions of society, the power that corporations exercise is not burdened with concomitant constitutional responsibilities to the body politic that is the United States. Their original public purpose and dependence on government, although still true in fact, has been covered over with a counterpane of privateness, permitting the corporations, as Adams commented, to refuse to recognize the "principle of righteousness, candor, courtesy, or indeed, any of the personal virtues, except energy and enterprise, which according to the old English economists, are assumed to be essential to continued business success."[17] In other words, corporations have the benefits of personhood without the burdens.

Americans are curiously ambivalent about corporations. Business, particularly big business, is low on the hierarchy of articulated public values. At the same time, however, there is a tacit recognition that business provides jobs and, ultimately, pensions. Moreover, there is a widespread desire for a continuing, even mounting, flow of consumer goods from the cornucopia of business enterprise. We thus appear to want things both ways: we know, at least intuitively, about the power of business and fear it; at the same time, few wish to forgo the bounty that corporate enterprise provides. States, furthermore, compete with each other for the establishment of new factories—as in the recent General Motors automobile factory in Tennessee—and seek to lure established business to relocate.

Corporations were the primary influence that changed the nature of property in the United States from tangible land and chattels to intangible promises, such as corporate stocks and bonds. John Locke, the putative intellectual father of the Constitution, provided the philosophical basis for the protection of property as "the great and *chief end* . . . of Mens uniting into Commonwealths, and putting themselves under Government."[18] "Preservation of their Property"—Locke's language—was uppermost in the minds of those who drafted the Constitution in 1787.[19] Since that date, much of the exegesis of the document, by the Supreme Court and other authoritative decision makers, was aimed at furthering the Lockean prescription—what Edward S. Corwin called "vested rights," which he said was the basic doctrine of U.S. constitutional law.[20] Surely Corwin was correct. The point for present purposes, however, is that what Locke perceived as property was transformed by technology and business enterpreneurship into a quite different form. But the protections originally accorded to tangible property, although still remaining intact, were neatly transferred to the new forms of wealth (of property).[21] Nor was that all: those with property (in corporate form) received not only the protection of the public law of the Constitution; they also were the recipients of analogous shields against monetary loss by the judicial invention of such private law doctrines as assumption of risk, contributory negligence, and the fellow servant rule.[22] No one should wonder about this favored position of property and business. If law is reflective of society and if, as Lord Bryce wrote, "business is king" in the United States,[23] then law and legal institutions are inevitably going to benefit those with the most social power. Oliver Wendell Holmes knew this; he wrote in 1873:

Whatever body may possess the supreme power for the moment is certain to have interests inconsistent with others which have competed unsuccessfully. The more powerful interests must be more or less reflected in legislation; which, like every other device of man or beast, must tend in the long run to aid the survival of the fittest.[24]

That, of course, was social Darwinism pure and simple, a jurisprudential system that evidenced Thomas C. Cochran's 1972 remark: "In the nearly four hundred years of American history, business would seem to have been as continuously present and important as any social institution."[25]

The rise and dominance of new forms of property during the past century means, as Adolf Berle observed, that we live under a system described "in obsolete terms."[26] Americans assume, usually without thought, that their economy is based on "private property." But most industrial property is no more private than, say, a Postal Service mail truck. We heatedly deny that we are collectivist, when it should be obvious, with a moment's reflection, that a substantial portion of American enterprise is possible only because it is collectivist. The state, to be sure, does not do the collectivizing generally, but that is a mere detail. The state provides the protective umbrella under which the institutions of corporate capitalism can flourish. As Gianfranco Poggi said, "The possession of capital is a legally and politically protected means to the creation and reproduction of de facto relations of dominations between individuals belonging to different classes."[27] The state, which is the source of all power relations within the nation, guarantees power relations that emanate from the ownership of capital.

Moreover, Americans continue to believe that the stockholders own corporations; yet Berle and Means were surely correct when they wrote in *The Modern Corporation and Private Property* that all that is owned is merely a transferable piece of paper, a promise by management to pay dividends when the managers so desire.[28] Criticisms have, to be sure, recently been heaped on the Berle and Means thesis of the divorce of ownership and control. That, however, is not the present point. The individual stockholder may own a share or even many shares of, say, Southern Bell or any other telephone company but would be ill advised to try to make off with a telephone pole. The stockholder does not own any part of it; the corporation owns that pole. And the corporation is a disembodied entity that can speak no word, think no thought, and do no deed by itself. It—the corporation—can act only through its managers and others in the corporate hierarchy. These people operate, as John Davis remarked, under a dual system of ethics: there is the ethical norm system of the manager or employee qua natural person; and there is the ethical system of the firm. The two systems can and often do conflict. A corporate manager may be a pillar of the community, the

very personification of personal rectitude, but when he or she enters the boardroom or the office of the chief executive officer of a corporation, his or her
values may well change. The manager then follows what may be called the
principle of *raison de groupe*, rather like political officers adhere to the principle
of *raison d'état*.[29] Whatever property meant to Locke, to the modern corporate
manager it is the means by which the firm's profits are maximized.[30] Profit,
Arjay Miller, former head of Ford Motor Company, maintains, is the bottom
line of corporate enterprise.[31]

The *Santa Clara* fiat marked a major constitutional revolution, all the more
significant because it came unanimously and only a few years after the Supreme
Court had refused to extend the protections of the Fourteenth Amendment to
business firms.[32] Since 1886, too few scholars have studied the corporation, and
particularly the supercorporation, as something that is *sui generis* in the U.S.
constitutional order—something that could not have been even remotely in the
minds of the men who drafted the Constitution. This book is an effort to help
redress the imbalance in the scholarly literature. By no means, however, is this
a complete assessment of the role and nature of the supercorporations. The
chapters deal in the main with the power and responsibility of corporate behemoths, yesterday and today. The subject matter deserves the continuing attention
of anyone concerned with the political economy of the United States—and,
indeed, of the entire world. For it is truistic to say that all business firms of any
consequence are now multinational in the scope of their operations.

Several significant issues of legal and constitutional policy are posed by the
supercorporations, none of which has been sufficiently analyzed as yet. It will
suffice here to mention some of the more important of these questions.

First is the problem of legitimacy. If corporations do govern us, as Davis and
others have maintained, what is the source of their right or title to rule? That,
in net, is the question of corporate legitimacy. In the past, legitimacy was attained
by political officers by theories of divine right or blood succession or, in a nation
that calls itself a democracy, by being elected by popular vote. Who elected
corporate managers to rule over us—or if not to rule, to exercise enormous
influence over the way that social affairs in the United States are conducted?
The answer, given the private nature of corporations, is that they selected themselves. They therefore have only an extremely thin claim to constitutional
legitimacy.

Next is the question of bureaucracy. The supercorporations are private bureaucracies; as such, they act in much the same manner as any other bureaucratic
organization. With the burgeoning of a relatively large public governmental
bureaucracy during the past half-century, a new constitutional phenomenon has
appeared: the rise of the bureaucratic state. Natural persons must routinely deal
with corporative collectivities; this cannot be avoided in modern America. A
new constitutional milieu has thus been created, one in which natural persons
are overwhelmed by the power of bureaucracies, both public and private.

Since individualistic theories of law and of constitutionalism are applied to corporations, the United States is left, as John P. Diggins has remarked, "without a sense of moral community and pluralism without a sense of national purpose."[33] This in turn means that the original conception of the Constitution—liberal individualism and liberal pluralism (liberal democracy, in short)—has had its social basis all but obliterated. Corporations operate as states within the state, which means that pluralism, long the accepted belief system of political scientists, is in disarray. Community values, furthermore, are lost as corporations go their individual ways with little actual control from the state.

Corporations have rent the traditional divisions of political power asunder. Federalism is an example. The fifty states still exist as political units, but all except two or three (California, Texas, and perhaps New York) are overwhelmed in assets and in power by the supercorporations. The states are not so much sovereign entities as a source of senators. So, too, with the supposed separation of powers in the national government (which, as Richard Neustadt has said,[34] are really separated institutions sharing power—quite a different thing). The important separation in the U.S. constitutional order is between political and economic power centers—not that of Congress, the president, and the courts.

Supercorporations rule in part through the medium of "contracts of adhesion," which somewhat resemble traditional contracts but in fact differ markedly. A contract of adhesion is one that a natural person or a small firm must accept on a take-it-or-leave-it basis; he must "adhere" to standardized forms produced by lawyers for the supercorporations. Since many industries, and indeed the economy itself, are dominated by corporate giants, this means a diminution in status of the natural person. He can no longer bargain as an equal. In other words, the rise of huge corporate enterprises has turned Sir Henry Maine's famous apothegm upside down. In 1861, Maine asserted that the movement of progressive societies was from status to contract—from, that is, an individual's freedom sharply limited by his station in society to one of persons freely contracting with each other. Only a little over a century later, the movement in industrialized societies has been, and continues to be, from contract to a new form of status. Contracts of adhesion, moreover, should be viewed as a form of private legislation, with the supercorporations having delegated power from the state to be lawmakers in fact.

Another legal-constitutional question posed by the giant firms is the nature and effect of their planning apparatus. In *The New Industrial State*, John Kenneth Galbraith invited attention to the fact that those companies, taken together, constitute the planning system of the United States.[35] It is true that corporate managers, at least in their public rhetoric, assert an abhorrence of economic planning. Galbraith's point, however, is that they merely dislike planning by public government. So they do: they cannot avoid short- and long-term planning in their own corporate communities.

Corporations have become multinational in scope. This provides the social pressure that is leading toward the slow but steady erasure, in fact although not in theory, of national boundaries—and thus of national sovereignty. Americans are already in a position where no important public policy issue can be viewed as being entirely domestic or wholly foreign. Each such issue unavoidably contains both aspects. The meaning for a Constitution drafted largely for the resolution of domestic affairs is an as yet unanswered question.

These and similar questions must be answered by economists and lawyers, political scientists and sociologists. There is a pressing need for a useful theory of conscious economic cooperation and of the relationship of the supercorporations to public government, one that will jibe with the enduring values of U.S. constitutionalism. No one has produced one thus far. This book seeks to further the debate of a generation ago, a debate that has, with a few exceptions, been allowed to languish. In 1959 a collection of essays edited by Edward Mason was published under the title of *The Corporation in Modern Society*. No other book of comparable stature and range has been published since then. Many scholarly articles and some books have been written about the corporation and its role in the U.S. political economy. But most scholarship tends to be of a technical nature. The chapters in this book differ; they treat the corporation as an institution—the most important of all nongovernmental institutions—and assess its power and social responsibility. The hundredth anniversary of the Supreme Court's decision in *Santa Clara* provides an appropriate focal point for such an inquiry.

NOTES

1. W. Adams & H. Gray, Monopoly in America 2 (1956).

2. Lekachman, A Cure for Corporate Neurosis, Saturday Rev., January 21, 1978, quoted in L. Brown, Building a Sustainable Society 322 (1981).

3. E.g., Gibbons v. Ogden, 9 Wheat. 1 (1824). See A. Miller, The Supreme Court and American Capitalism 25–50 (1968).

4. J. Galbraith, The New Industrial State (1967).

5. T. Cochran, Business in American Life: A History 76 (1972).

6. Santa Clara Cy. v. So. Pac. R.R. 118 U.S. 394 (1886).

7. H. Adams, Relation of the State to Industrial Action, and Economics and Jurisprudence (J. Dorfman ed. 1954) (two essays, the first published in 1887 and the second in 1897).

8. A. Bentley, The Process of Government (1908).

9. Reprinted as a paperback in 1961 under the editorship of Abram Chayes.

10. Id., at 264.

11. Id., at 268.

12. See G. McConnell, Private Power and American Democracy (1966); R. Dahl, A Preface to Economic Democracy (1985).

13. Davis, supra note 9, at 246.

14. Adams, supra note 7, at 145.

15. See, for discussion of courts as part of the governing coalition in the United States, M. Shapiro, Courts: A Comparative and Political Analysis (1981).

16. See The Economy as a System of Power (W. Samuels ed. 1979) (two volumes).

17. Adams, supra note 7, at 147.

18. J. Locke, Two Treatises of Government ch. 9, Book II, para. 124 (P. Laslett ed. 1960) (paperback edition) (first published in 1690).

19. See C. Beard, An Economic Interpretation of the Constitution (1913). For discussion, see Diggins, Power and Authority in American History: The Case of Charles A. Beard, 86 Am. Hist. Rev. 701 (1981).

20. Corwin, The Basic Doctrine of American Constitutional Law, in American Constitutional History: Essays by Edward S. Corwin 25 (A. Mason & G. Garvey eds. 1964) (the essay was first published in 1914).

21. See Hamilton, Property—According to Locke, 41 Yale L.J. 864 (1932).

22. Cf. Schwartz, Tort Law and the Economy in Nineteenth-Century America: A Reinterpretation, 90 Yale L.J. 1717 (1981).

23. Quoted in Cochran, supra note 5, at 1.

24. Holmes, The Gas-Stokers Strike, 7 Am. L. Rev. 582 (1873).

25. Cochran, supra note 5, at 1.

26. A. Berle, Power without Property 27 (1958) (paperback ed.).

27. G. Poggi, The Development of the Modern State: A Sociological Introduction 94–95 (1978).

28. First published in 1932; revised edition published in 1968.

29. For preliminary discussion, see Miller, Reason of State and the Emergent Constitution of Control, 64 Minn. L. Rev. 585 (1980). See also C. Friedrich, Constitutional Reason of State (1957).

30. For a present-day example of *raison de groupe* as applied to a large U.S. drug company, see M. Mintz, At Any Cost: Corporate Greed, Women, and the Dalkon Shield (1985) (an exposé of how A. H. Robins & Co. followed the principle of what was good for the enterprise was the sole criterion of policy).

31. A. Miller, How Business Should Respond to the New Pro-Business Climate 7–8 (1982).

32. E.g., Munn v. Illinois, 94 U.S. 113 (1876).

33. J. Diggins, The Lost Soul of American Politics 5 (1985).

34. R. Neustadt, Presidential Power (1960).

35. Galbraith, supra note 4.

I. DOCTRINAL ORIGINS

2

SANTA CLARA REVISITED: THE DEVELOPMENT OF CORPORATE THEORY

Morton J. Horwitz

The 1886 decision of the United States Supreme Court in *Santa Clara Co. v. Southern Pacific Railroad*[1] has always been puzzling and controversial. From the time Progressive constitutional historians began to mount their attack on the Supreme Court after the *Lochner* decision in 1905,[2] the *Santa Clara* case became one of the prominent symbols of the subservience of the Supreme Court during the Gilded Age to the interests of big business.[3]

The *Santa Clara* case held that a corporation was a person under the Fourteenth Amendment, and thus entitled to its protection. That holding has been affirmed by the Supreme Court dozens of times, notwithstanding a famous announcement by Justices Black and Douglas in 1949 that recent historical writing had led them to conclude that the *Santa Clara* case was wrongly decided.[4] In our own time, in *First National Bank v. Bellotti*,[5] a five-to-four majority of the Supreme Court treated the *Santa Clara* case as if it in effect had already decided that corporations, like individuals, were entitled to the protection of the First Amendment.[6] As far back as 1925, the Supreme Court assumed that the free speech clause was incorporated into the ''liberty'' protected by the Fourteenth Amendment.[7] In *Bellotti* the majority spoke as if it were simply axiomatic that the *Santa Clara* case settled the view that the free speech doctrine had been extended to corporations.[8]

For such a momentous decision, the opinion in the *Santa Clara* case is disquietingly brief—just one short paragraph—and totally without reasons or precedent. Indeed, it was made without argument of counsel. It declared:

> The court does not wish to hear argument on the question whether the provision in the Fourteenth Amendment to the Constitution, which forbids a State to deny to any person within its jurisdiction the equal protection of the laws, applies to these corporations. We are all of opinion that it does.[9]

Can it be that so casual a declaration as this did in fact represent a major controversial step in American constitutional history? Did the decision actually represent a significant departure from American constitutional jurisprudence? I think not. The *Santa Clara* decision was not thought of as an innovation but instead was regarded as following a line of cases going back almost seventy years to the *Dartmouth College* case.[10]

But my interest in the *Santa Clara* case extends far beyond the question of whether it was consistent with previous constitutional decisions. Whatever the Supreme Court justices had in mind, the case is usually thought to express a new theory of the corporation or, as it soon became fashionable to call it, a new theory of corporate personality. The *Santa Clara* case is thus asserted to be a dramatic example of judicial personification of the corporation, which, it is argued, radically enhanced the position of the business corporation in American law.[11] There can be no doubt that recent cases like *Bellotti*, which recognizes a constitutional right of corporations to spend money to influence elections, *have* contributed enormously to the political and economic power of big business.

But the question remains whether the *Santa Clara* case did in fact proceed from a theory that the corporate entity was no different from the individual in its constitutional entitlements. To answer this question, I will attempt a long excursion into the history of the theories of the corporation that were prevalent when the *Santa Clara* case was decided. I hope to show, first, that the so-called "natural entity" or "real entity" theory of the corporation that the *Santa Clara* case is supposed to have adopted was nowhere to be found in American legal thought when the case was decided; second, that those who argued for the corporations as well as Supreme Court Justice Stephen Field, who decided in favor of the corporation in two elaborate circuit court opinions below,[12] clearly had no conception of a natural entity theory of the corporation; and, third, that when the natural entity theory emerged about a decade later, it was only then gradually absorbed into the *Santa Clara* precedent to establish dramatically new constitutional protections for corporations.

So initially, I wish to show not only that the real meaning of the *Santa Clara* decision has not been understood, but also that it did not express the pro–big-business theory of the corporation that only came to fruition shortly before the First World War.

Yet, finally, this focus on the *Santa Clara* case and on the history of corporate theory is designed to explore a still more difficult question about the role of legal theory in legal decision. For almost forty years after 1890, American jurists, like their German, French, and English counterparts, were preoccupied with the theory of the corporation, or, as it was then frequently called, with corporate personality. Then the issue suddenly vanished from controversy. The last great analysis of the question, which is sometimes thought to have permanently put it to rest, appeared in a 1926 *Yale Law Journal* article,[13] by the philosopher John Dewey. Writing in sympathy with the powerful contemporaneous Legal Realist attack on "conceptualism"[14] Dewey sought to show that theories of corporate personality were infinitely manipulable and that at different times the same theories had been used both to expand and to limit not only corporate but trade union powers. Let me quote Dewey's argument. "Each theory" of group personality he maintained "has been used to serve . . . opposing ends."

[I]t has been employed both to make the state the Supreme and culminating personality in a hierarchy, to make it but *primus inter pares*, and to reduce it to merely one among many. . . . Corporate groups less than the state have had real personality ascribed to them, both in order to make them more amenable to liability, as in the case of trade-unions, and to exalt their dignity and vital power, against external control. . . . The group personality theory has been asserted both as a check upon what was regarded as anarchic and dissolving individualism, to set up something more abiding and worthful than a single human being, and to increase the power and dignity of the single being as over against the state.[15]

There are very few discussions of corporate personality after Dewey. The Legal Realists in general had succeeded in persuading legal thinkers that highly abstract and general legal conceptions were simply part of what Felix Cohen, quoting von Jhering, derisively called "the heaven of legal concepts."[16] Only more concrete statements of functional relations, Cohen argued, were useful in deciding legal questions.

In our own time, the debate over concepts had revived once more within the Critical Legal Studies Movement where one dominant trend had been to demonstrate the indeterminacy of concepts.[17] The issue is whether any abstract conception—"freedom" or "security" or "rights" are often used as examples— has any entailment in terms of more concrete legal doctrines or rules.[18]

By contrast, I will argue that most important controversial legal abstractions do have determinate legal or political significance. In the jargon of the current Critical Legal Studies debate, I wish to deny that legal conceptions are infinitely "flippable" and instead to insist that they do have "tilt" or influence in determining outcomes. Thus, for example, I wish to dispute Dewey's conclusion that particular conceptions of corporate personality were just as easily used to limit as to enhance corporate power. Instead, I hope to show that, for example, the rise of a "natural entity" theory of the corporation was a major factor in legitimating big business and that none of the other theoretical alternatives could provide as much sustenance to newly organized concentrated enterprise.

I do not wish to be understood to disassociate myself from those brilliant critical or Legal Realist attacks on legal reasoning.[19] The central thrust of the Realist legacy to which we are all still indebted ultimately derives from Holmes' classical statement, "General propositions do not decide concrete cases."[20] Holmes as well as John Dewey and Felix Cohen after him were attacking the formalist claim that one could deductively and without discretion reason from a general concept to a particular application. As a matter of legal *logic* their attack on formalism continues to be as powerful today as it was fifty years ago. But their attempt to discredit the then orthodox claim to a non-political, non-discretionary mode of legal *reasoning* led them to ignore the obvious fact that when abstract conceptions are used in specific historical contexts they have more limited meanings and more specific argumentative functions. We have spent too much effort repeating the demonstrations of the indeterminacy of concepts in a logical vacuum; but not enough time trying to show that in particular contexts the choice of one theory over another is not random or accidental because history and usage have limited their deepest meanings and applications.

THE SANTA CLARA CASE IN CONTEXT

The Real Meaning of the Santa Clara Decision

The *Santa Clara* case, along with several companion cases, came to the United States Supreme Court from California.[21] They presented the question whether the equal protection clause of the Fourteenth Amendment barred California from taxing corporate property—in this case railroad property—differently from individual property.

These California tax cases were clearly regarded as important and momentous events in giving meaning to the newly enacted Fourteenth Amendment. Above all, they represented another effort mounted by business interests after their narrow failure to get the Supreme Court to broadly construe the Fourteenth Amendment in the *Slaughterhouse Cases*.[22] In that decision, Justice Samuel Miller, speaking for a five-man majority not only offered an extremely narrow construction of the ''privileges and immunities'' clause but he also construed the ''equal protection clause'' as limited to protecting the status of recently freed slaves. In dissent, Justice Stephen Field, who argued for a much more expansive definition of each of the provisions of the fourteenth amendment, sought, in effect, to create a general federal charter of constitutional rights.[23]

The central issue in the *Slaughterhouse* case was whether the Fourteenth Amendment had radically altered the constitutional relationship between the states and the federal government. Justice Miller's ''race theory'' interpretation of the Fourteenth Amendment reinforced traditional fears of centralized power and was meant to produce as little change in the federal balance of power as possible. By contrast, Justice Field interpreted the Fourteenth Amendment as ratifying a dramatic alteration in the federal system as a consequence of the Civil War.[24]

So when the California tax cases came before Justice Field, sitting on circuit, the most basic and controversial question before him was whether it was possible after the *Slaughterhouse* decision to construe the equal protection clause to extend to non-race related questions. The central thrust of his decision was to continue his battle, which was eventually successful, to expand the meaning of the amendment beyond the boundaries of race relations. Indeed, the real significance of the Supreme Court's decision in *Santa Clara* may be precisely that it did go beyond Justice Miller's *Slaughterhouse* effort to confine the scope of the equal protection clause.

But our inquiry needs to focus elsewhere. How did Justice Field justify applying the equal protection clause to corporations when the language of the amendment was written to protect "persons"?

Let us turn to the major argument in the brief on behalf of the corporation before the United States Supreme Court. Written by the eminent California lawyer, John Norton Pomeroy, the central argument was that the Fourteenth Amendment protects the property rights not of some abstract corporate entity but rather of the individual shareholders. As Pomeroy declared in his brief, provisions of state and federal constitutions "apply . . . to private corporations, not alone because such corporations are 'persons' within the meaning of that word, but because *statutes violating their prohibitions in dealing with corporations must necessarily infringe upon the rights of natural persons.* In applying and enforcing these constitutional guaranties, *corporations cannot be separated from the natural persons who compose them.*"[25]

"That this conclusion *must* be true," Pomeroy argued, "appears from the following principle:"

Whatever be the legal nature of a corporation as an artificial, metaphysical being, separate and distinct from the individual members, and whatever distinctions the common law makes, in carrying out the technical legal conception, between property of the corporation and that of the individual members, still in applying the fundamental guaranties of the constitution, and in thus protecting rights of property, *these metaphysical and technical notions must give way to the reality.* The truth cannot be evaded that, *for the purpose of protecting rights, the property of all business and trading corporations* IS *the property of the individual corporators.* A State act depriving a business corporation of its property without due process of law, does in fact *deprive the individual corporators of their property.* In this sense, and within the scope of these grand safeguards of private rights, there is no real distinction between artificial persons or corporations, and natural persons.[26]

Justice Field made exactly the same point in his circuit court opinion in the companion *San Mateo* case:[27]

Private corporations are, it is true, artificial persons, but . . . they consist of aggregations of individuals united for some legitimate business. . . . It would be a most singular result if a constitutional provision intended for the protection of every person against partial and discriminating legislation by the states, should cease to exert such protection the moment the person becomes a member of a corporation. . . . On the contrary, we think that it is well established by numerous adjudications of the Supreme Court of the United States . . . that whenever a provision of the constitution, or of a law, guarantees to persons the enjoyment of property . . . the benefits of the provision extend to corporations, and that the courts will always look beyond the name of the artificial being to the individuals whom it represents.

The arguments of Pomeroy and Field are very different from a "real entity" or "natural entity" theory of corporate personality that is often ascribed to the *Santa Clara* case but which in fact only emerged some time after *Santa Clara* was decided. Only this later theory can truly be said to personify the corporation and treat it "just like individuals."

Corporate Theory in the Late Nineteenth and Early Twentieth Centuries

The theory of corporate personality attributed to the *Santa Clara* case—the natural entity theory—was not really available at the time the case was decided. This is clear after reviewing the American legal struggle to reconceptualize the corporation and the philosophical debates that arose in the late nineteenth and early twentieth century on the nature of corporate personality.

The Philosophical Debates

There was a flood of writing on the subject of "corporate personality" in Germany, France, England, and America near the turn of the century. Why should so metaphysical a subject, even if it attracted the speculative instincts of German and French jurists, have appealed to the practical, earth-bound sensibilities of English and American legal thinkers?

The intellectual history of the subject is quite clear. It was introduced into Western thought by the publication of the German legal theorist Otto Gierke's great 1887 book on the history of associations in German legal theory.[28] By 1900, there were dozens of books written in French and German on "group personality," "corporate personality," or, as the French liked to call it, "moral personality."[29] It became accessible to English and American thinkers after 1900 when Maitland, the great English legal historian, published a portion of Gierke's work under the title, *Political Theories of the Middle Ages*,[30] to which Maitland contributed an introduction. Between 1900 and 1904 Maitland published four other articles on the early history of corporations, culminating in his paper, "Moral Personality and Legal Personality,"[31] which sought to advance Gierke's idea that corporations were "real" or "natural" entities that possessed legal personalities deserving of recognition. In America, Gierke's work was first noticed by German-born and trained University of Chicago Professor Ernst Freund, who in 1897 published *The Legal Nature of the Corporation*.[32]

If the intellectual history of the subject is relatively clear, the question remains why so abstruse an inquiry should have engaged the attention of Anglo-American lawyers? Maitland, wrongly it turns out, lamented the fact that the English could not care less. He wondered, "Why we English people are not interested in a problem that is being seriously discussed in many other lands," and his article, "Trust and Corporation,"[33] sought to explain how the Trust "enabled us to construct bodies which were not technically corporations and which yet would be sufficiently protected from the assaults of individualistic theory."[34]

Americans, in fact, were especially receptive to questions involving group theory. Even before Gierke was known or Maitland's writings had crossed the

Atlantic, American legal thinkers had begun to wrestle with the problem of conceptualizing group personality, and, in particular, the corporation. Beginning in the 1890s they too sought to develop a picture of the corporation as a "real" or "natural" entity as well as to explain or justify the inscrutable holding of the United States Supreme Court in the *Santa Clara* case.

What united all of these inquiries, whether German, French, English, or American, was the spectacular rise to prominence during the late nineteenth century of the business corporation as the dominant form of economic enterprise. In 1890, Justice Stephen Field estimated that three-quarters of the wealth of the United States was controlled by corporations.[35] This growth in the corporate form of economic enterprise presented essentially two fundamental challenges to traditional Western legal theory. First, in all of these countries the corporation was treated as a "legal fiction" or an "artificial entity" created by the state. Gierke and his successors devoted themselves to showing that the corporation—indeed, group activity generally—was "real" and "natural," not "artificial" or "fictional." The proponents of Realism ranged all the way from overt apologists for big business, whose primary objective was to free the corporation from a theory that justified special state regulation, to those who for a variety of reasons wished to attack nineteenth century liberal individualism.

The challenge to individualism produced a second fundamental set of questions. On the continent, individualism was under attack, first, by romantic conservatives, who loathed the atomistic features of modern industrial life and yearned for a return to a pre-commercial, organic society composed of medieval status and hierarchies.[36] They were joined in their attacks by socialists who wished to transcend the anti-collectivist categories of liberal social and legal thought.[37] While the attack focused on the rise of corporations, it also sought to take account of the recent prominence of labor unions and trade and professional associations.[38] And even Maitland, whose legal history was devoted to affirming the liberal vision of individual property holding against the collectivist historians' search for pre-modern forms of communal property,[39] promoted the real entity theory and sympathetically regarded the trust as a fictional device covertly designed to evade "the assaults of individualistic theory."[40]

The corporation, in short, was the most powerful and prominent example of the emergence of non-individualistic or, if you will, collectivist legal institutions. The artificial entity theory of the corporation, by contrast, sought to retain the premises of what has been called "methodological individualism," that is, the view that the only real starting point for political or legal theory is the individual. Groups, in this view, were simply artificial aggregations of individuals. On the other hand, it was the goal of the Realists to show that groups, in fact, had an organic unity, that the group was greater than the mere sum of its parts. In all the Western countries, therefore, theories of corporate personality were associated with a crisis of legitimacy in liberal individualism arising from the recent emergence of powerful collective institutions.

The American Legal Struggle to Reconceptualize the Corporation

By the late nineteenth century in America, fundamental changes had already taken place in the legal treatment of the corporation. First, and by far the most important, was the erosion of the so-called "grant" or "concession" theory of the corporation, which treated the act of incorporation as a special privilege conferred by the state for the pursuit of public purposes.[41] Under the grant theory, the business corporation was regarded as an "artificial being" created by the state with powers strictly limited by its charter of incorporation. As we shall see, a number of more specific legal doctrines were also derived from the grant theory in order to enforce the state's interest in limiting and confining corporate power.

The political mechanism used to enforce the grant theory was the special charter of incorporation, passed by the state legislature after negotiation between private interests and the state. During the Jacksonian period, special charters were denounced for their encouragement of legislative bribery, political favoritism, and, above all, monopoly. As a result, the movement for "free incorporation" laws that would break the connection between the act of incorporation and political favoritism and corruption triumphed between 1850 and 1870.[42] Gradually, by making the corporate form universally available, free incorporation undermined the grant theory. Incorporation eventually came to be regarded not as a special state-conferred privilege but as a normal and regular mode of doing business.

The problem faced by legal thinkers during the late nineteenth century was how to reconceptualize the corporation after the demise of the grant theory. On one hand, free incorporation provided the opportunity to treat the corporation under ordinary contractual categories familiar to partnership law. On the other hand, many of the special attributes[43] of the corporation could not be explained or defended by partnership analogies. As a result, during the last quarter of the nineteenth century, the legal literature is filled with discussions of the nature of the corporation—whether, like a partnership, it is a mere "aggregate" of individuals or whether, instead, it is an "entity," separate from the individuals who compose it.

Up through the 1880s, there was a strong tendency to analyze corporation law not very differently from the law of partnership.[44] Indeed, many of the rules involving the internal governance of the corporation were borrowed from partnership law, the most important of which was the requirement of shareholder unanimity for "fundamental" changes in corporate purpose.[45] Moreover, the erosion of the grant theory seemed to leave no choice but to create a conception of the corporation with powers flowing from the bottom up—from shareholders to directors to officers. This basic model of the corporation, emphasizing the property rights of shareholders, is the one put forth in *Santa Clara* by John Norton Pomeroy and Justice Field.

Later, shortly before the First World War, the partnership conception could not equally accomplish the task of legitimation when the court turned to less material, less property-centered claims of corporate constitutional rights against unreasonable search and seizure and self-incrimination. Here, it was difficult to reduce the constitutional claim of the corporation to the constitutional rights of the shareholders. In constitutional law, therefore, the first Supreme Court "natural entity" opinion was the 1905 decision in *Hale v. Henkel*[46] extending Fourth Amendment protections to the corporation. But the Court's continuing reluctance to entirely personify the corporation is underlined by its decision in the same case refusing to extend Fifth Amendment protection against self-incrimination to corporations.

Despite the Supreme Court's continued hesitancy, by 1900 the "entity" theory had largely triumphed and corporation and partnership law had moved in radically different directions. The success of legal thinkers in reconceptualizing the corporation seems to have had important consequences for the legitimacy of the corporate entity.

The triumph of the entity theory parallels another development in late-nineteenth-century corporate law—the tendency to shift power away from shareholders, first in favor of directors and later to professional managers.[47] By contrast, in 1875, by analogy to the partnership, American law tended to conceive of directors as agents of shareholders. After 1900, however, directors were more frequently treated as equivalent to the corporation itself.[48] This realignment of legal powers within the corporation thus made the entity theory ever more plausible. In turn, the entity theory produced court decisions that promoted oligarchical tendencies within the business corporation.

The collapse of the grant theory eventually produced the best of all possible worlds for the expansion of corporate power. By rendering the corporate form normal and regular, late-nineteenth-century corporate theory shifted the presumption of corporate regulation against the state. Since corporations could no longer be treated as special creatures of the state, they were entitled to the same privileges as all other individuals and groups. While the state thus lost any special claims—arising out of the original theory of corporate creation—to regulate corporations, the once powerful grant theory did make it easier to continue to conceive of the corporation as a supra-individualistic entity. As a result, late-nineteenth-century entity theorists drew on the early history of corporations to justify their assertion of its organic and collective nature at the same time as they disavowed the completely subordinate position that that theory had created for the corporation.

Thus, one can clearly see that the natural entity theory of the corporation ascribed to the *Santa Clara* case was only just being formulated at the turn of the century. In 1886 corporate theory was in a state of flux both legally and intellectually and the natural entity theory really was not yet available to justify the holding in the *Santa Clara* case. It was only afterwards that theorists began to recognize the reality of corporate growth.

THE CONCEPT OF CORPORATE PERSONALITY
AND ITS DETERMINATE LEGAL SIGNIFICANCE

Corporate Personality

The corporation occupied an anomalous position in American law throughout the nineteenth century. In a legal system whose categories were built around individual activity, it was not at all easy to assimilate the behavior of groups. Inherently individualistic legal conceptions like "fault" and "will" were difficult to apply to corporations. "How is it possible," Ernst Freund asked in 1897, "upon any other basis [than the individual person], to deal with notions that are constantly applied to the holding of rights, and which explain their most important incidents: intention, notice, good and bad faith, responsibility? How can we establish, unless we have to deal with individuals, the internal connection between act and liability?"[49]

Any conception of corporate rights, Freund emphasized, would involve "a departure from well-settled principles."

> If the individual, private, and beneficial right is to measure and govern all rules relating to rights of whatsoever nature, then the corporate right will continue to be abnormal and illogical. If, on the other hand, we emancipate ourselves from the absolute recognition of one form of right as orthodox, . . . we may well arrive at the conclusion, that in dealing with associations of persons we must modify the ideas which we have derived from the right of property in individuals, and what has first seemed to be an anomaly will appeal simply as another but equally legitimate form of development.[50]

The corporation also stood in clear contradiction to a legal culture dominated by Lockean ideas of pre-social natural rights. In post-revolutionary America, there was no better example of the social creation of property than the chartered business corporation. As natural rights theories grew in power and scope after the Civil War,[51] the corporation thus seemed to constitute a standing contradiction to any claims to the pre-social character of property rights.

Three conceptions of the legal organization of the corporation competed for dominance after 1880. The traditional conception, derived from the ante-bellum grant theory, as well as older English corporation law, characterized the corporation as "an artificial entity created by positive law."[52] But as the movement for free incorporation eroded the force of the grant theory, two other conceptions of the corporation began to emerge with radically different implications for the development of corporation law. In substantially different ways, these two newer theories sought to convey the idea that incorporation was a normal and natural mode of business organization, not a special privilege bestowed by the state.

In reaction to the grant theory, some legal writers during the 1880s began to put forth a polar opposite conception of the corporation as a creature of free contract among individual shareholders, no different, in effect, from a partnership. In this conception, the corporation was not a creature of the state but of individual initiative and enterprise. It was "private," not "public."

A third theory which emerged during the 1890s also sought to represent the corporation as private, yet neither as "artificial," "fictional," nor as a creature of the state. This "natural entity" theory soon began to be projected onto the ambiguous opinion of the Supreme Court in the *Santa Clara* case.

The term "corporate personality" is itself an important clue to the intellectual crisis. The "aggregate" or contractual view of the corporation seemed capable of restricting corporate privileges and, in particular, the rule of limited liability. That there was a close relationship between the justification for limited liability and a conception of the corporation as a separate (though "artificial") entity distinct from its shareholders was clear to Chief Justice Taney as early as 1839. If the entity were disregarded, Taney wrote,

and . . . the members of a corporation were to be regarded as individuals carrying on business in their corporate name, and therefore entitled to the privileges of citizens in matters of contract, it is very clear that they must at the same time take upon themselves the liabilities of citizens and be bound by their contracts in like manner. The result of this would be to make a corporation a mere partnership in business, in which each stockholder would be liable to the whole extent of his property for the debts of the corporation; and he might be sued for them in any state in which he might happen to be found.[53]

Not only did Taney believe that there was a logical connection between an entity theory and limited liability; he also maintained in perfectly straightforward Jacksonian fashion that every effort of corporations to claim that they were constitutionally "entitled to the privileges of citizens" would erode the entity theory by forcing courts to turn to the rights of shareholders. There was a trade-off, he supposed, between the grant of corporate privileges and the claim of shareholder constitutional rights. He could not yet even imagine that the fictional entity itself could plausibly claim constitutional privileges. The effort to protect corporate property in *Santa Clara* through a conception of shareholder rights thus raised precisely the danger that Chief Justice Taney identified—it might undermine the justification for limited liability.

The effort of some legal thinkers beginning in the 1880s to treat the corporation as no different from a partnership was reinforced in a series of anti-consolidation cases in which courts looked behind the corporate entity to treat the shareholders as the real legal actors in the corporation. The most famous of these cases was the attack on the Standard Oil Trust by the State of Ohio.[54] Ohio brought *quo warranto* proceedings against the Standard Oil Company, maintaining that it had acted beyond its corporate powers in joining the trust. Since a majority of the individual shareholders had voted to transfer their stock to the trust, the corporation maintained that only the shareholders, not the corporation, had acted. In piercing the corporate veil, Ohio Supreme Court Justice Minshall treated the idea "that a corporation is a legal entity apart from the natural persons who compose it" as "a mere fiction."

It appears that the intense efforts of most judges and legal writers during the 1880s and 1890s to equate the corporation with its stockholders was motivated by a delegitimating strategy, deriving from anti-corporate and anti-consolidation sentiment. Of course, the defendants of corporate property in *Santa Clara* also made use of this theory, which seemed to them at the time more favorable to the corporation than the traditional "artificial entity" theory. Yet, given the structure of American legal ideas, it may have seemed the only way to turn once the implications of the demise of the grant theory rendered the entity conception of the corporation more problematic.

Ultra Vires

[U]nfortunately, there is now in this country a newer growth of corporation lawyers and authors, fostered and fashioned in the same school, who would confuse the subject by regarding the rights, duties and powers of a corporation as identical with the rights, duties and powers of the individuals composing it. To recognize such an anomalous position would clearly nullify, in great measure, the whole doctrine of *ultra vires*.

Reuben A. Reese, *The True Doctrine of Ultra Vires in the Law of Corporations* (1897)[55]

The doctrine that a corporation cannot act beyond its legal competence is perhaps the best reflection of the traditional legal conception of the nature of the corporation. At one pole, to the extent that the corporation is fully thought of as an artificial entity created by the state, we would expect courts strictly to construe powers granted in the corporate charter and refuse effect to corporate activity regarded as beyond the powers conferred. At the opposite pole, to the extent that a corporation is regarded simply as a convenient device for conducting business activity, not as a privilege or concession derived from the state, we would expect the death of the ultra vires doctrine.

Before the Civil War, in fact, the ultra vires doctrine was strictly applied by American courts, thereby voiding most transactions held to be outside the grant of a corporation's powers.[56] By 1930, the ultra vires doctrine was, if not dead, substantially eroded in practice,[57] reflecting the triumphant view that corporate organization was a normal and natural form of business activity.

During the half century after 1880 we can trace the tension between those doctrines that reflected the old vision of corporate powers as a state-conferred privilege and the emergence of newer theories designed to represent the corporation as a "natural" form of business organization. It also represents one of many technical expressions of the conflict over political economy between small entrepreneurs and emergent big business over the legitimacy of large scale enterprise. In this setting, the doctrine of ultra vires provides us with one measure of conflict.

At first glance, the doctrine of ultra vires was still a powerful judicial tool as late as 1900, despite the seemingly contrary message of state general incorporation laws, which had become the norm between 1850 and 1870. Yet there was still a long ideological distance to travel between the first general incorporation laws, which continued to impose many restrictions on corporate financing and structure, and the New Jersey incorporation law, first enacted in 1889, whose major premise was that a corporation could do virtually anything it wanted.[58] Even within the context of early general incorporation, therefore, the state did not entirely renounce its role as creator and regulator.

While judicial decisions during the last decades of the nineteenth century thus continued to invoke the ultra vires doctrine and its underlying conception of the corporation as an artificial entity, many important changes in corporation law had strengthened the view that the ultra vires doctrine was an anachronism "now honored more in the breach than in the observance."[59] Even in jurisdictions that still dealt harshly with ultra vires acts, the definition of legitimate corporate powers had for a long time been expanding. "The courts," wrote William W. Cook in his 1894 treatise on corporation law, "are becoming more liberal, and many acts which fifty years ago would have been held to be *ultra vires* would now be held to be *intra vires*. The courts have gradually enlarged the *implied* powers of ordinary corporations until now such corporations may do almost anything that an individual may do, provided the stockholders and creditors do not object."[60]

Even concededly ultra vires activity had begun to receive recognition by the courts. Since corporations already had been made liable in tort as well as prosecuted criminally for ultra vires acts, the doctrine had increasingly reflected considerable internal contradiction. The exceptions, many commentators noted, were beginning to eat up the rule. Even within the last remaining bastion of the ultra vires rule, the law of contracts, courts after the Civil War had begun a retreat. While they continued to refuse to enforce "executory" contracts—those where neither party had performed—they now refused to intervene to upset property rights acquired under "executed" ultra vires contracts. By the 1880s, the majority of state courts had gone one step further to enforce even contracts that, despite lack of corporate power, had been performed by one side to the agreement.[61] Yet, the United States Supreme Court, after a short flirtation with a "liberalized" ultra vires rule during the 1870s, became the most ardent defender of traditional doctrine, consistently rejecting the majority view that partially performed contracts could be enforced.[62] Until at least 1930, the Supreme Court continued to resist the trend of state decisions[63] as well as the appeals of legal scholars for relaxing ultra vires limitations.[64]

The contradictions and inconsistencies in ultra vires doctrine were becoming unmanageable. "The doctrine of *ultra vires* is disappearing," wrote William W. Cook in 1898. "The old theory that a corporate act beyond the express and implied corporate powers was illegal and not enforceable, no matter whether any actual injury had been done or not, has given way to the practical view that the parties to a contract which has been partially or wholly executed will not be allowed to say it was *ultra vires* of the corporation."[65] While judges thus continued to sound like ante-bellum grant theorists when they were deciding executory contract cases, the vitality and coherence of the grant theory and the regulatory premises that underlay it had long been eroded.

Foreign Corporations

Despite the advent of general incorporation laws by the 1870s, we have seen that the Supreme Court continued into the twentieth century to treat the corporation as an artificial entity subject to ultra vires constraints.[66] It was only a series of state corporation statutes buttressed by Legal Realist attacks that finally destroyed most ultra vires limitations during the 1920s.

A second set of doctrines provides another measure of the gradual shift in the conception of the corporation from an artificial to a real or natural entity. They deal with the power of a state to exclude foreign corporations—corporations chartered in another state—from doing business within its boundaries.

The "original fountain head of the law of foreign corporations"[67] was Chief Justice Taney's decision in *Bank of Augusta v. Earle*[68] (1839), which represents as clear a statement of the artificial entity theory as any in American law. The corporation "exists only in contemplation of law, and by force of the law," wrote Taney. Since it is "a mere artificial being" of the state of its creation, "where that law ceases to operate, and is no longer obligatory, the corporation can have no existence."[69] Thus, a state was not constitutionally obliged to allow foreign corporations to do business within its boundaries.

The doctrine of *Bank of Augusta v. Earle* was vigorously reaffirmed after the Civil War[70] and continued to find favor in the United States Supreme Court throughout the nineteenth century, even in the face of the Court's assumption that the corporation was a "person" under the Fourteenth Amendment. By the end of the nineteenth century, however, there were signs of increasing strain not only between an expanding Supreme Court protection of interstate commerce and the foreign incorporation doctrine but also between the latter and the natural entity conception that was emerging in legal thought. And yet it was only in a group of cases in 1910 that the Supreme Court really put to rest the doctrine of *Bank of Augusta v. Earle*.[71] From that time on, expanding Fourteenth Amendment protections of the corporation swept aside Taney's vision of the business corporation as an artificial creature of the state.

As with the history of ultra vires, we see that it was not the Supreme Court of the Gilded Age that renounced the artificial entity theory of the corporation but rather the judges and legal writers of the early twentieth century who came to understand the corporation as a normal and natural mode of doing business. And, as we shall see, it was a group of Legal Realist legal thinkers who developed and articulated this new conception of the corporation.

From the era of general incorporation onward, legal writers commented on the disparity between the reality of free incorporation and those "artificial" and "unrealistic" restrictions on corporate power that continued to derive from the ante-bellum grant theory. Yet, in the Supreme Court, an "old" conservative majority perpetuated the Jacksonian tradition of competitive capitalism and suspicion of corporate power[72] not only by continuing to invoke legal doctrines derived from the artificial entity theory but by giving a strict literalist reading to the Sherman Anti-Trust Act.[73] Around 1910 or 1911, the "new" conservatives finally overthrew the strict construction of the Sherman Act in the *Standard Oil* case;[74] they also reversed those doctrines in corporation law based on a conception of the corporation as a creature of the state.

The "Inevitability" of Concentration

Are the large combination of capitalists and corporations known as "trusts" a logical and therefore proper development of the present economic system, or are they abnormal excrescences that can and should be eradicated by legislation?

Question to Professor William W. Folwell of the University of Minnesota by a Committee of the Minneapolis Socialist Labor Party (1888).[75]

The efforts by legal thinkers to legitimate the business corporation during the 1890s were buttressed by a stunning reversal in American economic thought— a movement to defend and justify as inevitable the emergence of large-scale corporate concentration.

Until the late 1880s, prevailing American economic thought refused to accept either the inevitability or the naturalness of large-scale concentrations of capital. Most discussion of the "monopoly problem" during the 1870s and early 1880s focused on the railroad, which was treated as something of a special case.[76] Whether defenders and opponents of railroad consolidation emphasized the "overproduction" of lines after the Civil War or whether they argued about a "natural monopoly" analysis of the railroad, they tended to regard the problem as unique. Before the late 1880s, few saw in the railroad problem any more general pattern of industrial concentration.

Popular attention began to be drawn to the question of industrial concentration with the publication of Henry D. Lloyd's muckraking articles on monopoly. His first magazine article, "The Story of a Great Monopoly,"[77] in 1881, was an attack on the Standard Oil Company. "As early as 1884 he asserted that combinations were dominating, most, if not all, industries in the country, from coffin-making to iron pipe foundries."[78] Above all, the attention paid to formation of the notorious "trusts" during the 1880s, raised more general questions concerning the causes of industrial concentration.

In 1882, the first great trust, the Standard Oil, was born, after "the sharp mind of Standard's legal counsel, S. L. T. Dodd, conceived of the new trust form of organization."[79] The trust was designed to bring about corporate consolidation while avoiding the prohibition under state corporation laws of one corporation holding the stock of another. Since the individual shareholders of the consolidating corporations tendered their stock to trustees in exchange for trust certificates, the resulting trust was not incorporated and hence was thought to be immune from the limitations of corporation law.

Five other successful, nationwide trusts were organized during the 1880s: the American Cotton Oil Trust (1884), National Linseed Oil Trust (1885), the National Lead Trust (1887), the Whiskey & Sugar Trusts (1889). The "trust problem" therefore became a central issue of public policy only a few years before the Sherman Act was enacted in 1890. The Act itself reflected the still widely shared orthodox laissez-faire position that industrial concentration was an unnatural interference with the laws of free competition and could only be achieved through conspiracy or illicit financial manipulation. Except for the relatively rare case of "natural monopoly," it was thought that the "laws" of the market—especially the "law of diminishing returns"—would continue to prevail.

Some orthodox theorists traced the causes of monopoly to illegitimate governmental interference in the economy—through tariffs and other intrusions on free competition, governmental grants to railroads, grants of corporate privileges, and the operation of the patent laws. But most were complacently confident that monopoly was inherently impermanent. " 'Trusts', as a rule, are not dangerous," the Dean of the Columbia Law School, Theodore W. Dwight, wrote in 1888. "They cannot overcome the law of demand and supply nor the resistless power of unlimited competition."[80] Indeed, the intellectual paralysis of laissez-faire theorists in the face of combination was captured best in 1891 by Judge Seymour Thompson of St. Louis, a vocal opponent of the Trust.

The problem . . . of restraining corporate and individual combinations and monopolies, is the problem of restraining a species of communism; it is communism against communism, and the question is, how far communism ought to go in restraining communism. The general rule is that it ought not to go at all. The general rule is that commerce should be free.[81]

Beginning in the late 1880s, however, several writers began to ponder the question of whether large-scale enterprise was inevitable. Perhaps the earliest was Arthur T. Hadley, whose book, *Railroad Transportation* (1885), was the first to generalize from railroad consolidation to the inevitability of industrial concentration. Seeing "the present age" as "an age of industrial monopoly," Hadley argued that the American economy was moving away from free competition. Yet, the existing system of thought blinded men to the changes that were occurring.

All our education and habit of mind make us believe in competition. We have been taught to regard it as a natural if not necessary condition of a healthful business life. We look with satisfaction on whatever favors it, and with distrust on whatever hinders it. We accept almost without reserve the theory of Ricardo, that, under open competition in a free market, the value of different goods will tend to be proportional to their cost of production.[82]

But, ultimately, Hadley's analysis was limited by his effort to generalize from the railroad problem. He sought to explain the particular forms of "cut-throat competition" that enabled railroads to cut prices below marginal costs, but he did not propose any general analysis of how industrial concentration could be explained in terms of economic theory. That task fell to another writer, Henry C. Adams, the chief statistician for the newly formed Interstate Commerce Commission.

Adams' brilliant and influential tract, "The Relation of the State to Industrial Enterprise" was the best expression of the new anti-laissez faire sentiment behind the recently formed American Economic Association.[83] It sought to define the conditions under which governmental regulation would be legitimate. Seeking to explain industrial concentration, Adams invoked John Stuart Mill's tripartite distinction among industries that displayed "constant," "diminishing," or "increasing" returns to scale. While the railroad was "a good illustration of this third class of industries,"[84] there were also "many other lines of business which conform to the principle of increasing returns, and for that reason come under the rule of centralized control."[85]

Such businesses are by nature monopolies. We certainly deceive ourselves in believing that competition can secure for the public fair treatment in such cases, or that laws compelling competition can ever be enforced. If it is for the interest of men to combine no law can make them compete. For all industries, therefore, which conform to the principle of increasing returns, the only question at issue is, whether society shall support an irresponsible, extra-legal monopoly, or a monopoly established by law and managed in the interest of the public.[86]

Though it was thereafter expressed in many different ways, the argument for the inevitability of industrial concentration always represented some variation on Adams' original insight about increasing returns to scale.

Among the earliest to proclaim the inevitability of industrial concentration were social thinkers who were influenced by European socialism and Marx's prediction of the inevitability of monopoly capitalism. In 1889, President E. Benjamin Andrew of Brown University declared that the competitive system was fast disappearing and giving way to trusts and combinations.[87] Although competition had "hitherto been assumed as the certain postulate of all economic analysis and generalization," in fact "in a great variety of industries, perhaps a majority of all, permanent monopolies may be maintained, apart from any legislative or special aids. . . . No economic laws prevent the permanent existence of monopolies."[88]

In the same year, the Christian Socialist Edward Bellamy pronounced with satisfaction the "doom" of the competitive system. Competition was at odds with the fundamental principles of Christianity. "[T]he competitive system tends to develop what is worst in the character of all, whether rich or poor. The qualities which it discourages are the noblest and most generous that men have, and the qualities which it rewards are those selfish and sordid instincts which humanity can only hope to rise above by outgrowing."[89]

Moving from the "moral iniquities of competition,"[90] he turned to an analysis of the causes of consolidation. "It is a result of the increase in the efficiency of capital in great masses, consequent upon the inventions of the last and present generations. . . . The economies in management resulting from consolidation, as well as the control over the market resulting from the monopoly of a staple, are also solid business reasons for the advent of the Trust."[91]

The few economists who still seriously defend the competitive system are heroically sacrificing their reputations in the effort to mask the evacuation of a position which, as nobody knows better than our hard-headed captains of industry, has become untenable. . . . While the economists have been wisely debating whether we could dispense with the principle of individual initiative in business, that principle has passed away, and now belongs to history.[92]

Except for his conclusion, Bellamy's vision of the inevitability of economic concentration was echoed by the new titans of industry. In 1888, the President of the American Cotton Oil Trust, John H. Flagler, defended the development of trusts as a reflection of "a steady, logical and wise evolution, or improvement in the method of conducting industrial affairs." There was an historical evolution in the conduct of business which passed through "successive stages of development" from individual to partnership to corporation and, now, to the trust. "This progressive development in the machinery for the conduct of business was impelled by the growing and ever-increasing demand for larger facilities, greater capital, greater energy, combination of activities, skill and intelligences."[93]

The courts did not yet agree. Beginning in the late 1880s, six different states brought *quo warranto* suits to revoke the charters of corporations that had become constituents of one of the great trusts.[94] The most famous lawsuits involved the successful Ohio and New York attacks on, respectively, the Standard Oil and Sugar Trusts.[95] In both cases, the courts dealt a set-back to any "entity" theory of the corporation, holding that the act of the individual shareholders in joining the trust was really the act of the corporation.

As the attacks on the trust form mounted, corporation lawyers realized that the earlier strategy of simply evading the restrictions of corporation law would no longer work. "It was considered wise to yield in the matter of form. The trusts were transformed into companies."[96] In the words of the biographer of one of these lawyers, William Nelson Cromwell, "[t]he vulnerability of the trust arrangement to the combination and conspiracy concept of the Sherman Act and to the legal analysis of the Ohio and New York decisions led to the finding of new legal techniques. The need was met by an amendment to the Corporation law of New Jersey."[97] Several corporation lawyers connected with Cromwell's firm "were among those active in the drafting of this amendment."[98] And, as Alfred D. Chandler has written, "The New Jersey legislature quickly obliged."[99]

The New Jersey Act of 1889,[100] which permitted incorporation "for any lawful business or purpose whatever," was among the first to allow one corporation to own the stock of another, thus legalizing the holding company and making the trust device unnecessary. Cromwell, himself, seems to have been the first lawyer to use the New Jersey provisions. As counsel to the Cotton Oil Trust, he appears to have conceived of the need for the New Jersey law after a lower court in Louisiana in 1889 sustained the state's effort to dissolve several of the Trust's constituent corporations.

Pending the appeal of an adverse decision, Cromwell called special meetings of all of the constituent corporations, obtained the necessary proxies and quietly dissolved the Louisiana corporations and transferred all their assets to a Rhode Island corporation set up for that purpose, whose stock was held by the trustees. When the appeal came on, he announced to the consternation of the Attorney General of Louisiana that the relief requested was no longer necessary for the Corporations were no longer in existence.[101]

In the same year, the American Cotton Oil Trust was reorganized once more as a New Jersey holding company, perhaps the first major enterprise to take advantage of the change in New Jersey law. The successful New York attack on the Sugar Trust also led it to reorganize as a New Jersey corporation. It soon received the additional benefit of immunity from the Sherman Anti-Trust Act, when the United States Supreme Court held in the *E.C. Knight Case*[102] that the Act could not constitutionally reach "manufacturing."

After the passage of the New Jersey Act, the entire expenses of the state of New Jersey were paid out of corporation fees. "[S]o many Trusts and big corporations were paying tribute to the State of New Jersey," noted New York corporation lawyer Charles F. Bostwick, "that the authorities had become greatly perplexed as to what should be done with [its] surplus revenue."[103] "[T]he relation of the state toward the corporations resembles that between a feudal baron and the burghers of old, who paid for protection," observed William W. Cook.[104] Lincoln Steffens simply called New Jersey "the traitor state."[105]

The passage of the New Jersey Corporation Act, followed by a rapid capitulation of many other states, marked the end of all serious efforts to use corporation law to regulate consolidation. Urging repeal of many New York restrictions on corporations, New York lawyer Charles F. Bostwick noted "the sudden exodus of hundreds upon hundreds of millions of dollars, controlled by corporate interests and financiers from New York into the State of New Jersey"[106] during the decade after the passage of the New Jersey law. "New York, although disclaiming any intention of entering into legislative competition for the securing of corporate capital within its jurisdiction, is, in fact, one of the most ardent bidders," Bostwick wrote.[107] For example, only three years after the passage of the New Jersey law, "the State of New York could no longer withstand the temptation, and the incorporation laws of this State were radically amended" to match the single most attractive New Jersey provision allowing holding companies. "[B]ut this came too late to get back any fugitive capital and still it continued to go elsewhere."[108]

The lesson, for Bostwick, was to further remove most restraints on corporations. "The *laissez faire* doctrine is good in government, and similar doctrine applied in politico-economic life is equally good," he concluded.[109] As state legislatures during the 1890s outbid each other in passing ever more "liberal" corporation laws that removed many of the remaining legal barriers to consolidation, the focus of those who hoped to preserve competition shifted to the Sherman Act.

But the New Jersey law confirmed the views of those who saw consolidation as inevitable, and during the 1890s, in both legal and economic writings, there is a marked shift towards the inevitability thesis.[110] By 1891, William W. Cook could declare that concentration was the result of "an established principle of economics." "It is a law of nature," he proclaimed. "These great concerns arise because by doing business on a large scale they can do it more cheaply."[111] "[M]ost of the younger economists of the country who have studied the question thoroughly," Von Halle reported in 1896, were "in favour of combinations." "Under the influence of historical thought, they feel convinced that the movement is an unavoidable step in an organic development, and that it finds its justification in the tendencies of modern capitalism."[112]

For the first time, the full implications of general incorporation laws began to be developed, and the view that legal forms cannot interfere with the natural evolution of the economy gained ascendancy. Commenting on the failure of legislation to check consolidation, Cook began the fifth edition of his celebrated treatise on corporation law with the aphorism, "The laws of trade are stronger than the laws of men."[113]

In these writings on corporations, we find the earliest articulation of that contempt for legal form that eventually came to characterize Legal Realism. "Whether true or false, the maxim 'combination is the life of trade,' is an economic and in no sense a legal proposition," wrote Arthur J. Eddy, the author of a well-known legal treatise on Combination, in 1901. "If sound, economic forces will protect it; if unsound, neither legislative enactments nor judicial utterance can give it life . . . the courts might as well try to conserve Gresham's law, the Malthusian theory, Ricardo's doctrine of rent, or any other economic, scientific or philosophic notion."[114]

Legal structures merely reflect the underlying economic substructure. "[T]he corporate form of co-operation has been like all other industrial, commercial, social and political forms a matter of development," Eddy explained. "[I]n some sort it existed prior to its recognition by law . . . the law simply sanctioned a form of organization which the commercial and industrial world found useful and indispensable." Even if there were no laws creating corporations, "men would necessarily act together . . . in joint associations." "Since the law is simply the application of common sense and reason to existing conditions . . . the law would follow the economic tendency, [and] the collective bodies would be recognized . . . there would inevitably spring up in a progressive community organizations in form similar to the modern corporation."[115] The large industrial corporation was, in short, a natural reflection of the rational economic tendency towards combination. "Consolidation," concluded William W. Cook, "is the spirit of the age, moving on resistlessly, regardless of human laws and hostile public sentiment."[116] Those who "disapprove of trusts and combinations [for] general anti-centralistic and individualistic reasons," wrote the economist Ernst von Halle in 1896, "play into the hands of socialism."[117]

Consolidation and Majority Rule

If the private law of corporations—that is, the law regulating relations within the corporation as well as with private parties—had not changed after 1880, it is difficult to imagine how the enormous corporate consolidation of the next thirty years could have taken place. For until the First World War—by which time the centralization of the American economy was largely accomplished—state corporation law was centrally involved in the question of corporate consolidation.

After 1880, ultra vires doctrines continued to limit the power of corporations to consolidate. While courts still refused to enforce ultra vires executory contracts, they generally were not willing to unravel contracts that had already been performed. Most judicial decisions that stood in the way of corporate consolidation did so on the grounds that a corporation had no power to lease its property to another corporation or to transfer its stock to a holding company. The single area that dominated Supreme Court ultra vires decisions between 1880 and 1900 were cases involving railroad consolidations. In a series of opinions during the last two decades of the nineteenth century, the Court consistently struck down as beyond corporate power arrangements by which one railroad leased all of its facilities to another line. The terms of these leases almost always exceeded the productive life of the assets transferred under them. Indeed, the Court occasionally gave its approval to the truly Draconian rule that the lessor under a void ultra vires agreement could not sue to recover the leased property or its value.[118] While these "loose" forms of consolidation confronted various legal impediments, an outright sale of corporate assets to produce a merger rarely ran afoul of ultra vires limitations since by the time the transactions were challenged in court they had already become "executed" contracts.

Some state courts were even noticeably unreceptive to the Supreme Court's views on leases used for consolidation. In 1886, the New Jersey Supreme Court treated such a lease as a fully executed contract that could not be interfered with.[119] And following a series of decisions generally hostile to the ultra vires doctrine, the New York high court in 1896 enforced the terms of a public utility lease, denouncing "the rank injustice" produced by the Supreme Court's ultra vires rule.[120] William W. Cook, the treatise writer on corporation law, cheered the New York decision as "breaking away entirely from the decisions of the Supreme Court of the United States and of the English courts on this subject." "The court," he wrote, "will not declare a contract void merely to satisfy a superannuated principle of law."[121] The lease cases caused even Judge Seymour Thompson of St. Louis, in his 1899 treatise on corporation law, to denounce "the abominable doctrine of *ultra vires*."[122]

It is quite clear that the Supreme Court's strict attitude towards ultra vires doctrine during the late nineteenth century was substantially related to hostility to corporate consolidation. An "old conservative" majority, favoring small competitive units of production and fearing large-scale enterprise, never really abandoned the traditional view of the corporation as an artificial creature of state power. It thus consistently deployed the ultra vires doctrine for the purpose of preventing further concentration.

There were essentially three stages in the efforts of corporations to achieve consolidation. The first stage, the "pool," represented a "loose" form of agreement employed by railroads, beginning in the 1870s, to fix rates and regulate traffic. Through a combination of ultra vires and anti-trust attacks, this form of cartelization was eventually defeated, though it had already largely proved unstable and impossible to enforce.[123]

A second effort, the "trust" or holding company, was fiercely attacked by state *quo warranto* decisions brought against the constituent companies. The New Jersey Corporation Law of 1889 was drafted to save the trusts, since it was among the first statutes to allow corporations to own shares in other corporations.[124] But even before the federal power was successfully deployed against holding companies in the *Northern Securities* case[125] (1904), the trust form had lost favor, and was replaced by direct merger.

The merger movement of 1898–1903 seems to have been based on the legal conclusion that courts might not deploy the Sherman Act to attack consolidation if it took the form of outright purchase of other businesses. Arthur Eddy wrote in 1901:

The Courts having condemned simple combinations [e.g. pools or price fixing agreements] and the trust form of combination as contrary to public policy the corporate form naturally suggested itself as a possible escape from the force and effect of the many decisions adverse to the other forms. It was argued that while the courts might deny the right of individuals, firms or corporations to meet together to form associations, pools or agreements with the intent to control prices and outputs, no court would deny the right of an individual, or of a partnership, or a corporation to purchase outright the assets, business and good-will of any individual, firm or corporation engaged in the same line of trade or manufacture. . . . So long as the state sanctions the creation of corporations without limitations as to power and capital, then it would seem to follow that within their chartered rights corporations have the same power to acquire property as has an individual.[126]

It was the task of legal theory to show that there was no difference between the rights of individuals and corporations to acquire property.

With the merger movement beginning in 1898, corporate strategists thus turned to outright consolidation. This strategy was undoubtedly encouraged by the unwillingness of both state and federal courts to use the ultra vires doctrine to unravel already consummated transactions.[127] While the Supreme Court throughout the 1890s had regularly supported attacks on "loose" forms of consolidation by refusing to enforce arrangements for long-term lease of corporate assets, the merger movement rendered ultra vires constraints practically irrelevant.

The new legal pressure point in attacks on corporate consolidation shifted to the common law rule that unanimous shareholder consent was necessary for sale of corporate assets or, indeed, for any "fundamental" change in corporate purposes.

During the 1880s, nearly all courts required unanimous shareholder consent to corporate consolidations as well as to other "fundamental" corporate changes.[128] The rule of unanimous consent, it should be noted, is a dramatic example of the extent to which partnership-contract categories governed important aspects of corporation law in the period immediately after the Civil War.[129] Any fundamental corporate change was regarded as a breach of the individual shareholder's contract as well as, in effect, an unconsented "taking" of his property.[130]

The obstacle that unanimous shareholder consent presented for consolidation was seen as early as 1887 by New York lawyer William W. Cook whose successive treatises on corporation law proclaimed the inevitability of economic concentration. With respect to the legal rule permitting any shareholder to object to a sale of assets, Cook accurately predicted in 1887, that "large interests will require and in some way will obtain a removal of the legal right of stockholders to object to the changes toward which the times are rapidly approaching."[131]

By the time the merger movement began, nearly all the states had passed general consolidation statutes applicable to railroad corporations.[132] These statutes permitted consolidation of lines with less than unanimous shareholder consent. In addition, by 1901, fourteen states, including Delaware (1899), New York (1890), and New Jersey (1896), had authorized any corporation "carrying on any kind of business of the same or similar nature" to merge with less than unanimous shareholder agreement.[133] The earliest consolidation statutes, therefore, permitted "horizontal" integration, while still denying corporations the power to engage in "vertical" mergers among different lines of business.

Vertical integration, therefore, came about not through statutorily authorized consolidations but through sale of assets. It still had to confront the general common law rule that any sale of corporate assets to achieve consolidation required unanimous agreement of the shareholders.

There was one small exception to the unanimity rule, which was first exploited by consolidating corporations to avoid the consequences of the rule. Where a corporation was insolvent and had no prospects of profit, courts had permitted a simple majority of shareholders to wind up the business and sell all of its assets. In the wake of the merger movement, courts began simply to "rubber stamp" the claims of the majority that the business was a failing one.[134] As a leading proponent of corporate consolidation put it in his 1902 treatise on Consolidation:

> It has been urged that this power of a majority to wind up a corporation, and to dispose of its assets for such purpose, exists only in the case of failing concerns. The distinction is not well drawn. . . . The very best time to wind up the affairs of a corporation may be in view of future uncertainties when it is most prosperous and has accumulated a large surplus. The determination of the question when this action should be taken, must rest in the discretion of the majority.[135]

This position was soon adopted by courts. Since it was clear that a majority could dissolve an insolvent corporation, "must [they] wait until the stockholders' investment is all lost before taking action?" the New Hampshire Supreme Court asked in 1912. "If the majority may sell to prevent greater losses, why may they not also sell to make greater gains?"[136] As a student of the subject has concluded: "In many [cases], it was . . . clear that the losing business was not being abandoned but was instead being continued by the new corporate owner of the assets. . . . By steps, then, these asset sales became de facto consolidations."[137]

At the same time as the judiciary was "sliding ineluctably toward majoritarianism in major corporation decisions involving shareholders,"[138] state legislatures began to take the lead in passing statutes allowing a majority to sell corporate assets. One of the earliest was a New York statute of 1893, which overruled the leading New York case expounding the unanimity rule.[139] In addition, Delaware in 1899 and New Jersey in 1902 passed legislation providing for appraisal and "buy out" of the shares of dissenting minority stockholders.[140] By 1926, there was "hardly a state . . . where the dominant common law rule . . . ha[d] not been abrogated by statute or decision."[141]

The shift to majority rule in fact made the merger movement legally possible. It not only made consolidations much easier to effect, it also dealt the final blow to any efforts to conceptualize the corporation as a collection of contracting individual shareholders.

When the rule of unanimous shareholder consent began to be widely articulated by courts around the time of the Civil War, the leading treatise on corporations still regarded business corporations as "little more than limited partnerships, every member exercising through his vote an immediate control over the interests of the body."[142] As late as 1890, the leading decision of the United States Supreme Court did "not see that the rights of the parties in regard to [sale of] the assets of [a] corporation differ from those of a partnership on its dissolution."[143] It referred to a treatise on Partnership before reaffirming the rule of unanimity.

In his brilliant study, *The Legal Nature of Corporations* (1897), Ernst Freund understood that the emergence of majority rule within a corporation could only be justified by some entity theory of the corporation that moved beyond contractualism and conceptions of individual property rights. How could the "corporate will" be identified with a simple majority of shareholders, Freund asked.

The true corporate will would be expressed by unanimous action resulting from common deliberation and mutual compromise and submission; but for purposes of convenience the law stops the process of reaching the conclusion halfway, and is satisfied with the concurrence of the greater portion of those acting. The justification of this legal expedient lies in the fact that the will of the majority may be presumed to express correctly what would be the result of forced unanimity; a presumption not always agreeable to fact, but convenient and more practicable than any other. . . . In so far as the presumption fails to be correct, it cannot be denied that a will which is not identical with the corporate will is imputed to the corporation, just as we impute the will of the agent to the principal without insisting that it should in all cases accord with the principal's will. The same view must be taken of the acts of other corporate organs; they may likewise be presumed to voice correctly the corporate will, but their will is not the corporate will strictly speaking.[144]

While Freund was tempted to derive majority rule from unanimous shareholder consent, he was forced to admit that it was a fiction "not always agreeable to fact." He turned instead to a theory of a separate corporate entity, "imput[ing]" to the corporation the "will" of the shareholders. Above all, majority rule was another example of Freund's conclusion "that in dealing with associations of persons we must modify the ideas which we have derived from the right of property in individuals, and what has first seemed to be an anomaly will appear simply as another but equally legitimate form of development."[145]

Attack on the Entity Theory

The first sustained effort to reconceptualize the corporation in the light of the triumph of general incorporation laws began during the 1880s.

In 1882, Victor Morawetz published *A Treatise on the Law of Private Corporations*, which proposed a radical reinterpretation of the legal status of the corporation. The corporation, Morawetz wrote, "is really an association formed by the agreement of its shareholders, and . . . the existence of a corporation as an entity, independently of its members, is a fiction."[146]

Morawetz treated corporations as virtually indistinguishable from partnerships. "[T]here is no reason of immediate justice to others, why a number of individuals should not be permitted to form a corporation of their own free will, and without first obtaining permission from the legislature, just as they may form a partnership or enter into ordinary contracts with each other."[147]

General incorporation laws "to a great extent . . . leave the right of forming a corporation and of acting in a corporate capacity free to all, subject to such

limitations and safeguards as are required for the protection of the public.'' The
only argument for restricting corporate powers, he claimed, was that notice of
limited liability of shareholders needed to be communicated to potential creditors.
''And this seems to be the chief office of the general incorporation laws which
are now in force nearly everywhere.''[148]

The source of corporate power was, for Morawetz, in the shareholders. The
principle of majority rule was derived, as in a partnership, from *unanimous*
shareholder consent. So the majority could not go outside of the purpose specified
in its charter without the unanimity of shareholders. Thus, the doctrine of ultra
vires, originally derived from the grant theory of the corporation, should be
replaced by the requirement of unanimous shareholder agreement, as in a partnership. Regulation of the corporate activity would come, not from the state,
but from the shareholders.

Morawetz' effort to ''disaggregate'' the corporation into freely contracting
individuals must have seemed at the time the only entirely logical conclusion to
draw in light of the triumph of general incorporation law. It not only dispensed
with an increasingly fictional conception of the corporation as a creature of the
state, it also made it possible to fit corporation law into the now dominant
individualistic mode of private contract law.

The tendency to reconceptualize the corporation along partnership-contractualist lines continued during the 1880s. In 1884, two years after Morawetz'
treatise, Henry O. Taylor, another New York lawyer, wrote *A Treatise on the
Law of Private Corporations* which was aimed, he said, at ''dismissing this
fiction'' of the ''legal personality'' of the corporation, so that ''a clearer view''
of individual rights and interests could be determined ''without unnecessary
mystification.''[149]

Taylor was supported by John Norton Pomeroy, the California lawyer who
was simultaneously putting forth this argument on behalf of the corporation in
the *Santa Clara* case. Pomeroy emphasized the significance of general incorporation laws in rendering older conceptions of incorporation anachronistic. ''The
common-law conception of the 'legal personality' of the metaphysical entity
constituting the corporation, entirely distinct from its individual [members], arose
at a time when corporations were all created by special charters,'' Pomeroy
wrote. All this had changed under general incorporation laws in which ''persons
complying with a few formal requisites can organize themselves into a company
for almost any business purpose . . . these associations differ very little in their
essential attributes from partnerships.''[150]

It is not entirely clear to what extent the legal thinkers who advocated a
partnership-contractualist conception of the corporation during the 1880s were
motivated by any particular political vision or attitude towards corporations.
Overtly, they seemed only to wish to bring corporation law into line with the
new reality of free incorporation. Pomeroy and Justice Field clearly believed
that the partnership theory offered the greatest chance of success in protecting
the corporation under the Fourteenth Amendment. Yet, their individualistic lan-

guage harkened back to earlier Jacksonian criticisms of corporations as "special privileges" and monopolies. And despite the fact that the clear tendency of attacks upon the traditional theory that corporations were creatures of the state was to undermine any claims to special state control of corporations, the partnership theory was soon treated as supporting an anti-corporate position.

Perhaps that was a correct understanding of its ultimate tendency. For example, Henry O. Taylor, the New York lawyer and corporate law treatise writer, appears to have been aware that his effort to dismiss the "fiction" of corporate personality for producing "unnecessary mystification" might also call into question the legitimacy of limited shareholder liability. Like Chief Justice Taney,[151] Taylor observed that limited liability was "the logical outcome of the notion of a corporation as a person, as a subject of rights and liabilities distinct from its members,"[152] a notion he was doing his best to undermine.

There were many suggestions during the 1890s that a contractual theory might subvert corporate privileges. Writing in 1892, Dwight A. Jones focused on the delegitimating tendency of the partnership theory.

[T]he main value of a corporate charter arises from the fact that powers and privileges are thereby acquired which individuals do not possess. It is this that makes the difference between a business corporation and a partnership. In the former there is no individual liability.... There is no death.... It is not policy therefore for a corporation to break down its own independent existence by burying its original character in the common place privileges of the individual.... *Any mingling of corporate existence with the existence of the stockholders will weaken corporate rights.*[153]

Indeed, opponents of corporate consolidation during the 1890s often advocated elimination of the corporate form and return to the partnership. One of the most influential American economists, Henry C. Adams, saw in the extension of the corporate form the root cause of the growth of economic concentration that was destroying competitive society. "[T]hese corporations," he wrote in 1894, "assert for themselves most of the rights conferred on individuals by the law of private property, and apply to themselves a social philosophy true only of a society composed of individuals who are industrial competitors."[154] Adams' solution was to limit the benefits of the corporate form to those "natural monopolies" that could actually demonstrate "increasing returns" to scale.[155]

Was there not good reason, then, to suspect that any contractualist theory of the corporation was only the first step toward attacking the corporate form itself? In 1900, Christopher G. Tiedeman published his *Treatise on State and Federal Control of Persons and Property in the United States*,[156] a greatly expanded and retitled version of his influential *Treatise on the Limitation of Police Power* (1886). The later book is filled with the anguish of the old conservative witnessing the rise of industrial concentration. Tiedeman wrote:

It does not take a very keen observer to note that, for the past fifteen or twenty years, the tending to the establishment of all-powerful and all-controlling combinations of capital

. . . has been increasing year by year in this country. . . . The rapid accumulation of vast fortunes has inspired some of their possessors with the desire for the acquisition of power through the control of industries of such great extension and scope, that they may earn the appellation of *kings* instead of *princes* of industry. If this economic tendency were left unchecked, either by economic conditions or law, the full fruition of it would be a menace to the liberty of the individual, and to the stability of the American States as popular governments.[157]

Finally Tiedeman brought the power of incorporation itself into focus.

[A]ll attempts to suppress and prevent combinations in restraint of trade must necessarily prove futile, as long as the statutes of the State permit the creation of private corporations. . . . The grant of charters of incorporation . . . only serves to intensify the natural power which the capitalist in his individual capacity possesses over the noncapitalist, by the mere possession of the capital. I advocate, as a return to a uniform recognition of the constitutional guaranty of equality before the law, the repeal of the statutes which provide for the creation of private corporations.[158]

The contractualist view of the corporation as essentially no different from a partnership began to come under attack from the moment it was presented. Its most forceful claim was that any entity theory of the corporation was a fictional and anachronistic carryover from a bygone era of special corporate charters. Yet, the picture of the corporation as a contract of individual shareholders was itself becoming a nostalgic fantasy at the very moment the partnership view was most forcefully put forth.

Some of the contractualists seemed to have in the back of their minds an ideal of what in a later age would be called "shareholder democracy." But during the 1880s it was beginning to become clear that management, not shareholders, were the real decision-makers in large publicly owned enterprises.[159] Ironically, Morawetz published his contractualist theory in the same year as Standard Oil was organized into the first of the great Trusts. Soon, the "oligarchic" tendency of the Trusts became a point of standard observation.

During the 1880s, the judicially imposed requirement of shareholder unanimity for fundamental corporate changes continued to provide the doctrinal foundation for a "partnership" theory of the corporation. But during the 1890s, several states including the commercially significant jurisdictions of Delaware, New York, and New Jersey, passed statutes that overthrew the unanimity rule for corporate consolidations. Many of these statutes also substantially enhanced the power of the board of directors to initiate such action.[160]

By the time of the First World War, it was common for legal writers to observe that "the modern stockholder is a negligible factor in the management of a corporation."[161] "It cannot be too strongly emphasized," another wrote, "that stockholders today are primarily investors and not proprietors."[162]

The Demise of the Trust Fund Doctrine: The New
Relationship of the Shareholder to the Corporation

One of the best measures of the shift in the conception of shareholders from "members" to "investors" in the corporation is the demise of the so-called "Trust Fund Doctrine" beginning in the 1890s. The demise of the Doctrine was paralleled by the growth of corporations, diversification in corporate ownership, and the subsequent expansion of the stock market.

The rise of the "natural entity" theory, at the same time, presented a picture of the corporation that legitimated the Doctrine's demise.

The origin of the Doctrine goes back to Justice Story's celebrated opinion in *Wood v. Dummer*[163] (1824) declaring that the capital stock of a corporation was a trust fund for the benefit of corporate creditors. Its central significance was to make the shareholders of an insolvent corporation liable for their failure to pay the full or par value of any stock to which they subscribed from a corporation.[164] This question of the extent of shareholder liability for "watered stock"—stock issued for less than par value—represented one of the two or three most important issues in corporate law during the late nineteenth century and generated hundreds of cases and thousands of pages of legal writing.

Accusations of widespread corporate fraud and financial manipulation focused on the "watered stock" question. And amid the wreckage of the 1893 Depression, judges and legal writers faced the fact that enforcement of the Trust Fund Doctrine had "punished the innocent and unsettled hundreds of millions of dollars of investments."[165]

In one case, prior to the Depression, the United States Supreme Court held stockholders liable on "watered stock" more than twenty-five years after the company failed.[166] In observing the changes that the Depression had produced, William W. Cook wrote: "Corporation ruin has created corporation law."[167]

History of Limited Shareholder Liability

It is not usually appreciated that truly limited shareholder liability was far from the norm in America even as late as 1900.[168] Though by the time of the Civil War the common law had evolved to the point of presuming limited shareholder liability in the absence of any legislative rule, in fact most states had enacted constitutional or statutory provisions holding shareholders of an insolvent corporation liable for more than the value of their shares. The most typical provision, which first appeared in the 1848 New York statute providing for general incorporation of manufacturing companies,[169] imposed "double liability" on shareholders. By the end of the nineteenth century, this provision "ha[d] been copied, in its essential features, in almost every State in the Union."[170] Many other constitutional or statutory enactments imposed even more extensive potential liability on shareholders.[171] As a result, the distinction between the liability of the "members" of a corporation and a partnership, so clear to modern eyes, was still regarded rather as a matter of degree than of kind throughout the nineteenth century. And even within the strictist of limited liability jurisdictions, the Trust Fund Doctrine promulgated by courts made innocent shareholders potentially liable for the difference between the par value and the purchase price of their shares.

When the Doctrine came under attack during the 1890s, its defenders emphasized that its main function was to protect creditors who had a right to suppose that the stated capital stock of a corporation reflected its real value. For a corporation to sell shares at discount was, they argued, a fraud on subsequent creditors. But unlike its original "partnership" rationale this argument for the Trust Fund Doctrine already conceded that corporations were separate entities and that the stockholders were only investors, not owners, managers, or members of a corporation. If the Trust Fund Doctrine was simply designed to give notice to protect creditors, the Doctrine's opponents replied, it can only apply to subsequent creditors since existing creditors could not have relied on a subsequent issue of watered stock.

By degrees, courts beginning in the 1890s gradually eroded the Trust Fund Doctrine. One of the most important immediate influences in producing the change was the rise of a national stock market, which definitively converted shareholders into impersonal investors. Yet, this was only the culmination of a long-term transformation by which shareholders, once regarded as "members" of a corporation, not fundamentally different from partners, came to be treated as completely separate from the corporate entity itself.

The Structural Transformation of the Corporation

In order to comprehend the changes in legal doctrine during the 1890s, we should first understand the dramatic changes in the structure of the business corporation as well as the market for stock that took place during the 1880–1900 period.

The major changes were in the size and scale of industrial companies. Before 1890, only railroads constituted "large, well-established, widely known enterprises with securities traded on organized stock exchanges, while industrials, though numerous, were small, scattered, closely owned, and commonly regarded as unstable."[172] Most of the manufacturing enterprises of the 1880s have been described as "small" companies, with net worth under $2 million. For the sake of comparison, there were extremely few "very large" companies worth more than $10 million, and even enterprises classified as "large" (worth between $5 million and $10 million) were also "fairly rare."[173] By contrast, "each of the country's ten largest railroads had more than $100 million of net worth and the largest of them all, the Pennsylvania Railroad, had over $200 million."[174]

In manufacturing, "the partnership form of organization predominated. . . . Where enterprises were incorporated, and, therefore, had outstanding securities, these were generally held by a small group of persons and were infrequently offered for sale to the public."[175]

Most of the leading manufacturing companies were family-owned. Even two of the "very large" companies, Singer Manufacturing and McCormick Harvesting Machine, were controlled by and had a majority of their stock owned by the family. And Andrew Carnegie's combined steel interests, which constituted among the very largest of manufacturing enterprises, were organized as closely owned partnerships until they converted to the corporate form in 1892.[176]

Nearly all of the distributive enterprises—wholesalers like Marshall Field in Chicago, R. H. Macy's in New York, and John Wanamaker in Philadelphia—were organized as partnerships as were companies in gold mining and oil drilling. And while the processing branch of industry—oil refining, sugar refining, lead smelting—was the first category in which large-scale publicly owned enterprises (besides railroads) developed during the 1880s, the meat processing giants, Swift and Armour, retained the partnership form well into the 1880s.

Before 1890 a man with excess capital to invest was likely to put his money into real estate. If he chose to buy securities, he had a relatively narrow range from which to select. The principal type of security investment was in railroading. Industrial securities, except in the coal and textile industries, were almost unknown.[177]

Those industrial securities that did exist were usually exchanged only in "direct person-to-person sales."[178] Between 1890 and 1893, however, industrials began to be listed on the Stock Exchange and to be traded by leading brokerage houses. And only after 1897, in the midst of the merger movement, did companies publicly offer shares of stock, replacing the system of "private" subscriptions that had prevailed throughout the nineteenth century. It is perhaps at this moment that we can clearly identify the beginning of the shift away from "the traditional point of view" of shareholders as "the ultimate owners, the corporate equivalent of partners and proprietors."[179]

The Overthrow

When Seymour Thompson published his six-volume treatise on corporation law in 1895, he lamented the fact that the Trust Fund Doctrine had only recently "been greatly modified" by American courts—"so much so, that it may now be doubted whether the capital of a corporation is a trust fund for its creditors in any different sense than the sense in which the property of a private person is a trust fund for his creditors."[180]

Beginning in 1887, the New York Court of Appeals overthrew the Trust Fund Doctrine.[181] And, in a widely followed opinion, the Minnesota high court held in 1892 that only fraud could permit a creditor to recover against a holder of "watered stock."[182] The most important consequence of this shift to a fraud theory was that in a majority of jurisdictions only subsequent creditors—those who presumably had relied on representations about the capital stock of the corporation—could sue on "watered stock."[183]

But the most controversial departures from the Trust Fund Doctrine appeared in a series of cases decided by the United States Supreme Court in 1891 through

1893. In the leading case of *Handley v. Stutz*[184] (1891), the high court, while purporting to reaffirm the Trust Fund Doctrine, distinguished between the original subscription to corporate shares, to which traditional trust fund shareholder liability applied, and a subsequent issue of shares at a discount by a "going concern," which created nonliability. Even Seymour Thompson conceded that where an established corporation "finds itself in urgent need" of money, "it would be a hard and perhaps a mischievous rule that would prevent it from reselling the shares at their market value."[185] Yet, he protested that, taken together, Supreme Court decisions had "overturn[ed] all former rulings" of the Supreme Court and "totally obliterat[ed]"[186] the Trust Fund Doctrine.

Handley v. Stutz and companion cases provided the opportunity for those who wished to attack the Trust Fund Doctrine. In its different treatment of the original and subsequent stock issues, wrote George Wharton Pepper, the Supreme Court had undertaken "the impossible task of distinguishing on principle between the status of two sets of stockholders."[187] Based on the Court's decisions, he concluded, the Trust Fund Doctrine "is neither a theory nor a doctrine."[188]

The seeming incoherence of the Court's distinction between the liability of different classes of shareholders encouraged advocacy of the more restricted fraud theory of liability.[189] Indeed, between 1891 and 1893, the Supreme Court itself wavered between theological reaffirmation of the Trust Fund Theory and statements that went to the verge of overruling the Doctrine.[190]

The root of the problem was that the relationship of the shareholder to the corporation had begun fundamentally to change during the 1890s. "[T]he liability of the stockholder to pay in full for his stock was an obligation placed upon him because of his relation to the corporation." Under "the traditional point of view," the shareholders were "the ultimate owners, the corporate equivalent of partners and proprietors."[191]

But as the market for shares widened, the relation of the shareholders to the corporation began to be redefined. For example, one of the major limitations on the Trust Fund Doctrine began to take shape even before *Handley v. Stutz* was decided. Was a subsequent bona fide purchaser of "watered stock" liable to creditors? No, answered the influential jurist, John F. Dillon in an 1879 railroad stock case. "Millions of dollars of stocks are sold in this country every week," Dillon wrote, "and there is no practice on the part of purchasers, and no understanding that the law requires of them that they shall ascertain . . . that certificates of full-paid stock have, in fact, been fully paid. . . . Besides, on what principle is it that a purchaser of the company's shares is to be held to be the guardian of the rights of the company's creditors and bound to protect them?"[192]

As the marketing of corporate shares moved away from formal "private" subscriptions, the meaningfulness of the Supreme Court's distinction between original and subsequent issues of stock began to collapse. So too, as Judge Dillon had suggested, the difference between bona fide purchasers of original and subsequent shares. "Certificates of stock have become such important factors in trade and credit, and general investment by all classes," wrote William W.

Cook in 1898, "that the law is steadily tending towards the complete protection of a *bona fide* purchaser of them in open market. . . . The constant tendency of the courts to increase the negotiability of certificates of stock will probably establish the rule that the purchaser in good faith of a certificate of stock is not liable on any unpaid subscription price thereof, unless such liability is stated on the face of the certificate itself. Indeed, even now this may be said to be the established rule."[193]

With the development of investment banking after 1900, even the marketing of original shares of corporate stock no longer entailed a formal relationship between the corporation and a subscriber. The original investor who purchased shares in the market for less than par value now was in a position no different from the subsequent bona fide purchaser whom courts had already been protecting against creditors.[194]

The establishment of a complete market for stock thus made an anachronism of the Trust Fund Doctrine. Indeed, New York in 1912 and Delaware in 1917 permitted the issue of stock without par value, and by 1924 thirty-four states had followed suit.[195] The Delaware law "in effect though not in form . . . cut off the creditors' remedy of shareholders' liability" when stock was issued for property or services.[196] By 1925, James C. Bonbright noted "that many lawyers with a long and extensive practice in corporation cases have never had a single suit involving a shareholder's liability on watered stock."[197] Little more than a generation earlier, by contrast, such suits had been the stock in trade of legal writing on corporation law.

When the Trust Fund Doctrine first came under attack during the 1890s, George Wharton Pepper noted that "many fundamental questions in regard to the legal status of corporations are still unsettled. . . . [I]t may be doubted whether any six learned judges would to-day give explanations even substantially similar of the difference between corporations and joint stock companies or statutory partnerships."[198] Indeed, as Pepper noted, one of the theories that might make the Trust Fund Doctrine coherent was a partnership theory, "the view that the corporation is identical with the members that compose it."[199] But the tendency of courts to distinguish between prior and subsequent purchasers of "watered stock"—a shift from the trust fund to the fraud doctrine—had already begun to erode such a conception.

When George Wharton Pepper introduced Maitland's work on Gierke to an American audience in 1901, he was quick to notice that a natural entity theory of the corporation made the Trust Fund Doctrine "unnecessary."[200] And a year later, a critic of the Doctrine charged the Supreme Court with "refus[al] to accept the consequences" of an entity theory of the corporation, which meant, he believed, overthrow of the Trust Fund Doctrine.[201]

The natural entity theory of the corporation thus emerged at virtually the same moment as the Trust Fund Doctrine began to collapse. As we have seen, one of the major organizing premises of the natural entity theory was to posit the existence of a sharp distinction between the corporate entity and the shareholders.

It was precisely this picture that ultimately subverted the coherence of the Trust Fund Doctrine.

The Corporate Entity and the Power of Directors

At some point at the beginning of the twentieth century, Americal legal opinion began decisively to shift to the view that "the powers of the board of directors . . . are identical with the powers of the corporation."[202] Earlier, the dominant view, as expressed by the United States Supreme Court, was that "when the charter was silent, the ultimate determination of the management of the corporate affairs rests with its stock holders."[203] "The law," said one federal court in 1881, "recognizes the stockholders as the ultimately controlling power in the corporation."[204] But modern corporate legislation, passed during the first quarter of the twentieth century, ratified a new "absolutism" that courts themselves had already begun to bestow upon corporate directors.[205]

Writing in 1895, Seymour Thompson identified "three radically different views"[206] that were still entertained by courts and legal thinkers concerning the nature and limits of the powers of corporate directors.

1. That the directors, being chosen representatives of the corporation, constitute, for all purposes of dealing with others, *the corporation itself*; hence, that within the scope of the objects and purpose of the corporation they have all the powers of the corporation itself. 2. That the directors have all the powers of *general agents* in the management of corporate affairs. 3. That they have only the powers of *special agents*.[207]

In an early Supreme Court case involving the Bank of the United States, the Court, per Justice Story, had clearly rejected, over a dissent by Chief Justice Marshall, the first, most expansive, definition of the powers of directors.[208] "In ordinary business corporations," Thompson conluded, "the powers of the board of directors . . . fall far short of being co-equal with the powers of the corporation."[209] In England, the judges had limited the directors' powers even further by classifying them within the most restrictive category of special agents. "On the whole," Thompson concluded, "judicial theory, at least in America, greatly preponderates in favor of the proposition that the directors of a business corporation are its *general* or managing agents."[210]

The classification of directors as agents itself underwent some important changes. The leading antebellum treatise on corporation law, by Angell and Ames, best reflects the earlier understanding of the limited legal position of the board of directors in the corporation. Whereas Judge Thompson's 1895 treatise devoted almost 500 pages to the legal status of directors, there is not even a separate chapter on the subject in the 1861 edition of Angell and Ames. Their discussion of directors is scattered throughout a chapter on "Agents of Corporations," which indiscriminately lumps together officers and directors. They confidently declared that, in the absence of any contrary legal provisions, "the power to appoint officers and agents rests, of course, like every other power, in the body of the corporators'' or shareholders.[211] And, most importantly, they announced the widely held view that directors have no inherent power ''to appoint subagents to contract for the corporation . . . and accordingly contracts made by such subagents will not be binding on the corporation.''[212]

In his 1877 treatise on corporation law, George W. Field observed that it was ''usual'' for corporations to confer the authority for managing the business ''upon a limited number of the members usually called directors or managers, who act, in most respects . . . as agents for and in place of the corporation, and of the stockholders.'' In the absence of any other legal provision, wrote Field, ''it is evident, on general principles, that the corporators [stockholders] would possess such power.''[213] However, when in 1897 Professor Ernst Freund addressed the question of whether the relation between the board of directors and ''the members at large of the corporation'' was the same as or different from ''that of principal and agent,'' he concluded that ''both views have found judicial support.''[214] While Freund saw that the agency analogy broke down to the extent that a majority shareholder resolution could not supersede the managing authority of the board, he did insist that, logically, unanimous shareholder action was the ultimate authority in the corporation. Indeed, Freund seemed to have endorsed ''the view that the members at large are the true and ultimate holders of the corporate rights.''[215]

The judicial reaction to the idea that corporate directors, being agents, could not delegate their powers to subagents is perhaps the best litmus for identifying the changing legal status of directors. Only in the early twentieth century did courts widely assert that, because the directors were ''the primary possessors of all the powers which the charter confers,'' the board's powers were therefore ''original and undelegated'' and hence could be conferred upon agents.[216]

The leading twentieth-century treatise on the power of corporate directors was written to reflect this shift in legal opinion. ''The enlargement of facilities for the purchase and sale of corporate securities,'' wrote Howard Holton Spellman in 1931, ''the tendency toward combinations of corporations, and the consequent desirability of diversification of individual investments have joined to create a class of stockholders who regard themselves as investors rather than co-entrepreneurs. . . . Accordingly, modern decisions tend toward an emphasis of the directors' absolutism in the management of the affairs of large corporations; the board of directors has achieved a super-control of corporate management and of the corporation's legal relations.''[217]

This shift in the internal constitution of the corporation was among the most important reasons for the demise of the partnership-contract theory of the corporation after 1900. Ernst Freund's ''representation'' theory of the corporation, for example, was directly dependent on ''the view that the members at large are the true and ultimate holders of the corporate rights.''[218] In 1897, Freund could still suppose that the realities of internal corporate organization could support such a theory. Yet, he already saw that ''where the whole sum of corporate

powers is vested by law directly in a board of directors . . . such an organization
. . . allows us to see in a large railroad, banking or insurance corporation rather
an aggregation of capital than an association of persons."[219]

The Natural Entity Theory

For orthodox legal writers of the 1880s, it still seemed sufficient to quote John
Marshall's view of the corporation as an "artificial entity" in order to combat
the partnership theory. They could also cite an abundance of Supreme Court
ultra vires decisions which continued to treat the corporation as a creature of the
state.

Above all, the artificial entity theory stood in the way of corporate consolidation. For those who, like Arthur Eddy, wished to argue that "corporations
have the same power to acquire property as has an individual,"[220] it was essential
that the artificial entity theory be overthrown. For Eddy, theories such as that
of the New York Court of Appeals in the celebrated Sugar Trust Case, amounted
to "a positive restriction of that liberty which is guaranteed by free institutions."
The New York court had written:

It is not a sufficient answer to say that similar results may be lawfully accomplished; that
an individual having the necessary wealth might have bought all these sugar refineries,
manned them with his own chosen agents, and managed them as a group, at his sovereign
will; for it is one thing for the state to respect the rights of ownership and protect them
out of regard to the business freedom of the citizen, and quite another thing to add to
that possibility a further extension of those consequences by creating artificial persons to
aid in producing such aggregations. The individuals are few who hold in possession such
enormous wealth, and fewer still who peril it all in a manufacturing enterprise; but if
corporations can combine and mass their forces in a solid trust or partnership, with little
added risk to the capital already embarked, without limit to the magnitude of the aggregation, a tempting and easy road is opened to enormous combinations, vastly exceeding
in number and strength and in their power over industry any possibilities of individual
ownership; and the state, by the creation of the artificial persons constituting the elements
of the combination . . . becomes itself the responsible creator, the voluntary cause, of an
aggregation of capital which it simply endures in the individual as the product of his free
agency. What it may bear is one thing; what it should cause and create is quite another.[221]

During the 1890s, one finds a growing movement to attack this "artificial
entity" theory of the corporation. Perhaps the original appeal of the contractualists to the underlying meaning of general incorporation laws had begun to
sink in. Or, perhaps, the casual declaration by the Supreme Court in 1886 that
the business corporation was a "person" under the Fourteenth Amendment was
beginning to have an effect, though the real significance of that doctrine was
still in the future. More probably, the phenomenal migration of corporations to
New Jersey after 1889 made legal thinkers finally see that, in fact as well as in
theory, corporations could do virtually anything they wanted to. The literature

of the 1890s on the inevitability of concentrated enterprise reflected this new reality by emphasizing for the first time the epiphenomenal nature of legal forms.

Beginning in the 1890s and reaching a high point around 1920, there is a virtual obsession in the legal literature with the question of corporate "personality."[222] Over and over again, legal writers attempted to find a vocabulary that would enable them to describe the corporation as a "real" or "natural" entity whose existence is prior to and separate from the state. What the contractualists first tried to express, with only the vocabulary and concepts of natural rights individualism then available to them, the entity theorists completed.

Along with the contractualists, they sought to represent the corporation as entirely separate from the state and therefore really "private." Contrary to the contractualists, they insisted that groups were just as "real" as individuals and that, in addition, the corporation was separate and distinct from its shareholders.

The earliest group of these "natural entity" theorists, writing in ignorance both of Gierke and Maitland, simply repeated over and over again that the corporation was not fictional, but "real," and that it was a "fact" like any other holder of rights.[223] Corporations were "autonomous, self-sufficient and self-renewing bod[ies]," and "they may determine and enforce their common will." "[N]either the group nor its functions is created by the state."[224]

The most brilliant of these early efforts to express the reality of groups was University of Chicago Professor Ernst Freund's *The Legal Nature of Corporations* (1897). Influenced by the work of Gierke on the nature of the corporation, Freund sought to translate Gierke's Hegelian analysis for a practical-minded and antimetaphysical American Bar.

For Freund, the basic conflict was between the fiction theory, which denied the idea of a distinct legal personality in the corporation, and the organic theory, propounded by many German jurists, "who insist that the distinctiveness of the corporate personality is as real as the individuality of a physical person."[225] The proponents of the fiction theory, by contrast, argued that a corporate entity "is nothing but the sum of its parts,"[226] ultimately reducible to the reality of individual wills.

Running through Freund's argument is the effort to overcome the traditional private law emphasis on the individual character of legal rights. "If the individual, private and beneficial right is to measure and govern all rules relating to rights of whatsoever nature, then the corporate right will continue to be abnormal and illogical."[227] On the other hand, the organic theory was "illusory" in encouraging "the impression that . . . corporate personality possesses an absolute unity and distinctiveness."[228] Its emphasis on the psychological cohesiveness and organic unity of groups did not really describe the business corporation, whose members were "without any noticeable psychological connection" even though they "may easily exercise common rights."[229] Above all, German organicist theory had lost itself "in metaphysical speculations and refined distinctions of little substantial value."[230]

Between individualism and organicism, Freund presented a theory of "representation,'' which portrayed the corporation as a representative democracy governed by majority rule. When ''we speak of an act or an attribute as corporate, it is not corporate in the psychologically collective sense, but merely representative, and imputed to the corporation for reasons of policy and convenience.''[231]

But Freund acknowledged the radical break with individualism he was proposing for corporate theory. He was, after all, attempting to justify the power of the corporate majority to bind the minority.

That each person should fully answer for all his acts, and should not answer for the acts of others, is indeed a maxim of extraordinary importance, and it seems to be violated in the admission of representative action not resting upon express delegation. Against this it can only be urged that the maxim without modification is unjustifiable, because it antagonizes or prevents the full protection of joint interests, which, as we have seen, demand representation. The foundation of all liability upon principles of moral responsibility is a legal conception which may be carried to excessive lengths; even if fully justified where liability is penal and the moral quality of the act is of the essence of its legal aspect, it may be inadequate where it is simply a question of adjusting conflicting interests in accordance with prevailing ideas of justice and equity.[232]

Yet, as with the earlier contractual theorists, Freund had his greatest difficulty in accounting for the oligarchic tendencies that were already becoming dominant within the large corporation. Many statutes vested corporate powers directly in the board of directors, he noted. At that point, he acknowledged, ''corporate capacity would thereby be shifted from the members at large to the governing body. . . . Such an organization reduces the personal cohesion between the [shareholders] to a minimum, and allows us to see in a large railroad, banking or insurance corporation rather an aggregation of capital than an association of persons.''[233]

At the very moment, then, at which Freund sought to derive the corporate personality from majority rule of the shareholders, the corporate entity itself was becoming virtually independent of the shareholders. It required a still more abstract justification of corporate personality, divorced entirely from any pretense that, ultimately, the shareholders ruled.

Two years after Freund wrote, Henry Williams attempted that justification. In an article in the *American Law Register*, he asserted that shareholders ''possess no actual existing legal interest . . . whatever'' in a corporation. Even in the case of dissolution, ''when their actual legal rights first accrue,'' shareholders' rights were ''entirely subsidiary'' to creditors. ''The stockholders,'' he concluded, ''are in the position of the heirs, or next of kin or residuary legatees of a living person.''[234]

In the flood of articles on corporate personality after the turn of the century, legal writers continued to reinforce the notion that a group must be treated as ''an organic whole . . . which cannot be analyzed into the mere sum of its parts.''[235] The corporation, these writers insisted, was a ''real'' entity, a ''fact,'' not a "fiction."[236] University of Chicago Law Professor Arthur W. Machen summed up these views in an influential 1911 article, emphasizing "the naturalness and indeed inevitableness of the conception of a corporation as an entity."

In these days it has become fashionable to inveigh against the doctrine that a corporation is an entity, as a mere technicality and a relic of the Middle Ages; but nothing could be further from the truth. A corporation is an entity—not imaginary or fictitious, but real, not artificial but natural.[237]

Following the inevitability theorists, Machen underlined the new view that the corporation existed prior to law. "All that the law can do is to recognize, or refuse to recognize, the existence of this entity. The law can no more create such an entity than it can create a house out of a collection of loose bricks."[238]

What was the political significance of the thousands of pages devoted to the question of corporate personality? The argument between entity and contractual theorists during the 1880s and 1890s was, at bottom, a conflict over whether the individual or group was the appropriate unit of economic, political, and legal analysis. Some contractualists were openly hostile to big business and offered the partnership model as an alternative to the corporate form, to which they ascribed most of the evils of consolidation and monopoly. But other contractualists were not so much opposed to the corporation as they were to its oligarchic tendencies. Contractualism was, for them, a way of reasserting the primacy of shareholder control.

In one important respect, contractualism prepared the way for the triumph of the natural entity theory. Reasoning from individualist premises so prominent in the decades immediately after the Civil War, the contractualists were the first to see the anomalous character of the "artificial entity" theory of the corporation, not only because it clashed with the underlying spirit of general incorporation laws, but also because of its hostility to any theory of natural rights. Every bit as much as the natural entity theorists, the contractualists worked from a conception of property as existing prior to the state. By contrast, the artificial entity theory represented a standing reminder of the social creation of property rights.

The main effect of the natural entity theory of the business corporation was to legitimate large-scale enterprise and to destroy any special basis for state regulation of the corporation that derived from its creation by the state. Indeed, the demise both of the ultra vires doctrine as well as of constitutional restrictions on foreign corporations was an expression of the triumph of the natural entity theory. An entity theory was also helpful for advocating even more limited shareholder liability while justifying the growing irrelevance of the shareholders in the modern business corporation. Finally, it obliterated the claim that corporate mergers were different from individual acquisitions of property.

In their emphasis on corporate "personality," early natural entity adherents attempted simply to capitalize on the language of natural rights individualism by portraying the corporation as just another right-bearing person. Most later progressive legal thinkers, however, followed Ernst Freund's more "realistic" effort, dismissing the idea of corporate "personality" as merely a "metaphor." But the progressives were at one in seeking to demonstrate the "real" and "natural" character of corporations.

If the natural entity theory arose to legitimate emerging large scale enterprise, it became in the hands of Progressive thinkers a way of being realistic about social and economic trends. Large corporations were here to stay, and, as one of the ablest Progressive legal writers, Gerard Henderson, put it in 1918, the natural entity theory "looks upon a corporation . . . as a normal business unit, and its legal personality as no more than a convenient mechanism of commerce and industry. . . . [T]he material basis is the growing internationalism of business, of trade, of investment."[239]

By the time Henderson wrote, Progressives had struggled to emancipate themselves from legal conceptions rooted in natural rights individualism. If the central goal of earlier natural entity theorists had been to extend the natural rights of individuals to the corporate "personality," the Progressives instead sought to show that all rights, both corporate and personal, were entirely the creature of the state. "When we speak of a corporation being the subject of rights," Henderson wrote, "we mean that it has the capacity to enter into legal relations— to make contracts, own property, bring suits. Rights, in this sense, are pure creatures of the law. . . . There is no reason, except the practical one, why, as some one has suggested, the law should not accord to the last rose of summer a legal right not to be plucked."[240]

Thus, the "corporate device" was "not an expression of any philosophic quality in the group—of any group will or group organism. It is no more than a convenient technical device . . . to achieve the practical results desired, of unity to action, continuity of policy [and] limited liability."[241]

Both the "fictional" and the "realist" schools had unnecessarily assumed that only "persons" could be the bearers of legal rights, Henderson argued. "The assumption that a person alone can be the subject of rights is based on the conception of a right as a philosophic entity, springing out of the nature of man, independent of the law and anterior to it."[242] This view, "modern jurisprudence has very generally rejected."[243]

Henderson echoed Pound in arguing that there were, in fact, not "rights" but "interests."[244] Thus, the "practical" recognition of the corporate entity in no way implied special privileges or protections for corporations. "The social purposes for which legislation may override private interests are of the broadest sort, and fortunately their scope is constantly growing. . . . All legislation must be tested . . . by the fundamental criterion whether it is reasonably adapted to securing these interests."[245]

However often the Progressives ridiculed discussions of corporate "will" and "personality" as a metaphysical inquiry derived from outmoded natural rights conceptions, they were not indifferent to whether the corporation should be treated as a real entity. Here they stood together with earlier "realist" thinkers in insisting that the recognition and protection of group interests was a "practical" necessity of modern life. "The commercial world," wrote Henderson, "whose habits of thought so largely influence the development of law, has come to regard the business unit as the typical juristic entity, rather than the human being. . . . New economic phenomena, railroads, industrial combinations, the emergence of hitherto disregarded social classes, determine its growth."[246]

It was the task of Realist legal thinkers to adjust legal conceptions to these changes. For example, the earlier conception that the stockholders constitute the corporation, Henderson wrote, "is of no value under modern conditions. The modern stockholder is a negligible factor in the management of a corporation."[247] Standing behind the pragmatism of the Progressive view of corporations, then, was an acceptance of the recent triumph of the corporate form as "a normal business unit."[248] No longer was it necessary to resort to "metaphysics" to establish the legitimacy of the business corporation. It had become a *fait accompli*.

CONCLUSION

The *Santa Clara* case did not represent the triumph of a "natural entity" theory of the corporation. In 1886, when old conservatism still dominated the world view of Supreme Court justices, any such conception of corporate personality would have been received with hostility by a court still actively suspicious of corporate power and the emergence of concentrated enterprise. The 1905 case of *Hale v. Henkel*[249] underlines how late it was before the Supreme Court ambivalently began the move towards a "natural entity" theory in corporate constitutional jurisprudence. Its opinion that the search and seizure provisions of the Fourth Amendment apply to the corporation while the Fifth Amendment's self-incrimination clause does not, still wavers between the past and the future.

In *Santa Clara* a "natural entity" theory was unnecessary for the immediate task of constitutionalizing corporate property rights. An "aggregate" or "partnership" or "contractual" vision of the corporation—with well-established roots going back to the *Dartmouth College Case*[250]—was sufficient to focus the conceptual emphasis on the property rights of shareholders. Either a partnership or natural entity view could equally successfully have subverted the dominant "artificial entity" view of the corporation as a creature of the state.

If the choice between a "natural entity" and partnership theory was a toss-up when *Santa Clara* was decided, other nonconstitutional considerations soon pushed American legal theory toward the entity conception.

First, by 1900 it was no longer easy to conceive of shareholders as constituting the corporation. Changes in the conception of the shareholder from active "owner" to passive "investor" weakened the evocative power of partnership theory. Moreover, the entity theory was better able to justify the weakened position of the shareholders in internal corporate governance.

Second, the partnership theory represented a threat to the legitimacy of limited liability of shareholders. The entity theory, by contrast, emphasized the distinction between corporations and partnerships.

Third, while the partnership theory pushed in the direction of requiring shareholder unanimity for corporate mergers, the entity theory made the justification of majority rule possible.

Fourth, the entity theory was superior to the partnership theory in undermining Chief Justice Taney's foreign corporation doctrine which represented a substantial legal threat to the emergence of national corporations doing business in each of the states. The foreign corporation doctrine's reversal, shortly before World War I, can be associated with the triumph of the entity theory.

Finally, let me now remind you of why, if I am correct, these conclusions are important for general legal theory.

While it might be possible at some high level of abstraction divorced from concrete social understandings to demonstrate that the partnership theory could be manipulated to accomplish any of the legitimating tasks for which I have claimed the natural entity theory was superior, in many of the specific historical contexts I have identified the two conceptions of corporate personality did not have equal evocative or persuasive power. Indeed, they carried with them considerable legal and intellectual baggage that did not permit random deployment or infinite manipulability.

While John Dewey may have been correct in identifying the contradictory or random deployment of these conceptions as applied to labor unions and business corporations, he could not, I believe, have successfully demonstrated that each theory of *corporate* personality could have equally legitimated the practices of emergent large scale business enterprise.

An important task of legal theory, then, is to uncover the specific historical possibilities of legal conceptions—to "decode" their true concrete meanings in real historical situations. We have spent much too much intellectual energy in the increasingly sterile task of discussing legal theory in a historical vacuum. That is one of the reasons why Anglo-American jurisprudence constantly seems to get no further than repeated rediscoveries of the wheel. By contrast, in more specific settings, one finds that legal theory does powerfully influence the direction of legal understanding.

NOTES

1. Santa Clara County v. Southern Pacific R.R., 118 U.S. 394 (1886).

2. Lochner v. New York, 198 U.S. 45 (1905) (state regulations limiting the hours of employment in bakeries violate the right to freedom of contract guaranteed by U.S. Const. 14th amend.).

3. See Graham, Justice Field and the Fourteenth Amendment, 52 Yale L.J. 851, 853 (1943); Graham, The "Conspiracy Theory" of the Fourteenth Amendment, 47 Yale

L.J. 371, 403 (1938). See also C. Beard, Contemporary American History: 1877–1913 208, 210–13 (1936).

4. Connecticut Gen. Life Ins. v. Johnson, 303 U.S. 77 (1938); Wheeling Steel v. Glander, 337 U.S. 562, vacated, U.S. Gypsum Co. v. Glander, 337 U.S. 951, rev'd, 337 U.S. 951 (1949).

5. First Nat'l Bank of Boston v. Bellotti, 435 U.S. 765 (1978), reh'g denied 438 U.S. 907 (1978).

6. Id. at 780 n. 15.

7. Gitlow v. New York, 268 U.S. 652 (1925).

8. Bellotti, 435 U.S. at 778 n. 14 (referring to Justice Rehnquist's dissenting opinion at 822). See id. at 780 n. 15.

9. Santa Clara, 118 U.S. at 396.

10. Dartmouth College v. Woodward, 17 U.S. (4 Wheat.) 518 (1819).

11. Graham, supra note 3, 52 Yale L.J. at 853.

12. Santa Clara v. Southern Pac. R.R., 18 F. 385, 402–05 (C.C. Cal. 1883); San Mateo v. Southern Pacific R.R., 13 F. 722, 746–48 (1882) (companion cases).

13. Dewey, The Historical Background of Corporate Legal Personality, 35 Yale L.J. 655 (1926).

14. Fuller, American Legal Realism, 82 U. Pa. L. Rev. 429 (1934).

15. Dewey, supra note 13, at 669–70.

16. Cohen, Transcendental Nonsense and the Functional Approach, 35 Colum. L. Rev. 809 (1935).

17. See, e.g., Dalton, An Essay in Deconstruction of Contract Doctrine, 94 Yale L.J. 997, 1006–07 (1985); Kennedy, Form and Substance in Private Law Adjudication, 89 Harv. L. Rev. 1685, 1731–38 (1976); Singer, The Player and the Cards: Nihilism and Legal Theory, 94 Yale L.J. 1, 9–25 (1984); Unger, The Critical Legal Studies Movement, 96 Harv. L. Rev. 561, 568–70 (1983).

18. Kennedy, The Structure of Blackstone's Commentaries, 28 Buffalo L. Rev. 205 (1979).

19. Cohen, The Ethical Basis of Legal Criticism, 41 Yale L.J. 201, 215–19 (1931); Dewey, Logical Method and Law, 10 Cornell L. Rev. 17 (1924).

20. Lochner, 198 U.S. at 76 (1905).

21. San Mateo, 13 F. 745; Sacramento v. Central Pac. R.R., 18 F. 385 (1883) (for taxes of 1882); California v. Northern Ry., 18 F. 385 (1883); California v. Central Pac. R.R., 18 F. 385 (1883); California v. Southern Pac. R.R., 18 F. 285 (1883); Santa Clara, 18 F. 385.

22. The Slaughterhouse Cases, 83 U.S. (16 Wall.) 36 (1873).

23. Id. at 100–01.

24. Id. at 104–05.

25. Argument for Defendant, San Mateo v. Southern Pac. R.R. Co., 116 U.S. 138 (1882) (collected in Cases and Points at 12 (available in Harvard Law School Library)) (emphasis in original).

26. Id. at 10 (emphasis in original).

27. San Mateo, 13 F. at 743–44.

28. O. Gierke, Das Deutsche Genossenschaftsrecht (1887).

29. For a good bibliography, see 4 R. Pound, Jurisprudence 200–01 (1959) (unnumbered note).

30. O. Gierke, Political Theories of the Middle Ages (F. W. Maitland ed. 1900).

31. F. W. Maitland, Collected Papers (H. A. L. Fisher ed. 1911).

32. E. Freund, The Legal Nature of Corporations (1897).

33. F. W. Maitland, supra note 31, at 321.

34. Id. at 317.

35. See 1 S. Thompson, Commentaries on the Law of Private Corporations vi (1st ed. 1895).

36. Frug, The City as a Legal Concept, 93 Harv. L. Rev. 1057, 1083–90 (1980).

37. Laski, The Personality of Associations, 29 Harv. L. Rev. 404 (1916); See generally W. Y. Elliott, The Pragmatic Basis of Politics (1928).

38. See R. Wiebe, The Search for Order: 1877–1920 (1967); Galambos, Technology, Political Economy, and Professionalization: Central Themes of the Organizational Synthesis, 57 Bus. Hist. Rev. (1983); Galambos, The Emerging Organizational Synthesis in Modern American History, 44 Bus. Hist. Rev. (1970).

39. I. P. Vinogradoff, Outlines of Historical Jurisprudence 147–48 (1920); White & Vann, The Invention of English Individualism, 8 Social History 345, 352–54 (1983); D. Sugarman & G. R. Rubin, Towards a New History of Law and Material Society in England, 1750–1914 in Law, Economy and Society 28–30 (1984) (Rubin & Sugarman eds.).

40. F. W. Maitland, supra note 30, at 317.

41. Dartmouth College, 17 U.S. (4 Wheat.) at 636, quoted in J. Hurst, The Legitimacy of the Business Corporation in the Law of the United States, 1780–1970 at 9 (1970).

42. Id.

43. See infra note 53 and accompanying text.

44. See infra notes 146–50 and accompanying text.

45. See infra note 120 and accompanying text.

46. Hale v. Henkel, 201 U.S. 43 (1905). As late as 1904, the Supreme Court declared: "A corporation, while by fiction of law recognized for some purposes as a person, and for purposes of jurisdiction as a citizen, is not endowed with the inalienable rights of a natural person." Northern Securities Co. v. United States, 193 U.S. 197, 362 (1904). And in 1906 it stated that "the liberty guaranteed by the fourteenth amendment against deprivation without due process of law is the liberty of natural, not artificial persons." Western Turf Assoc. v. Greenberg, 204 U.S. 359, 363 (1906) (citing Northwestern Life Ins. Co. v. Riggs, 203 U.S. 243, 255 (1906)).

This way of thinking began to crumble with Hale, 201 U.S. 43, and was finally put to rest in 1910 in a series of "unconstitutional conditions" cases involving foreign corporations. See infra note 71, and G. Henderson, infra note 67, at 132–47.

47. A. Chandler, The Visible Hand: The Managerial Revolution in American Business 161 (1983).

48. See infra note 202 and accompanying text.

49. E. Freund, supra note 32, at 10.

50. Id. at 48.

51. See generally, C. G. Haines, The Revival of Natural Law Concepts (1930).

52. The most dramatic, largely because it seems so out of place, is Chief Justice Marshall's effort in Bank of United States v. Devereaux, 9 U.S. (5 Cranch) 61 (1809) to base the diversity jurisdiction of corporations on the residence of its shareholders. By the 1840s this approach was abandoned with Louisville R.R. v. Letson, 43 U.S. (2 How.) 497 (1844). A more far-reaching act of disaggregation—which remained ambiguous and

muted—was the implied distinction in the Dartmouth College case between, on the one hand, the artificial and socially created corporation and, on the other hand, the vested rights of the shareholders. See also J. Hurst, supra note 41, at 15–22.

53. Bank of Augusta v. Earle, 38 U.S. (13 Pet.) 519, 586 (1839).

54. State v. Standard Oil Co., 49 Ohio St. 137, 30 N.E. 279 (1892).

55. R. Reese, The True Doctrine of Ultra Vires in the Law of Corporations 2 (1897).

56. See Colson, The Doctrine of Ultra Vires in United States Supreme Court Decisions I, 42 W. Va. L.Q. 179, 184–89 (1936).

57. Id.

58. See infra note 95.

59. 5 S. Thompson, supra note 35, at 4629.

60. 1 W. Cook, Treatise on Stock and Stockholders, Bonds, Mortgages, and General Corporation Law 971–73 (3d ed. 1894).

61. 5 S. Thompson, supra note 35, at 4664–78.

62. Compare National Bank v. Matthews, 96 U.S. 258 (1877) and San Antonio v. Mehaffy, 96 U.S. 312 (1877) with Thomas v. West Jersey R.R., 101 U.S. 71 (1879); see also Colson, supra note 56, at 207–09, 213 (1936).

63. See Colson, The Doctrine of Ultra Vires in United States Supreme Court Decisions II, 42 W. Va. L.Q. 297, 330 (1936).

64. See Carpenter, Should the Doctrine of Ultra Vires Be Discarded? 33 Yale L.J. 49 (1923).

65. 1 W. Cook, Treatise on the Law of Corporations Having a Capital Stock, vii-viii (4th ed. 1898). "In the federal courts . . . the old rule against ultra vires contracts is upheld in all its rigor and applied with all its severity. The tendency of modern jurisprudence to relax on that subject finds no favor in the federal courts" (7th ed. 1913).

66. See Colson, supra notes 56 and 63.

67. G. Henderson, The Position of Foreign Corporations in American Constitutional Law 42 (1918).

68. Bank of Augusta, 38 U.S. at 587–88.

69. Id. at 588.

70. Paul v. Virginia, 75 U.S. (8 Wall.) 168 (1868).

71. Western Union Telegraph Co. v. Kansas, 216 U.S. 1 (1910); Pullman Co. v. Kansas, 216 U.S. 56 (1910); Ludwig v. Western Union Telegraph Co., 216 U.S. 146 (1910); Southern Ry. v. Greene, 216 U.S. 400 (1910).

72. Horwitz, Progressive Legal Historiography, 63 Or. L. Rev. 679 (1984).

73. United States v. Trans-Missouri Freight Ass'n, 166 U.S. 290 (1897); United States v. Joint Traffic Ass'n, 171 U.S. 505 (1898); Hopkins v. United States, 171 U.S. 578 (1898); Anderson v. United States, 171 U.S. 604 (1898); Addyston Pipe & Steel Co. v. United States 175 U.S. 211 (1899). The clearest statement of this "literalist" interpretation was given by Justice Peckham in Trans-Missouri: "When, therefore, the body of an act pronounces as illegal every contract or combination in restraint of trade or commerce among the several States, etc., the plain and ordinary meaning of such language is not limited to that kind of contract alone which is in unreasonable restraint of trade, but all contracts are included in such language, and no exception or limitation can be added without placing the act that which has been omitted by Congress." Trans-Missouri, 166 U.S. at 328.

74. Standard Oil Co. v. United States, 221 U.S. 1 (1911).

75. See 3 J. Dorfman, The Economic Mind in American Civilization 138 (1949).

76. See, e.g., S. Dillaye, Monopolies: Their Origin, Growth and Development (1882).

77. Lloyd, The Story of a Great Monopoly, 47 Atlantic Monthly 317 (1881).

78. H. Thorelli, The Federal Antitrust Policy: Origination of an American Tradition 134 (1954) (citing Lloyd, Lords of Industry, 138 N. Am. Rev. 535–53 (1884)).

79. A. Chandler, supra note 47, at 323.

80. Dwight, The Legality of Trusts, 3 Pol. Sci. Q. 592, 631 (1888).

81. S. Thompson, The Power of the People over Corporate and Individual Combinations and Monopolies, in Proceedings of the Ill. State Bar Ass'n 81, 84 (1891). Thompson concluded that "as a general rule, we may safely trust to the operation of natural laws and to the inherent weakness of every human combination, for a sufficient remedy." Id. at 90.

82. A. Hadley, Railroad Transportation—Its History and Its Laws 69 (1885).

83. T. Haskell, The Emergence of Professional Social Science (1977).

84. Adams, The Relation of the State to Industrial Action, 1 Publications of the Am. Econ. Ass'n 7, 61 (1887).

85. Id. at 64.

86. Id.

87. Andrews, Trusts According to Official Investigations, 3 Q.J. Econ. 117 (1889).

88. Andrews, The Economic Law of Monopoly, 26 J. Soc. Sci 1 (1890).

89. E. Bellamy, Plutocracy or Nationalism—Which? 2 (1889).

90. Id. at 3.

91. Id. at 5.

92. Id. at 1, 5.

93. Address by Mr. John H. Flagler Before the Commercial Club of Providence, Rhode Island (December 15, 1888).

94. People v. Chicago Gas Trust Co., 130 Ill. 268, 22 N.E. 789 (1887); People v. North River Sugar Refining Co., 22 Abb. N. Cas. 164 (1889); State v. Nebraska Distilling Co., 29 Neb. 700, 46 N.W. 155 (1890). See Louisiana v. American Cotton-Oil Trust, 1 Ry. & Corp. L.J. 509 (1887); California v. American Sugar Refining Co. 7 Ry. & Corp. L.J. 83 (1890).

95. See North River Sugar Refining Co., 22 Abb. N. Cas. 164.

96. E. Von Halle, Trusts or Industrial Combinations and Coalitions 94 (1895).

97. Dean, A Tribute to William Nelson Cromwell: An Address Delivered at the Cromwell Library of the American Bar Foundation, Chicago, Illinois (February 22, 1955) 69.

98. Id. at 70.

99. A. Chandler, supra note 47.

100. N. J. Laws, Ch. 269, § 4 at 414 (1889).

101. See supra note 97, at 99.

102. United States v. E. C. Knight Co., 156 U.S. 1 (1894).

103. C. Bostwick, Legislative Competition for Corporate Capital 22 (1899).

104. W. Cook, supra note 60 at vi.

105. Steffens, New Jersey: A Traitor State, 25 McClure's Magazine 41 (1905).

106. C. Bostwick, supra note 103, at 1.

107. Id. at 4.

108. Id. at 15.

109. Id. at 11.

110. W. Letwin, Law and Economic Policy in America 71–85 (1965).

111. W. Cook, The Corporation Problem 226 (1891).

112. E. von Halle, supra note 96, at 113.

113. See W. Cook, supra note 65, at vii.

114. 1 A. Eddy, The Law of Combinations, 665–66 (1901).

115. Id.

116. W. Cook, supra note 60, at vii (5th ed. 1903).

117. E. von Halle, supra note 96, at 113.

118. Compare St. Louis, Vandalia & Terre Haute R.R. v. Terre Haute & Indianapolis R.R., 145 U.S. 393 (1892) with Pullman's Palace Car Co. v. Central Transp. Co., 171 U.S. 138 (1898). See Harriman, Ultra Vires Corporation Leases, 14 Harv. L. Rev. 332 (1900); W. C. Noyes, A Treatise on the Law of Intercorporate Relations 349–52 (1st ed. 1902).

119. See Camden & Atlantic R.R. v. May's Landing & Egg Harbor City R.R., 48 N.J.L. 530 (1886).

120. Bath Gas Light Co. v. Claffy, 151 N.Y. 24, 34, 45 N.E. 390, 395 (1896).

121. W. Cook, supra, note 60, at viii.

122. 7 S. Thompson, supra note 35, at 7032 (2nd ed. 1899).

123. H. Thorelli, supra note 78, at 73–76.

124. See supra note 100 and accompanying text.

125. Northern Securities Co. v. United States, 193 U.S. 197 (1904).

126. 1 A. Eddy, supra note 114, at 601–02.

127. Metcalf v. American School Furniture Co., 122 F. 115 (W.D.N.Y. 1903).

128. See, e.g., Mason v. Pewable Mining Co. 133 U.S. 50 (1890); State ex rel. Brown v. Bailey, 16 Ind. 46 (1861); McCray v. Junction R.R., 9 Ind. 358 (1857); Stevens v. Rutland & Burlington R.R., 29 Vt. 545 (1851); see also Carney, Fundamental Corporate Changes, Minority Shareholders and Business Purposes, Am. Bar Found. Research J. 69, 88–89 (1980).

129. See Angell & Ames, Treatise on the Law of Private Corporations 537, 569 (11th ed. 1882).

130. 1 V. Morawetz, A Treatise on the Law of Private Corporations iii (2d ed. 1886); see also Carney, supra note 128, at 77–78.

131. W. Cook, supra note 60 (1st ed. 1887).

132. See statutes cited in W. C. Noyes, supra note 118, at 29 n. 1.

133. W. C. Noyes, supra note 118, at 36 n. 1 and at 84 n. 2. These states were: Alabama (1896), Colorado (1891), Connecticut (1901), Delaware (1899), Illinois (1895), Kentucky (1894), Louisiana (1874), Maryland (1888), Missouri (1889), Nevada (1883), New Jersey (1896), New York (1890), Pennsylvania (1901), Utah (1898). Noyes' list of thirteen states does not include the Pennsylvania statute of 1901. Actual dates of enactment for Colorado (1877), Illinois (1872), Kentucky (1893), and Utah (1896) are found in the following compilations of state laws: Mills, Mills' Annotated Statutes of the State of Colorado 688 (1891); 2 W. C. Jones & K. H. Addington, Annotated Statutes of the State of Illinois 1588–89 (1913); J. Barbour & J. Carroll, The Kentucky Statutes 350 (3rd ed. 1903); Young, Smith & Lee, The Revised Statutes of the State of Utah 163 (1897).

134. Metcalf v. American School Furniture Co., 122 F. 115; Traer v. Lucas Prospecting Co., 124 Iowa 107, 99 N.W. 290 (1904); Tanner v. Lindell R'y Co., 180 Mo. 1, 79 S.W. 155 (1904); Beidenkopf v. Des Moines Life Ins. Co. & National Life Ins. Co., 160 Iowa 629, 142 N.W. 434 (1913); Lange v. Reservation Mining and Smelting

Co., 48 Wash. 167, 93 P. 208 (1908); Butler v. New Keystone Copper Co., 10 Del. Ch. 371, 93 A. 380 (1915).

135. W. C. Noyes, supra note 118, at 174–75.

136. Bowditch v. Jackson Co., 76 N.H. 351, 82 A. 1014, 1017 (1912).

137. See Carney, supra note 128, at 88–89.

138. Id. at 90.

139. See In re Timmis, 200 N.Y. 177, 93 N.E. 522 (1910) for the New York statutory history. The leading case on shareholder unanimity is Abbott v. American Hard Rubber Co., 33 Barb. 578 (1861).

140. The Delaware statute appears in W. C. Noyes, supra note 118, at 94 n. 4. The New Jersey statute, broadening an 1896 law, appears in W. C. Noyes, supra note 118, at 232 n. 2 (2d ed. 1909). These appraisal statutes, Noyes wrote, "are probably broad enough to be available in aid of a reorganization through the transfer of corporate assets in exchange for stock." Id. at 232.

141. Weiner, Payment of Dissenting Stockholders, 27 Colum. L. Rev. 547 (1927).

142. Angell & Ames, supra note 129, at 166 (6th ed. 1858).

143. Mason v. Pewabic Mining Co., 133 U.S. 50, 59.

144. E. Freund, supra note 32, at 10.

145. Id. at 48.

146. 1 V. Morawetz, supra note 130, at iii.

147. Id. at 24 (1st ed. 1882).

148. Id.

149. H. Taylor, A Treatise on the Law of Private Corporations Having Capital Stock iv (1884).

150. Note, The Legal Idea of a Corporation, 19 Am. L. Rev. 114, 115 (1885).

151. See supra note 53 and accompanying text.

152. See H. Taylor, supra note 149, at 12.

153. D. Jones, A Corporation as "A Distinct Entity," 2 Counsellor 78, 79 (1892).

154. Adams, Relation of the State to Industrial Action and Economics and Jurisprudence: Two Essays by Henry Carter Adams (ed. J. Dorfman) intro. essay at 47–48 (1954).

155. Adams, Suggestions for a System of Taxation, Publications of the Michigan Political Science Ass'n (Ann Arbor, Mich.) 1, no. 2, 60 (May, 1894).

156. 1 C. Tiedeman, A Treatise on State and Federal Control of Persons and Property in the United States (2d ed. 1900).

157. Id. at 382–83.

158. Id. at 609–10.

159. Shiras, Classification of Corporations, 4 Yale L.J. 97, 99–100 (1895).

160. Beardstown Pearl Button Co. v. Oswald, 130 Ill. App. 290, 294–95 (1906).

161. G. Henderson, supra note 67, at 169.

162. J. Carter, The Nature of the Corporation as a Legal Entity 160 (1919).

163. Wood v. Dummer, 3 Mason 308, 30 Fed. Cas. 435 (1824). The Supreme Court adopted the Trust Fund Doctrine in Sawyer v. Hoag, 84 U.S. (17 Wall.) 610 (1873).

164. A second question was whether, in the absence of a national bankruptcy law, the trust fund doctrine prevented an insolvent corporation from exercising a preference about the order in which it paid its creditors, since it was concededly legal for an insolvent individual to exercise such discretion.

165. 1 W. Cook, supra note 60, at vii.

166. Hawkins v. Glenn, 131 U.S. 319 (1889); Glenn v. Liggett, 135 U.S. 533 (1890);

Glenn v. Taussig, 135 U.S. 533 (1890); Pincoffs, Corporations: Capital Stock a Trust Fund For Creditors, 26 Am. L. Rev. 100, 102 (1892).

167. 1 W. Cook, supra note 60, at v(4th ed. 1898).

168. The emphasis in histories of limited shareholder liability has been on identifying the periods in which shareholder liability to creditors of an insolvent corporation diverged from unlimited partnership liability. From this perspective, any limitation on otherwise unlimited liability is significant. See, e.g., Dodd, The Evolution of Limited Liability in American Industry: Massachusetts, 61 Harv. L. Rev. 1351, 1379 (1948) (identifying when the American common law diverged from England and assumed limited liability as the norm in the absence of a legislative provision for liability). As a result, scholars have tended to underemphasize the fact that, in most jurisdictions throughout the nineteenth century, the usual statutory provision made the shareholder liable for much more than—normally twice—the value of his shares.

169. 1848 N.Y. Laws, ch. 40.

170. 1 W. Cook, supra note 60, at 203–06.

171. See 3 S. Thompson, supra note 35, at chs. 46, 50 (1st ed. 1895).

172. Navin & Sears, The Rise of the Market for Industrial Securities, 1887–1902, 29 Bus. Hist. Rev. 105, 106 (1955).

173. Id. at 109.

174. Id. at 109 n. 4.

175. Id. at 109.

176. Id. at 109–10.

177. Id. at 106.

178. Id. at 137.

179. A. A. Freidrich, Stocks and Stock Ownership, 14 Encyclopedia of Social Sciences 403 (1937).

180. 1 S. Thompson, supra note 35, at vii (1st ed. 1895).

181. Christensen v. Eno, 106 N.Y. 97, 102, 12 N.E. 648 (1887); Southworth v. Morgan, 205 N.Y. 293, 93 N.E. 490 (1912); Jeffrey v. Selwyn, 220 N.Y. 77, 115 N.E. 275 (1917). See generally W. Cook, Treatise on the Law of Corporations Having a Capital Stock (4th ed. 1898).

182. Hospes v. Northwestern Mfg. Co., 48 Minn. 174, 50 N.W. 1117 (1892).

183. Ballantine, Stockholders Liability in Minnesota, 7 Minn. L. Rev. 79, 88 (1923); Note, The Nature of the Stockholder's Liability for Stock Issued at a Discount, 29 Harv. L. Rev. 854, 856 (1916).

184. Handley v. Stutz, 139 U.S. 417 (1891). See Also Clark v. Bever, 139 U.S. 96 (1891); Fogg v. Blair, 139 U.S. 118 (1891).

185. 2 S. Thompson, supra note 35, at 1295 (1st ed. 1895).

186. Id. at 1296.

187. Pepper, Recent Development of Corporation Law by the Supreme Court of the United States II, 34 Am. Law Reg. 448, 457 n. 2 (1895).

188. Id. at 456. See also Pepper, The "Trust Fund Theory" of the Capital Stock of a Corporation, 32 Am. Law Reg. 175 (2d ser.) 6 (1893).

189. See, e.g., Harriman, Corporate Assets as a "Trust Fund for the Benefit of Creditors," 3 N.W. L. Rev. 115, 206 (1894); McMurtrie, Is Unpaid Capital a Trust Fund in Any Proper Sense? 25 Am. L. Rev. 749 (1891).

190. Compare Camden v. Stuart, 144 U.S. 104 (1892) with Hollins v. Brierfield Coal & Iron Co., 150 U.S. 371 (1893). See Pepper, supra note 187, at 450.

191. Note, supra note 183, at 856.

192. Steacy v. Little Rock R.R., 5 Dill. 348, 373–74, 22 F. Cas. 1142, 1152 (E. D. Ark. 1879) (No. 13, 329).

193. 1 W. Cook, supra note 60, at 498 n. 1 (4th ed. 1898). This idea first appeared in Cook's treatise, Section 257, n. 2, as early as 1889 (2d ed.), except that he predicted that "some time hereafter" the rule of full negotiability would be established. The statement in the text, from the third edition (1895), was the first to declare it as "the established rule." By the eighth edition in 1923, Cook eliminated the statement that it had already become the "established rule," and simply cited cases for the proposition that it was "the better opinion, and the one most in accord with the usages and demands of trade." 2 W. Cook, supra note 60 at 854, section 257 n. 2.

194. See Navin & Sears, supra note 172, at 137–38.

195. 1 W. Cook, supra note 60, at 291 n. 4, 5; Bonbright, The Dangers of Shares without Par Value, 24 Col. L. Rev. 449, 458 (1924).

196. Bonbright, supra note 195, at 460.

197. Id. at 432

198. Pepper, Recent Development of Corporation Law by the Supreme Court of the United States I, 34 Am. Law Reg. at 296 (1895).

199. Pepper, supra note 187, at 453.

200. Pepper, A Brief Introduction to the Study of the Law of Associations, 40 Am. Law Reg. 255, 267 (o.s.) 49 (1901).

201. Hunt, The Trust Fund Theory and Some Substitutes for It, 12 Yale L.J. 63, 67 (1902).

202. H. Spellman, A Treatise on the Principles of Law Governing Corporate Directions 237 (1931).

203. Union Pacific R.R. v. Chicago R.R., 163 U.S. 564, 596 (1896).

204. Cass v. Manchester Iron & Steel Co., 9 F. 640, 642 (W.D. Pa. 1881).

205. H. Spellman, supra 202, at 6 n. 24.

206. 3 S. Thompson, supra note 35, at 2878 (1st ed. 1895).

207. Id. at 2878–79.

208. Bank of the United States v. Dandridge, 25 U.S. 64, 76, 78, 114–15 (1827).

209. 3 S. Thompson, supra note 35, at 2881.

210. Id. at 2881–82.

211. Angell & Ames, supra note 129, at 257.

212. Id. See also 3 S. Thompson, supra note 35, at 2862–63.

213. G. Field, Law of Private Corporations (1877).

214. E. Freund, supra note 32, at 53.

215. Id. at 48.

216. Manson v. Curtis, 223 N.Y. 313, 322, 119 N.E. 558, 562 (1918). H. Spellman, supra note 202, at 9–12. The leading case on the subject became Hoyt v. Thompson's Exec., 19 N.Y. 207 (1859), which was largely ignored by the New York courts until it later became a favorite "old" citation for recognizing plenary power in the board of directors. See Beveridge v. New York Elevated R.R. Co., 112 N.Y. 1, 22–23 (1889); People ex rel. Manice v. Powell, 201 N.Y. 194, 200 (1911); Manson, 223 N.Y. at 322, 119 N.E. at 562. A second early favorite, frequently cited in the twentieth century, was an opinion by Chief Justice Shaw in Burrill v. Nahant Bank, 43 Mass. 163 (1804). More typical cases reflecting the early view of directors as agents who could not delegate their powers are Mechanics Bank v. New York & New Haven R.R. Co., 22 N.Y. 258, 295

(1860) (opinion of Selden, J.); Brokaw v. New Jersey Railroad Co., 32 N.J.L. 328, 332 (1867).

217. H. Spellman, supra note 202, at 4–5.

218. E. Freund, supra note 32, at 58.

219. Id. at 60.

220. 1 A. Eddy, supra note 114, at 602.

221. New York v. North River Sugar Refinery, 121 N.Y. 582, 625 (1890).

222. See, e.g., W. Jethro Brown, The Personality of the Corporation and the State, 21 L.Q.R. 365 (1905).

223. D. Jones, supra note 153, at 80–81.

224. Davis, The Nature of Corporations, 12 Pol. Sci. Q. 273, 278 (1897).

225. E. Freund, supra note 32, at 13.

226. Id. at 11.

227. Id. at 48.

228. Id. at 51.

229. Id.

230. Id. at preface, 5.

231. Id. at 52.

232. Id. at 47.

233. Id. at 59–60.

234. Williams, An Inquiry into the Nature and Law of Corporations, 38 Am. L. Reg. (n.s.) 1, 3 (1899).

235. Brown, supra note 222, at 379.

236. See Raymond, The Genesis of the Corporation 216 (1906).

237. Machen, Corporate Personality, 24 Harv. L. Rev. 253, 261–62 (1911).

238. Id.

239. G. Henderson, supra note 67, at 3.

240. Id. at 166.

241. Id. at 167.

242. Id. at 165–66.

243. Id. at 165.

244. Id. at 174.

245. Id.

246. Id. at 5, 8.

247. Id. at 169.

248. Id. at 3.

249. Hale v. Henckel, 201 U.S. 43 (1905). See also cases supra note 46.

250. Dartmouth College, 17 U.S. (Wheat.) 518.

3

THE SHERMAN ANTITRUST ACT AND THE CORPORATE RECONSTRUCTION OF AMERICAN CAPITALISM, 1890–1914

MARTIN J. SKLAR

In the course of the history of the United States, the law and jurisprudence have adapted to and reinforced the changing forms and requirements of private property, property rights, and the market in the context of incessant capitalist development. The law has also placed limits on property rights on behalf of the public interest and the general welfare as determined by public policy. The long-term tendency of the law, however, has been to favor those emergent property forms, property rights, and contractual obligations that were suited to, or associated with, developmental change embracing productive, distributional or technological innovation, as against older property forms, vested rights, or contractual obligations, anchored in past or obsolescent market or production relations.[1]

From the late 1880s to 1914, both public and private law underwent changes suited to the protection and extension of the emergent corporate reorganization of capitalist enterprise.[2] But the adaptation proceeded along two not entirely concurrent lines: that of the law of property and contractual liberty and that of the law of restraint of trade. The law of property and contractual liberty converged rather directly with the corporate reorganization of business enterprise, but the law of restraint of trade negotiated an indirect route, with sharp turns and long delays before arriving at an adaptive destination. For about fifteen years, until mid–1911 with the U.S. Supreme Court's decisions in the *American Tobacco* and *Standard Oil* cases, the corporate reorganization of U.S. capitalism proceeded within an incongruent legal order, the law in part expediting and in part obstructing its progress.

With respect to the law of property and contractual liberty, the Supreme Court in the landmark *Santa Clara* case extended to corporations due process protections, both substantive and procedural, accorded to natural persons under the Fifth and Fourteenth amendments of the federal Constitution, and on that basis the Court endowed corporations with the rights and privileges it ascribed to the meaning of contractual liberty. The Court's rulings on both fronts together protected the pursuit and exchange of intangibles (earning power and titles to earnings) as well as tangibles (physical assets) and thereby facilitated the rise of capital markets in industrials, without which the corporate reorganization of capitalist property ownership would have been difficult and halting, even if not impossible.

The Court's *Santa Clara* decision, along with subsequent decisions in the 1890s relating to property and contractual liberty, protected corporations against deprivation by either federal or state government of their life, liberty, assets, or earnings without due process of law. In endowing corporate property with a claim to liberty similar (though not identical) to that enjoyed by white male persons, however, the new jurisprudence also sustained the older legal tradition under which corporations, as peculiarly the creatures of the law, were to remain responsible before the law and hence subject to public policy and judicial process. But in establishing a legal doctrine of substantive and procedural due process and applying it to corporations, now defined as persons at law, a definition made explicit in the Sherman Act itself, the Court widened the sphere of liberty attached to corporate property and operations. The Court thereby set limits on the reach of the law while extending the reach of the corporation. In effect, to the limited liability of the stockholder, it now added the limited liability of the corporation in the face of the legislative and executive powers of government.[3]

Concurrent with the changes in the legal concepts of property and contractual liberty in the late 1880s and the 1890s, the federal law regulating the market increasingly superseded state law as an ever-growing number of firms extended business operations across state lines as well as into foreign markets. The Interstate Commerce Act of 1887 and the Sherman Antitrust Act of 1890, by inaugurating regulative and judicial processes for the determination of the range and limits of the disposal of property in interstate and foreign commerce, established at the national level a governmental regulatory framework for the corporate reorganization of the market. In both the railway rate and the due process cases, the Supreme Court considerably strengthened the nationalization of the law of property, along with the law of the market, by stipulating positive federal standards of property rights and imposing them upon the states. At the same time, in new legislation designed to accommodate corporate reorganization of property ownership and market mechanisms, New Jersey and Delaware, in the years 1886 through 1896, followed by New York and other states, eased or lifted restrictions on corporate interstate ownership of stock and assets, reduced or rescinded corporate taxes, and liberalized regulations concerning stock issuance and indebtedness. In effect, these state laws placed corporations that availed themselves of interstate holdings and engaged in interstate trade more firmly within the primary jurisdiction of the commerce power of the federal government. By the opening of the last decade of the nineteenth century, federal and state law together was tending strongly to sanction the growing nationalization of the market and to modify the meaning of property, which, so far as it went, provided the corporate form of property ownership in industry and commerce with an appropriate legal environment.

The legal redefinition of property and contractual liberty, and the trend toward the nationalization of the law of property and the market, in a manner favorable to the corporate reorganization of industry, did not represent a fortuitous imposition of some *lex-ex-machina*; neither was it preordained by the Constitution, nor the result of a peculiarly activist, or constructive, or pro-corporation, Supreme Court. Indeed, legal revision in this period was not uniformly favorable to the corporate reorganization of enterprise. With respect to the law of restraint of trade, in particular, the Supreme Court from 1897 to 1911, in its construction of the Sherman Antitrust Act, rendered the law as positively forbidding corporate-administered markets, a rendering that conflicted with its pro-corporate rulings in the law of property and contractual liberty. Legal revision, including its inconsistencies, arose from the conflicts and contracts in the market among property owners and other parties; it resulted from the litigative and legislative activity of capitalists, lawyers, legislators, and others and only then from decisions of judges, who acted upon the corresponding legislation and legal arguments brought before them in cases. It was, in short, the outcome of an evolving social movement and the opposition it aroused. It was the emergence and rise of this great social movement in conflict with its opponents that made the decade of the 1890s the watershed of U.S. history that historians take it to be. Populism was not the only great social movement of the 1890s; so was the movement for corporate capitalism. It was the conflict between the two, to mention no others, that made the accommodation of the law to corporate capitalism something less than a tidy, linear affair.[4]

PROPERTY AND CONFLICTING FORMS OF CAPITALISM

In the period of about 1890 to 1914, as proprietary capitalist property and market relations came into conflict with and were being displaced or transformed by emergent corporate property and market relations, the law of market relations in its legislative and juristic phases became a major field of conflict and hence a central question in national politics. The law of restraint of trade came to center stage, while the law of money and banking, of railroad regulation, of labor organization and working conditions, and of other market relations played major roles as well. All these involved the question of regulating, or administering, the market, as against the old competitive mechanism. Although the law of property accommodated promptly and without significant resistance to corporate instruments of property ownership and control, the law of restraint of trade became a storm center of political contention and, before the turn of the century, fell out of phase with the emergent corporate reorganization of the market and property relations. The politics of the antitrust question centered on the law of restraint of trade.

The drafting of the Sherman Antitrust Act (1889–1890) and its subsequent early enforcement and judicial construction (1890–1911) became a critical field of conflict between advocates of small-producer (proprietary) capitalist property and corporate-capitalist property and correspondingly between those favoring a regulated market suited to preserving and strengthening proprietary capitalism and those favoring a regulated market suited to encouraging, protecting, and legitimizing corporate capitalism.[5] Cutting across these differences were those over the role of government and the role of such private arrangements as pools, cartels, cooperatives, or corporations in the regulation process, as well as differences over the broader question of the state-society relation. Once the law and the market were brought back into correspondence, the trust question receded from the center of politics, a major accomplishment of the Wilson administration. After 1914, with the passage of the Federal Trade Commission and Clayton Antitrust Acts, which in effect gave legislative and administrative embodiment to the Supreme Court's rule of reason decisions in the *Standard Oil* and *American Tobacco* cases of 1911, the trust question remained a large issue at law but became, and has ever since remained, a peripheral, or minor, however histrionic, issue in national party politics. The respective regulatory roles of government and private parties, and the state-society relation remain, of course, central political questions but detached from the antitrust issue as such.

Legal historians have shown the need to understand the relation of changes in the law to changes in the uses and conceptions of property and to economic development in a market society. Their work has been particularly rich and effective in their study of eighteenth-century and antebellum U.S. history.[6] By and large, however, historians, including legal historians, have understood the Sherman Act and its early judicial construction within the limits of such static conceptions as competition versus monopoly, centralization versus decentralization, protection of a consumer interest in efficiency, prevention of undue wealth transfers, and the trade-production distinction rooted in constitutional principles of dual (federal-state) jurisdiction. In so doing, they have shed much light on the subject, but they have ignored and obscured some aspects as well.[7] The Sherman Act and its early judicial construction invite study from a historical standpoint, such as that employed with good effect by legal historians in other cases, and, specifically, from the standpoint of a more detailed history of the changes in the market and in uses and conceptions of property accompanying the passage of the U.S. political economy from the proprietary-competitive to the corporate-administered stage of capitalism.[8]

INTERPRETATION OF THE SHERMAN ACT

The prevailing understanding of the drafting and early judicial construction (1890–1911) of the Sherman Antitrust Act, among specialists and generalists alike, runs something as follows.

1. The Sherman Act as drafted and passed was either fraudulent, inept, or regressively utopian. That is, either it was a political sham, or it was a confused, vague, and hence ineffective statute in the absence of judicial legislation, or it was an anachronistic

embodiment of the doctrine of competitive capitalism and of the policy of restoring and enforcing an obsolescent competitive market. In any case, the act as passed was not to be taken seriously.

2. The Supreme Court, in *E. C. Knight* (1895) and in the three leading cases of 1897–1899 (*Trans-Missouri*, *Joint Traffic*, and *Addyston Pipe*), taken together with the Court's strictures upholding contractual liberty, made the Sherman Act, whatever the intent of the several justices, ineffective against tight—that is, corporate—consolidations in industry.

3. Through its construction of the Sherman Act, the Supreme Court arrogated to itself, as against a feckless Congress, policy-making power respecting restraint of trade.

The usual story, though intriguing and though enjoying the assent of scholars of widely differing persuasions, and from left to right on the political spectrum, is wanting on all counts. Let us briefly address each in order.

Sherman Act as Sham or Ineffective

As passed by Congress, the Sherman Antitrust Act was neither a political sham, nor a piece of legislative shoddy, nor an instrument of the restoration of the classical competitive market. Nor did it represent an attempt to prevent corporate mergers or corporate-administered prices and investment. The drafting of the act and the interpretive contention that proceeded thereafter were indeed fields of conflict between small-producer and pro-corporate partisans in the marketplace and in politics. As passed, however, the act represented an effective and sophisticated attempt at legislating a legal order appropriate to permitting and regulating the rise and development of corporate capitalism. This conclusion is to be drawn from an examination of the *Congressional Record* and other sources of the act's legislative history,[9] viewed in the context of proximate judicial doctrines on restraint of trade and the commerce power of Congress under the Constitution.

Prior to the enactment of the Sherman Act, federal law on restraint of trade, apart from constitutional construction and the law of common carriers, rested not on public law or legislation but on common law adjudicated in British courts and in state and federal courts of the United States. By 1890, the common law as enunciated in the leading cases held that reasonable restraints of trade were valid and enforceable in the courts and that unreasonable restraints were invalid and enjoinable but in the absence of legislation were not punishable. Reasonable restraints were those among parties to agreements that restricted competition or production or trade without interfering with the right of others, not party to such agreements, to compete or produce or trade, without contravening public policy as stated in legislation or as interpreted by the courts, and without endangering the health, safety, welfare, or morals of the community (that is, without running afoul of the police powers of the state). Monopoly was in essence an extreme form of restraint of trade and, at law, was not to be understood in either the dictionary or in the literal economic meaning of the word. The common law protected the right to compete, but it did not stipulate the compulsion to compete. Although by 1890, there was no distinct federal body of common law on restraint of trade and for the most part the states occupied the field, the courts in the United States, both federal and state, construed common law principles respecting restraint of trade with a general consistency, while at the same time rendering decisions on the basis of these principles that were not similarly consistent or routinely predictable. The common law principles themselves, however, were rather clearly defined and uniformly acknowledged at the bench.[10]

The plain terms of Senator John Sherman's (R., Oh.) original draft bill, which he introduced into the U.S. Senate in late 1889, would have compelled competition and made illegal any attempt by private parties to regulate the market in any significant manner. His bill was, in this respect, similar to those introduced by populists, such as that of Democratic Texas Senator John H. Reagan, and it was intended thereby to appeal to them and attract their votes. Sherman stated, however, in floor debate, that he expected the courts to interpret the act in accordance with common law doctrine—in such a way, that is, as to protect the right to compete, to permit corporate combinations and other reasonable restraints of trade, and to eschew any absolute compulsion to compete. Certain senators who favored corporate enterprise and who were better versed in legal technique and judicial process than was Sherman took the unusual step on the Senate floor of removing the bill from Sherman and his Finance Committee and assigning it to the Judiciary Committee, where Senator George F. Edmunds (R. Vt.) drafted the better part of what became the Sherman Antitrust Act. The latter employed the terms that were absent from Sherman's draft bill but were habitually used in common law cases and given definite meaning by the courts: the terms *restraint of trade*, *monopoly*, and *conspiracy to restrain trade or monopolize*. In floor debate, Senator Edmunds and Judiciary Committee co-drafters like Senator George F. Hoar (R., Mass.) emphasized that their bill was intended to give federal legislative embodiment to the common law doctrine on restraint of trade and thus permit the courts gradually to enunciate permissible regulatory norms, or restraints of trade, among private parties in the market. The bill was ultimately passed by Congress exactly as it was reported from the Senate Judiciary Committee.[11]

In the next seven years (1890–1897), the federal courts construed the Sherman Act as having embodied common law doctrine on restraint of trade.[12] An attempt to repeal the Sherman Act being impolitic and in many ways counterproductive to their cause, small-producer anticorporate partisans concentrated their efforts on having the act construed literally, that is, as having superseded the common law, and as thereby outlawing reasonable as well as unreasonable restraints of trade. It was this view that the Supreme Court in the cases of 1897–1899 adopted, thereby not only reversing lower federal court decisions of the previous seven years but also embracing a fundamental, if not revolutionary, departure from traditional U.S. (and Anglo-American) law of restraint of trade.[13]

To construe the Sherman Act as having embodied the common law was in effect to assign to judge-made law a leading authority in regulating the market and to give it legislative sanction. That, in turn, meant permitting private law, and hence private parties, to determine to a large extent the regulation of the market within a framework of judicial process. Hence, the common law construction of the Sherman Act embodied the policy of allocating to private parties the primary role in regulating the market, and to the government, through executive oversight and judicial process, a secondary role. It meant, in the specific historical context of the time, a policy of permitting and regulating a corporate-administered market.[14] Conversely, to construe the Sherman Act as having superseded the common law was in effect to hold that only the federal government, through public law—that is, through legislation and executive administration—could regulate the market, either to the exclusion, or with only a secondary role, of private parties and private law. Since Congress in these years could not be brought to pass legislation expressly permitting corporations or other private parties to regulate the market, nor could Congress be brought to repeal or amend the Sherman Act, the Court's construction of the act as having superseded the common law meant that either American business in interstate and foreign commerce must remain entirely and compulsively competitive or it must be regulated, if at all, by the federal government to the exclusion of both the states and private parties. The alternatives, in short, were unrestricted competition or statist command.

Sherman Act as Ineffective

The Supreme Court's decision in *E. C. Knight*, taken together with the cases of 1897–1899, did not make the Sherman Act ineffective against tight corporate consolidations. *E. C. Knight* turned essentially on the issue of federal-state jurisdiction rather than on that of restraint of trade. On the heels of *Coe v. Erroll* (1886) and *Kidd v. Pearson* (1888) and in view of the post-Reconstruction settlement of national party politics based in part on institutional racialism (states' rights) and in view, furthermore, of the close and extended attention accorded the issue of dual jurisdiction during congressional debate on the Sherman Act, the outcome of the case could hardly have been different, given its presentation by the Department of Justice under Attorney General Richard Olney. The decision did not exempt from the reach of the Sherman Act the corporate form of combination as such. It held, rather, that consensual consolidations, though entirely vulnerable to prohibition by state law, at the state's discretion, did not per se violate the act unless it directly involved an unreasonable restraint of interstate or foreign commerce, something Olney's brief had failed to show. The decision turned, therefore, on whether either the sugar corporation's behavior or the corporate form of its consolidation could be reached in the manner argued by Olney. In his decision for the Court, Chief Justice Melville W. Fuller held that it could not. The decision embodied the view that the Sherman Act was to complement, not preempt, state authority in regulating restraints of trade within a state, while it left in place the prevalent lower federal courts' common law construction of the term *restraint of trade* as used in the act. It is usually overlooked, moreover, that in *E. C. Knight*, Fuller enunciated and affirmed the principle of plenary congressional power to regulate interstate and foreign commerce. That part of his decision became an essential element in the later majority opinions against defendants in the Sherman Act cases of 1897–1899, opinions in which Fuller joined.[15]

In his decisions for the Court in *Trans-Missouri*, *Joint Traffic*, and *Addyston Pipe*, Justice Rufus W. Peckham, who had delivered *Allgeyer*, substantially qualified the latter's liberty and due process principles, in effect, and indeed explicitly, subordinating them to Congress's power to regulate interstate and foreign commerce. The Court's position in these cases, and in all subsequent Sherman Act cases until the rule of reason decisions of 1911, held that the Sherman Act superseded the common law and thereby made illegal reasonable as well as unreasonable restraints of trade. Its position was, therefore, that because Congress had, under the commerce clause of the Constitution, full power to regulate interstate and foreign commerce and to limit liberty to the extent thereby implied in enacting the Sherman law, Congress had decided to retain exclusive power to regulate the interstate and foreign market by forbidding such regulation to private parties (the states being already excluded). In American interstate or foreign trade, private parties could not legally refrain from competition; they were compelled to compete. Although consolidation, or "bigness," per se, did not violate the law (as in *E. C. Knight*), any consolidation that directly and not merely ancillarily ended a competition that would otherwise have existed in interstate or foreign commerce, that prevented another from entering or remaining in competition, or that conferred a power to control prices or in any other way to regulate interstate or foreign commerce, did violate the law. Such, in the Court's view, was the public policy enacted by Congress.[16]

Put somewhat differently, the Sherman Act as construed by the Court took regulatory authority out of the market, where one-dollar-one-vote ruled, and placed it in the political arena where (theoretically) one-person-one-vote ruled. Hence, just as with the national banking and currency laws (before the Federal Reserve Act of 1913), which kept ultimate control of the money supply in the hands of the national state (Congress and the Treasury Department), subject to electoral politics, and out of the hands of private parties, so with the law regulating commerce and industry: regulation was to remain lodged with the federal government and forbidden to private parties. If the market were not to remain freely competitive, then it was to remain politicized—that is, subject to electoral politics.

The Court's construction of the Sherman Act readily reached tight corporate consolidations as well as those of the looser sort, as the *Northern Securities* case and the decisions in the lower courts in the *Standard Oil* and *American Tobacco* cases clearly demonstrated. Hence the construction of the Sherman Act by the

Court, or by the Harlan-led majority of the Court, from 1897 to 1911 put the nonstatist corporate reconstruction of American capitalism, then in process, beyond the pale of the law. The corporate reorganization of the economy in those years went forward within the framework of an incongruent legal order. Since the law and the market in a modern capitalist society are so intimately interrelated, the legal incongruity directly translated itself into a political conflict that became central to national politics in what historians refer to as the Progressive era.

Role of the Supreme Court

The generally held view that the Supreme Court in the 1890s and early years of the twentieth century assumed the policy-making role with respect to restraint of trade is well stated by J. Willard Hurst: "Inertia, slow perception of fast-moving business change, and ignorance of what to do about it figured in Congress's failure to generalize policy fast and effectively concerning the concentration of private industrial and financial power; within the context of lagging and vague legislation the United States Supreme Court thus became the principal maker of antitrust policy."[17]

It does not seem to be historically accurate, however, to describe Congress's action in passing the Sherman Act in 1890 as laggard, inept, or ineffective. By 1890, corporate consolidation on a scale large enough to regulate the market was still in an inchoate state in industry, finance, and commerce. Even among railroads, where "natural monopoly" added to the regulatory capacities of large-scale corporate organization, competition still raged. The states retained full power, unequivocally affirmed by the U.S. Supreme Court, to break up interfirm combinations domiciled within their respective jurisdictions.[18] Passage of the Sherman Act in 1890, then, should be viewed as a rather prompt response of the federal legislature to constituents' opinion and changing conditions. The drafting of the bill was, indeed, a matter of multifaceted contention and negotiation among small-producer and pro-corporate partisans, and it was further complicated by the constitutional law of federal-state jurisdiction, but the result—the act as passed—was neither vague nor inept. Rather, its terms constituted a sophisticated embodiment of a definite policy of permitting, and regulating through judicial process, corporate combination and enterprise.[19]

It is, of course, the Supreme Court's (and in general the judiciary's) routine and proper function, within the U.S. constitutional system, to interpret the meaning of a law in cases brought before it. Judicial interpretation, however, is not necessarily equivalent to policy making. From 1890 to 1911 (and thereafter), the Supreme Court acted as the principal interpreter of the meaning of the Sherman Act, and in that sense it is accurate to say that from 1890 to 1897 it shared with Congress and the executive the role of a principal maker of policy. But from 1897 to 1911, the principal maker of policy on the trust question was neither Congress nor the Supreme Court (or the judiciary) but the executive. Presidents McKinley, Roosevelt, and, to a lesser extent, Taft refused to accept the Court's non–common law construction of the Sherman Act as sound policy, and by controlling the prosecutorial process and, in Roosevelt's case, by establishing a rival, executive, agency—the Bureau of Corporations—and entering extralegal understandings with corporate executives, they took determination of antitrust policy away from the judiciary and, in the face of congressional inability to act, lodged it with the executive.[20]

Although the executive assumed the principal policy-making role on the trust question from 1897 to 1911, nevertheless, throughout this period, the executive and the Court were at loggerheads and engaged in a running battle over the nature of policy with respect to the regulation of the market. This debate made for uncertainty of the law, the bane of commerce, and hence for a crisis, or at least a growing crisis psychology, in the market and in politics. Corporate executives, investment bankers, small enterprisers, and labor unionists could not know for certain where they stood with respect to the law of market relations and practices, in the near or far future, and therefore in the present as well. The Court's majority might change; the next election might bring an executive with a different policy or a Congress ready to act in an unwanted way.

Under pressure to resolve the crisis of the legal order, President Roosevelt came in effect to accept the Court's definition of the alternatives: either a freely competitive market or statist regulation. In an evolving but by no means premeditated policy, first through executive action of the Bureau of Corporations (established 1903) and then through introduction of the Hepburn amendments to the Sherman Act in 1908, which died in Congress, and culminating in Roosevelt's public statements and writings, private policy planning, and presidential campaigning over the next four years, Roosevelt ultimately sought to legalize the corporate reorganization of the economy under direct state command. His efforts proved unsuccessful, and many earlier supporters of his policy backed off as they perceived more clearly its statist implications. President Taft opposed the statist solution of the trust question, as did Wilson. In restoring the common law construction of the Sherman Act, in its rule of reason decisions of 1911, the Supreme Court laid the juridical basis for what I call the corporate-liberal solution, one that Taft and Wilson affirmed and sought as presidents, in different ways, to strengthen and develop, with ultimate success—Wilson with considerably greater political success than Taft.[21]

CAPITALISM AND THE LAW

For its normal functioning and development, capitalism requires both certainty and predictability in the sociopolitical environment, and particularly in the law and the legal order. At the same time, capitalism requires openness to rapid change (development, growth). Hence, the law must provide for the play of continuous change on a field of relative certainty and predictability. The strength of common law jurisprudence lay precisely in its flexibility composed of these two virtues intertwined. That is, judge-made law, based on precedent and rational-instrumental reasoning rooted in experience, has allowed for both predictability and change. By its very nature, moreover, it is a predictability and change that has corresponded in general with the outlook, values, and interests of the litigants and hence with those propertied and contracting parties making regular use of the courts. Judge-made law in a capitalist society, then, has normally tended to express, arbitrate, and enforce the social dominance of capitalist property and capitalists as a class, but in the United States in particular, it has tended ultimately to validate that form of capitalist property and those capitalists that were ascending in the market and the society at large. The common law and, even better, its legislative embodiment, as in the Sherman Act properly construed, have thereby facilitated change as American capitalism has developed while validating the certainty and security of capitalist property and social relations as such. It has had one other virtue: it has sustained the principle and practice of a large autonomy of the market from party politics and state command, and hence the principle and practice of the supremacy of society over the state. It has therefore been peculiarly suited to serving as a powerful ally of the liberal form of capitalism, while no less amenable to serving, in a similar manner, the needs of a liberal form of socialism.

The corporate-liberal alternative, as embodied in the rule of reason decisions and as fleshed out in the legislation of 1914 and since, accomplished two basic conditions: it depoliticized the market in the sense of removing the regulation of the market from determination by electoral politics or by the exclusive or paramount power of the state, and apart from common carriers, public utilities, and other "natural monopolies," it ensured primary regulation of the market by the contractual relations of private parties and private law (that is, by private parties subject to judicial process) while assigning to the state the secondary regulatory role through prosecutory action or administrative policing subject to judicial review, in either case, judicial process based on common law doctrine and precedent.

The adaptation of the legal order to corporate capitalism was an integral phase of the corporate reorganization of American capitalism in general; it represented a signal achievement of the Progressive era. The adaptation was based in part on the recognition of the corporation as a person at law, both in constitutional constructions of the Supreme Court and in the Sherman Act itself. The adaptation was also based on the ultimate judicial construction of the Sherman Act as embodying the common law. Sherman Act jurisprudence represented one among a number of areas in the adaptation of the law to corporate capitalism, areas that included transportation, banking, labor, agricultural credits, and foreign trade. Neither in its realization nor in its form was the adaptation a foregone conclusion. It was an outcome of political contention stretching over twenty-five years (and beyond), a contention that saw the rise of significant populist and socialist party politics, the temporary splitting apart of both major parties (the Democrats in the 1890s and the Republicans in 1912), and more lasting political realignments. It was, finally, an outcome of a great social movement for corporate capitalism that rejected a statist for a liberal form.

NOTES

1. T. Veblen, The Theory of Business Enterprise 128–43, (1904; 1958); Commons, Legal Foundations of Capitalism (1924; 1957), 6–7, 11–46 et passim (1924, 1957). J. Hurst, The Legitimacy of the Business Corporation in the Law of the United States, 1780–1970 (1970); J. Hurst, Law and the Conditions of Freedom in the Nineteenth-Century United States (1956); J. Hurst, Law and Economic Growth: The Legal History of the Lumber Industry in Wisconsin, 1836–1915 (1977); J. Hurst, Law and Markets in United States History: Different Modes of Bargaining among Interests (1982), esp. ch. 1; M. Horwitz, The Transformation of American Law, 1780–1860 (1977); S. Kutler, Privilege and Creative Destruction: The Charles River Bridge Case (1971); L. Friedman, A History of American Law (1973), Part II, chs. 3, 5, 6, Part III, chs. 1, 4, 5, 8, 9; W. Nelson, Americanization of the Common Law: The Impact of Legal Change on Massachusetts Society, 1760–1830 (1975), esp. chs. 1, 8; T. Freyer, Forums of Order: The Federal Courts and Business in American History (1979); G. White, The American Judicial Tradition: Profiles of Leading American Judges (1976), especially chs. 2–7; Presser, "Legal History" or the History of Law: A Primer Bringing the Law's Past into the Present, 35 Vand. L. Rev. 849–90 (1982), especially pp. 858–62, 870–83. The generalization in the text refers to nonslave property; slave property involves a different order of historical phenomenon and is subject to different generalization. Cf. M. Tushnet, The American Law of Slavery, 1810–1860: Considerations of Humanity and Interest (1981); R. Cover, Justice Accused: Antislavery and the Judicial Process (1975); P. Finkelman, An Imperfect Union: Slavery, Federalism, and Comity (1981); Keir Nash, Reason of Slavery: Understanding the Judicial Role in the Peculiar Institution, 32 Vand. L. Rev. 8–218 (1979); E. Genovese, Roll, Jordan, Roll: The World the Slaves Made 25–49 (1974; 1976); Genovese, Slavery in the Legal History of the South and the Nation, 59 Tex. L. Rev. 969–98 (1981).

2. The corporate reorganization of capitalist (or business) enterprise here means not simply the formal incorporation of a business but the change from the competitive to the administered or "oligopolistic" market under the auspices, most typically in the United States, of the large corporation, in which ownership is lodged with holders of equity stock and may or may not be closely attached to management.

3. Santa Clara County v. Southern Pacific R.R., 118 U.S. 394 (1886); aff'd at Minneapolis & St. Louis Ry. Co. v. Oliver Beckwith, 129 U.S. 26 (1888). Cf. San Mateo County v. Southern Pacific R.R., 13 Fed. 722 (1882). Justice Field, sitting on circuit, delivering the decision of the court; argued but not decided, at 116 U.S. 138. The leading subsequent cases from 1890 to 1898 elaborating the revised view of property and liberty included Chicago, Milwaukee & St. Paul Ry. Co. v. Minnesota, 134 U.S. 418 (1890), Intersate Commerce Commission v. Cincinnati, New Orleans, and Texas Pacific Ry. Co., 167 U.S. 479 (1897), Allgeyer v. Louisiana, 165 U.S. 578 (1897), Smyth v. Ames, 169 U.S. 466 (1898). The Supreme Court's decision in St. Louis & San Francisco Ry. Co. v. James, 161 U.S. 545 (1896), extended to holding companies the right of interstate intercorporate stock ownership that it had upheld earlier for operating

companies in United States v. E. C. Knight Co., 156 U.S. 1 (1985); see T. Freyer, supra note 1, p. 112.

4. The foregoing rests on the assumption that the rise and ascendency of corporate capitalism was not simply a matter of technology or optimum efficiencies but a socio-political movement as well as a technoeconomic phenomenon in the narrow sense. Cf. James, Structural Change in American Manufacturing, 1850–1890, 43 J. Econ. Hist. 433–59 (1983), esp. 449–51. For the nationalization of the market and the law of the market, see J. Commons, supra note 1, at 11–18; J. Hurst (1970), supra note 1, at 45, 65, 68–73, 148–49, 156; T. Freyer, supra note 1, at 99–102; L. Friedman, supra note 1, at 454–55, 457–59; J. Jenks, The Trust Problem 80–84, 99–101 (1929, 5th ed.); Meade, Financial Aspects of the Trust Problem, 16 Annals 6–12 (1900); Navin and Sears, The Rise of a Market for Industrial Securities, 29 Bus. Hist. Rev. 126–27 (1955); Davis, The Investment Market, 1870–1914: The Evolution of a National Market, 25 J. Econ. Hist. 386–87, 393 (1965); Conant, Securities as a Means of Payment, 14 Annals 43 (1899); A. Link, Wilson: The Road to the White House 134 (1947); A. Berle, Jr., and G. Means, The Modern Corporation and Private Property 136–37, 203–6 (1933); Compton, Early History of Stock Ownership by Corporations, 9 Geo. Wash. L. Rev. 125 (1940); Cary, Federalism and Corporate Law: Reflections upon Delaware, 83 Yale L.J. 663–705 (1974).

5. As this implies, among the dominant disputants the controversy over the Sherman Act and its judicial construction was not about laissez-faire versus regulation or about competition versus monopoly, though concern for these issues was far from lacking on all sides, but about what kind of regulation and controlled by whom. It is essential that the small-producer, or proprietary, outlook not be confused or equated with an advocacy of either laissez-faire or free competition, or the pro-corporate outlook with antiregulation. It is equally essential to avoid the widespread error of equating the meaning of such technical-legal terms as *restraint of trade*, *competition*, and *monopoly* with their meaning in either common discourse or economic theory. In this chapter, the term *pro-corporate* means the outlook of those who affirmed, whether as desirable or unavoidable, the rise of large corporations to dominance in the American economy; it does not imply some special corporative theory or ideology. For further discussion of these matters, see M. Sklar, The Corporate Reconstruction of American Capitalism, 1890–1916: The Market, the Law, and Politics (Cambridge University Press, forthcoming).

6. Supra note 1.

7. See, e.g., H. Thorelli, The Federal Antitrust Policy: Origination of an American Tradition (1955); D. Dewey, Monopoly in Economics and Law (1959); W. Letwin, Law and Economic Policy in America: The Evolution of the Sherman Antitrust Act (1965); E. Jones, The Trust Problem in the United States (1926); O. Knauth, The Policy of the United States towards Industrial Monopoly (1914); Bork, Legislative Intent and Policy of the Sherman Act, 9 J. Law & Econ. 7–48 (1966); Lande, Wealth Transfers as the Original and Primary Concern of Antitrust: The Efficiency Interpretation Challenged, 34 Hastings L.J. 67–151 (1982); McCurdy, The *Knight* Sugar Decision of 1895 and the Modernization of American Corporation Law, 1869–1903, 53 Bus. Hist. Rev. 304–42 (1979); D. Morgan, Congress and the Constitution: A Study of Responsibility 140–59 (1966).

8. Cf. A. Chandler, Jr., The Visible Hand: The Managerial Revolution in American Business (1977); J. Hurst (1970), supra note 1; M. Sklar, supra note 5; Parrini and Sklar, New Thinking about the Market, 1896–1904: Some American Economists on Investment

and the Theory of Surplus Capital, 43 J. Econ. Hist. 559–78 (1983); A. Eichner, The
Emergence of Oligopoly: Sugar Refining as a Case Study (1969); D. Noble, America by
Design: Science, Technology, and the Rise of Corporate Capitalism (1977); W. Williams,
The Contours of American History pt. 3 (1961).

9. H. Thorelli, supra note 7, at 164–232; W. Letwin, supra note 7, at 85–89; D.
Morgan, supra note 7, at 140–59; McCurdy, supra note 7, at 323–28; Bork, supra note
7, at 14–48; Lande, supra note 7, at 82–106; and infra note 11.

10. Horner v. Graves, 7 Bingham 735 (1831); Central Ohio Salt Co. v. Guthrie, 35
Ohio State 666 (1880); Skrainka v. Scharringhausen, 8 Missouri Appeals Reports 522
(1880); Dolph v. Troy Laundry Machinery Co., 23 Fed. 553–59 (1886); Central Shade-
Roller Co. v. Cushman, 143 Mass. 353 (1887); Mogul Steamship Co., Ltd. v. McGregor,
Gow & Co., 21 Q.B.D. 544 (1889), aff'd 1892, A.C. 25. See also Judge Walter H.
Sanborn's discussion of these and other common law cases at United States v. Trans-
Missouri Freight Ass'n et al., 58 Fed. 71–72. Cf. Dewey, The Common-Law Background
of Antitrust Policy, 41 Va. L. Rev. 759–786 (1955).

11. 21 Cong. Rec. 2455–72, 2604, 2610–11, 2726–31, 3145, 3146, 3148, 3151–53,
4086–96, 6922. Thorelli (supra note 7, pp. 169–76, 180–81, 206–10, 226–28), McCurdy
(supra note 7, at 323–28), W. Letwin (supra note 7, at 94–97), Lande (supra note 7, at
83–96), and Bork (supra note 7, at 14–17), note or discuss the differences between the
express terms of Sherman's bill and the Judiciary Committee's bill but fail to discern the
difference in meaning relating to the common law and reasonable restraints of trade,
holding that the two bills, though wholly different in terms, were basically the same in
substance. Such casual attention to technical-legal terms is unusual, or at least unexpected,
in legal and legal-history scholarship. D. Morgan (supra note 7, at 143–48) notes the
basic difference between the two bills on the question of state-federal jurisdiction (pro-
duction-trade distinction) but does not address the common law question. Bork and Letwin
understand that the Sherman Act as passed was not intended by its framers to compel
competition, but they miss the difference between the two bills in this respect nevertheless.
All these authors note the centrality of the common law meaning of the Sherman Act's
terms in the minds of the drafters of the Judiciary Committee's bill, but none embraces
an understanding of the significance of that meaning precisely similar to that presented
here.

12. United States v. Jellico Mountain Coke and Coal Co. et al., 43 Fed. 898–99
(1890), 46 Fed. 432–437 (1891); United States v. Nelson et al., 52 Fed. 646–48 (1892);
United States v. Greenhut et al., 50 Fed. 469–71 (1892); In re Greene, 52 Fed. 104–19
(1892); United States v. Patterson et al., 55 Fed. 605–42 (1893), 59 Fed. 280–84 (1894);
United States v. Trans-Missouri Freight Ass'n et al., 53 Fed. 440–59 (1892), 58 Fed.
58–100 (1893); United States v. Joint Traffic Ass'n, 76 Fed. 895–98 (1896), 89 Fed.
1020 (1897); United States v. Addyston Pipe & Steel Co. et al., 78 Fed. 712–24 (1897).

13. United States v. Trans-Missouri Freight Ass'n, 166 U.S. 290–374 (1897); United
States v. Joint Traffic Ass'n, 171 U.S. 505–78 (1898); United States v. Addyston Pipe
& Steel Co., 175 U.S. 211–48 (1899).

14. On common law and private party regulation, cf. Horwitz, The Emergence of an
Instrumental Conception of American Law, 1780–1820, 5 Perspectives in American
History 285–326, at p. 288 (1971); G. White, supra note 1, at 113–15.

15. Coe v. Errol, 116 U.S. 517 (1886); Kidd v. Pearson, 128 U.S. 1 (1888); United
States v. E. C. Knight Co., 156 U.S. 1 (1895), esp. at 11, 12, 16. Note, for example,
Herbert Knox Smith's assessment of Knight, in an office memorandum he wrote in early

1905 for the Bureau of Corporations while serving as deputy commissioner under Commissioner of Corporations James R. Garfield. Citing "the very common misinterpretation of the Knight case," Smith observed that "the legal point actually decided merely was that production does not *necessarily* imply interstate commerce. The Court did not say, nor did it decide, that there is never any connection between production and commerce." (Smith's emphasis.) H. K. Smith, Memorandum on Paper by James H. McIntosh on the Power of Congress to Regulate Industrial Corporations (paper read before the Nebraska Bar Association, January 9, 1903), February 18, 1905, U.S. Bureau of Corporations, National Archives, Record Group 122, Numerical File, 1903–1914, File No. 2480. Cf. McCurdy, supra note 7; Raymond, The Federal Anti-Trust Act, 23 Harv. L. Rev. 353–79, at 376–77 (1910); also, McCurdy, American Law and the Marketing Structure of the Large Corporation, 1875–1890, 38 J. Econ. Hist. 631–49 (1978); and Freyer, The Federal Courts, Localism, and the National Economy, 1865–1900, 53 Bus. Hist. Rev. 343–63 (1979).

16. Trans-Missouri, Joint Traffic, and Addyston Pipe, supra note 13; also, Hopkins v. United States, 171 U.S. 578 (1898); Anderson et al. v. United States, 171 U.S. 604 (1898); United States v. The Coal Dealers' Association of California et al., 85 Fed. 262 (1898); Bement v. National Harrow Co., 186 U.S. 70–95; Montague & Co. v. Lowry, 193 U.S. 38–48 (1904); Chesapeake & Ohio Fuel Co. v. United States, 115 Fed. 610–624 (1902); United States v. Swift, 122 Fed. 529 (1903), esp. at 529–34; United States v. Swift & Co. et al., 196 U.S. 375 (1905); Northern Securities Co. v. United States, 193 U.S. 197–411 (1904); Shawnee Compress Co. v. Anderson, 209 U.S. 423–35 (1908); Loewe v. Lawlor, 208 U.S. 274–309 (1908); United States v. American Tobacco. et al., 164 Fed. 700–28 (1908); United States v. Standard Oil Co., 173 Fed. 177–92 (1909).

17. Hurst, Legal Elements in United States History, 5 Perspectives in American History 3–92, at 71 (1971). Elsewhere in the same essay (p. 15), however, Hurst offers a guideline that I have tried to follow and with which I fully agree: "A history of anti-trust law proper might stick to the Sherman and Clayton Acts and rulings of the courts and the Federal Trade Commission. But a history of the law's relations to market structure and procedures and of the results for resource allocation must invite some economic theory and economic history, as well as materials from political science and sociology." Cf. Hurst (1982), supra note 1, ch. 2.

18. McCurdy and Morgan, supra note 7.

19. Cf. Morgan, supra note 7, at 149, for an evaluation of Senate debate on the Sherman Act as having been of a "high caliber" and at a "high level" of thought and legal expertise (also at p. 157 et passim). The famous statement of Republican Senator Orville H. Platt (Conn.) that "the whole effort has been to get some bill headed 'A bill to punish trusts' with which to go to the country" (21 Cong. Rec. 2731) has been cited time and again as evidence of the fraud or ineptness of the Sherman Act. But Platt, who in Senate debate argued in favor of permitting reasonable restraints of trade, made that statement about, and during the debate on, Sherman's original bill, not the Judiciary Committee's bill (not the act as passed), which he voted for. Cf. W. Letwin, supra note 7, at 53n.3; Bork, supra note 7, at 23, 23n.43; H. Thorelli, supra note 7, at 197–99, 201.

20. On the extralegal understandings, see Wiebe, The House of Morgan and the Executive, 1905–1913, 65 Amer. Hist. Rev. 49–60 (1959).

21. See Sklar, supra note 5; Sklar, Woodrow Wilson and the Political Economy of Modern United States Liberalism (1960), reprinted in a New History of Leviathan (1972)

7–65 (R. Radosh & M. Rothbard eds.); Seltzer, Woodrow Wilson as "Corporate-Liberal": Toward a Reconsideration of Left Revisionist Historiography, 30 W. Pol. Q. 183–212 (1977); Hawley, The Discovery and Study of a "Corporate Liberalism," 52 Bus. Hist. Rev. 309–20 (1978); R. Lustig, Corporate Liberalism: The Origins of Modern American Political Theory, 1890–1920 (1982).

4

THE ONE BEST SYSTEM? A POLITICAL ANALYSIS OF NEOCLASSICAL INSTITUTIONALIST PERSPECTIVES ON THE MODERN CORPORATION

MICHAEL BARZELAY AND ROGERS M. SMITH

The corporation has almost always been a controversial institution. But today academic justifications for the modern corporation's dominance in the American politicoeconomic system are perhaps the strongest they have been in decades as a result of the innovative efforts of a small group of economists and jurists connected to the University of Chicago. Unlike some of their predecessors, these writers do not stake their case on the apparent tendency of market systems to safeguard liberties, as did Hayek and Friedman. Nor do they simply argue that a market system enchances economic welfare, as do most neoclassical economists. Instead these contemporary writers, including Michael Jensen, Eugene Fama, William Meckling, and Richard Posner, are attempting to justify the corporation per se by eschewing the academic norm of analyzing capitalist economies as if these were market systems in which owners managed and managers owned.[1] They believe the corporate form can be shown to be the most efficient existing organizational structure even though such union of management and ownership has become rare.

In this chapter, we will argue that their justification relies in part on implausible views of how economic institutions arise historically. In brief, these writers, whom we term the neoclassical institutionalists, wrongly assume that through some invisible hand the most economically efficient organization form available in an era will inevitably come to predominate. We will survey basic developments in U.S. corporate law during the nineteenth century to show that the story of the corporation's ascendancy, in particular, is inadequately described by this approach.

THE NEOCLASSICAL INSTITUTIONALIST VIEW

Judging by their strong claims about the efficiency of the corporate form of organization, the neoclassical institutionalist writers have subverted the older neoclassical paradigm principally in order to save its fundamental prescriptions. Since Berle and Means published their famous study of the separation of management and ownership in widely held corporations some fifty years ago, many critics of the corporate system have emphasized the wide gap between neoclassical models of the market system and the realities of the U.S. corporate economy.[2] Meanwhile, few mainstream economists have addressed fully the contention that because of the separation of ownership and control, the strong results about how markets promote economic welfare derived from many neoclassical models do not apply to market systems in which the modern corporation is the dominant organizational form. However, by integrating recent developments in organization theory, the economic analysis of law, and corporate finance, the neoclassical institutionalists now claim that the modern corporation behaves nearly as efficiently as the owner-managed firm of earlier neoclassical theory. Moreover, based on their theory of institutional evolution, these writers contend that the corporation is the one best way to organize economic activity in a modern industrial market economy.

The new institutional economists depart from the neoclassical theory of the firm, first, by distinguishing the roles of managers, creditors, and shareholders in modern corporations. Many of their specific models analyze how these types of economic agents adjust to one another as each strives to maximize their wealth. Jensen and Meckling, for example, show how a manager's efforts to raise capital from a potential creditor who is wary of managerial discretion, opportunism, or excessive on-the-job consumption will likely lead to bonding and monitoring activities, as specified contractually in the credit instrument. Because these contractual devices can reduce actual managerial discretion, Jensen and Meckling argue that credit markets diminish substantially the central difficulty that they believe arises from the separation of ownership and control: inefficient managerial behavior.[3]

The existence of equity markets is also said to reduce inefficient management practices. Based on the conventions of corporate finance theory and some—though by no means all—of the pertinent empirical findings, the neoclassical institutionalists argue that the stock market values corporations accurately. More specifically, the market value of the tradable residual claims issued by a corporation is said to be an unbiased estimate of the net present value of the corporation's future free cash flows, which can be distributed as dividends.[4]

The neoclassical institutionalists argue that since the capital market values corporations in an unbiased manner, the effects of current or anticipated inefficient behavior by managers will always be discounted in the prices of tradable residual claims. A few other mechanisms, such as the market for managers' human capital, are also said to encourage managers to maximize the value of their firms, although these mechanisms are far less elaborately analyzed. Drawing on these lines of argument, the neoclassical institutionalists claim that corporate managers have every incentive to choose efficient investment decisions and make efficient operating expenditures.[5]

In sum, the neoclassical institutionalists contend that capital markets ensure the rational social control of corporate enterprises.[6] The entitlements that undergird credit markets encourage creditors and managers to restrict managerial discretion, while those entitlements embodied in tradable residual claims enforce efficient managerial behavior through the pricing of these claims in equity markets.[7]

CRITIQUE

Resting as it does on modern finance theory and transactions-cost economics, this analysis represents a powerful attempt to justify the predominant role of the corporation in organizing economic affairs. Moreover, many critics of corporate capitalism and advocates of alternative market systems have yet to address this neoclassical institutionalist program. For instance, David Schweikart, a prominent advocate of worker-controlled enterprises, ignores the claim that private capital markets are necessary social instruments for economizing.[8]

Although we are skeptical about how closely the neoclassical institutionalist models of corporate behavior correspond to the reality of the corporate system, we find generally persuasive the relatively narrow claim that perfect capital markets would militate against inefficient managerial behavior. By itself, this claim does not imply that the corporate system is firmly justified, since such a justification requires a wide-ranging political, social, and moral inquiry. Yet in a society that values material prosperity, the purported efficiency of the corporate form does go some way toward supporting its defensibility. This defense is greatly strengthened by the apparent neoclassical institutionalist contention that the modern corporation is uniquely adapted to the exigencies of efficient capital accumulation in an industrial market economy.

The validity of this last contention is far from obvious. In eighteenth- and nineteenth-century America, England, and France, a great variety of nonincorporated forms were employed, including limited partnerships, the *société en commandité*, and business trusts. Arguably, these and other organization forms could have supplied many of the advantages provided by incorporation.[9] Furthermore, Barzelay and Thomas have argued recently that a form of enterprise can be designed that utilizes the markets for tradable residual claims and debt as social instruments for economizing but that permits substantial employee control.[10] Drawing upon the analysis of manager-investor interactions presented in Jensen and Meckling's theory of the firm and taking into account their published objections to labor-managed organization forms, Barzelay and Thomas claim that a non-capitalist, private, market-oriented enterprise can be designed that is as efficient as the modern corporation.[11]

It is here that the neoclassical institutionalists' views on how economic institutions develop and change historically are crucial to their justifications for present arrangements. The noncorporate organization forms of the nineteenth century did not become standard in the United States. Moreover, as far as we know, the form Barzelay and Thomas proposed does not exist, although it is similar in some respects to several actual types of enterprise. Because these alternative organizational forms are not currently employed, some members of the neoclassical institutionalist school would surely argue that they must be inefficient. This contention follows from the neoclassical institutionalists' account of institutional change. According to Douglass North, "Competition in the face of ubiquitous scarcity dictates that the more efficient institution, policy, or individual action will survive and the inefficient ones perish."[12] Recognizing the importance of legal decisions in shaping organization structures, Richard Posner argues similarly that judges and legislators select only those rules and entitlements that foster the most efficient forms of organization for the time.[13] Essentially, then, the neoclassical institutionalists claim that particular types of economic organizations come to prevail in law and life because they best further wealth maximization.

Advocates of this position acknowledge that the vision of legal decision making and institutional change it proposes is artificially simple and abstract, just as all other elegant theories are. Posner, for example, recognizes that we can see much more in legal reasoning than estimates of the economic consequences of a particular rule. But for him, following Milton Friedman, the test of a theory is not its descriptive validity; it is its predictive or explanatory utility.[14] The neoclassicals' economic model of the evolution of rules and institutions is, on this score, the "most promising positive theory of law extant," for Posner insists that historically the law "uncannily follows economics."[15] Thus Posner believes that in some sense the deep structure of decision making and institutional change is described by the pursuit of social wealth maximization, even if those who shape institutions are neither capable of pursuing nor willing to pursue this goal to the exclusion of all other social ends.

Proponents of this perspective on institutional evolution have not yet examined closely the emergence of the private corporation as a generally available legal device for organizing economic activity during the first half of the nineteenth century.[16] It is plausible to infer, however, that the neoclassical institutionalists would claim that the corporate form emerged because it is uniquely efficient for organizing most kinds of economic activity in a complex market economy.[17] This claim must be disputed if organization forms that are not prevalent can plausibly be held to be as efficient as the modern corporation. In doing so, it is first necessary to see why the neoclassical institutionalists lack credibility when they appeal to efficiency to explain the evolution of legal entitlements, such as those constituting the corporation. Then we must seek an empirically valid model of decision making and institutional change that shows how legal decision makers choose among alternative rules that shape a society's economic organization.

A DIFFERENT VIEW: THE ROLE OF IDEOLOGY

It is true that all theories necessarily distort reality. But the neoclassical theory of the evolution of legal entitlements distorts reality beyond recognition, as its most eminent practitioners increasingly acknowledge. Having tried to suggest various mechanisms to account for the claimed efficiency of the common law, Richard Posner now admits that he still lacks a "good reason" why this claim is valid, though he remains convinced of its veracity.[18] In contrast, Douglass North, who in his earlier works also tried to use the neoclassical approach to account for changes in economic institutions, now argues—in explicit opposition to Posner—that neoclassical economics "does not and cannot explain the dynamics of change."[19] A brief survey of their unsuccessful efforts will help to clarify what direction a more plausible approach to institutional change than neoclassical analysis must take.

In 1973, Posner suggested that judge-made common law rules tend to promote efficiency because judges have sometimes self-consciously chosen to do so and because when they have not, their inefficient rules have eventually been displaced in one of two ways. In areas of law where voluntary relationships among disputants exist, as in contracts and much of property and tort, economically rational private actors evade judicially favored inefficient rules by writing contrary, efficient arrangements into their express agreements with each other. In other areas of the law, political pressures exerted by economically rational interest groups eventually bring about legislative preemption of inefficient judge-made laws.[20]

Davis and North offer precisely this sort of historical explanation when they hypothesize that general incorporation laws resulted from lobbying by manufacturers who sought to make incorporation less costly.[21] While Posner has not elaborated any pertinent historical claims, he would undoubtedly agree that over time, judges and legislatures have adopted and altered legal definitions of the corporation's nature and powers in order to ensure its efficient functioning under changing conditions. Posner explains both the attributes of the modern corporation and its predominance over other types of business organization forms by appeal to its economic advantages. Thus he contends that the corporation represents the "normal solution that the law and business practices have evolved to meet the problems" of economic organization in industrial market systems.[22]

Posner's general account of why legal entitlements are efficient is, however, unpersuasive. First, his claim that legislatures will correct inefficient judicial rules contradicts his own stated conception of the legislative process. Posner typically portrays legislatures as dominated by special interest groups that trade their economic and political support for legislative protection in the "electoral market." Such legislation may at times further overall social wealth while advancing the economic goals of the special interests involved, but Posner believes that legislation will usually be anti-competitive and hence an obstacle to efficiency.[23] For this reason, Posner should not expect that inefficient judge-made rules will be replaced by efficient legislative ones or, more specifically, that the statutes governing corporations necessarily advance any interests besides those of the corporations themselves.[24] There are similar problems with the notion that the writing of express contrary agreements will ensure efficiency. The disparate interests of private parties may prevent them from choosing arrangements that maximize social wealth. Even if these arrangements happen to be efficient, they could be misconstrued by "misguided," noneconomically minded courts.

Apparently recognizing these difficulties, Posner has subsequently tried to explain the alleged efficiency of legal entitlements by pointing to the dominance of utilitarian ideology in the heyday of the common law. For Posner to stress the role of ideology in decision making is risky, however, in part because he does not believe that utilitarianism always yields wealth-maximizing results. More important, Posner's recent position provides no guarantee that legal decision making will be efficient if nonutilitarian ideologies are prevalent among judges. In this event, the claim that decision making is somehow governed by efficiency standards would have to be discarded. In the face of these difficulties, Posner asserts that there are many explanations for the claimed efficiency of the common law, while conceding that it is an embarrassment that no single explanation seems to do the job.[25]

In his earlier writings with Lance Davis and Robert Paul Thomas, Douglass North tried to prove that the historical evolution of institutional rules could be explained by the Posnerian neoclassical assumption that judges and other lawmakers, when confronted with political or legal conflicts created by changing circumstances, choose to maximize economic growth.[26] These earlier accounts were unsatisfactory for several reasons. Alexander Field argues that these models treated legal doctrines and institutional structures as both exogenous and endogenous, undermining the clarity of their causal arguments.[27] Moreover, in practice their authors often failed to specify how changes in exogenous variables altered actual historic choices faced by legal decision makers. Hence, the approach remained more asserted than demonstrated. North himself erred most by neglecting the visible role of ideological values in helping historical decision makers resolve the ambiguity of the conditions they faced and the uncertainty surrounding the consequences of the alternative rules they considered.

Subsequently his careful studies of actual historical decisions appear to have led North to accept such criticisms. He now contends, against neoclassical approaches, that one cannot account for how legal decision makers deal with the uncertainties of the choices they confront without recognizing the often dominant role ideology plays. North holds this predominance of ideology to be especially true for judges, who are relatively insulated from interest group pressures and so are freer to act upon their own beliefs.[28]

The decision-making analyses of both Posner and North, then, point to the centrality of judicial ideology in shaping legal decisions. North correctly notes that ideology provides individuals with a worldview that simplifies decision making; that ideology is inextricably interwoven with moral and ethical judgments about fairness and worth; and that people often alter their ideological perspectives when their experiences are cognitively inconsistent with their ideology.[29] North, however, has yet to provide a specific account of how ideology or shared values shape institutional change. We will now offer such an account of decision making and institutional development and then apply it to the evolution of the corporation in the nineteenth century.[30]

THE REFORMATION OF IDEOLOGY

Students of the history of political ideas have taught that ideologies shape notions of desirable individual and collective aims, understanding of how individuals within a political community are connected to one another, and beliefs about how fundamental social institutions enhance or frustrate the ideologically sanctioned aims. By implication, ideology influences legislative and judicial decisions in at least three ways: by clarifying decision makers' aims, by providing a relatively simple conception of social relations so that decision makers can comfortably reason about social causation, and by sanctioning core beliefs about the value of social arrangements and institutions.

In turn, the decision makers' products augment and often alter broader ideological perspectives. They contribute specific conceptions, doctrines, and policies that are frequently retained and applied in later, somewhat different, contexts, where they may prompt adjustments in more general perspectives. And they contribute to other social, economic, and political developments, often in unexpected ways. These developments can foster ideological revisions. In a changing world, perhaps the only certainty is that neither ideologies nor social institutions will remain wholly static. But the history of corporate law confirms that the specific ways in which social institutions are reshaped in dynamic environments depend in significant measure on the particular traditions of discourse, or dominant legal and political ideologies, that are culturally available to strategic decision makers, such as Supreme Court justices.

The legal theorist Ronald Dworkin has provided the most influential analysis of the ways in which important legal decisions are linked to ideological outlooks. Contemporary jurisprudence now appears to accept his claims about decision making in hard cases—those in which the applicable legal rules are in conflict or manifest contradictions between well-established rules and newly dominant values. Here Dworkin argues, courts are forced to turn from black-letter law to "principles" and to judges' interpretations of the political theory and morality of the legal system in which they operate.[31]

Similarly commentators ranging from the classical legal realists to contemporary students of hermeneutics suggest that different readings of the law ultimately reveal conflicts between competing visions of a desired political and socioeconomic system.[32] In his recent survey of jurisprudence, for example, Lief Carter argues that at "virtually every point in constitutional history some inchoate theory, some enveloping vision of national need, does seem to drive constitutional decisions."[33] Few would disagree with Dworkin's claim that political visions influence common law adjudication as well. Because Dworkin focuses on how judges decide, he does not go on to explore how their decisions contribute to a reshaping of legal rules and broader social behavior in ways that may alter the political ideologies they have employed. His recent stress on their need to "construct" and not simply "discover" adequate theories encompassing their decisions indicates, however, that he would certainly expect this to be the case.[34]

This notion that broader political visions influence legal decision making and are influenced by the results can be usefully elaborated by drawing upon Sheldon Wolin's acclaimed analysis of the role these visions play in relation to formal political theories.[35] In *Politics and Vision*, Wolin argues that political theories usually express a general perception of how people in a given community are connected to one another and a sense of how their political, social, and economic arrangements serve to "mark out paths along which human motions can proceed harmlessly or beneficially."[36] Visions of these interconnections and arrangements—what Wolin calls "political space"—contain broad, almost intuitive notions of how rights and duties, legal restraints, and social mores can be crafted to promote desired social ends. Most political theorizing takes place within such frameworks of root assumptions. The resulting positions theorists defend are in many ways sets of measures designed to realize the social and political structure he or she thus envisions.[37]

When a political community's external environment changes, however—due to economic development, geographic expansion, or social disorders, for example—its members may be compelled to reconceive some or all of the elements of their envisioned political world. Robert Wiebe's impressive recent survey of antebellum U.S. history shows, for instance, how the growth of economic opportunity in areas distant from established social organizations produced substantially reconfigured notions of American political space in that era.[38] A new sense of the extraordinary possibilities of American life arose, and these positive outlooks were intertwined with diffuse resentments toward the confining, gentry-dominated social and politicoeconomic order constructed by the Federalists and Jeffersonians. In the 1820s and 1830s, these sentiments strengthened the Jacksonians' emerging, more democratic vision of America. The institutionalization of this vision was achieved, in part, through legislative and judicial actions.[39]

Wolin notes that dramatic transformations in material and social conditions, such as were underway in this period, often give rise to truly great, imaginative political theorizing—though he would certainly add that philosophic writings are only the most elaborate examples of how basic ideological outlooks are altered in response to the actual changes that political theorists, lawmakers, and ordinary citizens experience. Although a theorist's detailed articulation of a political vision may be too abstruse for common discourse, Wolin contends that such visions themselves, with their fundamental norms and premises, can be and indeed must be matters of shared public knowledge in all genuine political communities.[40] In other terms, all members socialized within a community, including lawmakers and ordinary citizens, inevitably have some common understanding of their mutual interconnectedness and of desirable social arrangements. This understanding is always put under stress by changes in their material and social environments (which may, of course, have resulted from their own previous actions).

We can accordingly interpret the rule-making decisions of judges and legislators in the face of new controversies as efforts, like the innovations of political theorists, to preserve and adjust the meaning of their shared conceptions of political space. A model of institutional change must therefore capture how lawmakers craft social institutions as they adjust their ideologically conditioned perceptions and aims to the changing social world around them.

In examining how lawmakers resolve conflicts generated, for example, by new technologies, expanding market trading areas, and the diffusion of institutional innovations, one must especially investigate the tensions usually inherent among the elements of the dominant visions or ideologies they employ. Virtually all influential ideologies, including those of the nineteenth century, contain an array of inherently competitive notions of humans and society, each of which can point to quite different policy implications in given circumstances.[41] Depending upon its particular architecture, a prominent ideology will incline its adherents to regard some changes in social conditions as more problematic than others and to view certain programs and institutional changes as compelling while other will seem unacceptable. An excellent illustration of how ideologies demarcate options and difficulties for legal decision makers is provided by the Jacksonians. The Jacksonian legislators and judges relied on but also rearranged the elements of civil republican ideology in expressing and institutionalizing their emerging vision of the United States as a democratic society in the 1830s and 1840s.

The Jacksonian experience also affirms that opportunities for lawmakers to institutionalize their visions of political space are often pressed upon them by critical political and legal controversies, such as hard cases. In explaining the sequence of legal rules adopted by authorities, it is therefore necessary to indicate how the resolution of such controversies is shaped by particular legal articulations of dominant ideological strains. It is equally important to explore how factual circumstances in hard cases, along with inherited legal rules, constrain the institutionalization of these ever-changing ideologies and the aims they countenance. Factual circumstances frame the specific choices to be made. Inherited legal categories are relatively binding, in part because lawmakers typically respond to complex new situations by choosing principles that are plausibly consistent with past beliefs and practices. Because of these factual and legal constraints, institutional rules at any given time are never fully consistent, giving the law a certain patchwork quality.[42] Yet as streams of decisions are made in the face of the multiple interrelated tensions that typically develop among principles when societies undergo rapid change, even fundamental legal and political categories can experience substantial shifts in their meanings.[43] Any discussion of the role of ideology in shaping institutional change must capture both the patchwork and dynamic qualities of the law.

Accordingly, a general account of institutional change, especially by judicial decision making, must be four-step process. First, the material, political, ideological, and institutional context in which critical legal controversies arise must be sketched, indicating which political and ideological forces have succeeded in placing proponents of their political visions on the bench. Second, the ways in which those who hold one or another dominant ideology are likely to regard these controversies must be described. Third, an adequate account must explain how a judge's decision to adopt a particular rule expresses (and sometimes revises) his or her general ideological outlook. Finally, the consequences of his or her decision for both the general pattern of legal doctrines and for later social and political developments must be identified—an inquiry that often reveals that decision makers produce results quite different from those they intended.

In applying this general account to the evolution of the corporation, we must therefore first attend to the various material and social circumstances that structured the initial political space of the United States, including its dominant ideologies, and identify how corporations were understood in this setting. We must then see how this environment produced legal disputes concerning corporations, how the adherents of the dominant ideologies responded to those issues, and how judges fashioned and refashioned corporate rules and entitlements in accordance with their general ideological commitments. We must be aware of how these actions gradually produced ideological and legal transformations while also altering the material and social worlds, generating further legal issues. This complex historical process eventually led to the general incorporation acts and to the specific question of corporate personality posed in the *Santa Clara* case. The story is in fact too complex for us to be able to provide more than a general sketch here; but that sketch should be sufficient to confirm, as North argues, that the historic processes of institutional change in question cannot be adequately grasped by the neoclassical institutionalist approach.

IDEOLOGIES AND THE CORPORATION

In 1800, only a clairvoyant could have foreseen that within eighty years the limited liability corporation would become a dominant form of organization for the pursuit of private business purposes. Corporations were relatively uncommon in the United States at the turn of the nineteenth century, and most older corporations were cities, boroughs, churches, charities, or colleges. With the exception of banks, insurance firms, and transportation companies, business enterprises were rarely incorporated. These business corporations, moreover, were not considered private entities in either the law or the popular thought of the time. The corporation was primarily conceived of as a legal device by which to extend public powers to private individuals.[44] Given this legal conception and its embodiment in such public agencies as municipalities, the term *private corporation* might well have struck many contemporaries as an oxymoron.

As with municipalities and other corporations, the granting of charters to business enterprises was seen to be the best way for state legislatures to induce private individuals to undertake activities they believed would directly enhance the public good. Since only some endeavors met this standard, state legislatures approved each corporate charter individually, through a special incorporation act. It was only through special incorporation that a group of individuals could possess legal personality, which enabled the corporate entity to withstand changes in or the demise of the original members for at least a limited number of years. Those who received a charter were considered to be members of the "little republic" that the state had authorized, just like the inhabitants of municipalities.[45]

As justified by their quasi-public status, corporation members sometimes enjoyed a variety of privileges, such as limited financial liability, legal protection from competitive injury, and other immunities. Depending upon its specific line of business, moreover, a corporation might receive the right to condemn private property by means of the power of eminent domain. In return, state legislatures sometimes insisted on strict control and participation in corporate ownership and profits.[46]

By 1880, the notion of a private corporation was almost as commonly accepted as it is today. In many states, general incorporation acts made it possible for investors to form corporations in practically any area of business activity, subject only to perfunctory legislative approval. With the enormous expansion of incorporated businesses, the earlier common understanding that corporations were arms of the state withered away. The idea that a corporation was composed of members had also given way to the radically different notion that these entities were composed of individual investors in transferable stock. Furthermore, several previously contingent features of the corporate form had become part of its constitution, including limited financial liability, full protection from uncompensated public takings, and the same limited liability in tort then granted to individuals.[47] On the other hand, what had been an essential feature of the corporate form—protection from competitive injury—was swept away by legislative practice and judicial rulings in the years leading to the general incorporation acts.[48]

How did the corporation emerge as such a dominant form of business organization, with a dramatically altered legal status and incidents that made it much more clearly private than public? To explain this transformation, we must probe how U.S. lawmakers, during a period of extraordinary change, adapted their ideological visions, their understandings of political space, and we must relate these adaptations to the shifting meanings they gave to corporations.

In the aftermath of the Revolution, Americans' political space was highly circumscribed. They dwelled on the edges of largely unexplored frontiers. Roads and other means of transport were extremely limited. Most trade was consequently carried on between population centers and their hinterlands, not among the different regions of the new country. These market arenas narrowed Americas' conceptions of their political space, yet they were not the only factor that did so. Despite the colonials' common struggle against the British, states and localities remained the focus of social solidarity and political community. These sentiments of local attachment were reinforced by an important institutional reality: state legislatures assumed many of the powers that had previously been vested in the king-in-Parliament.[49]

Having recently experienced the upheaval of revolution, leaders of state governments were unsure how strong their experimental republican institutions would be. Seeking security and dignity for these regimes, leaders of many state governments began to use their authority to promote material progress.[50] Generating new wealth would certainly help gain the enduring political support of those who benefited directly from such promotional activities. Moreover, since these activities would be undertaken by the states against the contrasting historical backdrop of burdensome British political and economic controls, even those people who did not benefit directly would likely become highly loyal to the new, more benign governmental institutions.

Among the obstacles to employing public power to promote material progress was the longstanding resistance of the population to the debts and taxes that might be needed to finance state investments. At the time, the huge public debts incurred during the Revolution weighed heavily on the minds of the people, as well as on the public finances of the several states. High taxes, too, were as unpopular after the Revolution as before, as indicated by the fact that the Massachusetts tax for current expenses remained fixed at $133,000 for a quarter-century (1795–1820).[51]

There were however, few ideological barriers to governmental actions aimed at fostering economic growth. In the new American polity, two interrelated but distinguishable ideologies, or visions of political space, chiefly competed for primacy. These outlooks tended to be aligned roughly with their proponents' places in the federal structure of the new regime. State leaders often stressed the civic republican or commonwealth tradition that favored small governments dominated by popular legislatures. National elites frequently stressed a Lockean liberalism that envisioned a central government securing personal liberties, especially property rights, for all.[52]

In the post-Revolutionary period, both strains of political thought encouraged political leaders to see a connection between material progress and political stability, and both contained rationales for employing public authority on behalf of economic aims. Although each of these systems of thought feared the absolutist possibilities of an extensive role for government, the republican belief that the economy should be ordered to further the common good and Locke's liberal endorsement of efforts to promote the productive uses of property together provided ample ideological support for various forms of public economic intervention that were considered at the time.[53]

There were nonetheless elements within both republican and Lockean thought that—in a somewhat different social, political, and economic milieu—could be used to oppose governmentally conferred economic privileges or extensive regulation. For centuries, republican or commonwealth views had taught that if governments became entangled with venal financial elites, corruption would ensue. Early American republicans adapted Adam Smith's laissez-faire doctrines to bolster their vigilance against corruption, though they used these doctrines selectively. The Jeffersonian republicans challenged the mercantilist national programs of the Hamiltonians but not state developmental measures, which they generally favored. The emphasis in Locke's liberal views on the sanctity of private property rights and the propriety of allowing productive activity to reap its rewards could also be used to circumscribe governmental intrusions into the economy.[54]

These anti-interventionist elements remained inert during the post-Revolutionary period, when it was generally popular to use public powers to stimulate investments and activities that appeared visibly to benefit the general welfare. To do so without incurring debts or raising taxes, state governments needed to induce groups of private investors to undertake risky investments in banks, bridges, turnpikes, canals, and the like.[55] One way to create the necessary inducements was to extend certain powers of public agency to these private individuals.

According to the English common law tradition, the king-in-Parliament could confer legal personality on groups of individuals, thereby creating clerical eleemosynary, or civil corporations.[56] Clerical corporations were churches and church offices. Eleemosynary corporations were privately initiated institutions dedicated to charitable purposes, such as hospitals and colleges. Most civil corporations were municipalities, although even in early nineteenth-century England some of these were business enterprises.[57] In the United States, the common legal and popular conception that corporations contributed directly to the public good helped push state legislatures to employ this technique in promoting certain economic activities.

The question of whether these corporations were essentially public or private bodies could not be answered by reference to the common law traditions inherited by colonial Americans and adopted by the post-Revolutionary regime. Rooted in English conceptions of the proper social order during the medieval era, the common law still largely derived the rights and duties of ordinary people, nobles, and the king from bonds of kinship and vassalage. These categories had little relationship to the emerging modern conceptions of public and private. At common law, actions could be public or private, but persons and corporations were both.[58] The ambiguity and arguable irrelevance of these categories persisted to the end of the eighteenth century, as illustrated by the notions that the king-in-Parliament or a state legislature was necessarily one of the founders of every corporation.[59]

The difficulty of characterizing early American business corporations as either public or private also stemmed from their frequent possession of privileges of public agency, including limited liability in tort and contract, powers of eminent domain, and freedom from competitive injury. Limited financial liability was rare initially, but it eventually proved to be a magnet for investors, especially in an era when courts favored strict liability in tort. Among other sovereign privileges extended to corporations, the most formidable in the late eighteenth and early nineteenth centuries was the right of eminent domain. In crossing private lands, for instance, corporations building turnpikes and canals were protected from legal actions demanding compensation for damages. Well into the nineteenth century, growth-minded state courts responded to such actions by invoking the commonwealth principle that the "general good is to prevail over partial individual inconvenience." Accordingly, courts ruled that these takings were "part of the price to be paid for the advantages of the social condition" and therefore constituted "damages without injury." State legislatures, as well as the courts, further protected the early corporations by extending to them some immunities from injurious competition. Such privileges were provided not only to natural monopolies, such as turnpikes and canal companies, but to chartered mining and manufacturing companies as well.[60]

However settled the English common law of corporations may have been, in the new American nation, rapid growth in the numbers and activities of business corporations generated a series of difficult legal controversies. Predictably, corporations attempted to use the courts to enhance their public powers and immunities, as well as to protect themselves against legislative interference. The cases resulting from these efforts raised difficult technical legal questions over whether business corporations should be considered essentially public or private and how far they should be regarded as persons or citizens in their own right rather than as mere aggregates of natural persons or citizens. Resolution of these technical legal problems was frequently inconsistent from case to case.

Legal adherents of both republican and liberal views sometimes found it useful to emphasize the public purposes corporations served; at other times, these same parties chose to focus on the private property rights of corporate entities and of individual corporation members. Stress on the public character of corporations often served the aims of Federalist champions of liberal mercantilism, as well as those of republicans who sought to sustain the legislative powers needed to create and regulate corporations. But Federalists sometimes insisted on the private character of corporations instead, especially when they feared legislative encroachments on economic liberties, and at times the laissez-faire strain in Jeffersonian republican thought took similar stances. Legal advocates of these ideological strains were also inconsistent in their favored conceptions of the corporation's legal standing. Both Jeffersonian republicans and Federalists who believed strongly in individual property rights sometimes argued that a corporation was a mere legal fiction and that courts should recognize the rights of the natural persons of which it was comprised. In some cases, however, Federalist lawyers discovered that corporate legal rights could not be effectively defended unless the corporation were granted more independent legal personality. In others, republicans found their defense of legislative powers could be aided by that same step.

Many of these difficulties were visible in Chief Justice Marshall's struggles with questions of the corporation's nature and entitlements. John Marshall was a staunch Federalist, a Lockean advocate of mercantilist promotional measures, and an ardent defender of vested property and contractual rights.[61] In attempting to embody these general commitments in legal doctrines, Marshall repeatedly wrestled with cases that turned on the meaning of corporate personality.

In 1809, the Supreme Court considered *Bank of United States v. Deveaux*, which required it to decide whether a corporation could sue or be sued in the courts of the United States. Since federal jurisdiction under Article III, section 2 granted such standing only to citizens and states, Marshall apparently would have to deem the corporation a citizen in order to give it the protection of the federal courts. But if a corporation were deemed a citizen, the law would stress its legislatively created legal personality rather than the rights of its private owners. Marshall was reluctant to take this step because he feared giving primacy to legislative actions rather than to individual economic rights. The chief justice therefore ruled that the corporation was an "invisible, intangible, artificial being," a "mere legal entity" that was "certainly not a citizen." Despite this definitional dictum, Marshall still allowed the corporation to sue in federal court as if it were a citizen, for this could be seen as enabling members of corporations to exercise their rights as citizens. Marshall also conceded that state legislatures could treat corporations as citizens "under certain circumstances."[62]

Chief Justice Marshall took a further step toward granting the corporation full legal personality in the famous case of *Dartmouth College v. Woodward* (1819), which primarily raised the related question of whether corporations were essentially public or private.[63] At stake was the right of the state of New Hampshire to alter unilaterally the college's corporate charter. The New Hampshire legislature had assumed control of the college and appointed its own board of overseers. The college's trustees sued to overturn what they viewed as a usurpation of their chartered powers. In ruling against the Dartmouth trustees, the state trial judge deemed the college a public corporation. The objects for which the corporation was created—education and religion—were, he thought, "matters of public concern."[64]

On appeal, Marshall reversed the state court's ruling by focusing instead on the origins of this eleemosynary corporation. Dartmouth's founders were private individuals who had used their private resources for their own charitable purposes. Marshall contended that these facts justified deeming the college a private corporation, whose trustees were properly empowered to supervise the perpetuation of its original purposes, just as visitors appointed by a charity's private founders always had been at common law. The fact that the college served public objects did not make it a public corporation, Marshall argued, because all corporations served some public purposes.[65]

In Marshall's view, private corporations served public purposes through the exercise of private rights, which the courts had to defend. The vehicle for upholding those rights was the contract clause, which Marshall generally regarded as the chief constitutional instrument for protecting property rights. In *Dartmouth College*, Marshall had common law precedents to justify the assertion that a corporate charter was a contract. He held accordingly that charters, at least those of private, eleemosynary corporations, were protected by the contract clause and hence must be treated with the solicitude owed private property.[66] This line of reasoning helped Marshall to rule in favor of the Dartmouth College trustees and against the New Hampshire legislature.

Marshall still faced one hurdle in the case before reaching that conclusion, and it caused him to wrestle once again with the perplexing legal identity of the corporation. To avoid burdening the courts with meaningless litigation, a contractual right ordinarily would not be enforced unless the complainant had some "beneficial"—typically pecuniary—interest at stake. Because Dartmouth's unpaid trustees appeared to have no financial interest in maintaining their control over the corporation, Marshall could not reverse the decision by focusing on their individual property rights as members of the corporation. Thus he was compelled, as in *Deveaux*, to emphasize the independent legal identity—the "individuality"—of the corporation more than he was usually inclined to do. Although he continued to stress that private corporations had no political character Marshall held that the special charitable nature of eleemosynary corporations meant that the rights and interests of their original donors attached to the enterprises themselves. Those corporate legal rights were protected by the Constitution under the contract clause. Hence Marshall could at last conclude that the legislature's act must be overturned. This precedent made it easier to assign independent legal personality to other types of corporations as well.[67]

Marshall was undoubtedly willing to enhance corporate legal personality in this case because the result furthered his most fundamental judicial aims. At a time when the special privileges of corporations were becoming more controversial, *Dartmouth College* signaled that the Court would protect the vested rights of all private corporations, including business corporations, against antagonistic popular legislatures.[68] This position was of a piece with Marshall's strong support for vested rights generally. No doubt this course reflected Marshall's beliefs about what would promote economic growth in the young nation, but those beliefs almost certainly stemmed more from his general Lockean outlook than from any actual economic calculations about the consequences of his decision. He was surely also aware of the considerable assistance his ruling would give to the economic and political interests of the gentry groups he had always favored.[69]

Whether Marshall's decision was legally or economically correct, it was certainly politically sensitive, for it was handed down just as antiprivilege perspectives that Marshall feared were becoming increasingly prominent in U.S. politics. The seeds of these new political outlooks were sown, ironically, by the long-standing enthusiasm for state promotional charters, which had led to the creation of some 1,500 new corporations by 1816. These corporations, in turn, furthered the geographical expansion of settlement, diversified economic activities, generated new forms of economic interconnectedness, and transformed their predominantly gentry investors into wealthy corporate elites. Moreover, as charters were increasingly given to competing ventures and to incipient manufacturing enterprises, it became more difficult for people to see how specific corporate activities strengthened the commonwealth in a direct way.[70]

The newer, competing businesses often took advantage of technological innovations and of opportunities in newly opened regions that were neglected by established gentry-run enterprises. Resentments developed when the established corporations insisted on their legal rights to monopoly status, creating obstacles to the realization of the new regions' aspirations. Those resentments were increasingly less muted by deferential habits of behavior because the fragmentation of older social and economic forms of integration had shattered much of the practical and moral potency of the traditional gentry financial, political, and kinship networks. After the depression of 1819–1821 had damaged faith in the capacity of existing institutions to guarantee prosperity, extensive popular hostility toward elites emerged. This hostility provided the emotional fuel for the movements that would become Jacksonianism.[71]

In this extraordinarily dynamic environment, perceptions of how the corporation was located in political space also began to change fundamentally. Instead of a few isolated efforts to provide a public spur to economic growth in undeveloped lands, corporations increasingly appeared as a swarm of competitive, profit-seeking, and thus more clearly private entities. Understandably adherents of the dominant American political ideologies interpreted this widely shared new perception in quite different ways. Small businessmen, rising entrepreneurs, and western farmers who resented the established corporations found in republican thought ample material to portray their foes as illicit beneficiaries of special privilege who were corrupting the public-spiritedness of the general government and the body politic.[72]

The corporations and their political supporters, on the other hand, often did not oppose the new legal and ideological stress on the private character of the older chartered enterprises, for Lockean liberalism suggested that if corporations were private property, they ought to be protected against arbitrary legislative regulations and takings. When corporate "members" were seen less as bearers of a public trust than as merely private owners of property that took the form of stock, their juridical champions, John Marshall included, could more easily defend them as holders of sacredly guarded property rights. Similarly, it seemed increasingly less appropriate to make investors bear responsibility for all the actions and debts of the corporations whose stock they happened to purchase.[73]

But in the transformed conditions of the Jacksonian era, the adherents of the republican outlook acquired the political power to offer several distinct types of opposition to such vested rights. Once good times returned after 1825, state governments continued to promote growth as enthusiastically as ever, but now they did so more often through purely public roads, canals, and other public works. When they did rely on private corporations, state legislatures displayed increased suspicion of the companies' tendencies to pursue private interests instead of the public good and, accordingly, reasserted their powers to regulate the enterprises in question with greater firmness. Chartered banks, for instance, were sometimes directed by a legislature to assist its preferred developmental projects.[74]

Although stricter intentional control was one route to reform embedded in the ideology of the new political elite, it was not the only one. As the numbers of corporations grew, both legislatures and courts drew increasingly on the strong suggestion in laissez-faire thought that competition could serve as an indirect, even epiphenomenal, control on corporate abuses and therefore should be encouraged. Republican thought, thus augmented, helped push legislatures to confer new private charters and courts to construe the rights of both old and new enterprises in ways that ensured increased competition.[75]

The common result of all these strategies was a surge of further legal battles over the status of the corporation. In particular, with the development of the first railroads in the 1830s, the courts were flooded with actions by older turnpike and canal companies, which asserted that their corporate property rights were being infringed by the new grants of railroad charters. But the established corporations, though their position was embellished by both Marshall's legal doctrines of vested rights and Locke's mercantilist ideology, soon found themselves on the defensive. The new general perception of its private nature meant that the corporation would never again possess quite the same aura of public benefactor it previously had in both politics and law. As the 1820s ended, moreover, the opponents of the older vested privileges succeeded in placing Jackson in the White House, where he eventually won his great symbolic battle against the keystone of national gentry mercantilism, the Bank of the United States.[76]

His political movement came to have a decisive impact on legal doctrines after Jackson replaced John Marshall with his own attorney general. It fell to this new chief justice, Roger Taney, to apply the political vision of the Jacksonians to the question of the corporation's legal status and powers. He did so prominently in the landmark case of *Charles River Bridge v. Warren Bridge* in 1837. The Massachusetts legislature had chartered a second bridge in close proximity to the forty-seven-year-old Charles River Bridge, linking Boston to Charlestown. The Charles River Bridge corporation charged that this second grant represented an unconstitutional infringement of its original charter, which it interpreted as granting an exclusive franchise.

Like the Jacksonians generally, Taney was no opponent of the sanctity of property rights, and with Marshall he was quite willing to construe a corporate charter as a contract within the meaning of the Constitution's contract clause. But Taney quickly showed that he was indeed the heir of the republican or commonwealth views the Jacksonians favored. "The object and end of all government," he argued in clear republican tones, "is to promote the happiness and prosperity of the community. While the rights of private property are sacredly guarded, we must not forget that the community also has rights." The Massachusetts court had made the judgment, which Taney found quite plausible, that economic progress would be better served by encouraging new endeavors guided by the "light of modern science" instead of remaining wedded to the "improvements of the last century." Given that there was not any explicit grant of monopoly status in the Charles River Bridge's original charter and that such charters should be interpreted in the light of this conception of the public interest, Taney upheld the legislature's action and the state court ruling.[77]

The *Charles River Bridge* decision was unquestionably one that its author believed would be beneficial, even necessary, for furthering economic growth. But some see it as ratifying the desirability of competition in a way that aided "emergent entrepreneurial and commercial groups," though not necessarily the general welfare, while others contend that the political motive to set the legal "balance against privilege" was decisive.[78] Justice Joseph Story's vehement dissent in the case provides further evidence that its result cannot be attributed to economic reasoning alone, for Story was as concerned about economic efficiency as any one else. But he adhered to the not-implausible liberal mercantilist belief that security for granted privileges remained most essential for this end. Accordingly Story thought that the prerogatives of the original bridge should be upheld. It therefore seems beyond doubt that estimations of economic efficiency alone cannot account for this judgment either. *Charles River Bridge* is explicable only as a product of the full set of economic and political assumptions and aspirations that comprised Taney's Jacksonian outlook.

Paradoxically, however, just as Marshall's concern to protect corporate rights led him to endow corporations with fuller legal identity, so Taney's desire to assert limits on corporate powers pushed him in the same direction. In *Bank of Augusta v. Earle* (1839), Taney had to decide the extent of the contractual powers of private corporations—specifically whether a corporation chartered in one state had as much right as any citizen to enter into contracts in another state. The chief justice ruled that barring any positive state action to prevent it from doing so, a corporation could enter into such interstate contracts, but he strove to deny that its rights were equal to those of natural citizens. Specifically, he did not wish to grant corporations all that might be implied by Article IV, section 2's privileges and immunities clause. To do so he had to stress the corporation's independent legal personality. He argued that although a corporation "is indeed a mere artificial being, invisible and intangible, yet it is a person, for certain purposes in contemplation of law." Thus, when it makes a contract, "it is the contract of the legal entity; of the artificial being created by the charter; and not the contract of the individual members." That meant the corporation could have no contractual powers beyond those authorized in its charter, and if these were more limited than those of its natural members, the limitations were perfectly legitimate.[79]

The decision, then, once again expressed Taney's characteristic Jacksonian aim of sustaining state legislative authority over corporations, but it also propelled the movement of the law toward seeing the corporation as something other than a mere aggregate of natural persons. The Taney Court carried that trend an important step further in an 1844 decision rendered by Justice Wayne: *Louisville, Cincinnati, and Charleston Railroad v. Letson*. This case announced what Chief Justice John Marshall had not quite been willing to say in *Bank of United States v. Deveaux*: that "for the purpose of suing and being sued," a corporation is a citizen of the state in which it is incorporated. Marshall had held only that a corporation could exercise the citizenship of its stockholders, but as corporations had become less like small clubs owned by a few gentry, the probability that its owners would all be citizens of the same state had decreased. Hence if corporations were to be assigned a citizenship in order to maintain their rights to sue, another rule was necessary. The Court had little difficulty in deciding that the place of incorporation should be decisive. It simply noted that a "corporation created by a state to perform its functions under the authority of that state" seemed to have been clearly accepted by the law as "a person, though an artificial one, inhabiting and belonging to that state." So it was appropriate that it be "deemed a citizen of that state" for the limited purposes of exercising its chartered powers: to contract and to sue and be sued.[80]

As these decisions indicate, even as Taney and the adherents of Jacksonian democracy wished to assert state authority over corporations, they also wished to maintain corporate legal powers sufficient for the companies' effective operation. This seemed a necessity, as corporations were continuing to do much of the work of economic development, and continued economic expansion multiplied demands for new charters even more quickly through the 1840s. The states had suffered some failures with direct investments, moreover, and so they were once more inclined to leave the financing and operation of economic enterprises in private hands.[81] In addition, the rapid development of the railroads in the 1840s and 1850s helped cement the corporation's preeminence. These first truly large-scale corporations served as national instruments for capital investment as well as transportation and trade, and their magnitude dramatized the potential of the corporate form.[82]

Political opposition to giving corporations special privileges through charters also gained momentum in this era, however—in part because the increased involvement of legislatures with developmental companies had bred extensive corruption, in accordance with the long-standing fears of laissez-faire republican Jacksonians. Also significant was the great nationwide depression of 1837–1843, which caused several states to default on their corporate bonds and unleashed new hostility toward corporations and their wealthy beneficiaries. The belief that special charters fostered corruption was probably accurate, for in another example of unexpected consequences, the Jacksonian democrats' very insistence on confining corporations to the powers explicitly granted in their charters—expressed in the legal doctrine of ultra vires—meant corporations faced with changing conditions constantly had to win new favors from legislatures augmenting their powers. They usually found ways to do this.[83]

But the opposition to special charters pointed in two different directions. On the one hand, resentful unincorporated businessmen, angry consumers, and working groups supported efforts, visible in states as disparate as New York and Louisiana, to amend state constitutions in order to limit the legislature's powers to grant special charters. In the light of the demands for new economic organizations, this approach was probably quixotic, and it eventually proved unworkable. Corporations persuaded legislatures and courts to find loopholes to even constitutional limits on the powers they were granted. The other solution was to end the special character of charter privileges, making them available to all through general incorporation laws.[84]

This was the answer that eventually prevailed: general incorporation laws began to grow in popularity in the late 1840s and had become the norm by 1900.[85] The complex history of the movements for various forms of these laws in the several states cannot be reviewed here in detail, but certain points should be stressed. In retrospect, a policy of easy general incorporation may appear to represent an embrace of the escalating inequalities in corporate wealth and power of the Gilded Age, but that was far from what was usually intended. It must be recalled that the United States did not experience its industrial revolution until the late nineteenth century. In the 1840s, the potent corporate empires, enormous wealth differentials, and harsh working conditions it would breed were imaginable to very few.

In perhaps the greatest irony of the many in this area, general incorporation laws initially appeared instead as democratizing measures, both economically and politically. The special charters had bred favoritism, political corruption, and privileged elites, and they had been barriers, albeit increasingly ineffective ones, to new enterprises. By making the corporate form almost universally available, the government would no longer be a source of immoral services to special interests but would once more be encouraging private endeavors by all that would serve the public good. The laissez-faire strain in Jacksonian thought argued that if economic competition were made more open to everyone, the results would include not only increased efficiency but equal opportunities for all conscientious, industrious Americans to obtain their own thriving businesses, thus enriching the nation as a whole without creating durable forms of excessive economic dependence.[86] Since the common man could be counted on to take commendable advantage of his economic possibilities, general incorporation would produce a distribution of wealth that would be more conducive to political equality.[87]

Existing corporate and financial elites, on the other hand, favored general incorporation laws on less public-spirited grounds. They saw such laws simply as useful devices to facilitate the operation and proliferation of their enterprises. But they were able to give their concerns broader appeal by evoking the fears in Lockean ideology about extensive governmental regulation in order to support pro-market policies.[88]

The corporate elites proved more successful in realizing their aims. The rosy republican scenario of increased opportunity and equality made possible by general incorporation laws, like so many other predictions of political and judicial lawmakers, was radically different from the eventual results. The further spread of corporations, combined with new transportation and industrial technologies, formed part of an industrial revolution that generated far more sweeping transformations in the nation's physical, economic, and political environment than ever before. Those transformations were also reflected in its prevailing ideologies and in views of the corporation. Once corporations chartered in one state could operate elsewhere in the country, states began competing to have the most permissive incorporation laws in the nation.[89] Consequently, while American republicanism's laissez-faire strain flourished, the last legal vestiges of older commonwealth beliefs that corporations had special public responsibilities were soon eradicated. Culminating the direction in which the Supreme Court had felt driven to move, corporations were now defined as purely private, competitive, limited liability, profit-maximizing economic devices, treated as legal persons essentially to permit the trading of their shares.[90]

These corporate persons were the targets of important populist and labor protests that drew in part on antiprivilege republican themes.[91] The protest movements were not very successful at shaping enduring legal doctrines, however, so our purposes require us only to note that corporate interests came to defend and to be defended by a significantly novel economic and legal ideology, usually termed social Darwinism. A harsher view than either Lockean or Jacksonian laissez-faire doctrines, both of which promised that even the average day laborer would share in economic growth, this outlook portrayed the market as an arena of competition in which the fittest should be allowed to struggle and survive— thereby benefiting society in the long run, though not the many present-day losers in the contest.[92] It may well be, as Morton Horwitz suggests in chapter 2, that when the Supreme Court took it for granted in the *Santa Clara* case of 1886 that the personhood of corporations meant that they were also persons within the meaning of the postwar Fourteenth Amendment, it was only continuing the Jacksonians' limited recognition of the corporation's legal personality. That recognition was not inconsistent with extensive governmental regulation, as we have seen. But as the broad guarantees of the Fourteenth Amendment, especially the due process clause, became vehicles for social Darwinist legal ideas, corporate economic rights of personhood, defined with the assistance of the best legal counsel wealthy corporations could provide, grew more and more extensive.

This development is quite explicable, for both the liberal and republican strains in American political thought had always contained powerful notions of the centrality of economic freedoms that provided ample material on which to build. Decisions of the Marshall and Taney courts had, for different reasons, increasingly identified the corporate form as an autonomous bearer of such rights and freedoms. Hence it became possible to attribute to corporations virtually absolute contractual and vocational liberties that could be used to oppose both governmental regulatory efforts and union activities. As a result, the evolution of the law toward acceptance of the private nature of corporations and of their independent legal pesonality, meant that the legal doctrines comprising the American law of corporations came in the late nineteenth century to serve as suitable bases for the dawn of the rhetorically laissez-faire and effectively pro-corporation *Lochner* era in American law. They played that role despite their origins in very different political visions. Neither Marshall nor the Jacksonians foresaw the triumph of these vastly influential corporate persons, with their extensive range of legal powers, or the development of a broader legal and political ideology in which private corporations would play such a pivotal role. Yet each helped to bring it about.

CONCLUSION: THE LIMITS OF EFFICIENCY ANALYSIS: LAW, IDEOLOGY AND SYSTEMIC CHANGE

This narrative demonstrates how much the evolution of the corporation in nineteenth-century America was the product of ongoing changes in the realities and the prevailing conceptions of the nation's political space, changes that both produced and were produced by innovations in legal doctrines. Over time, decision makers adapted these conceptions to the enormous social alterations of those decades, including the vast expansion of settlement, the strengthening of republican and later democratic institutions, and the development of a buoyant commercial economy. Their adaptations of corporate doctrines represented, however, political choices, not neutral, economically functional revisions. In their efforts to adjust to these changing material and social circumstances, lawmakers and others drew intellectual and moral sustenance from the two dominant ideological strains that formed America's young tradition of political discourse.

The liberal vision, in particular, helped link the private corporation to the emerging modern category of the private as part of a Federalist, mercantilist program to safeguard corporate property rights against extensive regulation by the state legislatures that created these legal persons. The republican vision, which attained dominance after corporations became vehicles for the gentry's privileged socioeconomic position, also gave a push to the private corporation. But unlike the liberal vision's emphasis on private property rights, the republican vision understood the utilization of this institutional device as a means to make American society more democratic.

While the evolution of the corporate form generally reflected these shifts in lawmakers' conceptions of political space, legal decision makers faced substantial difficulties in successfully institutionalizing their visions of the good society. In the short run, inherited legal categories and factual circumstances were constraints, as evidenced by the complexities Marshall faced in reaching his desired result in *Dartmouth College*. Over the course of time, such specific factual circumstances and the inherited meanings of legal categories were more easily evaded and hence were much weaker constraints on legal decision making. But in the long run, lawmakers were not necessarily any more able than in the short run to craft social institutions that actualized their evolving notions of political space. Marshall's protection of corporate vested rights, for example, helped fuel the Jacksonian political movement, whose democratic conception of American society was greatly at odds with the political order he had hoped to sustain. Similarly, the Jacksonians' efforts to institutionalize their visions of a democratic society—in part through the passage of general incorporation acts—helped to create the late nineteenth-century social and ideological order, which bore little resemblance to their republican vision of a good society.

It is worth speculating on the extent to which the consequences of decisions, such as those made by Marshall and Taney, were hidden from their view by the particular timing of political and economic developments in the nineteenth century. It seems quite important, and yet contingent, that the Jacksonian aversion to privilege and corruption became the dominant political force well before the industrial revolution. Had the emergence of expressive egalitarianism and industrialism coincided, it is possible that the Jacksonian republican vision might have led key lawmakers to weaken the entitlements and legal personality of the corporate form. Ideologies, then, certainly cannot by themselves determine social developments; but they provide intellectual resources that can play a crucial role in defining the options decision makers perceive in dealing with social problems as they understand them.

This account of how ideology mediates between social conditions and institutions provides more specificity to Douglass North's recent critique of the neoclassical theory of institutional evolution. It also demonstrates just how tenuous is the argument of Richard Posner and others when they hold that the deep structure of social processes leads lawmakers to achieve the goal of structuring social institutions exclusively to further economic efficiency. Although pro-development sentiments were embedded in nineteenth-century judicial and political ideology, the governing strata's intertwined commitments to liberalism and republicanism capture more fully the aims and strategies of those who most shaped the evolution of the corporate form.

The weakness of the efficiency theory of the corporation's evolution means, in turn, that the neoclassical institutionalists cannot defend their position by arguing that the modern corporation must be efficient because it has prevailed, or, conversely, that alternative organization forms that do not now exist cannot possibly be as efficient as the modern corporation. History shows that the corporation's definitive prerogatives obtained political and legal support, not that they were proved most conducive to social wealth maximization. Since the static analyses of Jensen, Fama, and Meckling also cannot demonstrate that the modern corporation is uniquely efficient,[93] the neoclassical institutionalist program for defending the corporation against the challenges raised since Berle and Means appears to be deeply flawed.

Perhaps the difficulties of arguing that the modern corporation is the one best way to organize economic activity (at least where assets are specific, lumpy, and risky) explain why earlier Chicago school economists, such as Knight, Hayek, and Friedman, did not attempt so ambitious a task. These social philosophers generally argued in favor of relying on the market system to achieve social coordination while skirting the issue of whether any particular organization form is most efficient or otherwise desirable. Although silent on the vital issues raised by Berle and Means and on organizational questions generally, the conventional neoclassical position is, for that very reason, to some extent more plausible in its most basic thrust—as well as more open to alternative ways of organizing the market system—than the institutionalist reformulation. The plausibility of the neoclassical position, however, is bolstered by the strategy of forgoing any attempt to claim that the specific form of the modern corporation is uniquely efficient. A younger generation has decided to take up this challenge. If advocates of noncapitalist market systems employ some of the analytical tools they have developed, an unanticipated consequence of their decision may be to motivate a better-informed search for alternatives to the corporate form.

NOTES

1. See Jensen and Meckling, Theory of the Firm: Managerial Behavior, Agency Costs, and Ownership Structure, 4 J. Fin. Econ. 305 (1976); Fama and Jensen, Separation of Ownership and Control, 26 J. L. & Econ. 301 (1983); Fama and Jensen, Agency Problems and Residual Claims, 26 J. L. & Econ. 329 (1983); R. Posner, Economic Analysis of Law 300–5 (2d ed. 1977); summarized in Barzelay and Thomas, Is Capitalism Necessary? A Critique of the Neoclassical Economics of Organization, 7 J. Econ. Behav. & Org. 111 (1986).

2. A. Berle and G. Means, The Modern Corporation and Private Property (1932).

3. Jensen and Meckling, supra note 1. Attempts by creditors to control managers through the structuring, bonding, and monitoring of contracts is admittedly costly, but according to the authors, capitalist entitlements encourage managers to minimize these agency costs.

4. Tradable residual claims entitle their owners to a pro-rata share of dividend distributions but not necessarily to the voting rights that ordinarily attach to common stock.

5. Jensen and Meckling, supra note 1; Fama, Agency Problems and the Theory of the Firm, 88 J. Pol. Econ. 289 (1980); R. Posner, supra note 1. Some of these claims may be weakened by recent developments in financial economics that call into question the belief that financial markets are perfect in the sense intended by the neoclassical institutionalists. See, e. g., Symposium on Some Anomalous Evidence Regarding Market Efficiency, 6 J. Fin. Econ. 95 (1978).

6. On instruments for rational social control, among them the price system, see R. A. Dahl and C. E. Lindblom, Politics, Economics, and Welfare (1953).

7. Efficient risk spreading requires unrestricted, tradable, residual claims, since these financial instruments can be held in small quantities by a large number of investors, while the indivisible specific assets they finance cannot be. When capital investments are financed in this way, in theory the particular risk preferences of managers are irrelevant to the selection of investments; investment decisions consequently can be made according to the market value rule. Cf. Arrow, The Role of Securities in the Optimal Allocation of Risk, 31 R. Econ. Stud. (1964); E. Fama & M. Miller, Theory of Finance (1972); Fama and Jensen, supra note 1.

8. D. Schweikart, Capitalism or Worker Control? (1980). For skeptical commentaries on neoclassical institutionalist economics, see J. Pratt & R. Zeckhauser, Principles and Agents (1985).

9. Handlin and Handlin, Origins of the American Business Corporation, 5 J. Econ. Hist. 1–23 (1945); L. Friedman, A History of American Law 176–77 (1973); N. Rosenberg and L. Birdzell, How the West Grew Rich 189–210 (1986).

10. Barzelay and Thomas, supra note 1.

11. Jensen and Meckling, Rights and Production Functions: An Application to Labor-Managed Firms and Codetermination, 42 J. Bus. 469 (1979).

12. D. North, Structure and Change in Economic History 7 (1981). See also Alchian, Uncertainty, Evolution, and Economic Theory, 59 J. Pol. Econ. 211 (1950). For critiques, see Winter, Economic "Natural Selection" and the Theory of the Firm, 4 Y. Econ. Essays 225 (1964); Field, The Problem with Neoclassical Institutional Economics, 18 Explor. Econ. Hist. 174 (1981).

13. This proposition holds so long as a people enjoys basic civic and political liberties.

14. R. Posner, supra note 1, at 12.

15. Id. at 18–19, 21; Posner, Some Uses and Abuses of Economics in Law, 46 U. Chi. L. Rev. 281 (1979); R. Posner, The Economics of Justice 5 (1983).

16. The closest to an attempt to analyze the general incorporation acts in neoclassical institutionalist terms is L. Davis & D. North, Institutional Change and American Economic Growth 76–77, 168–71 (1971). "Although the relationship is not perfect, there is a significant correlation between the passage of general incorporation laws and the importance of manufacturing in a state's economy. Granted the weakness of the evidence, it appears likely that the potential of scale economies in the new manufacturing technology engendered a potential effort by manufacturers to change the law to make that incorporation less costly. We leave it to interested political historians to test this tentative hypothesis." Id. at 171.

17. The claim is implicit in R. Posner, supra note 1, at 289–313. Consequently, Robert Gordon has contended, much as we do, that the approach of modern "lawyer-economists" like Posner, who believe that "common law rules have tended to become more and more efficient," assumes that the "corporate form developed in order to fulfill the need for capital accumulation during the period of industrial take-off." Gordon terms this economic approach a version of "evolutionary functionalism." Gordon, Critical Legal Histories, 36 Stan. L. Rev. 65, 69 (1984).

18. R. Posner, Economics of Justice, supra note 15, at 103.

19. D. North, supra note 12, at 57.

20. R. Posner, supra note 1, at 415–17, 439–41.

21. L. Davis & D. North, supra note 16, at 171.

22. R. Posner, supra note 1, at 292. Posner also endorses the neoclassical institutionalists' answers to concerns about the separation of management and ownership, and so he labels this a false issue (at 300–3).

23. Id. at 404–9.

24. Thus Robert Gordon notes that Posner's type of account has difficulty explaining "what look like a large number of anticapitalist rules, such as those restricting corporate powers, capitalization, and attempts to limit liability." Gordon, supra note 17, at 80.

25. Posner, Economics of Justice, supra note 15, at 106–7, 114–15.

26. L. Davis & D. North, supra note 16, at 44–45, 254–56; D. North & R. Thomas, Rise of the Western World (1973).

27. Field, supra note 12, at 174.

28. D. North, supra note 12, at 174.

29. Id. at 49.

30. In recent years, various members of the Conference on Critical Legal Studies have similarly explored the role of ideology in legal decision making. In so doing, they have rejected traditional Marxist accounts that portray legal doctrines as thinly veiled expressions of the interests of a single ruling capitalist class. Instead they stress the multiplicity of influences on law and its relative autonomy from other socioeconomic structures, which law nonetheless does reflect and shape.

Some of these scholars remain, however, closer to Marxian models than others. Mark Tushnet, for example, maintains that "we can still expect the law to embrace positions that are required by the interests of the ruling class as a whole, even if they are inconsistent with the interests of individual members of that class. The law remains linked to the relations of production directly through the political perception of advanced segments of the ruling class and indirectly through the political principles that are ultimately rooted in those relations." M. Tushnet, The American Law of Slavery 27–28, 30 (1981).

In contrast, Robert Gordon stresses that the "course of historical development" and the "causal relations between changes in legal and social forms are likewise radically undetermined." Neither is law a "neutral technology" that automatically adapts to social "needs." Legal rules are "political products that arise from the struggles of conflicting social groups" with disparate resources. But they do not change instantly with every shift in those forces. In part because of the interests of the legal profession, in part because of the organizational characteristics of the legal system, they have, again, some "relative autonomy" from the dominant coalitions of the moment. That relative autonomy makes it worthwhile to view legal doctrines as "ideologies" whose "peculiar internal structures" are partly "independent variables" in social development. Gordon, supra note 17, at 100–2.

The analysis we offer seems to us to be basically of the sort Gordon proposes—and as he notes, it is thus little different from that of many intellectual historians of political ideas, such as Quentin Skinner and even the young Louis Hartz. Our account may lay more stress than Gordon does on law's interconnections with broader political ideologies and less on legal doctrines as themselves relatively autonomous ideologies or producers of ideology. On this point we are closer to Ronald Dworkin. It is in the end hard to be certain how much these features really separate us from Gordon, however; although he terms attention to law as ideology a "promising approach," he does not provide the type of model for exploring law and ideology historically that we sketch here. Gordon, supra note 17, at 102, 111–12 n. 120, 119 n. 31.

31. R. Dworkin, Taking Rights Seriously 26–28, 67–68, 106–7, 117, 149 (1977).

32. R. Smith, Liberalism and American Constitutional Law 227–28 (1985).

33. L. Carter, Contemporary Constitutional Lawmaking 28 (1985).

34. R. Dworkin, Law's Empire 52–53, 89–90 (1986). This work appeared too late for its argument to be incorporated fully into our analysis here, but we believe our use of Dworkin's earlier writings remains justifiable.

35. Dworkin similarly links legal decision making to political theorizing. Id. at 90–93, 380, 409–10.

36. S. Wolin, Politics and Vision 15 (1960).

37. Id. at 16.

38. R. Wiebe, The Opening of American Society 255–56, 265–90 (1984).

39. Id. at xiv, 131, 141–43, 155, 165; M. Meyers, The Jacksonian Persuasion (1957).

40. S. Wolin, supra note 36, at 66.

41. R. Smith, supra note 32, at 36–59. This does not prove that all ideologies lack any determinate gravitational pull in particular directions or that they are all inherently crippled by insuperable internal contradictions, as the most radical contemporary analyses of law and ideology sometimes suggest. Those claims must be demonstrated in regard to each particular ideology examined.

42. Id. at 4, 63–66, 228–29.

43. See generally M. Horwitz, The Transformation of American Law, 1780–1860 (1977). Both the patchwork and the dynamic qualities of law were not lost on Oliver Wendell Holmes: ''The truth is, that the law is always approaching, and never reaching, consistency. It is forever adopting new principles from life at one end and it always retains old ones from history at the other which have not been absorbed or sloughed off. It will become entirely consistent only when it ceases to grow.'' O. W. Holmes, The Common Law 32 (1963/1881).

44. English legal thought included an older medieval strand that viewed corporations chiefly as a species of monopolistic property and a later conception that traced monopolistic privileges to the public nature and purposes of corporations. This latter view, emphasized by Blackstone, was predominant in late eighteenth-century America. M. Horwitz, supra note 43, at 110, 115, 117. See also O. Handlin and M. Handlin, Commonwealth 87, 91–92 (1969); L. Friedman, supra note 9 at 169.

45. W. Blackstone, I Commentaries on the Laws of England 455–56 (1979); L. Friedman, supra note 9, at 166–68.

46. L. Friedman, supra note 9, at 170–71; Rosenberg & Birdzell, supra note 9, at 198.

47. O. Handlin & M. Handlin, supra note 44, at 147, 158–59, 180; J. W. Hurst, The Legitimacy of the Business Corporation in the United States 65–66 (1970).

48. M. Horwitz, supra note 43, at 135–39; L. Friedman, supra note 9, at 172–73.

49. O. Handlin & M. Handlin, supra note 44, at 51, 61, 70, 77; L. Friedman, supra note 9, at 157–58; M. Horwitz, supra note 43, at 110–12; R. Wiebe, supra note 38, at 152–53.

50. Id.

51. O. Handlin & M. Handlin, supra note 44, at 51, 62; M. Horwitz, supra note 43, at 112; L. Friedman, supra note 9, at 158–61.

52. J. G. A. Pocock, The Machiavellian Moment 506–52 (1975); Appleby, The Social Origins of American Revolutionary Ideology, 64 J. Am. Hist. 935–58 (1978); R. Smith, supra note 32, at 140–45.

53. O. Handlin & M. Handlin, supra note 44, at 134–36; J. G. A. Pocock, supra note 52, at 387, 390–91; R. Wiebe, supra note 38, at xiii, 152–54; R. Smith, supra note 32, at 133–44.

54. R. Wiebe, supra note 38, 62–63, 152, 156; O. Handlin and M. Handlin, supra note 44, at 137; J. O. Appleby, Capitalism and the New Social Order 46–47, 88–90 (1984); R. Smith, supra note 32, at 143–46; M. Horwitz, supra note 43, at 134.

55. O. Handlin & M. Handlin, supra note 44, at 77, 79; M. Horwitz, supra note 43, at 63–108.

56. This power was assumed by state legislatures after the revolution.

57. W. Blackstone, supra note 45, at 458–59, 468–70.

58. Handlin & Handlin, supra note 9, at 19–20.

59. W. Blackstone, supra note 45, at 458–59, 468–70; L. Friedman, supra note 9, at 166.

60. M. Horwitz, supra note 43, at 63–108, 110; L. Hartz, Economic Policy and Democratic Thought 40 (1948); Lansing v. Smith, 8 Cow. 149 (1828) (quoted in M. Horwitz, supra note 43, at 72–73).

61. G. E. White, The American Judicial Tradition 22 (1976); R. Faulkner, The Jurisprudence of John Marshall (1968).

62. Bank of the United States v. Deveaux, 5 Cranch 61, 86, 91 (1809).

63. Dartmouth College v. Woodward, 4 Wheat. 518 (1819).

64. Trustees of Dartmouth College v. Woodward, 1 N.H. 116–17 (1817); F. Stites, Private Interest and Public Gain: The Dartmouth College Case 53 (1972).

65. Dartmouth College, 4 Wheat. at 633–39; F. Stites, supra note 64, at 61–62, 79–80, 101.

66. Dartmouth College, 4 Wheat. at 643–50; F. Stites, supra note 64, at 79.

67. Dartmouth College, 4 Wheat. at 629–30, 636, 641–43; F. Stites, supra note 64, at 80–81. Even so, in later cases Marshall still stressed that a corporation's individuality extended to something approaching citizenship only for purposes of standing under the Constitution's diversity of citizenship jurisdiction clause (Article III, section 2). He explicitly denied that incorporation created citizens in a manner parallel to naturalization, a position later courts have maintained. See, e.g., Osborn v. Bank of United States, 9 Wheat. 827–28 (1826); Paul v. Virginia, 75 U.S. 168, 177 (1869).

68. Justice Story's concurring opinion in Dartmouth College attempted to improve on Marshall's account of what constituted private corporations, arguing that while the popular mind equated "public" with "serving public purposes," at law "public" meant government ownership. So long as a corporation was privately held, it was private, though a legislature could reverse the right to regulate it further by so stipulating in the initial charter. This definition of public and private lacked much legal foundation. The application of the public-private distinction to corporations seems really to have begun with Story's own opinion in Terrett v. Taylor, 9 Cranch 52 (1815). But Story's argument in Dartmouth College did underline that businesses were private corporations, while leaving legislatures a regulatory loophole they eventually exploited. Dartmouth College, 4 Wheat. at 668–72; F. Stites, supra note 64, 83–84; L. Friedman, supra note 9, at 174–75.

69. L. Friedman, supra note 9, at 174; R. Wiebe, supra note 38, at 229; R. Smith, supra note 32, at 147–48.

70. O. Handlin & M. Handlin, supra note 44, at 191, 243; R. Wiebe, supra note 38, at 152–53.

71. O. Handlin & M. Handlin, supra note 44, at 159, 189, 191, 243; R. Wiebe, supra note 38, at 152–56; M. Horwitz, supra note 43, at 111–12, 128–31.

72. O. Handlin & M. Handlin, supra note 44, at 144, 152, 154, 158, 213; M. Horwitz, supra note 43, at 114, 137.

73. O. Handlin & M. Handlin, supra note 44 at 144, 147, 158; M. Horwitz, supra note 43, at 113–14; N. Rosenberg & Lo Birdzell, supra note 9, at 196.

74. L. Friedman, supra note 9, at 169–70; R. Wiebe, supra note 38, at 154–56.

75. Id.

76. O. Handlin & M. Handlin, supra note 44, at 157, 159, 180, 191, 194–95; M. Meyers, supra note 39, at 61–97, 109–15; R. Wiebe, supra note 38, at 154, 156, 164–67, 203–4, 257–60.

77. Charles River Bridge v. Warren Bridge, 11 Pet. 420, 547–48, 553 (1837). See

also F. Stites, supra note 64, at 105–7; M. Horwitz, supra note 43, at 132–37; R. Wiebe, supra note 38, at 242–43; R. Smith, supra note 32, at 148–49.

78. M. Horwitz, supra note 43, at 143–49, takes the first view; O. Handlin & M. Handlin, supra note 44, at 194–98, take the second.

79. Bank of Augusta v. Earle, 13 Pet. 519, 587–89 (1839).

80. Louisville, Cincinnati and Charleston R. R. Co. v. Thomas Letson, 43 U.S. 497, 555, 558–59 (1844); J. H. Kettner, The Development of Amerian Citizenship 264 n. 52 (1978).

81. L. Friedman, supra note 9, at 172, 477.

82. A. Fishlow, American Railroads and the Transformation of the Ante-Bellum Economy (1965); Chayes, Introduction, in J. W. Davis, Corporations xii (1961); M. Horwitz, supra note 43, at 137; R. Wiebe, supra note 38, at 380–81. N. Rosenberg & L. Birdzell, supra note 9, at 202, suggest alternatively that problems associated with the use of trusts to organize large-scale, unincorporated enterprises served to spur broader corporation laws later in the century.

83. L. Hartz, supra note 60, at 57; Berle, Historical Origins of American Corporations, in W. Cary & M. Eisenberg, Corporations: Cases and Materials (1980); Chayes, supra note 82, at viii; L. Friedman, supra note 9, at 169–74, 447; R. Wiebe, supra note 38, at 245; N. Rosenberg & L. Birdzell, supra note 9, at 199.

84. L. Friedman, supra note 9, at 171–73, 447–49.

85. Id. at 447, 449. N. Rosenberg & L. Birdzell, supra note 9, at 199–202, argue that the corporate form did not become dominant until well after 1890. Other authorities appear to accept earlier dates.

86. M. Meyers, supra note 39, at 30–32, 180–84, 202–5, 219–21.

87. "The desire for business expansion created an irresistible demand for more charters; and it was believed that under general laws embodying safeguards of universal application that scandals and favoritism incident to special incorporation would be avoided." Justice Brandeis in Liggett Co. v. Lee, cited in W. Cary & M. Eisenberg, supra note 83, at 6; see also L. Hartz, supra note 60; O. Handlin & M. Handlin, supra note 44, at 213, 217, 243; L. Friedman, supra note 9, at 172–73.

88. O. Handlin & M. Handlin, supra note 44, at 224–25, 243–44; L. Friedman, supra note 9, at 447, 459–65; M. Horwitz, supra note 43, at 262–66.

89. Brandeis, supra note 87; J. W. Hurst, supra note 47, at 63–65.

90. O. Handlin & M. Handlin, supra note 44, at 159–61, 191, 218; M. Horwitz, supra note 43, at 317; Chayes, supra note 82, at ix–xii.

91. L. Goodwyn, The Populist Moment 275, 318–19 (1978).

92. R. Hofstadter, Social Darwinism in American Thought 39, 41, 46–47 (1955); R. Smith, supra note 32, at 150.

93. Barzelay & Thomas, supra note 1.

II. Legal Language as Social Control and Economic Planning

5

THE IDEA OF THE CORPORATION AS A PERSON: ON THE NORMATIVE SIGNIFICANCE OF JUDICIAL LANGUAGE

Warren J. Samuels

DEFINITIONS AND SOCIAL POLICY

The objective of this chapter is to discuss, perhaps to answer, such questions as: Of what significance is it for the corporation to be thought of as a person? Of what significance is it for the corporation to be treated as a person? The focus of the chapter, then, is not on the corporation as a person as such but on the idea of the corporation as a person and its social role. To this end, an analysis of more universal applicability is brought to bear on this question. There are therefore two levels of discussion: the general analysis and its application to the idea of the corporation as a person. The argument is that ideas (such as the idea of the corporation as a person) are inexorably embodied in legal definitions in such ways as to influence our view of the world and therefore economic and political behavior, policy, and performance, and that in consequence of this recognition, the embodiment of certain ideas in law becomes an object of control.

THE CORPORATION AS SOCIOLOGICAL REALITY

The corporation is a remarkable institution. It has proved functional for the accumulation of financial and material capital, for the organization both for and of production, and for the marshaling of diverse persons and interests in the pursuit of common purpose(s), purposes that often, if not typically, are worked out or identified through internal corporate processes. Most economic (production and exchange) activity is organized through the corporate form. The corporation is a mode of decision making and of defining reality and values. As a human institution, the corporation manifestly figures in the power structure and belief system of society. It is both a product of and a contributor to power structure

The author is indebted to Arthur S. Miller, A. Allan Schmid, James D. Schaffer, and Robert A. Solo for comments on an earlier draft of this chapter.

and to belief system. The corporation is an evolving phenomenon, a participant in change with regard to both power structure and belief system. As a mode of organizing human activity and focusing the human belief system, the modern corporation, or the modern corporate system,[1] has substantially replaced the church as the principal rival of government[2] in Western society and also augurs eventually to rival the nation-state system in what we still refer to, increasingly anachronistically, as international relations. Yet there exists both a symbiotic and a conflictual relationship between the corporation (or the corporate system) and government.

To say that the corporation figures prominently in the power structure and belief system of society is really to say that it is a social institution and that it thereby partakes inexorably of the characteristics and functions of a social institution. As an institution, the corporation is a sociological unit.[3] As a form of business, it is a sociological reality, a form of human bonding, an institution of "established integration of social elements," a mode of organizing production giving structure and color to the entire social system.[4] The idea of the corporation as a person is to be examined in this context.

MEANING AS A DEPENDENT AND INDEPENDENT VARIABLE

How are we to understand the corporation? It is one of the central arguments of this chapter that whatever answer we give to that question will have enormous consequences for the corporation and for the larger corporate and socioeconomic power and belief systems of which the corporation is a part. It is another central argument that the answer one tends to give will be profoundly influenced by the state of these systems in which we find ourselves and experience our lives. The purpose of this chapter, then, is to explore how it is possible for both of these arguments to be true and the means by which the consequences and influences work out. In order to accomplish this purpose, it will be necessary also to explore the economy and the law in their multifaceted relations with power structure and belief system.

Expressed somewhat differently, in *Santa Clara Co. v. Southern Pacific Railroad*,[5] the Supreme Court unanimously affirmed that the corporation was a person with respect to the Fourteenth Amendment to the U.S. Constitution. This is an answer to the question, What is the corporation? This particular answer has a complex legal and ideological history of its own, as the chapters by Morton Horwitz, Martin Sklar, and David Dale Martin to this book make amply clear. I do not propose to rehearse that story, although my discussion will touch upon what they and others have to say. I do propose to identify the situation in which any answer to the question, What is the corporation? has meaning and significance. That meaning has to be understood in terms of both power structure and belief system.

BELIEF AND POWER

That the corporation has to be explicated in terms of power structure and belief system should be indicative of the fundamental nature of the corporation in modern socioeconomic-political life. To say this is, of course, to take a position on the question of what is the corporation. Thus the discussion here, which affirms the critical importance of the corporation to the power structure and belief system of society, directly challenges all views that affirm the contrary and thereby minimize (and arguably obscure) the power structure and belief system significance of the corporation and the corporate system. Some of the many lines of reasoning by which we have come to know the corporation directly deny that corporations have power or are important to the belief system of modern society. (I have heard and read people discuss the belief system appropriate to the corporation and then treat certain beliefs as if they were, or were to be taken to be, truth in some transcendental sense. Some of these persons were aware, and others apparently unaware, of their performance of the high-priest role.[6]) To say, then, that the corporation is an important institution is to say something about what is the corporation, something that power structure and belief system often deny, sometimes in the interest of corporate power and facilitating belief.

Any answer to the question, What is the corporation? is itself functional in the evolution of the corporation. Thus answers are attractive and contrived because of their anticipated or desired consequences in that evolution. If positions on the question are inevitable, so is the functioning of answers to the question. The corporation is an important part of the economic power structure, and power players attempt to manipulate belief system in order to influence power structure and performance.[7] It is true both that ideas have a life of their own and that they are the object of control and manipulation by power players.

THE ECONOMY AS NORMATIVE ARTIFACT

The material bearing on the subject is vast and complex, ultimately involving theories of society and of history. A valuable point of entry is to understand the economy as an artifact (a product of human action) and therefore as a normative phenomenon and finally as the result of what is fundamentally a complex and subtle deliberative and nondeliberative decision-making process. Unlike the solar system or the system of plate techtonics, the economy is what it is because of human action, both individual and collective. The economy is made by human beings as they pursue their efforts to allocate resources, to produce, and to survive. But the economy can be formed and structured, and can operate, in a number of quite different ways. Accordingly and necessarily, the production of the economy as an artifact inexorably involves the making of explicit or implicit normative decisions, ultimately as to whose interests will count insofar as interests conflict. This also means that there must be a decision-making process, itself an artifact and ultimately normative, through which such decisions are made.

The economy, as a normative artifact produced through the exercise of deliberative and nondeliberative human choice, is therefore the product of whatever power structure and whatever belief system is brought to bear on or is operative through the decision-making process. One critical facet of this process is the prediction of the future. Actually the economic future is radically unknowable. It does not now exist and will not exist until human beings have made their economic future. It therefore cannot be known in advance; the basic data do not and cannot exist in the present; data are ex post, not ex ante, phenomena. The future is radically unknowable, but it is made by human beings, and it is made by them based on choices deliberatively and nondeliberatively made. These choices are themselves based in part on visions or preferences of the future. Actions based on certain desired or anticipated scenarios or states of the future tend to produce a future based thereon.[8] There is, of course, no one-to-one relationship between actions in the present and the future to which they give rise. The economy is, after all, subject to natural influences, and human actions are diverse and often contradictory. The actual future may be unintended and unexpected by any particular actor(s), being the result of the aggregation of their individual choices and subject to compositional relationships (for example, leading to the fallacy of composition). What is important is that, these latter considerations aside, the production of the future will be profoundly influenced by the structure of power and the regnant belief system in the present.

To the extent that the production of the future is based on some view of the future, leading to actions that pro tanto produce the future, then the key factors are (1) whose beliefs, desires, and view of the future are to count and (2) what are those beliefs, desires, and view of the future. To an extraordinarily enormous extent, the organization of society (and thereby the economy) is ultimately a matter of the determination of what power structure and what belief system will channel both the operation of existing relations between persons and the creation of the future. What ultimately is involved is the creation and recreation of economic (and social) order, either the reproduction of the existing order or the production, typically gradually and incrementally, of a new order. To no small extent, science, religion, common sense, law, and so on are fundamentally contributors to our conception of the economy and thereby help form the creation of the future. Operative within each, however, are structural conflicts as to which conception of the economy, and thereby which future, is to be advanced and thereby made operative in the normative artifact-creation process.

RIGHTS AND THE SOCIAL CONSTRUCTION OF LEGAL REALITY

What does it mean to say that someone, Alpha, has a right? There are at least two answers to such a question. First, it is a positive, descriptive proposition to say that Alpha has such and such a right. Such a view, of course, is considerably, if not grossly, incomplete: it lacks specification as to what the right covers, how it is to be protected, and so on; it lacks reference to the more or less correlative but conflicting rights of others that may in the ordinary exercise thereof impinge on this right or this right holder; and it lacks reference to any related conditions or duties that may limit the right or its exercise.

Second, although the grammatical form of the statement that "Alpha has a right" is that of an "is" rather than an "ought" proposition, there is ensconced in the statement a normative or prescriptive element. The relative weight of the normative element depends on who articulates the proposition. For me to say that my neighbor has such and such a right is a relatively strictly positive, descriptive proposition, not unlike my saying that he has a particular car in his driveway or that his children are playing volleyball on the lawn. For a court so to announce, however, is tantamount to the giving of legal status to an interest, and that is effectively normative; it is the legal recognition of and support for an entitlement, which is prescriptive and normative. The point is that to say that Alpha has a right is more than a positive, descriptive proposition, whether I say it or a court says it, although especially if a court does. For the "fact" that Alpha has a right constitutes a manifestation of the normative structure of society, which is a result of a complex legal-political decision-making process through which it has been decided that Alpha, rather than some Beta, has his interest protected, which means both that Beta's interest is not protected and moreover that Beta is exposed to the exercise of Alpha's right.

Rights, in other words, are the vehicle through which both ordinary and legal language establish and express protected interests and thereby correlative and conflicting unprotected, and exposed, interests. (The Hohfeldian system is one example of a more elaborate and to some extent more precise mode of expression but is not in ordinary use; nonetheless the same point applies to it.) For someone to have a right is to establish their normative status; rights are in se normative, even though statements about rights can be positive. (The statement "Alpha has a right" is, within limits, a testable, positive proposition without special normative import. In order to say that Alpha should have, or should not have, the right, one needs an additional normative premise.) For someone to have a right of economic significance is for that person to have a particular position in the parallelogram of protected interests, in the parallelogram of power—that is, the economy. To say that someone has a right, therefore, is to say something of the extant normative power structure of society and economy. For a court (or legislature) to say that someone has a right is for it to affect, not merely to discourse about, the normative power structure of society and economy. For the Supreme Court to affirm that the corporation is a person for the purposes of the Fourteenth Amendment is for it seemingly to make an "is" statement but effectively and more important to make a normative "ought" statement about the power structure of the economy.

THE TRANSFORMATION OF LAW

In the late nineteenth century, the foundations, typically expressed in terms of rights, were laid in the United States for the rise to dominance of the corporation and of what eventually became the corporate system. The foundations included legal provision of life in perpetuity, limited stockholder liability, and treatment of the corporation as a person for the purposes of the Fourteenth Amendment.

Numerous aspects of this topic are relevant to the present discussion: the transformation of American law facilitative of industrial capitalism[9] and restrictive of consolidations of social life antagonistic to it,[10] such as a predominantly agrarian or laboristic economy and society; the development of a business society and culture; the emergence of an ideology, or belief system, whose functions were to explain and legitimize that society and culture; the consolidation of industrial capitalism as a system of bourgeois power, a system increasingly organized through the corporate form;[11] and so on. Running throughout all these aspects are the interplay of ideology (belief system) and power and of both with law. Ideology became adjusted to power structure, and power structure was facilitated by ideology and promoted facilitative ideology. Law was channeled by ideology and by power structure (in part through differential access to government), and law abetted the development of ideology and power structure. Law, power, and belief system (ideology) interacted as part of the evolution of American culture along a particular, business, gradient. Some of this was unintended, and much was unexpected by many, but substantial efforts were made to recast power structure, law, and belief system along desired lines. One part of this grand tableau was the affirmation of the personhood of the corporation.

LEGAL DEFINITION OF SOCIOECONOMIC REALITY

The affirmation of the personhood of the corporation was one manifestation of an underlying aspect of law and the operation of the legal system. Law, including legal theory, performs (along with other institutions and processes) the function of defining socioeconomic reality. Law, including legal writing, is a technique for the shaping of images,[12] and, as with all governance and politics, it is both a system or process of meaning and an arena for efforts to control systems of shared meaning.[13] (Legal rights and rules are real for individual members of society; that is, they make social reality—not discover a preexistent and preeminent reality imposed on people—that is enforced by legal and other sanctions. Legal and theological pretense here is functional.) This sociolegal reality typically is defined in terms of rights and rules, but it is also defined in terms of chains of reasoning and by definitions, such as the definition of the corporation as a person. Law thus defines and redefines legal-economic reality, giving effect to countless forces and efforts to use the law for economic and/or other advantage. Legal definitions of reality encapsulate the fundamental tautologies at the basis of the economic system. These tautologies govern the structure of freedom and control (including hierarchy versus equality), the processes of continuity versus change, and the selective perception of interests to be given legal protection as rights. Legal control of the corporation (or of anything else) implies, or presumes, legal recognition and protection in other respects of that which is controlled. Legal definitions evidence, affirm, and reinforce the corporation at the same time legal treatment presumes the corporation.

THE CORPORATION AS PRIVATE AND AS PUBLIC PHENOMENON

The legal definition of the corporation as a person, as several other chapters in this book make amply evident, is part of a complex, kaleidoscopic, and revealing matrix of conceptions. The corporation may be and has been seen to be an instrument of government; in this respect, or in this sense, it is essentially a public or public sector (that is, governmental) phenomenon. The corporation may be and also has been seen to be an instrument of private incorporators, a collective extension of themselves, and thus essentially a "private" and decidedly nongovernmental phenomenon.

From one point of view, the corporation equates with the state and from the other with the individual. Here we have two different definitions of reality, each affecting our perception of what is the corporation and thereby also affecting the exercise of social control (especially through the adoption of one legal policy or another). Recognition of the corporation as private government as constituting governance would tend toward the imposition of the same checks on it as on public government; thus the marketing of the private character of the corporation is functional to the avoidance of these checks and indeed to the countering of government regulation even in the absence of that recognition.

The selective perception of the corporation as a public (or governmental) or as a private phenomenon is but one example of the selective attribution of content to the categories of private and public. It may or may not be true that these categories have no conclusive exclusive content (which I would affirm but is not at issue here), but what most people most of the time mean thereby is a matter of selective perception. The attribution of specific content to the open-ended categories private and public not only defines reality but channels the policy of the law.[14] Legal rights are obviously public in character (they are what they are at least in part because of government action or inaction), but they also are private in character in that they pertain to nominally private parties and they are arguably the result of a matrix of private pressures on government to resolve conflicts of interest in one way or another. In other words, rights are in some sense both private and public, and what is instructive is the selective way in which they are perceived and acted upon as one or the other.

The same is true of the corporation. It is a creature existing in some sense, as John Marshall put it, in the contemplation of law.[15] It is also the result of private action generative of the corporate form and corporate law to begin with and, further, of specific corporation-organizing activities generative of particular corporate entities, always within the existing state of the law of corporations and of other law. If personhood involves privateness, law governs privateness but—or, better, *and*—private interests influence and in a profound sense "govern" law. Law is not exogenously determined in some manner preexistently and preeminently independent of humans and society but is a normative artifact. The critical point is that legal definition of the corporation will give effect to one set of preconceptions of privateness and publicness or another, to one belief system or another, to one set of policy premises or another. Involved in all this is a language, a system of discourse. But more than a system of discourse is involved: there is also being created the normative artifacts that comprise and structure the economy. To the extent that the market works, these artifacts will govern how and to which (whose) ends the market works.

Although it is possible to perceive the corporation as a creation of the law, it also is possible to contemplate it as both the creation and instrument of the incorporators (as Justice Stephen Field did in a series of cases).[16] But it is also possible and arguably necessary to recognize that the law is what it is in part due to the actions of corporations and of those who promote the corporate form and particular corporations. The corporation and the corporate system are not natural givens but phenomena created through the deliberate use of government (including the playing off of certain states, such as Delaware and New Jersey in the late nineteenth century, to generate favorable terms of incorporation and existence). Government here as elsewhere was used to control and channel the opportunity set structure of the economy and thereby the distributions of opportunity and wealth. Thus even the conservative economist John Bates Clark wrote in 1899 of "the power of corporations to make the political machine their instrument and the legislator their servant" and of the "grip that corporations have on political machines and on the law-making power,"[17] and again in 1901, "Very insidious is the power that massed capital knows how to use in controlling the so-called representatives of the people, who are often rather the conscienceless substitutes for the people in the work of ruling."[18] Although modern mainstream economists tend to take the corporation and the corporate system as given in the working out of solutions deemed presumptively optimal, Clark and others were concerned, during the later years of the early modern history of the corporation, about the use of law to produce a particular corporate form of economic reality.

INDIVIDUALIST AND MANAGERIALIST CONCEPTIONS OF THE CORPORATION

The concept of the corporation as a person for constitutional purposes must be understood in the context of a larger matrix of doctrinal development of law and ideology. At least one aspect of this development is particularly ironical.

Given the development of the economy as a corporate system and its concentration of economic power in the hands of a relatively few giant corporations, there have developed two major, albeit conflicting, ideological rationales of the system.[19] In one, the corporation is interpreted along more or less traditional individualist lines as just another individual economic actor not very different from the sole proprietorship, especially in being subject to the overriding forces of the market. In the other, the corporation and its managers are recognized as having power not totally circumscribed by the market. Here the rationale is in terms of the important managerial functions performed by corporate officers in the aggregate. The combination of individualist and managerialist ideologies, notwithstanding their obvious conflicts, has proved powerful in the rationalization of the status quo structure of corporate power. In the one, the corporation is portrayed in the image of the individual; in the other, the corporate system is affirmed and applauded for its transindividual social functions.

The irony is that the affirmation of the personhood of the corporation, which gave constitutional standing to the identification of the corporation with individual human beings and thus facilitated and gave effect to the treatment of the corporation as an individual person rather than as part of something larger, came at a time when three critical developments in the organization and control of the economy were underway: the development of gigantic national and impersonal business firms; the rise of a managerial elite dominating economic decision making; and thus, as Joseph Schumpeter expressed it, the decline of individualist entrepreneurial capitalism and the rise of routinized, bureaucratized corporate capitalism.[20] Clearly the doctrine of the personhood of the corporation was a means of encapsulating into law the individualist ideology, which, neither paradoxically nor unintentionally, became a further means for the development of the corporate system, which thereby further reduced the realism of the individualist portrayal of the economy. The idea (some would say the myth) that the corporation is a person served the function of obscuring the putative fact that the corporation is by its nature a collective transindividual organization. In time the adjustment of ideology to power structure involved the formulation of the managerialist ideology, which came to coexist with the individualist ideology, one appealing to certain people and the other to other people, in both cases serving to legitimize the system, albeit through quite different, and conflicting, portrayals. The affirmation of the corporation as a person, however, served the ideological function (in addition to its legal functions) of reinforcing the perception of corporation in a manner consonant with the individualist ideology. Corporations were individuals, too, with the implication that they could and should be treated the same as human individuals rather than in a separate category. The role of selective perception is made evident by recognizing that neither labor unions nor cooperatives were so identified and defined. In the case of trade unions, for example, the Clayton Act antitrust exemption is effectuated by the language that for antitrust purposes labor is not to be considered a commodity,[21] both avoiding the personhood identification of a form of collective action arguably parallel to the corporation and providing the protection in both a lesser and negative way. In the case of the corporation, at any rate, a (giant) collective was defined as a single person.

PERSONHOOD AND THE LEGAL DEFINITION AND RECREATION OF REALITY

Law is a mode of regulating and integrating individual and collective human behavior. Such is its nature as a premier form of social control in the modern world. One subtle and inconspicuous way in which it performs this function is to help form the definition of reality and of values that generate action, govern policy, and mediate conflicts and thereby help determine economic reality itself. Belief affects individual and collective, private and public, behavior and thus the creation and recreation of the economy. In part this definition of reality by law, which is instrumental in the recreation of reality, is accomplished by selectively interpreting and therefore selectively reinforcing part of the status quo, thereby helping to reformulate or reconstruct reality.

The affirmation of the corporation as a person for the purposes of the Fourteenth Amendment (especially through substantive, as opposed to procedural, due process interpretations) participated in the transformation of the U.S. economy as both a dependent and an independent variable. As an independent variable, it helped reinforce certain power configurations rather than others. As a dependent variable, it was a means through which certain forces operated and was in a sense the product of those forces, the forces constituting the corporatization of the economy.

In both regards, it must be understood that while the affirmation of personhood was instrumental to the development of the corporate system as we have come to know it, antitrust law not only notwithstanding but arguably as a means thereto, both the affirmation of personhood and the corporatization of the economy were in a sense secondary to the fundamental capitalist or bourgeois or middle-class nature of the economy. Business would have come to rule, it seems, whether through the corporation abetted by a constitutional doctrine of its personhood or otherwise. Still, corporatization, abetted by the individualist ideology of personhood, did come about—and with it what Charles Lindblom has called the privileged position of business.[22]

PUBLIC AND PRIVATE GOVERNANCE

If the affirmation of personhood was a confirmation and reinforcement of the fundamental role of the corporation in capitalism (though not necessarily of bourgeois or business power, although certainly in fact usefully), it was also thereby a legal foundation of the corporation as an institution perceived in some sense to be independent of the state. If one means by governance the exercise of decision making over matters of fundamental concern in the ordinary business of life to others, then, both the imagery and the reality of the market as a governance system notwithstanding, one must juxtapose to public governance (the state) the corporate system as a mode of private governance. At the highest and most abstract, if not also most esoteric, levels of social analysis and notwithstanding their evident interdependence, the institutions of government (state), religion (church), and business (corporations), along with custom and belief system, with which they also interact, form the dominant social control or governance system of society. The affirmation of the corporation as a person for certain constitutional purposes ironically contributed to the elevation of corporate economic organization to the highest reaches of the governance system of society. Indeed, the argument affirming the corporation as a check against the power of the state in effect also affirms the corporation as private government.[23] The corporation, although denominated a person, is not only a collective agglomeration of capital but a governing institution. In one respect at least this is not exceptional: human individuals, too, are each in their own way part of the governance system of society, reinforcing one custom or another, producing and/or obeying one law or another, bringing one pressure or another on government, and so on. It remains both true and important, however, that corporations are in economic affairs especially useful and important organizations, especially in regard to the limits of the solitary individual.

OBFUSCATING MEANING

One role of the idea of personhood was to affirm that the corporation is neither a collective organization nor a governing institution, either of which would tend to render it subject to checks on its power and use of power. Here the private-public dichotomy, plus selective identification of the corporation as a private person, functions to obscure concentrated private power as private governance. Another critical role of the affirmation of the corporation as a person was to help facilitate the obfuscation and thereby the exculpation of the negative impacts—negative externalities, in the language of economics—generated by corporate decisions on others. This reinforced the distribution of costs to others through limited liability. Costs registered in the market are not given by nature but are channeled by legal rules, rights, and definitions, differences in which lead to differences in configurations or distributions of costs. Corporations, as institutions of private governance, are remarkable for the range of their externality-inducing effects and are abetted in this by law and by legal definitions, such as of personhood.

CORPORATE PERSONS AS COMPLEX ORGANIZATIONS AND MODES OF COLLECTIVE ACTION AND IDENTITY

It is also both ironic and important that the affirmation of the corporation as a person was eventually accompanied by the development of the corporation as an extraordinarily large and complex organization, with a decision-making process often encompassing hundreds of thousands of individuals in what John Kenneth Galbraith would later call the technostructure.[24] This decision-making process encompasses the formulation of corporate self-identify, ends, and means and provides an arena in which individuals both cooperate and conflict for positions of advantage and power.

The corporation, while legitimized as a person, became one of the principal institutions of collective action and identity. As an institution, the corporation developed or acquired characteristics that not only significantly differentiate it from ordinary persons but do so in a culturally specific manner. First, corporations—both specific corporations and the form per se—became objects of quasi-religious attachment by individuals seeking, establishing, or reinforcing self identification. Second, whereas in precapitalist societies, institutions or organizations that were principally kin, tribal, and/or religious in character also performed functions of economic organization and control, in modern capitalist society, economic organization through the corporation has come to perform other group functions. Third, the corporation has its own formal and informal hierarchic structure. Individual participation, obligations, and freedom take place within the total power structure of the corporation. Indeed, individual rights of economic significance, such as private pensions, are a function of status within particular corporations. Rights both with regard to and within the corporation are of critical importance to individual humans as part of the total body politic. Moreover, the corporation has contributed to and complicated, but not negated, the property system of a business society. The operative opportunity set for many persons lies substantially within the corporation for which (for whom, if it is a person) they work. Fourth, questions of the social responsibility of the business corporation arise that, ironically, are presented by some persons as if they are to be treated differently than in the case of individual human persons.

THE CORPORATION AS A GIVEN OR A VARIABLE IN ECONOMICS

The treatment of the corporation in economics seems inadequate to its subject but is generally functional for individualist ideology in several ways. First, static microeconomic theory generally reaches efficiency conclusions based on reasoning that takes the economic unit under scrutiny as a given, whereas in reality the corporation has undergone change and evolution—both as a generic institution and as particular organizations—in part as the result of power play and calculations of advantage within the corporation and within (or on) government. Corporations never have been and are not now static phenomena. Second, the legal treatment of the corporation as a person seems to have facilitated a mental climate in which corporations are seen by economists as having preferences (objective functions) without any correlative necessity to examine the collective decision-making process through which corporate identity and goals, as well as internal power structure itself, are formed and reformed.

The assumption of profit maximizing is not sufficiently robust to enable penetration of what goes on in corporations. Indeed, it obscures internal corporate decision-making problems. Individual firms are not unitary arrangements serving one goal—profit making—but are organizations within which individuals seek their own interests, whose specific goals emerge from interpersonal and subgroup interaction, and whose history and internal socialization processes channel individual goal-producing behavior and commitments.

Although Frank Knight once wrote that a competitive economy requires "every member of the society . . . to act as an individual only, in entire independence of all other persons,"[25] most other economists continue to identify the corporation as a single actor, thereby assuming the correspondence of the individual and the firm, a view facilitated by the idea of the corporation as a person. Yet although both individuals and corporations have legal attributes, the individual corporation is hardly an atomistic individual. The notion of the individual corporate firm cannot be taken as self-subsistent in the same way or sense as the individual human person. Economic theory, however, fails to account adequately for the ontological status of firms, taking them as given, individual economic units.

This is part of the mind-set of economists who resonate well with the anti-interventionist approach to government and thereby provide support for both legal reinforcement of already established power positions and those who would obscure the critical role of government in producing the status quo in order to control government for their own purposes. What is lacking in much contemporary economics is a theory of power, especially, although only in part, with regard to government. "Power relations, not market relations, are the heart of the corporation and its dealings with other corporations, government and labor, and often also with the consumer. Without a theory of power, no theory of the modern corporation can go beyond the anthropomorphism of the neoclassical view."[26] Ironically, this was the view of Adam Smith, who recognized the link between the form of the economy and the source and distribution of power. He recognized, for example, that the form in which property can be accumulated and intergenerationally transmitted is critical with regard to the locus of authority in society.[27]

It is not surprising that some economists have found the corporation to be violative of the principle of competition, as replacing the fluidity of the competitive market and the field of private activity with a ruling "mass of capital,"[28] thus replacing the market with what is here called private governance and influencing economic performance.[29] Thus, whereas the traditional theory of capital markets posits that efficient use of capital requires competitive resort to capital markets by enterprises seeking funds, the rise of the giant corporation, especially the conglomerate corporation, has meant the replacement of the market with internal decision-making processes that at best can only be considered market like and that partake more of power than the impersonal market.

Interestingly if not strikingly, the libertarian economist Friedrich A. von Hayek has made significant proposals to create a greater and more competitive market for capital. He proposes, first, that stockholders individually have the right to determine the distribution of profits between dividends and retained earnings and, second, the elimination of voting rights accompanying corporate ownership of stock in another corporation.[30] This perspective of institutional redesign is important for its emphasis on the competitive market rather than on established power positions (especially that of corporate management). It is also important because it points to the further dichotomy of those who see the existing corporate system as a system of private (or private-public) planning in contrast to those who envision a competitive process, if not structure. Some economists accept the inevitability of planning and want to democratize or constitutionalize it; others want to attack it through effective antitrust enforcement and other regulatory controls. Such considerations, which penetrate to the very nature of the individual economic unit, as well as to the question of the power structure forming and operating through the market, tend, however, to be absent from microeconomic theory, which largely assumes the economy to be competitive and takes the individual corporation qua person as a given.

CONCLUSION: THE FUNCTIONAL ROLE OF DEFINITION IN THE LEGAL CONSTRUCTION OF SOCIAL REALITY

How, then, are we to understand the corporation? What is the corporation? Of what significance is the judicial (or legislative) affirmation of the corporation as a person for the purposes of the Fourteenth Amendment?

The corporation is an institution. It is collective action in control and in liberation of individual action; it is a habit of thought. It is an artifact.

The corporation is both a product of and a contributing participant in the power structure and belief system of society. Beliefs about the corporation, including those encapsulated in law and in economic theory and analysis, are both a function of the existing corporate system and power structure and functional for the evolution of that system and that structure.

The corporation is a principal means of organizing and reorganizing the normative artifact called the economy (the system of collective production and exchange), in part giving effect to certain preferences and definitions of the future.

The doctrine of the affirmation of the corporation as a person is part of the matrix of legal concepts, principles, and lines of reasoning through which the legal system, as both dependent and independent variable, relates to the power structure and belief system of the economy. In adopting fundamental conceptions, such as the idea of the corporation as a person, the courts pro tanto define and legislate economic reality, determining the normative structure of the economy. By making, rather than finding or discovering, legal concepts, law, and constitutions, the legal process helps make economic reality. It does this sometimes or in some respects in an original fashion and sometimes or in some respects as ratifier of a reality largely produced through other means but also always as a matter of choice—choice as to which aspect of the status quo to reinforce and which to inhibit. Judicial affirmation of the corporation as a person is epistemologically only superficially a positive, descriptive matter. Much more fundamentally, it is a linguistic means of establishing normative premises functional for subsequent legal reasoning and choice and is thereby functional in the normative reformation of the economy. The idea of the corporation as a person says little or nothing about physical reality independent of human beings but much (to a point) about how human beings in our society embody in linguistic usages the normative premises of collective behavior and the normative consequences of collective choice through government (even when privateness is being affirmed). Recognition of the social construction of reality requires an understanding that ideas have consequences; ideas (along with general interpersonal interaction, technology, and so on) help generate the social substance we often take so readily as a given as natural. The idea of the corporation as a person points to nothing in nature independent of human beings but to much with respect to how ideas are variables in socioeconomic organization.

NOTES

1. The concept of the corporate system is developed in A. A. Berle & G. C. Means, The Modern Corporation and Private Property (1932); Berle, Modern Functions of the Corporate System, Colum. L. Rev. 433 (1962); G. C. Means, The Corporate Revolution in America (1962); E. S. Mason, ed., The Corporation in Modern Society (1959); A. S. Miller, The Modern Corporate State (1976); R. Nader & M. J. Green, Corporate Power in America (1973); 6 J. Econ. Issues 1 (1972); W. J. Samuels, ed., The Economy as a System of Power (1979); J. M. Blair, Economic Concentration (1972); R. Marris, ed., The Corporate Society (1974); R. Marris & A. Wood, eds., The Corporate Economy (1971); B. A. Mintz & M. Schwartz, The Power Structure of American Business (1985); E. S. Herman, Corporate Control, Corporate Power (1981); Interlocking Directorates among the Major U.S. Corporations, Staff Study, Subcommittee on Reports, Accounting and Management, Committee on Governmental Affairs, U.S. Senate, 95th Congress, 2d Session (January 1978); Disclosure of Corporate Ownership, Subcommittee on Intergovernmental Relations, and Budgeting, Management, and Expenditures, Committee on Government Operations, U.S. Senate, 93d Congress, 1st Session (December 27, 1973).

2. For the view that the corporation is to be understood as principally a check against the power of government, see Novak, God and Man in the Corporation, 13 Pol'y Rev. 9, 12, 28, et passim (1980).

3. A. Berle & G. C. Means, supra note 1, at 44.

4. Fairchild, Business as an Institution, 2 Am. Soc. Rev. 1, 4–7 (1937). See also Alvin Johnson, Essays in Social Economics 1 (1954), and M. G. Smith, Corporations and Society (1974) (corporations as established social units).

5. 118 U.S. 394 (1886) (that the provision in the Fourteenth Amendment to the Constitution, which forbids a state to deny to any person within its jurisdiction the equal protection of the laws, applies to corporations).

6. See Novak, supra, note 2 and, revealingly, Toward a Theology of the Corporation

(1981); see also M. Novak & J. W. Cooper, eds., The Corporation: A Theological Inquiry (1981).

7. See W. J. Samuels, Pareto on Policy (1974).

8. K. E. Boulding, The Image (1956) (decisions as choices among alternative perceived images of the future).

9. See, e.g., J. R. Commons, Legal Foundations of Capitalism (1924); M. Horwitz, The Transformation of American Law (1977); W. Nelson, Americanization of the Common Law (1975); M. Tigar and M. Levy, Law and the Rise of Capitalism (1977); and D. C. North, Structure and Change in Economic History (1981).

10. C. A. Auerbach, Law and Social Change in the United States, 6 UCLA L. Rev. 516 (1959).

11. See references, supra note 1.

12. R. A. Solo, Intra-Enterprise Conspiracy and the Theory of the Firm, 34 J. Bus. 153, 160 (1961).

13. P. C. Sederberg, The Politics of Meaning (1984); P. L. Berger & T. Luckmann, The Social Construction of Reality (1966); Samuels & Mercuro, The Role and Resolution of the Compensation Principle in Society: Part One—The Role, 1 Res. L. & Econ. 157 (1979).

14. Fraser, The Corporation as a Body Politic, 57 Telos 5 (1983), and Ratner, Corporations and the Constitution, 15 U. S. F. L. Rev. 11, 19ff, 27 (1980–1981).

15. "A corporation is an artificial being, invisible, intangible, and existing only in contemplation of law. Being the mere creature of law, it possesses only those properties which the charter of its creation confers upon it, either expressly, or as incidental to its very existence." Dartmouth College v. Woodward, 17 U.S. (4 Wheat.) 518, 636 (1819). See also in re Clarke's Will, 204 Minn. 574, 578, 284 N. W. 876, 878 (1939): "A corporation is not a person, but has a legal and real individuality. Neither is it artificial, save as it is a generation of law rather than nature. It is in simple fact a legal unit—a very real one—endowed by its creator with many of the rights and attributes of persons."

16. County of San Mateo v. S. Pac. R. R. Co., 13 Fed. Rep. 722, 743–44, 747–48 (1882) (see also, Sawyer, C. J., concurring opinion, at 757ff); County of Santa Clara v. S. Pac. R. R. Co., 18 Fed Rep. 385, 402–405 (1883); Pembina Consolidated Silver Mining and Milling Co. v. Pennsylvania, 125 U.S. 181, 189 (1888).

17. Clark, Trusts, Present and Future, 51 Independent 1076, 1079, 1080 (April 20, 1899).

18. Clark, The Society of the Future, 53 Independent 1649, 1650 (July 18, 1901). Even Justice Field noted the Court's awareness "of the opinion prevailing throughout the community that the railroad corporations of the state, by means of their great wealth and the numbers in their employ, have become so powerful as to be disturbing influences in the administration of the laws." County of San Mateo v. S. Pac. R. R. Co., 13 Fed. Rep. 722, 730 (1882).

19. F. X. Sutton et al., The American Business Creed (1956); R. J. Monsen, Modern American Capitalism (1963); and E. S. Mason, The Apologetics of Managerialism, 31 J. Bus. 1 (1958). On the putative inadequacy of "individualism," see the works of Novak, supra note 2; M. Janowitz, Education for Civic Consciousness (1983); and R. N. Bellah et al., Habits of the Heart: Individualism and Commitment in American Life (1985).

20. J. A. Schumpeter, Capitalism, Socialism, and Democracy (3d ed. 1950). See also

W. J. Samuels, A Critique of Capitalism, Socialism and Democracy, in R. D. Coe & C. K. Wilber, eds., Capitalism and Democracy: Schumpeter Revisited (1985).

21. "That the labor of a human being is not a commodity or article of commerce." 15 U.S.A. sec. 17. That such is not dispositive of the matter in other fields, see Ratner, supra note 14, at 25: "A majority of the Court sees a corporation as an entity with rights and interests of its own, while a union is simply an aggregate of people in which their individual rights are paramount."

22. C. E. Lindblom, Politics and Markets 170ff. (1977).

23. Novak, supra note 2, at 12, 28, et passim.

24. J. K. Galbraith, The New Industrial State (1967).

25. F. H. Knight, Risk, Uncertainty and Profit 78 (1921).

26. James K. Galbraith, Galbraith and the Theory of the Corporation, 7 J. Post-Keynesian Econ. 43, 59 (1984).

27. "One of the more striking features of Smith's argument is in fact the link which he succeeded in establishing between the form of economy prevailing (i.e. the mode of earning subsistence) and the source and distribution of power or dependence among the classes of men which make up a single 'society'. . . . We also find here a form of property which can be accumulated and transmitted from one generation to another, thus explaining a change in the main sources of authority as compared to the previous period." R. H. Campbell & A. S. Skinner, General Introduction, Adam Smith, 1 An Inquiry into the Nature and Cause of the Wealth of Nations 12–13 (1976).

28. F. A. Walker, quoted in J. P. Munroe, A Life of Francis Amasa Walker 254 (1923).

29. For example, although the precise relationship (if there is one) between the institution of the corporation and the propensity to save is uncertain, there have been at least two conflicting views. According to one, the institution of the corporation reduces risk and facilitates the accumulation of capital, and thus abets the propensity to save. Taussig, Is Market Price Determinate? 35 Q. J. Econ. 394, 408–9 (1921). According to the other, corporate organization tends to destroy "one of the strongest motives for saving" by generating a permanent fund of capital and reducing risk. A. Johnson, supra note 4, at 61.

30. F. A. Hayek, Studies in Philosophy, Politics and Economics 300ff. (1967). For quite different views on corporate reform, see Manne, Our Two Corporation Systems: Law and Economics, 53 Va. L. Rev. 259 (1967); Symposium, 24 Q. Rev. Econ. & Bus. (1984); Samuels, supra note 1; TRB, Productive Predators, New Republic 4, Mar. 25, 1985, at 4; and Four Ways to Change the Corporations, Nation, May 15, 1982; 575.

6

THE JURISPRUDENCE OF CORPORATE PERSONHOOD: THE MISUSE OF A LEGAL CONCEPT

John J. Flynn

A basic focus and purpose of legal systems is the regulation of relationships: the relationships between individuals; between governmental and private organizations; and among individuals, government, and private organizations. Whether the area of legal doctrine is property, torts, civil liberties, or corporate law, the central preoccupation of legal regulation in each is the definition of relationships and the implementation of the definitions arrived at through the invocation of governmental power. Much of the history of the legal systems of every culture can be viewed as the evolution of the regulation of relational interests in that culture and the social, economic, political, and other forces that have shaped and channeled that evolution. A central concern of jurisprudence is the study of the intellectual means and the institutional devices by which this evolution has been and can be achieved through law and legal institutions. It is on this basis that I shall examine the *Santa Clara* decision, some of the present-day implications of recognizing corporations as persons for purposes of constitutional law, and the jurisprudential implications of the use and misuse of the concept of corporate personhood.

LAW AND THE RECOGNITION OF COLLECTIVES

The Western legal system has always recognized the "entityness" of religious, social, political, and economic organizations for purposes of the legal analysis of relationships, be it the church, the state, the university, the guild, or the feudal estate. Indeed, Western legal development may be viewed as a reflection of the ongoing process of reconciling demands for protection of individualism with demands for legitimation of institutions designed to provide some degree of collectivism.[1] As part of the demand for collectivism, the legal system has also recognized the corporation as a person for a number of purposes—holding title to land, contracting, and suing or being sued—well before the Supreme Court's cryptic recognition of the corporation as a person for constitutional purposes[2] in *Santa Clara County v. Southern Pacific Railroad Co.*[3] As a practical matter, the legal system has little alternative but to recognize some type of institutional organization for economic activity if a society is to accomplish any economic activity through the joint action of its human members. Collective action is necessary to achieve a wide variety of economic, political, and social objectives in a modern and complex society. Modern technology and the integration of the world economy appear to be accelerating the need for collective action in the economic sphere if a nation is to prosper and deal effectively with a world economy and complex national and international systems for establishing enforceable relational interests among and between a bewildering array of collectives. If the legal system failed to recognize and accommodate this practical reality, it is difficult to see how such collective activity could take place at all.

Recognition of the corporation as a person for constitutional purposes is more significant, however, not because of some metaphysical debate over personhood[4] but because such recognition elevates this form of joint or collective action to a constitutional status with certain immunities from control by the community through government. Defining the scope of this immunity from governmental regulation is a central function of a constitution and the institution of judicial review in a free and democratic society. The Bill of Rights and the implementation of its values by an independent judiciary are thought to be crucial pillars of human freedom from governmental regulation of civil liberties, including the right of the individual to join with others for the exercise of specific collective rights. This kind of immunity, however, enlarges and shapes the discretion possessed by the institution or individual given constitutional immunity from government regulation—an enhancement of social, political, and economic power of great significance to a society and its citizens.[5]

In the case of recognizing some level of constitutional status for the corporate collective, the creation of a broad realm of collective discretion free from the regulation of government results in the narrowing of the power of the individual to enlist the aid of government against the activity of the corporate collective. It constitutes a shift in the balance of rights and power from an individualistic and rights basis for organizing society toward a collectivist and status basis for doing so. The striking of that balance is among the most basic functions of an organized society and its legal system in defining its social, political, and economic values and the character and quality of life a society deems ought to be the standard for its human members. It is a step that a society may not avoid as a practical and ethical matter in the process of adjusting basic values to new realities, but it is a step that ought not be taken casually and one that requires sensitive and reflective decision making by those charged with the high responsibility of making the choice.

The choice is an ethical choice: a question of ''ought'' requiring the considered and reflective weighing of the values of society, the balance of decision-making power in society and the consequences of the choice made. By long-standing acquiescence in the United States, the major responsibility for making the choice through constitutional interpretation—subject to the difficult-to-exercise power of Congress, the people, and the states to amend the Constitution—has been confided in the courts and the institution of judicial review. Unfortunately, too often judges charged with the responsibility of pouring meaning into constitutional language in the light of evolving reality, the moral values of society, and the consequences of their interpretation either have not engaged in a considered and deep reflection about the problem with which they are confronted or have engaged in a form of decision making that hides the reasons for the choices they make and the meaning they impose. Such has been the case with many of the decisions involving the personhood status of corporations for purposes of defining the scope of constitutional immunities for corporations from regulation by government.

MISUSE OF THE CONCEPT OF PERSON IN *SANTA CLARA*

Before oral argument in the *Santa Clara* case, Chief Justice Morrison Waite stated: ''The court does not wish to hear argument on the question whether the provision of the Fourteenth Amendment to the Constitution, which forbids a state to deny any person within its jurisdiction the equal protection of the laws, applies to these corporations. We are all of the opinion that it does.''[6] The issue arose because of a claim that California property tax laws treated railroads operating in more than one county differently from railroads operating in only one county and that the law treated all railroad corporations differently from other corporations and natural persons. Although the Court's opinion did not find it necessary to decide the equal protection issue because it affirmed Justice Field's lower court opinion holding the tax invalid on other grounds,[7] the *Santa Clara* case has been recognized ever since for having launched the doctrine of corporate personhood for purposes of constitutional analysis.[8]

There can be little doubt from a jurisprudential view that the Court's method for recognizing corporate personhood in *Santa Clara* constituted a serious misuse of concepts for legal purposes.[9] Indeed, it is difficult to characterize the Court's methodology as a form of legal analysis. It resembles a dictatorial edict issued without reason, explanation, or argument. The Court's conclusion sounds like an article of faith, the roots of which were not explained and the consequences of which were not explored.

Decision making of this sort gives credence to the average person's belief that lawyers and judges use words in mysterious and sometimes dishonest ways. The self-same word and the concept it normally generates seems to mean first one thing and then another in the hands of a lawyer or judge. Those apparently hard and concrete things we call facts normally associated with a fixed concept in our daily existence sometimes disappear in the hands of a lawyer or a judge, are deemed irrelevant in one circumstance and of great weight in another. Or they are said to mean first one thing and then another depending on the circumstances of the case. One might conclude that the primary function of lawyers and judges is to distort facts and manipulate concepts—in a word, to be liars on behalf of the interests they represent. "How the edifice of justice can be supported by the efforts of liars at the bar and ex-liars on the bench is one of the paradoxes of legal logic which the man on the street has never solved."[10]

The reason the person on the street may believe lawyers and judges are liars is a misunderstanding about how words, concepts, and facts are used in the legal process and the significance of the constraints imposed by role obligations on those participating in and controlling the process. In the process of legal analysis, words are not viewed as trustworthy symbols of the concrete or rigid definitions capturing the concept for an identifiable thing in reality. Instead they are recognized as tools in the process of legal analysis—tools generating amorphous concepts whose meaning and implications shift and change depending on the facts of each case, the policies thought to be involved in resolving conflict or planning one's course of action, and the consequences of employing the concept in a particular way in the circumstances of the case.[11] Concepts like "consideration," "property," and "person" are used to define the facts for purposes of the decision, as well as to denote the relevant policy in the circumstances of a dispute, to aid in defining and applying the concept. The concept is being used to link that segment of reality deemed facts to the policy found relevant in the light of the short- and long-term consequences of the decision in order to determine the moral question of what ought to be done in a particular case or circumstance. The process of reasoning involved results in the paradox that one must know the facts in order to know the policies, while also knowing the policies in order to know the facts. Thus every legal question is unavoidably an ethical one: a question of what ought to be done in a specific circumstance in the light of the moral values found relevant and all the consequences of the decision.

H.L.A. Hart has also pointed out[12] that concepts in law demand a special method of "elucidation":

1. They cannot be understood properly through a definition but must be viewed "in examples of typical contexts where these words are at work."
2. Concepts in law assume the existence of a legal system and also have a special connection with a particular rule in the system.
3. It makes a difference as to who is invoking the concept: whether the concept is invoked by a judge to decide a case or an attorney in arguing one.
4. Concepts attach identical consequences to any one of a large set of identical facts.

It may also be said that concepts in law are tools of analysis and prediction by which disputes may be resolved in a fair and predictable manner and law may be relied upon to act as a knowable constraint upon decision making in society.

Even the most mundane and routine legal question, like the enforceability of a properly executed note representing a debt, reinvokes several ethical judgments enshrined in the policies underlying the rule that one ought to abide by one's promise. In determining whether the rule is applicable in a given situation and what it means, a judge must first discover the rule and its relation to a host of other rules and in the light of institutional and role constraints binding the decision maker, a complex process itself; determine the meaning of the rule and the concepts used to express it in the light of the facts and policies found relevant to the circumstances; and then determine whether to apply the rule and the concepts it generates in this particular instance. The "fact" of the age of the promisor in a contract suit may not be a "fact" for the purpose of the analysis in one case, but it may become a "fact" for purposes of another case. In the latter instance, another rule (the age of consent), policy (the reasons for having a rule establishing an age of consent), and consequence (what ought to be the responsibilities of the young and the duties of the mature for their commercial relationships) may come to the fore through a process called legal reasoning or "thinking like a lawyer."

Legal reasoning should not be considered any different from the reasoning followed in art, the sciences, and other disciplines when thinking is done at its highest level.[13] It entails induction, deduction, and reasoning by analogy; definition and theory; creation and conservation. It requires a knowledge of the territory under consideration, a deep appreciation for the policies involved, and a healthy skepticism for determining what are facts for purposes of resolving a particular dispute or problem. In legal reasoning at this level, one must be engaged in the paradox of having to know the facts in order to know the law and give it meaning, while also knowing the law and its moral roots in order to know what the "facts" are. Too often, legal reasoning is viewed as a rigid deductive system in which one applies predefined and reified rules to fixed "facts" through a mechanical process of deductive reasoning to reach a preordained result. Such a naive and simplistic positivism is not unknown to other disciplines at both the level of mundane and routine decision making of applying the rules to the facts to decide the "is" of a particular dispute and in decision making at the higher level of determining what the rules "ought" to be and mean generally.

For example, economics in the hands of some schools of economic thought and some of the brokers of the program to wed law and economics[14] resembles a simplistic and mechanical version of legal reasoning. In philosophical terms, it is a discredited form of analytical positivism and a throwback to the legal formalism and conceptualism of the nineteenth century seeking to impose a hidden and a priori set of theological postulates on reality. It is a process dressed up in the supposed objective rigor of the scientific method rather than the more straightforward brute declarations of faith of the nineteenth century.[15] The unquestioned use of the abstract model entails the unexamined adoption of the model's rigid assumption of fact and value and produces a mind-set cloaked with blinders, resulting in the ruling out of consideration many other "facts" and competing value choices. Such reasoning is a form of epistemological decapitation of the process for determining what are the "facts" relevant to the decision and a form of intellectual castration cutting off consideration of competing value choices for determining what "ought" to be the meaning of a concept and the appropriate application of that meaning in a particular case. It is a gumball machine method of reasoning where the "facts" are inserted into the machine of a rigid model or a fixed definition and the lever of deductive reasoning is then pulled to produce the "right" answer—a perfectly round and smooth ball in conformity with the unrevealed, unrealistic, and narrow assumptions of fact and value that go into the construction of the gumball machine.[16] This is not to say that traditional economic theorizing is wrong. Although abstract theorizing can be a limited source of potential insights to be considered in the course of legal analysis, the use of abstract economic theorizing from a world where words and concepts are at rest, facts are fixed and static, and consequences are predetermined cannot be translated into a trustworthy tool of analysis in the real world of legal analysis. The obligation of legal analysis to resolve the "is" and "ought" of conflict in an imperfect and shifting world makes words, facts, concepts, reality, and the clash of moral values dynamic and not fixed. Words and concepts cannot be fixed and immutable in a decision-making process required to decide the "is" of a particular dispute and what "ought" to be the law in similar circumstances not before the decision maker in the light of the general policies of the law, the institutional and other purposes of the legal process, and the refusal of reality and societal values to remain constant and immutable.

In the case of the conservative-libertarian movement to wed law with neoclassical economic theorizing, the exercise is also a tautology because the process assumes what it sets out to discover. The model assumes the existence of a legal system and a set of property and other rights that "ought" to be protected by the legal system as an underlying assumption to be used in defining what ought to be the rules of the legal system for defining the scope of property and other rights.[17] The reasoning is circular and cuts off the kind of necessary fact and policy inquiry that is essential if the legal process is to achieve its functions of resolving disputes in society in accord with the realities of the dispute and the congeries of moral values the society expects its legal system to foster and protect.[18]

The *Santa Clara* case might be viewed as an example of this kind of reasoning. The Court, apparently without thought or reflection, appeared to be implementing mechanically a syllogism: Corporations are persons within the meaning of the Fourteenth Amendment; all persons are entitled to due process and equal protection under the Fourteenth Amendment; therefore the corporation is entitled to the guarantees of due process and equal protection found in the Fourteenth Amendment as limitations upon the power of government to regulate corporate activities. The Court failed to explain or support its major premise, a significant lapse of judicial responsibility to reveal its reasoning process, the "facts" deemed relevant to its decision, the values sought to be achieved, and the consequences the Court believes will follow from a major decision of long-term constitutional

dimensions and one having important social, political, and economic consequences. Logic in law should be understood as a tool for exposing assumptions
underlying premises and not a device for ignoring them or proving a desired
conclusion implicit in the premises.

A current reaction to this and other forms of excessive conceptualism, a
nineteenth-century form of analytical positivism very much with us today, is the
critical legal studies (CLS) movement. It is an ill-defined but vigorous school
of thought, attacking the reliability of language and concepts as predictable and
objective guides to just and fair decision making in law.[19] Its underlying political
assumptions are apt criteria for examining critically the methodology of the *Santa
Clara* case of 100 years ago:

Two main tendencies can be distinguished in the critical legal studies movement. One
tendency sees past or contemporary doctrine as the expression of a particular vision of
society while emphasizing the contradictory and manipulable character of doctrinal argument. . . . Another tendency grows out of the social theories of Marx and Weber and
the mode of social and historical analysis that combines functionalist methods with radical
aims. Its point of departure has been the thesis that law and legal doctrine reflect, confirm,
and reshape the social divisions and hierarchies in a type or state of social organization
such as capitalism.[20]

The recognition that legal concepts can be manipulated as devices to hide and
give effect to underlying ideological preferences of decision makers is a legacy
from the legal realist tradition.[21] The CLS movement has sought to go a step
further, however, by asserting that legal concepts are used intentionally to hide
the implementation of the shared value system and assumptions of the central
legal actors in a society at a given point in time,[22] a likely explanation and
description of the intellectual process at work in the *Santa Clara* case.

It is within the broad range between the rigid jurisprudence of positivism and
the open-ended, nihilistic, and ideological assertions of the CLS movement that
I wish to analyze the use and misuse of legal concepts in general and, more
particularly, the use and misuse of the concept of person for constitutional
purposes to describe the legal status of corporations. Concepts in law do have
content and meaning derived from the language used to invoke the concept,
other rules and the concepts they invoke in the analysis, the facts of the dispute,
the role of rules in the legal process, the traditions and culture of the society,
and the constraints of role definitions applicable to the decision maker. But words
and concepts in law are functional and mobile, not fixed and rigid definitions
for immutable concepts corresponding to some aspect of reality.[23] They are tools
of analysis for resolving conflict in a bewildering array of factual circumstances,
operating within a range of meaning, relevance, cultural, and linguistic constraints and institutional limitations. As such, they are complex tools requiring
sophistication and care in their use. Carelessness can create a misuse of words
and concepts in law to the damage of society, the parties to the dispute, the

long-term evolution of the concepts involved, the law they effect, and the central concepts by which a society defines itself and the values it seeks to achieve.

It is a misuse of legal concepts to treat them as axiomatic definitions with a predetermined and unchanging meaning to be mechanically applied to "facts" routinely served up for decision. And it is a misuse of legal concepts knowingly to use and manipulate them to conceal the selfish and narrow ideological objectives of a political elite bent on maintaining existing institutions and social arrangements or changing them for its own class benefit.[24] Worse still is the use and manipulation of legal concepts to achieve the unexamined and narrow ideological objectives of a decision maker oblivious to the reality that he or she is doing so. The first abuse is an indication of superficiality; the second can be an indication of either arrogance or dishonesty; and the third is an indication of ignorance.

ROOTS OF THE *SANTA CLARA* DECISION

The roots of the Court's cryptic statement in the *Santa Clara* case may never be known. One is, however, entitled to speculate. The conspiracy theory of the Fourteenth Amendment advanced by the Beards[25] has been persuasively discounted.[26] The decision to accord corporations constitutional rights as persons within the meaning of the Fourteenth Amendment was the product of court decisions reflecting a tide of contemporary economic and political events rather than the secret machinations of the draftsmen of the amendment or the persuasiveness or dishonest manipulations of the historical record by advocates like Roscoe Conkling.[27] Rather, the *Santa Clara* decision appears to be the product of an ideological elite seeking to impose its values on society during a time of revolutionary economic change through an institution whose role as a branch of government was changing dramatically. The Court's role was shifting from a subservient branch of government in economic policy making to that of the principal branch of government in defining both economic policy and the role of government in implementing the policy defined. The Court used that redefined role to impose its view of the appropriate role of government in regulating economic affairs and the economic theories by which that regulation must be measured on a constitutional basis.

In a series of cases leading up to the court's decision in *Santa Clara*, Justice Field, sitting as a circuit judge, had been actively and aggressively holding that the Fourteenth Amendment did not distinguish between different types of persons and therefore that its protections ought to be extended to all persons, not just to "newly-made citizens of the African race."[28] In making the leap from recognizing that the Fourteenth Amendment protected all persons to the conclusion that corporations were persons of the class of persons uniformly protected, Field asserted:

The argument that a limitation must be given to the scope of this amendment because of the circumstances of its origin is without force. Its authors, seeing how possible it was for the states to oppress without relief from the federal government, placed in the constitution an interdict upon their action which makes lasting oppression of any kind by them under the form of law impossible. . . .

Private corporations are, it is true, artificial persons, but . . . they consist of aggregations of individuals united for some legitimate business. . . . It would be a most singular result if a constitutional provision intended for the protection of every person against partial and discriminating legislation by the states, should cease to exert such protection the moment the person becomes a member of a corporation. We cannot accept such a conclusion. On the contrary, we think it is well established . . . that whenever a provision of the constitution, or of a law, guarantees to persons the enjoyment of property, or affords to them means for its protection, or prohibits legislation injuriously affecting it, the benefits of the provision extend to corporations, and that the courts will always look beyond the name of the artificial being to the individuals whom it represents.[29]

Field saw the function of Fourteenth Amendment personhood status for corporations not as a device for protecting individual rights of association for political or social ends but as a means for implementing a laissez-faire economic policy for business interests and establishing constitutional rights of property on an almost absolutist basis in the emerging capitalistic economy of the nineteenth century.[30] The fact that freeing business from government regulation did not include depriving business interests of the use of government and its courts to enforce their property and contract rights was not seen as an inconsistency in the laissez-faire philosophy being applied. Field believed that equating the human and corporate person for purposes of defining the scope of constitutional immunity from government economic regulation was all the consistency one needed. In doing so, Field misused the concept because he equated the corporate collective with an individual and did not reveal fully the underlying policies determining the meaning, use, and consequences of the concept or the reasons for not distinguishing between individual and collective activity regarding the powers of government. Nor did Field reflect, apparently, on the appropriate role of the judiciary in a government of constitutionally divided powers. Mesmerized by laissez-faire, classical economics and an absolutist view about the rights of property, Field converted the concept of corporate personhood into a tool for ruling out of consideration competing value choices, all of the facts, many of the potential consequences of the decision, and the appropriate role of the courts as a coequal branch of government.

Field, not a judge of subtle mind or conciliatory personality,[31] was the most "uncompromising judicial exponent of laissez faire in his time, perhaps in American constitutional history."[32] His concept of the basis for property rights appears to have been an almost theological one of a God-given right to do as one wished with one's property.[33] Yet it would be an overstatement to credit Field as being solely or even primarily responsible for the recognition of corporations as persons for constitutional law purposes. The conclusion in *Santa Clara* was unanimous, whatever the unspoken and unwritten rationale may have been, and one suspects unanimity was reached in spite of Field's personality and ability to persuade others to his point of view.

Personhood for corporations on a constitutional level came about as a by-product of several larger shifts and changes taking place during one of the great watersheds in our economic history—post–Civil War America. A capitalistic economy began to assert itself over the agrarian one substantially vanquished in civil war; the industrial revolution began to expand rapidly through the building of vast transportation and communications networks; a new social ethic exalting hard work, entrepreneurship, and the materialism of the Deity—Horatio Algerism in short—was riding high; and the riches of a still largely untapped continent awaited exploitation by a rapidly expanding population. The expression of these forces through some doctrine of constitutional law installing laissez-faire as the norm for defining the scope of the power of government and classical economics as the constitutionally mandated ideological base for government economic policy seems almost inevitable by hindsight. It has been observed:

Due Process was fashioned from the most respectable ideological stuff of the later nine-teenth century. The ideas out of which it was shaped were in full accord with the dominant thought of the age. They were an aspect of common sense, a standard of economic orthodoxy, a test of straight thinking and sound opinion. In the domain of thought their general attitude was on the present. In philosophy it was on individualism; in government, laissez faire; in economics, the natural law of supply and demand; in law, freedom of contract. The system of thought had possessed every other discipline; it had in many a domain reshaped the law to its teachings.[34]

At the same time, the conception of the judicial function as subservient to the legislative function (particularly in matters of economic policy) was giving way to a tradition of judicial supremacy in all matters of governmental economic policy. The courts assumed they had the final voice in measuring the wisdom of the exercise of regulatory power by government. They did so on yardsticks of substantive due process and freedom of contract; constitutional guarantees applied with far more zeal to the newly discovered persons of corporations than the newly liberated persons of slaves. The development of more sensible stand-ards for preserving the national interest in fostering a common market and limiting discriminatory local regulation, standards consistent with a more limited role of the judiciary in economic policy making, was effectively cut off by the frozen conceptualization of interstate and intrastate commerce and the persistence of dual federalism.[35] The Court's inclusion of corporations within the concept of person for Fourteenth Amendment purposes was the product of a superficial use of legal concepts as axiomatic definitions with a predetermined and unchanging meaning being applied mechanically to ''facts'' assumed to be routinely served up for decision.

The federal and state governments were viewed as separate and independent sovereigns whose sovereignty did not overlap. Each was confined to its specific jurisdiction by rigid concepts of intrastate and interstate commerce, with the states precluded from regulating the latter and the federal government precluded from regulating the former. Invalidating discriminatory local legislation on commerce clause grounds or through a preemption analysis, methods leaving ultimate policy making in the hands of the elective branches of government, were not effective tools available to the courts during this time of dynamic economic change. Constitutional personhood for corporations, a near-absolute freedom of contract, substantive economic due process, and equal protection became the inevitable conceptual vehicles for the courts to impose their version of laissez-faire and classical economics as constitutional restraints upon government in regulating economic relationships in post–Civil War America.

LEGACIES OF *SANTA CLARA*

The most obvious legacy of the *Santa Clara* decision is the continued recognition of the corporation as a person for purposes of several clauses of the Constitution. A less obvious legacy is the consequence of that recognition for the economic, political, and social development of twentieth-century America.[36] A still less obvious legacy is the ongoing misuse of legal concepts when it comes to the legal analysis of problems involving corporate personhood for purposes of determining the relevance and meaning of the concept in constitutional law, as well as for the use of the concept elsewhere in the law. It is this last legacy of *Santa Clara* I wish to explore. It is a legacy that has deflected a realistic evaluation of the purpose, consequence, and legitimacy of the modern corporation and one that continues to generate a misuse of the concept of corporate person in constitutional analysis and elsewhere.

A pattern of misuse of the legal concept of corporate personhood became evident and well established during the period of the Court's enchantment with substantive economic due process. The rise and fall of the Court's involvement with substantive due process is well chronicled and will not be repeated here save for that feature of it involving the repeated use of the concept of corporate personhood as a vehicle to carry out the Court's economic views and assert its power as final arbiter of the scope of governmental authority in the economic sphere.

During the era of substantive due process, the Court repeatedly engaged in the hypostatization of legal concepts, ''thingifying'' them as fixed concepts divorced from the facts of cases, the policies giving rise to the concept, the consequences of applying the concept in the circumstances involved, the role of the judiciary in relation to other branches of government in the light of the use being made of the concept, the meaning of other concepts in the firmament of the area of the law the Court was dealing with, and the moral implications of the decision being made. For example, the Court's concept of contract as a freely bargained and consensual relationship between two persons of equal bargaining strength was used in *Lochner v. New York*[37] to strike down a state statute limiting the hours of bakery and confectionary workers to sixty hours weekly. The Court viewed the statute as an interference "with the right to labor, either as employer or employee"[38] and as "mere meddlesome interference with the rights of the individual,"[39] all of which flowed from recognizing freedom of contract as a type of liberty protected by due process from "unreasonable" interference by the legislature. A fixed mental picture generated by the concept of contract so captured the majority that it cut off any consideration of the possibility that the contracts of employment might not have been bargained upon terms of employment because there was in fact no free bargaining between parties of equal strength. Nor did the Court pay any deference to the legislative rationale for adopting the statute or the consequences of its decision.[40] Instead, a rote and mechanical application of a fixed meaning of the contract concept to the statute in the light of "facts" dictated by the Court's assumption of fixed values underlying its concept of contracts and its fixed meaning of due process inexorably produced the Court's conclusion that the statute was unconstitutional.[41]

When the Court's fixed concept of contracts was applied to legislation restricting the right of an employer to fire employees for union activity in factual circumstances clearly involving a corporate employer, the Court took no note of the difference between an individual human person doing so and a powerful and far-flung corporate person doing so.[42] The doctrine of corporate personhood was so entrenched in the minds of the judges as to prevent the issue of whether contracts by corporate persons should be treated differently from contracts by natural persons from even being thought of, let alone from being raised as a fact that ought to be considered. The Court equated the corporate person with a natural person, a "category mistake"[43] confusing the legal and practical rationale for classifying individuals as persons for constitutional law analysis and the rationales for classifying corporations as persons generally. A fixed and rigid concept of personhood restricted the thinking of the Court and the litigants to such a degree that certain of the facts (the corporate nature of the person involved and the inequality of bargaining power under the circumstances) and the policy considerations they raised were kept from being facts for purpose of the analysis. A similar pattern was followed in the due process and equal protection cases,[44] with no attention paid to the possibility that the presence of a corporate person might make a difference to the reality the Court was dealing with and shift the content of the package of facts, values, and policies underlying the analysis to a different set of ethical considerations than those applied to similar conduct by human persons.

The Court's abdication of the role of czar of state and federal economic policy through the abandonment of the doctrine of substantive economic due process[45] did not carry with it an abandonment of the practice of including corporations within a fixed constitutional concept of person. Although it was not necessary for the Court to repudiate the doctrine of corporate personhood in order to escape the role of the economic and political czar of the economy, the close relationship between the initial decision to expand the concept of person to include corporations and the implementation of substantive economic due process to achieve the Court's economic and political ideology should have justified a reexamination of the use made of the concept of corporate personhood.[46] The concept was, after all, the primary vehicle by which the Court was able to transport its fixed concept of substantive economic due process into many of the cases challenging the economic and political wisdom of state and federal economic legislation. Instead the Court resisted calls for a reexamination of the inclusion of corporations as persons for purposes of constitutional analysis even while abandoning the authority to strike down state and federal economic regulation under the banner of substantive economic due process.

In *Wheeling Steel Corp. v Glander*,[47] a case striking down an Ohio ad valorem tax discriminating against foreign corporations on federal equal protection grounds, Justice Robert Jackson appended an explanation to his majority opinion explaining why that opinion "assumed without discussion that the protections of the Fourteenth Amendment are available to corporations":

It was not questioned by the State in this case, nor was it considered by the courts below. It has consistently been held by this Court that the Fourteenth Amendment assures corporations equal protection of the laws, at least since 1886, . . . and that it entitles them to due process of law, at least since 1889. . . .

In view of this record I did not, and still do not, consider it necessary for the Court opinion to review the considerations which justify the assumption that these corporations have standing to raise the issues decided.

Justice Jackson stated these views in response to a dissent in the case by Justices William Douglas and Hugo Black challenging Fourteenth Amendment personhood for corporations, only the second challenge opinion since the purported abandonment of substantive due process to the doctrine since its birth in *Santa Clara*.[48]

Although the Court had never openly reviewed the "considerations which justify the assumption" that corporations should be considered persons for purposes of the Fourteenth Amendment, Justices Douglas and Black did not attack the doctrine on that ground or on the more basic ground of the persistent misuse of the concept in legal analysis by ignoring the facts, policy, and consequences of recognizing corporate personhood under the circumstances. Instead they once again stressed that the definition of the concept was in error rather than that its use was erroneous in certain circumstances because of the meaning of the language of the amendment and its historical purpose. Quoting Arthur Twyning Hadley—"the Fourteenth Amendment was framed to protect the negroes from oppression by the whites, not to protect corporations from oppression by the Legislature"[49]—the dissenters argued that the meaning of the concept should be derived from the grammatical use made of the symbol for the concept—the word *person*.

Although one may agree that some of the meaning of a concept may or should be derived from the popular meaning of the symbol used for the concept,[50] it is just as much a misuse of a legal concept to base its sole meaning on a definition as it is to refuse to explain why a certain meaning is given a concept in a particular circumstance. Such a course fails to give the entire meaning of the concept as a tool of legal analysis or illuminate the policies sought to be implemented by employing the concept in the circumstances involved to achieve certain consequences. Justices Black and Douglas, leaders in the revolution of finding new meanings in the Fourteenth Amendment and the rest of the Bill of Rights in the civil liberties field, should have been among the first to recognize that the meaning of central legal concepts shifts and changes over time. The reality with which law must deal shifts and changes and new insights and new values come to the fore in the never-ending task of adjusting old concepts and enduring values to new realities and past divisions of governmental power to present political, social, and economic realities.[51]

Justice Douglas made a more considered criticism of the doctrine of corporate personhood in *Bell v. Maryland*,[52] a case explicitly asserting the Fourteenth Amendment rights of human beings and implicitly involving the Fourteenth Amendment rights of a corporate person. In that case, the defendants had been convicted of a criminal trespass for refusing to leave a corporately owned and segregated restaurant where they had sought service. The majority did not reach the question of whether the convictions violated the human defendants' Fourteenth Amendment rights by virtue of being state action denying them the equal protection of the laws because the state had passed laws abolishing the crimes of which the defendants had been convicted and establishing rights of public accommodation. Consequently, the Court remanded the case to the state court for its determination as to whether the repeal of the Maryland criminal trespass statute and adoption of a public accommodations law would result in vacating the convictions and dismissal of the criminal charges as a matter of state law.

Justice Douglas, concurring in the result, would have reached the merits of the case. Douglas saw the majority as confronting and then ducking the issue of whether a "person's 'personal prejudices' may dictate the way in which he uses his property and whether he can enlist the aid of the state to enforce those 'personal prejudices.' "[53] Indeed, the dissent by Justices Black, John Harlan, and Byron White came close to framing the issue in precisely this way.[54] According to Douglas, this was not the real issue. Instead, the real issue must be viewed in the light of the reality that "the corporation that owns this restaurant did not refuse service to these Negroes because 'it' did not like Negroes. The reason was because 'it' thought 'it' could make more money by running a segregated restaurant."[55] By framing the issue in this manner, Justice Douglas turned the analysis to a functional one of using the concept of corporate personhood to explore and link a different range of facts, policies, and consequences:

Here, as in most of the sit-in cases before us, the refusal of service did not reflect "personal prejudices" but business reasons. Were we today to hold that segregated restaurants, whose racial policies were enforced by a State, violated the Equal Protection Clause, all restaurants would be on an equal footing and the reasons given for refusing service to Negroes would evaporate. Moreover, when corporate restauranteurs are involved, whose "personal prejudices" are being protected? The stockholders'? The directors'? The officers'? The managers'? The truth is, I think, that the corporate interest is in making money, not in protecting "personal prejudices."[56]

By viewing the concept of corporate personhood functionally rather than as a rigid and fixed definition similar to that of human personhood, the Douglas opinion not only defined a different slice of reality as the facts relevant to the decision but also shifted the package of policies relevant to the decision to ones not considered by the majority. The fundamental moral question became the scope of property rights of a collective, permitted by the state to operate as a collective for a public purpose, and not the scope of individual property rights recognized by the state for a different range of moral objectives and historical reasons. Thus:

The problem with which we deal has no relation to opening or closing the door of one's home. The home of course is the essence of privacy, in no way dedicated to public use, in no way extending an invitation to the public. . . . The facts of these sit-in cases have little resemblance to any institution of property which we customarily associate with privacy. . . .

So far as the corporate owner is concerned, what constitutional right is vindicated? It is said that ownership of property carries the right to use it in association with such people as the owner chooses. The corporate owners in these cases—the stockholders—are unidentified members of the public at large, who probably never saw these petitioners, who may never have frequented these restaurants. What personal rights of theirs would be vindicated by affirmance? . . . Why should his interests—his associational rights—make it possible to send these Negroes to jail?[57]

Justice Douglas recognized the consequences, as well as the factual and policy differences, involved in extending human rights of association and privacy to corporations through the vehicle of the concept of person:

Affirmance finds in the Constitution a corporate right to refuse service to anyone "it" chooses and then get the State to put people in jail who defy "its" will.

More precisely, affirmance would give corporate management vast dimensions for social planning.

Affirmance would make corporate management the arbiter of one of the deepest conflicts in our society: corporate management could then enlist the aid of state police, state prosecutors, and state courts to force *apartheid* on the community they served, if *apartheid* best suited the corporate need; or, if its profits would be better served by lowering the barriers of segregation, it could do so.[58]

Justice Douglas also recognized that an interpretation rejecting the use of the concept of corporate personhood for some purposes did not necessarily mean that the concept of personhood should not be used for other purposes where the facts, policies, and consequences ''ought'' to require such in order to achieve a basic moral value of our society. Thus corporate personhood for purposes of constitutional analysis ''ought'' to be recognized to protect rights of free speech,[59] to uphold the policies of the Fourth Amendment,[60] or to assert political or other rights of the members of a collective peculiar to the type of organization involved and the circumstances of the demand by government treading on the constitutional rights of individual members of the organization.[61] To those convinced that legal analysis should function with the logic of a gumball machine, such a result may appear incomprehensible.[62] The word *person* means first one thing and then another and can no longer serve as a reliable and fixed vehicle for understanding what the law is. Such a belief overlooks the function of concepts in legal analysis to also determine what the law ought to be (based on the meaning of the language and concepts used in the light of the circumstances of the case, the values of the society, and the institutional role of the decision maker) and is part of the reason why one continues to see the misuse of the concept of corporate person-hood in constitutional analysis a century after its appearance in the *Santa Clara* case.

In *Allied Structural Steel Co. v. Spannaus*,[63] for example, the Court once again invoked a rigid concept of contract for purposes of the contract clause of the Constitution to strike down a Minnesota statute imposing obligations on employers of more than one hundred employees offering their employees a privately funded pension plan. The statute, a response to widespread pension abuses subsequently regulated by the Employee Retirement Income Security Act of 1974 (ERISA),[64] assessed a pension funding charge if the employer terminated the plan or closed its Minnesota office and the funds in its pension plan were insufficient to cover the full pensions of all employees who had worked ten years or more. Although the legislation significantly altered Allied Steel Company's obligations under the pension plan, the Court refused to explore Minnesota's objectives in adopting the statute, the realities surrounding the bargaining (if any) that had taken place in establishing the terms of the pension plan and each employee's participation in the plan, and the fact that the employer was a cor-porate employer. No examination of the meaning of the concept of contract for purposes of the contract clause in the light of these circumstances was engaged in, nor was the corporate character of the employer examined as a factor to be weighed in the calculus for giving meaning to the contract clause or for weighing the reasons for adoption of the statute. The fact that there had been widespread abuse of employee pension rights through termination of pension plans by cor-porate mergers and acquisitions received no notice. Instead the majority me-chanically applied their predetermined and fixed concepts of contract and corporate person to their predetermined and fixed facts to arrive at their prede-termined conclusion, a process all too reminiscent of the nineteenth-century analytical positivism many thought had died with the passing of substantive economic due process.

A similar simplistic reasoning process and misuse of legal concepts has been taking place with the recognition of First Amendment speech rights of corporations. In *First National Bank of Boston v. Bellotti,*[65] a majority of the Court held a Massachusetts statute prohibiting banks and business corporations from spending funds for the purpose of influencing the vote on referendum proposals violated the corporation's free speech rights protected by the First Amendment as applied to the states through the Fourteenth Amendment. The statute was expressly passed to suppress opposition by corporate interests to a state income tax proposal, a circumstance some have suggested made the statute particularly reprehensible and the Court's decision to strike it down understandable but one that should be read narrowly.[66] From the perspective of a concern about the necessary relationship between some level of constitutional protection of economic rights being essential to the realistic possession and exercise of civil rights,[67] the Massachusetts statute may be viewed as a suspect and probably bad statute.[68] Although one may agree that bad statutes may, on occasion, justify narrow decisions striking them down by a minor extension of existing rules or concepts, the Court's opinion in *Bellotti* was not a narrow one for the concepts of free speech and corporate personhood.

The majority opinion by Justice Lewis Powell shifted the issue from whether corporations have or ought to have First Amendment rights coextensive with those of natural persons to an issue of whether the statute "abridges expression that the First Amendment was meant to protect."[69] How one could decide the latter issue, implicitly recognizing for the first time a right of free speech by commercial corporations, without grappling with the meaning of corporate personhood in the light of the facts of the case, the lower court decision, and the statute enacted by Massachusetts was not explained. Instead, Justice Powell simply identified the speech involved as political speech, a type of speech clearly within the meaning of the concept of speech as that concept is used in the First Amendment. An implicit assumption resulting from stating the issue in this way is that it does not matter factually from what source the protected speech comes because the purpose of the First Amendment is to protect a marketplace of ideas rather than the right of the source of the ideas to exercise free speech.[70] The assumption leads to the inexorable conclusion that any state regulation interfering with the functioning of the undefined marketplace of ideas violates the First Amendment without regard to the implicit impact of the expansion of the meaning of corporate personhood on the political life of society, the balance between individualism and collectivism, and the long-term consequences of the decision for other state and federal regulation of corporations.

Not surprisingly, the remainder of the Powell opinion consists of a refutation of the state's arguments as to why corporations ought not be considered persons within the meaning of the First Amendment in the circumstances of this particular case. Left unclear is the affirmative side of the issue of why nonmedia commercial corporations should be considered persons protected from government regulation of political campaigning by the guarantees of the First Amendment and the scope of the right being recognized.[71] The crucial questions in decisions of such moment are when to ignore the differences and when to recognize the similarities between prior precedent protecting free speech by individuals and the corporate media. These are questions that can be answered only by deep reflection on the policies, moral values, and facts involved in the circumstances and by minds sensitive to the deeper implications of what they are doing.

Aside from glimpses of category mistakes equating the corporate person with human persons,[72] it would appear that the majority opinion is either a smoke-screen for implementing unstated economic, social, and political values of the majority or an unexplained and unjustified reflex reaction to what the majority believed was a heavy-handed and unacceptable state law. The Powell analysis rejected the Massachusetts court's limitation of corporate speech rights to subjects that derive from a corporation's property interests, noting that the lower court did not take the "extreme position" that corporations have only the rights granted them by the state.[73] The majority opinion justified rejection of the Massachusetts argument by noting that no such distinction had been recognized in prior corporate speech cases, cases generally involving media, religious, and civil rights entities. One suspects that the cited cases did not consider the speech rights of purely commercial corporations because the issue was not raised in those cases, a factual distinction between the instant case and the cited precedent based on policy considerations and consequences the Powell opinion choose to ignore without explanation.

Elsewhere in the majority opinion, in the process of backing into the recognition of a constitutionally protected right of free speech for all corporations, the majority asserted that if a legislature is empowered to restrict certain subjects of corporate speech to those topics related to its business interests, it can similarly limit the classes of speech for religious, charitable, and civic corporate collectives as well. Such an assertion denies the flexibility of legal concepts and the impact of different facts raising different policies and different consequences with a resulting shift in the meaning of a concept. One may agree that the lower court test for describing the scope of corporate speech rights as limited to those related to its business interests is an artificial and impractical test, and such a consideration is therefore a relevant consideration in deciding whether to recognize a right and the scope of the right recognized. It is not, however, legitimate to premise the reasoning on the alleged inflexibility of legal concepts, particularly in the course of a decision recognizing for the first time that all corporations, without regard for the circumstances, are protected from government regulation of their speech because they are persons within the meaning of the First Amendment.

The Powell opinion also portrays a simplistic view of the modern corporation by suggesting that shareholders in disagreement with the content of the speech their corporation chooses to make can make use of the mechanisms of corporate democracy to protect their interests or have resort to derivative suits to challenge improper corporate expenditures.[74] Writing as if Berle and Means never existed,[75] let alone the widespread knowledge of the powerlessness of shareholders[76] and their questionable claims of ownership in the modern public issue corporation,[77] reflects either a naive or a disingenuous understanding of the public issue corporation.

Whether the opinion is the product of a conscious or unconscious implementation of unidentified policies and values, the consequences of the misuse of legal concepts are the same: deprivation of an understanding of the underlying reasons for the Court's recognition of corporations as persons with free speech rights severely restricts one's understanding and use of both the concept of corporate personhood and the concept of free speech. It makes unpredictable the consequences of the decision, which may reach far beyond the resolution of the case before the Court. Absent that understanding and basis for prediction, one is left without a sufficient guide to predict the implications of the Court's decision or assess its wisdom and propriety. It would appear that the opinion is the product of an unthinking analytical positivism or is premised on a fixed political faith in nineteenth-century classical economics and a laissez-faire theory of government granting unelected judges the primary power to determine economic policy, a not unreasonable inference from subsequent decisions in this and other areas by the Burger Court.[78] If this is the case, the concept of corporate person and its misuse in the legal process have once again become central factors in a rebirth of substantive economic due process under other guises to impose judicially defined policies of laissez-faire and classical economics as constitutional constraints upon the powers of government.

CONCLUSION

The legitimacy of the modern public issue corporation has been a major issue in academic circles since Berle and Means published *The Modern Corporation and Private Property* in 1932.[79] The legal system has dealt with the reality described by Berle and Means and others through a variety of not necessarily coordinated responses. For example, federal and state securities regulation seek to control dishonesty in securities transactions and ensure some level of integrity of the markets where securities are traded; federal antitrust regulation has evolved in the direction of providing the means for government and private parties to control attempts to displace the competitive process through the individual and joint exercise of corporate power; environmental regulation seeks to control the power of corporate and other collectives to pollute with impunity; rate and other regulatory regulation control the power of natural monopolies and other entities, where market forces cannot or do not work, to realize monopoly profits or exclude competitors from related markets; and a wide range of complex health, safety, and other laws seek to protect the individual from the often overwhelming and otherwise uncontrolled power of collectives in our society.

Understanding of the nature and reality of corporate collectives is often clouded by the legal system "thingifying" the concept of the corporate person or by the treating of it as if it were the same as a human person without regard for all the facts, policies, and consequences of doing so. This has been particularly true in constitutional adjudication where the mysticism of corporate personhood remains with us and is being expanded in much the same manner as it was in the heyday of substantive due process. The Court continues to make and remake economic and political policy through its use of the concept of corporate personhood, but it is either refusing to acknowledge that it is doing so or is obfuscating the fact that it is doing so through the rote and mechanical use of the concept. The result is superficial decision making and a failure to examine fully the facts, policies, and consequences of the decisions being made.

The repeated failure of the courts to acknowledge several realities and moral implications about the modern corporation, as well as acknowledge the unavoidable making of policy choices inherent in the institution of judicial review under a written constitution, has prevented the development of a realistic and constructive understanding of the corporate collective in a variety of circumstances. Such an understanding of the modern corporation is necessary to the formulation of coherent legal standards regulating corporations, defining the scope of constitutionally protected collective economic freedom necessary for the realization of basic civil liberties, sensibly dividing the powers of government to regulate corporations, and predicting the implications of the definitions made for other values of society. Courts do not often recognize that not all corporations are the same. Some are like large political states with wide-ranging political and economic power that might justify subjecting them to the constraints of the Constitution as governments[80] rather than their liberation from governmental control as persons protected by the Constitution from government. Other corporations are the alter ego of an individual or small group of individuals, which might justify treating the entity as a human person in some circumstances. The consequences of equating or not equating commercial corporations with human beings for purposes of constitutional analysis are often of great political, social, and economic significance. The way in which the courts decide such issues implicitly involves the striking of the appropriate balance in economic policy-making authority among the branches of government and the striking of a balance between individualism and collectivism. A majority of the Court in *Bellotti*, for example, expanded federal judicial control over state economic regulation and significantly narrowed the role state and federal legislative bodies can play in the regulation of excessive and corrupting special interest campaign financing. The majority did so without exploring the full implications of its holding by examining the facts, policies, and consequences involved in a significant expansion of the attributes of corporate personhood.

Society too has generally failed to escape mesmerization by the concept of corporate personhood. Policy makers, for example, have failed to recognize fully the implications of the divorce of ownership and control in the large public corporation or that the statutes creating and regulating corporations are ''towering skyscrapers of rusted girders, internally welded together and containing nothing but wind.''[81] The legal conception of corporate personhood has captured popular and political thinking about the corporation to such a degree that proposals for constructive reform and sensitive thinking about the implications of the gradual shift in our society from one based on individualism to one based on collectivism are largely ignored.[82]

These are the most significant legacies of the *Santa Clara* decision and the consequences of the continued misuse of the concept of corporate personhood in legal analysis and the resulting broader misuse of the concept in law and in society generally. The legitimacy of the modern corporation remains an unresolved and fundamental legal and moral issue, trapped by a mind-set that refuses to view the concept of the corporate person functionally.[83] The concept of corporate personhood, like other concepts in law, must be understood as a functional tool to link facts to policy in the light of consequences, the moral values of society, the function and functioning of the legal process, the appropriate role of courts in the realm of economic and civil liberties policy making, and the basic tension every society faces of striking an appropriate relational balance between the demands for individualism and those for collectivism. The failure of the courts to use the concept of corporate personhood functionally constitutes one of the most significant and enduring misuses of a concept in the history of U.S. law and a misuse that must be rectified before any real progress can be made toward legitimizing the corporation, understanding the full implications of its evolution, and reforming the law that purports to regulate it.

NOTES

1. See generally, Pound, The New Feudal System, 19 Ky. L. Rev. 1 (1930) describing the tension between a rights-based legal system and a relational-interests-based one.

2. See W. Hurst, The Legitimacy of the Business Corporation 68 (1970).

3. 118 U.S. 394 (1886).

4. See Manning, Corporate Power and Individual Freedom: Some General Analysis and Particular Reservations, 55 Nw. U.L. Rev. 38, 40 (1960).

5. See Freidmann, Corporate Power, Government by Private Groups, and the Law, 57 Colum. L. Rev. 155 (1957).

6. 118 U.S. at 396.

7. County of Santa Clara v. S. Pac. R.R. Co., 18 Fed. 385 (1883).

8. For an exhaustive survey of the evolution of the concept of corporate personhood for constitutional purposes, see Graham, An Innocent Abroad: The Constitutional Corporate "Person," 2 UCLA L. Rev. 155 (1955).

9. The personhood status of corporations for various legal and social purposes has always been the product of a complex series of considerations: "considerations popular, historical, political, moral, philosophical, metaphysical and, in connection with the latter, theological." Dewey, The Historic Background of Corporate Legal Personality, 35 Yale L. J. 655 (1926).

It is a misuse of the concept for a court to reveal nothing about the reasons for its conclusion that a corporation is a person for Fourteenth Amendment purposes. Court decisions of major constitutional dimensions should be reasoned explanations of the interpretation made, not brute declarations of a major premise. One is deprived not only of a basis for understanding the interpretation but also of an understanding of how far the interpretation is to be carried, the wisdom and moral basis of the choice made, and its consequences for laws, policies, and relationships in circumstances not before the court but potentially involving the same concept.

10. F. Cohen, Field Theory and Judicial Logic, 59 Yale L.J. 238 (1950).

11. See F. Cohen, Transcendental Nonsense and the Functional Approach, 35 Colum. L. Rev. 809 (1935).

12. Hart, Definition and Theory in Jurisprudence, 70 L.Q. Rev. 37 (1954). For a criticism of Hart's views and those of others on the function of concepts in legal reasoning, see Simpson, The Analysis of Legal Concepts, 80 L.Q. Rev. 535 (1964).

13. See Terrell, Flatlaw: An Essay on the Dimensions of Legal Reasoning and the Development of Fundamental Normative Principles, 72 Calif. L. Rev. 288 (1984). See generally, G. Zukav, The Dancing Wu Li Masters, An Overview of the New Physics (1979).

14. See, e.g., R. Posner, Economic Analysis of Law (1972); R. Posner, Antitrust Law: An Economic Perspective (1976); R. Bork, The Antitrust Paradox: A Policy at War with Itself (1978). For an interesting assessment of Posner's consistency in applying the form of economic analysis of legal problems he advocated as a scholar now that he has become a judge, see Cohen, Posnerian Jurisprudence and Economic Analysis of Law: The View from the Bench, 133 U. Pa. L. Rev. 1117 (1985).

15. "Most current law and economics theory represents neoconceptualism strikingly similar to the classical conceptualism successfully undermined by the realists. The law and economics model is the model of free, value-enhancing exchange, yet . . . market exchanges are in fact a function of the legal order; the terms of so-called free bargains (and, taken collectively, the supposedly objective market price) are determined by the legally protected right to withhold what is owned. Exchange 'value' (and 'costs') is a function of that right, so that the rationale of exchange is ultimately as circular and self-referencing as the rationale for legal rights. The legitimacy of every exchange calculus depends upon the legitimacy of prior legal decisions; it neither establishes that legitimacy nor evades the problem of legitimacy by a purported ahistorical objectivity. Similarly, judges cannot escape responsibility for the distributional consequences of legal decisions. The exchange calculus cannot be divorced from the question of distribution, since exchange is a function of the existing distribution of legal entitlement, and every new legal decision (including those that rigorously apply the law and economics approach) will inevitably affect subsequent distribution and, in turn, affect subsequent exchanges, costs, values, etc. Like the older spheres of private and public, questions of market exchange and of distribution simply collapse into each other." Mensch, The History of Mainstream Legal Thought, in The Politics of Law: A Progressive Critique 37 (D. Kairys ed. 1982).

16. See Flynn, The Misuse of Economic Analysis in Antitrust Litigation, 12 Sw. U.L. Rev. 335 (1981). Critical legal studies (CLS) scholars (see notes 19–22 and accompanying text, infra) are particularly harsh in their criticism of the law and economics movement. See Heller, The Importance of Normative Decision-Making: The Limitations of Legal Economics as a Basis for a Liberal Jurisprudence, 1976 Wis. L. Rev. 385; Kelman, Choice and Utility, 1979 Wis. L. Rev. 769; Kelman, Consumption Theory, Production Theory, and Ideology in the Coase Theorem, 52 S. Cal. L. Rev. 669 (1979); Kennedy, Cost-Benefit Analysis of Entitlement Problems: A Critique, 33 Stan. L. Rev. 387 (1981).

For a thoughtful rejoinder, see Kornhauser, The Great Image of Authority, 36 Stan. L. Rev. 349 (1984).

17. See Mensch, supra note 15.

18. The Burger Court has not confined its unexamined manipulation of the concept of corporate personhood to constitutional questions. For example, in Copperweld Corp. v. Independence Tube Corp., 467 U.S. 752, 104 S.Ct. 2731 (1984), the Court held a parent and wholly owned subsidiary were not separate persons for purposes of the Sherman Act's prohibition of contracts, combinations, or conspiracies in restraint of trade. 15 U.S.C. §§ 1, et seq. Such a result is not in conformity with the formalisms of corporate personhood recognized in Santa Clara and its offspring. The Court reached its result in order to minimize the antitrust risk of operating a corporation through a parent-subsidiary structure, a structure that might be dictated by tax, business, or other considerations. A similar result is achieved with regard to intracorporate activity by the so-called intra-enterprise doctrine, holding that agreements reached within a corporation cannot be made the basis of a § 1 or § 2 claim under the Sherman Act. See L. Schwartz, J. Flynn, & H. First, Free Enterprise and Economic Organization: Antitrust 458–71 (6th ed. 1983). The Court's belief that antitrust risks can only be reconciled with legitimate business reasons for using the parent-subsidiary format and the corporate format generally is the product of analyzing whether a practice restrains trade under the concepts of contract, combination, or conspiracy rather than under the concept of restraint of trade. For a different approach under the Louisiana antitrust law see, Dussouy v. Gulf Coast Investment Corp. 660 F.2d 594 (5th Cir. 1981).

19. For excellent summaries of the Critical Legal Studies (CLS) movement, see generally, D. Kairys (ed.), The Politics of Law (1982); Boyle, The Politics of Reason: Critical Legal Theory and Local Social Thought, 133 U. Penn. L. Rev. 685 (1985); Singer, The Player and the Cards: Nihilism and Legal Theory, 94 Yale L.J. 1 (1984); Gordon, Critical Legal Histories, 36 Stan. L. Rev. 57 (1984); Hutchinson & Monahan, Law, Politics and the Critical Legal Scholars: The Unfolding Drama of American Legal Thought, 36 Stan. L. Rev. 199 (1984); Unger, The Critical Legal Studies Movement, 96 Harv. L. Rev. 649 (1984); White, The Inevitability of Critical Legal Studies, 36 Stan. L. Rev. 649 (1984); Note, 'Round and 'Round the Bramble Bush: From Legal Realism to Critical Legal Scholarship, 95 Harv. L. Rev. 1669 (1982).

20. Unger, supra note 19, at 563 n.1.

21. See White, supra note 19, at 652.

22. For a critique of this position, see Gordon, supra note 19.

23. There are boundaries on the mobility of the words and concepts used in law. The boundaries are derived from popular meaning of the words used and the way in which they are used, the history and purpose of the rule in which the words are used, the overall legal context in which the dispute arose, the role of decision makers in the circumstances, the facts and consequences of the decision, and other rules in the system of law involved. The tension between a functional and definitional role for concepts in legal decision making is an ongoing one and a source of continuing controversy in jurisprudence. Compare Cohen, supra note 11, and Hart, supra note 12, with Ross, Tu-Tu, 70 Harv. L. Rev. 812 (1957). See generally, Simpson, supra note 12.

24. Courts may, of course, be using legal fictions and other devices masking underlying policy choices for a variety of other objectives. For example, the concepts of standing and political question may be devices used to deflect decision making to other branches of government or to forestall deciding the underlying moral conflict involved in a particular

circumstance because the court or society is not yet ready to have the issue decided for institutional or other reasons. These uses of legal concepts are not manipulative or dishonest but a reflection of the necessary and creative use of the legal process in a democratic society by a court sensitive to the limitations of the judicial process. See W. Bishin & C. Stone, Law, Language and Ethics 394–402 (1972).

25. C. Beard and M. Beard, II The Rise of American Civilization 111–13 (1927).

26. See generally, Graham, The Conspiracy Theory of the Fourteenth Amendment, 47 Yale L.J. 371, 48 Yale L.J. 171 (1939).

27. Ibid.

28. The Railroad Tax Cases, 13 Fed. 722, 740 (Cir. Ct. D. Cal. 1882).

29. 13 Fed. at 740, 741, 743, & 744.

30. Field's natural law dissent in the Slaughterhouse Cases, 83 U.S. 36, 118 (1873), became the majority substantive due process standard in subsequent cases.

31. See R. McCloskey, Introduction to C. B. Swisher, Stephen J. Field, Craftsman of the Law (Phoenix Books ed. 1969) where Field is described as "willful," "stubborn," "dogmatic," "independent," "indomitable," "relentless," and "ambitious." McCloskey also notes that Field was not possessed of a subtle mind: "Field's mind was not one given to recognizing that there may be two or even more plausible sides to a question, still less to acknowledging that there may be many gradations between the right and the wrong, the good and the bad. It was a mind that saw truth as a series of broad, unmistakable generalities, and that entertained few doubts." Id. at xii-xiii.

32. Id. at xii.

33. See Sinking Fund Cases, 99 U.S. 700, 750 (1879)(Field, J., dissenting and suggesting that "property" is as sacred as the laws of God). See also the Field dissent in Munn v. Illinois, 94 U.S. 113, 136 (1877); Mendelson, Mr. Justice Field and Laissez-Faire, 36 Virginia L. Rev. 45 (1950). For a scholarly examination of the concept of property in Anglo-American law and the various attributes attributed to it over time, see Cohen, Property and Sovereignty, 13 Cornell L. Rev. 8 (1928).

34. Hamilton, The Path of Due Process of Law, 48 Ethics 269, 294–95 (1938). See also R. Hofstadter, Social Darwinism in American Thought (1955).

35. See Corwin, The Passing of Dual Federalism, 36 Va. L. Rev. 1 (1950). The concept of two distinct and separate sovereigns often resulted in neither being constitutionally capable of regulating the same type of economic activity. Compare Hammer v. Dagenhart, 247 U.S. 251 (1918)(commerce clause does not support federal authority to regulate labor standards of manufacturers) with Adkins v. Children's Hospital, 261 U.S. 525 (1923)(states precluded from enforcing minimum wage legislation because it violates due process).

36. Many of these implications are explored in the writings of Arthur S. Miller. See A. Miller, The Modern Corporate State: Private Governments and the American Constitution (1976); A. Miller, The Supreme Court and American Capitalism (1968). See also R. Nader and M. Green (Eds.), Corporate Power in America (1973); J. Cohen and M. Mintz, America, Inc. (1972); G. Bannock, The Juggernauts: The Age of the Big Corporations (1971).

37. 198 U.S. 45 (1905).

38. 198 U.S. at 59.

39. Id. at 61. The majority opinion provoked Holmes' well-known dissent where he observed: "This case is decided upon an economic theory which a large part of the country does not entertain. . . . The Fourteenth Amendment does not enact Mr. Herbert Spencer's

Social Statics. . . . A constitution is not intended to embody a particular economic theory, whether of paternalism and the organic relationship of the citizen to the State or of "laissez faire." Id. at 75–76.

40. See, e.g., Allgeyer v. Louisiana, 165 U.S. 578 (1897); Adkins v. Children's Hospital, 261 U.S. 525 (1923).

41. See Pound, Liberty of Contract, 18 Yale L.J. 454 (1909); Strong, The Economic Philosophy of Lochner: Emergence, Embrasure and Emasculation, 15 Ariz. L. Rev. 419 (1973).

42. See Adair v. United States, 208 U.S. 161 (1908); Coppage v. Kansas, 236 U.S. 1 (1915).

43. "A category-mistake . . . represents the facts of mental life as if they belonged to one logical type or category (or range of types or categories), when they actually belong to another." G. Ryle, The Concept of Mind 16 (1949).

44. The cases are collected in Mr. Justice Douglas's dissent in Wheeling Steel Corp. v. Glander, 337 U.S. 562, 576 (1949). See also Bell v. State of Maryland, 378 U.S. 226, 242 (1964)(Douglas and Goldberg, concurring).

45. The chronicle of that abandonment is well set forth in McCloskey, Economic Due Process and the Supreme Court: An Exhumation and Reburial, 1962 Sup. Ct. Rev. 34; Strong, supra note 41, at 419.

46. Justice Black's call for a reconsideration of the doctrine in his dissent in Connecticut General Co. v. Johnson, 303 U.S. 77 (1939), during the time that the doctrine of substantive due process was being dismantled, was ignored.

47. 337 U.S. 562 (1949).

48. The other being a dissent by Justice Black in Connecticut General Life Insurance Co. v. Johnson, supra note 46. The Black dissent stressed the history and language of the Fourteenth Amendment, concluding that its purpose was "to protect weak and helpless human beings." Id. at 87. Justice Black also stressed the plain meaning of the language of the amendment, concluding that "person" means a human being. Although the history of the amendment is clearly relevant to—though not necessarily conclusive of—the meaning of the amendment, Justice Black's "plain meaning" argument is significantly less persuasive. While legal language and the concepts it generates borrow from popular meaning, its use in the decision-making process remains primarily functional and not definitional. It is being used to link facts to policy in the light of consequences, a dynamic process that cannot take place when a definition replaces the tool of a functional concept in the process of decision making.

49. 337 U.S. at 578.

50. For an analysis of the process by which legal concepts gain meaning from popular usage, see Ross, Tu-Tu, supra note 23, at 812 (1957). For a criticism of Ross's views as an incomplete explanation, see Simpson, supra note 12.

51. A present-day example of shifts in the meaning of basic concepts is the controversy over abortion. It may appear to be a paradox that at the same time the Court is expanding the civil liberties of corporate persons, it is narrowing the rights of arguably human ones in the form of a fetus. The debate is a deeper and more difficult moral problem involving the concept of personhood for purposes of constitutional analysis: whether a fetus ought to be considered a person for some or all purposes of the Fourteenth Amendment and the scope of the personhood rights that ought to be recognized in pregnant women to control their own bodies and exercise rights of privacy in regard to the power of the state on such matters. Elsewhere I have expressed doubt about the way in which the Court

resolved this most fundamental moral conflict in Roe v. Wade, 410 U.S. 113 (1973). Treating a deep moral issue as a matter of science or the past status of a fetus at common law may be factors contributing to resolution of the conflict, but they should not be used as devices to cause a court to ignore the deeper underlying moral claims being asserted. On the other hand, it is sometimes essential to mask the underlying moral conflict because it is not capable of being resolved in the present circumstance. Masking the resolution of the conflict behind legalisms or the appeal to seemingly absolute sources of truth like science may be necessary to resolve the immediate dispute or nudge the society to reexamine the dimensions of the moral issues involved. See Flynn, Death Before Life: Abortion as a Moral Issue, A Response, 1 J. Contemp. L. 278 (1975).

Concepts like person may also be used as a necessary vehicle by which protection of newly recognized societal interests is incorporated into a constitutional level of protection so long as the moral rationale for doing so is made clear and the decision maker is aware that the concept is being used for a particular end. For an example of the use of the concept of person in this way to achieve safeguards for certain environmental values, see C. Stone, Should Trees Have Standing? (1974).

52. 373 U.S. 226 (1964).

53. 378 U.S. at 245.

54. "The crucial issue . . . is whether the Fourteenth Amendment, of itself, forbids a state to enforce its trespass laws to convict a person who comes into a privately owned restaurant, is told because of his color he will not be served, and over the owner's protest refuses to leave. We think that the question should be decided and that the Fourteenth Amendment does not forbid this application of the State's trespass laws." 378 U.S. 318.

55. Ibid.

56. 378 U.S. 246.

57. Id. at 253, 261–62.

58. Id. at 264–65.

59. Citing Grosjean v. American Press Co., 297 U.S. 233 (1936); New York Times v. Sullivan, 376 U.S. 254 (1964).

60. Citing Hale v. Henkel, 201 U.S. 43 (1906).

61. Citing NAACP v. Alabama, 357 U.S. 449 (1958)(enjoining state effort to compel disclosure of membership lists of civil rights organization).

62. See, e.g., Kelsen, The Pure Theory of Law, 50 L.Q. Rev. 474 (1934).

63. 438 U.S. 234 (1978). See also, Upjohn Co. v. United States, 449 U.S. 383 (1981)(significant expansion of the lawyer-client privilege in the context of the corporation-lawyer relationship without examination of the significance of corporate personhood in relation to human personhood in defining the scope of the privilege for corporations generally).

64. 29 U.S.C. §1001, et seq.

65. 435 U.S. 765 (1978).

66. See L. Tribe, American Constitutional Law 57–58 (1979 Supp.). See also O'Kelley, The Constitutional Rights of Corporations Revisited: Social and Political Expression and the Corporation After First National Bank v. Bellotti, 67 Geo. L. Rev. 1347 (1979).

67. See McCloskey, supra note 45, at 34, 45–50, arguing that certain forms of economic regulation can be just as destructive of civil liberties as direct regulation of civil liberties. I would go further and suggest that there is a basic level of economic freedom necessary to the exercise of political and social freedom. Indeed, fears of corporate power and corporate statism are premised upon such an assumption, as is the populist political

tradition and the antitrust movement. See generally H. Thorelli, The Federal Antitrust Policy—Origination of an American Tradition (1955). Defining the scope of economic freedom is a primary responsibility of the legislative process, which is better able—in normal times—than the courts to make a sensible and informed judgment on the matter.

I believe there are circumstances where the judgment should be made by courts on a constitutional basis. The corporate free press cases are an example. With the growing corruption of the legislative process by corporate, union, and other collectives' political action fund raising (a euphemism for what was once called bribery), there may well be an argument for increased judicial involvement to protect individualism rather than promote collectivism. Paradoxically, the Bellotti decision tilts the balance in favor of the collectives and against the individual by calling into serious question any effort to adopt campaign financing regulation designed to prevent the buying of elective offices. For an attempt to reconcile Bellotti with campaign financing regulations called into doubt by the decision, see O'Kelley, supra note 66, at 1375, et seq. For a thoughtful and wide-ranging examination of what constitutes and ought to constitute bribery in a criminal law sense, see Lowenstein, Political Bribery and the Intermediate Theory of Politics, 32 UCLA L. Rev. 784 (1985).

68. From the perspective of whether the Massachusetts statute promoted an open marketplace of ideas, see Patton and Bartlett, Corporate "Persons" and Freedom of Speech: The Political Impact of Legal Mythology, 1981 Wis. L. Rev. 494 (arguing the result of the decision will be the opposite of what the Court predicted).

69. 435 U.S. at 776.

70. The dissent by Justices White, Brennan, and Marshall asserted the basic purpose of the First Amendment speech clause is to protect the "use of communication as a means of self-expression, self-realization, and self-fulfillment." 435 U.S. at 804. Not surprisingly, the dissent's different view of the policies behind the concept of free speech led to quite a different view about the scope of the concept of corporate personhood and a right claimed in the name of the corporation to free speech.

The majority's marketplace of ideas conception treats speech as a commodity and the regulation of who may engage in producing the commodity as a governmental interference with the functioning of the marketplace for the free exchange of ideas in violation of the political principle of laissez-faire. The invocation of the market concept in a way analogous to the neoclassical economic concept of a market is as superficial and misleading as it is in economics. Reality does not equate with the factual assumptions underlying the model, and the model assumes the existence of a legal system with an existing distribution of rights entitled to protection while purporting to confront the question of what ought to be the rights protected. For a critical analysis of the marketplace approach, see Ingber, The Marketplace of Ideas: A Legitimizing Myth, 1984 Duke L.J. 1. See also M. Tushnet, Corporations and Free Speech, in The Politics of Law: A Progressive Critique 253 (D. Kairys ed. 1982).

71. The majority opinion expressly disclaimed any purpose to determine whether some other circumstance might justify a restriction on the speech of corporations, unions, or similar entities that would not be justified when applied to a natural person. 435 U.S. at 777, note 13.

72. For example: "The referendum issue that appellants wish to address." 435 U.S. at 765; "appellants proposed speech." 435 U.S. at 787. Chief Justice Burger's concurring opinion apparently justified recognition of a corporate speech right because such a right has been recognized for media conglomerates, and Burger could not see any facts that

justify treating media conglomerates differently from other conglomerates. 435 U.S. at 795. The Burger concurrence may be evidence of the use of concepts as rigid definitions rather than tools in the process of legal analysis. While a rose is a rose argument may have merit in some circumstances, it is less than insightful in significant constitutional law analysis. For an example of a rose is a rose type of analysis generating widespread uncertainty and expanding the Court's new substantive due process power to strike down state and federal economic regulation, see Virginia State Board of Pharmacy v. Virginia Citizens Consumer Council, 425 U.S. 748 (1976)(holding commercial advertising to be "speech" within the meaning of the First Amendment).

73. 435 U.S. at 778, note 14. Such an "extreme position" was stated long ago by Mr. Chief Justice John Marshall: "A corporation is an artificial being, intangible, and existing only in contemplation of law. Being the mere creature of law, it possesses only those properties which the charter of creation confers upon it, either expressly, or as incident to its very existence. These are such as are supposed best calculated to effect the object for which it was created." Dartmouth College v. Woodward, 4 Wheat. 518, 636 (1819). Although it may be unrealistic to analyze the modern corporation as a concession from the state or as a chip off the block of state sovereignty, it is equally unrealistic to reject out of hand these and other theories attempting to identify the nature of a corporation. It is also unrealistic to hypostatize the state to such a degree as to believe the state is an independent and antagonistic collective acting as a check on corporate collectives to which it gives birth. State control of corporate collectives through charter restrictions has been generally nonexistent for almost a century. Corporate control of state corporation laws has been a reality for almost as long. See First, Law for Sale: A Study of the Delaware Corporation Law of 1967, 117 U. Pa. L. Rev. 861 (1969). It is particularly unacceptable for a court to dispose of such considerations by simply characterizing them as extreme without explanation or reflection and then ignore them altogether.

74. The problem of defining the degree to which shareholders can be extended rights to control the expenditure of corporate funds for political activities of their corporation is considerably more complex than that allowed by the Court, and the complexity is attributable to the Court's simplistic approach to the issue in Bellotti. See Brudney, Business Corporations and Stockholders' Rights under the First Amendment, 91 Yale L.J. 235 (1981).

75. A. Berle and G. C. Means, The Modern Corporation and Private Property (Rev. ed. 1968).

76. See Hetherington, Fact and Legal Theory: Shareholders, Managers and Corporate Social Responsibility, 21 Stan. L. Rev. 248 (1969); Harbrecht, The Modern Corporation Revisited, 64 Colum. L. Rev. 1410(1964).

77. See J. Flynn, Corporate Democracy: Nice Work If You Can Get It, in Corporate Power in America 94 (R. Nader and M. Green eds. 1972).

78. See Central Hudson Gas & Electric Corp. v. Public Service Comm., 447 U.S. 557 (1980)(use of the Court's newly discovered "commercial speech" doctrine to strike down regulation of public utility bill inserts); Consolidated Edison Co. v. Public Service Comm., 447 U.S. 530 (1980)(ban on political inserts in utility billing envelopes held a violation of corporate First Amendment rights). See also Flynn, Trends in Federal Antitrust Doctrine Suggesting Future Directions for State Antitrust Enforcement, 4 J. Corp. L. 479 (1979), suggesting that the current Court is presiding over a rebirth of substantive due process under a variety of guises, including the recognition of commercial and corporate speech for First Amendment purposes, the narrowing of the state action doctrine

in antitrust, and the use of §1983 of the Civil Rights Act to protect corporate economic interests against discriminatory or unwise (in the Court's view) legislation.

Some have suggested that the Court should revive expressly the doctrine of substantive economic due process in order to protect and promote the neoclassical version of competition. See Wonnell, Economic Due Process and the Preservation of Competition, 11 Hast. Const. L.Q. 91 (1983). The observation that those who fail to learn the lessons of history are condemned to relive them should be considered in evaluating such proposals.

79. See generally J. Hurst, The Legitimacy of the Business Corporation in the Law of the United States—1780–1970 (1970).

80. See Miller, Toward "Constitutionalizing" the Corporation: A Speculative Essay, 80 W. Va. L. Rev. 187 (1978). Efforts to subject private public utilities to constitutional constraints in some of their decisions, on the ground that they are engaged in state action as regulated utilities, have failed. See Jackson v. Metropolitan Edison Co., 419 U.S. 345 (1974). Municipally owned utilities have been held to be subject to federal constitutional constraints under the state action doctrine. See Memphis Light, Gas & Water Div. v. Craft, 436 U.S. 1 (1978). Conceptualizing the class of large public issue corporations wielding economic, political, and social power as governments subject to the constraints of some constitutional values like due process is not as radical as one might think on first glance. Corporations are created by state law, and many of them possess far more power than the states that created them and those that attempt to regulate them. Compared to municipally owned utilities, many private corporations have much greater political, social, and economic power, and that power is growing rapidly after Bellotti.

81. Manning, Shareholder's Appraisal Remedy, 72 Yale L.J. 223, 244 n. 37 (1962).

82. See, e.g., C. Stone, Where the Law Ends: The Social Control of Corporate Behavior (1975).

83. For an example of a functional approach to a problem of corporate law, see Hamilton, The Corporate Entity, 49 Tex. L. Rev. 979 (1971)(circumstances in which court's do and "ought to" pierce the corporate veil).

7

THE PARADOX OF PATERNALISM AND LAISSEZ-FAIRE CONSTITUTIONALISM: THE U.S. SUPREME COURT, 1888–1921

Aviam Soifer

In 1898, the year Americans first sailed forth to fight in other countries to protect purported victims of imperialism, A. V. Dicey steamed into Harvard University to deliver his lectures on law and public opinion in England. Like William Blackstone, Vinerian Professor before him, Dicey deployed a number of memorable epigrams to capture basic truths of his day. Dicey's assertion that "protection invariably involves disability,"[1] in particular, appeared to state the obvious to Americans at the turn of the century.

In this chapter, I will consider how Dicey's epigram pertains to what the U.S. Supreme Court had to say during the tenures of Chief Justices Fuller and Edward White from 1888 to 1921 about the capacity of the individual in the United States to contract and care for himself. Americans need not have read or believed all of Herbert Spencer's *Social Statics*, of course, to fear governmental regulation and to celebrate the autonomy of vigorous, manly citizens free of invidious, paternalistic coddling. There has been considerable recent scholarly debate about the extent of social Darwinism in late-nineteenth-century America. Indeed, David Hollinger quipped, "Social Darwinism can now claim a dubious honor: that it has been shown *not* to have existed in more places than any other movement in the history of social theory."[2] Whatever terminology we choose to use, however,

This chapter is part of a larger project on the Thirteenth Amendment made possible in part by grants from Project '87, cosponsored by the American Historical Association and the American Political Science Association, and by the American Bar Foundation Fellowship in Legal History. A fellowship at the Legal History Workshop at the University of Wisconsin, summer, 1982, was also invaluable. Portions of this chapter were delivered at the 1983 Annual Meeting of the Organization of American Historians. I benefited from the comments of Russell Osgood, Herman Belz, and those in the audience.

I have been lucky for years with research assistants. But Margaret Geary was exceptionally helpful in writing this chapter. I am grateful to her, and to Janice Brown, Lance Cassak, Steve Lincoln, and Anita Mari, as well as to colleagues and friends at Boston University and faculty—particularly Stanley Kutler and Willard Hurst—and fellow Fellows at the University of Wisconsin.

legal materials from the period from the 1880s into the 1920s suggest that combating paternalism was a core concern among judges and lawyers. It may usefully be seen as an appealing surrogate for more explicit social Darwinistic rhetoric.[3]

As Charles Sanders Peirce put it, in an age pervaded by a "dominant gospel of greed," people "seemed to relish a ruthless theory."[4] The great race of life, premised somehow on the notion of an equal start, continued to have great appeal as a fundamental American image. The tendency to harden this egalitiarian image into ruthlessness gained strength from innumerable mutually enforcing influences, including bedrock Calvinist values; Ben Franklin–like homilies; Oliver Wendell Holmes, Jr.'s bitter deference to the cosmos; and the muscular Christianity of the period, which promoted the quest for manliness and godliness in the gymnasium, on distant battlefields, and within legal and economic combat.

A generation ago, Robert McCloskey suggested that during this era, "the major value of the Court . . . was the protection of the business community against government."[5] This still seems generally accurate today, even if we recall what Charles Beard used to tell his students: the historian's "best equipment" is to remember that the "very opposite of accepted faith may be true."[6] There is a generational pattern, of course, to today's revisions of revisionists; now scholars search for order in the period roughly from 1880 to 1920, and some profess little faith that we would know a Progressive or a robber baron if we saw one.[7]

The largely unexplored legal doctrine of the period provided the trellis on which influential lawyers and judges domesticated a thorny legal hybrid of Adam Smith and Herbert Spencer. Justices such as Field, Brewer, and Peckham enthusiastically went about breeding an American Beauty rooted firmly in first principles they announced they had discovered in the U.S. Constitution. Grant Gilmore's observation that "the few people . . . who have ever spent time studying the judicial product of the period have been appalled by what they found"[8] is an intriguing challenge in itself. A sampling of judicial decisions involving protection of those deemed unfit shows why the justices were caught in a bind of their own creation, forced to perform gymnastic feats to find and hold the line between the legal spheres they claimed they were obliged to separate. The paradox of paternalism may fill some of the void left by the shrinking of the orthodox view of laissez-faire constitutionalism.

In focusing on the Court from 1888 to 1921, I do not seek to demonstrate again that there is and always has been a chasm between law in books and law in action. Nor do I make any claim that paternalism was a new problem when Fuller succeeded Waite or a problem that had been resolved in 1921 when Howard Taft took the enlarged seat he coveted at the center of the Court. My thesis is that under the guise of a formalistic, unitary vision of categories such as individual autonomy and citizenship, the justices subdivided and manipulated legal doctrine in a way that arrogated tremendous discretionary power to themselves. In proclaiming both their authority and their ability to distinguish between people as individuals and as members of groups, the judicial brethren became the paternalistic patriarchs. It is revealing to consider to what extent those already on top benefited and those on or near the bottom suffered as a result of the process through which justices made their choices.

The justices manipulated the deductive pretensions of their categorical approach in several ways. As the courts aggressively protected the interests of corporations, which the justices proclaimed to have equal rights as persons, they acted paternalistically toward others, such as women, Indians, and sailors, whose claims for equal treatment they viewed as contrary to the natural order. Simultaneously, the Court disabled some citizens, such as blacks, by approaching their claims with extreme arms-length formality while declaring that black men already had achieved full legal equality.

Lochner v. New York,[9] nearly always invoked to categorize the entire era, is still shorthand in constitutional law for the worst sins of subjective judicial activism.[10] I will not fully rehearse the ways in which *Lochner* itself may have been anomalous.[11] But I am interested in the concept of autonomous individualism inherent in the notion of liberty of contract at stake in *Lochner*, that legal idea affords a means to examine how true the Court was to prevailing laissez-faire principles.[12]

Robert Gordon recently noted that Americans came to be "obsessively judge-centered"[13] in the late nineteenth century. I will explore a few elements of what that obsession might have entailed. The U.S. Supreme Court played only one part in the story, of course. The highest state courts generally competed with one another for the starkest application of freedom of contract and the truest belief in laissez-faire ideology. Unquestionably, state court decisions probably had the most immediate impact and did much to shape public consciousness about legal doctrine. Decisions such as those invalidating legislative interventions in aid of victims of fires and floods as overly paternalistic joined other holdings striking down legislative coddling such as aid to the blind, competitive merit scholarships for a state university, and standardized scales and scrip laws for miners and factory workers. There is something to Charles Warren's assertion, after he surveyed all the U.S. Supreme Court's decisions about state police powers from 1887 to 1911, that "the National Supreme Court, so far from being reactionary, has been steady and consistent in upholding all state legislation of a progressive type."[14] Moreover, we cannot know if, had they been polled, nearly all Americans—or even nearly all native-born, white male Americans—enthusiastically would have endorsed particular Supreme Court decisions or even the general pattern of such decisions.[15]

My claim is narrower and necessarily more impressionistic. In pursuit of an element of the mentalité or consciousness of legal opinion makers who gained professional ascendancy from the Gilded Age into the early Jazz Age—men from a cohort sharply reduced in numbers by the Civil War and perhaps hardened by it as well—I will consider the legal construct of the autonomous individual by focusing on judicial decisions that added to or subtracted from that legal fiction. The justices' mathematical machinations allowed them to become the nation's ultimate paternalists even as they devoted themselves tenaciously to rooting out paternalism whenever they perceived it.

In considering efforts to restrict what judges viewed as debilitating paternalism, masquerading as protection, I will use the following as a definition of paternalism: a decision made by someone for someone else, allegedly for the latter's own good. Paternalism relates directly to Dicey's formulation. Can one have protective legal intervention without making some statement about the disability of purported beneficiaries? To the modern eye, to even a mediocre anagrams player, there is an obvious connection between the loathed concept paternalism and the more neutral, if not positive, notion of parentalism. Yet *paternalism* remains one of our most powerful pejoratives.

Several themes emerge from scrutiny of a series of relatively obscure Supreme Court decisions handed down when laissez-faire thought was dominant. I will respond briefly to recent legal history revisionists as I examine the breakdown of the notion of unified U.S. citizenship. Then, confining my discussion largely to enforcement of contracts through a focus on Thirteenth Amendment challenges, I will explore what judges seem to have meant by individual freedom. Finally, I wish to argue that paternalism provided a convenient, almost infinitely distensible target: it enabled the justices to bull their way through complexities in order to constitutionalize their antipaternalistic notions and to act as if their ideas had been deduced from some deep structure of constitutional liberty.

In recent years, historians have begun to focus on the elusive concept of paternalism, largely but not exclusively in the context of slavery.[16] But the manipulability of the paternalism concept in constitutional law after the end of Reconstruction and the paradoxical results of such manipulation remain largely unexplored. A series of snapshots taken from Supreme Court decisions about the Thirteenth Amendment involves black people, but the cast of characters is more varied. In fact, it is reminiscent of *Peter Pan*.[17] Sailors, Indians, and others often considered eternal children found themselves before the Supreme Court in Thirteenth Amendment disputes.

SETTING THE STAGE

When lame duck President Grover Cleveland nominated Melville W. Fuller as chief justice in 1888, Fuller faced vigorous opposition from Republican senators who feared for the fruits of the Civil war victory under the constitutional guardianship of "disloyalists" like Fuller.[18] But Fuller had the advantage of being the "most obscure man ever appointed chief justice."[19] Moreover, he seemed quite safe on the issue of paternalism. In a book review for Chicago's fledgling literary magazine, the *Dial*, Fuller had written, "Paternalism, with its constant intermeddling with individual freedom, has no place in a system which rests for its strength upon the self-reliant energies of the people."[20] This widely shared, if not hackneyed, sentiment coincided with the views of Cleveland and most other Democrats; it was also not far removed from the proclamations of many Republicans.[21]

The legal harvest of Civil War reform in constitutional amendments and statutes basically had been lost already, however, in a remarkable string of Supreme Court decisions either invalidating or narrowing to the point of oblivion the constitutional commands and statutory protections enacted during the first decade after the war.[22] In the 1883 *Civil Rights Cases*, the Supreme Court declared that black citizens already had shaken off the effects of slavery, noting that their progress was now such that they should "take the rank of a mere citizen" and cease to be the "special favorites of the law."[23] By the time Fuller reached the bench, the Court had declared that corporations also were to enjoy fourteenth amendment protection.[24] Thus whites, blacks, and corporations were considered self-sufficent equals before the law. Judges would ensure formal equality; no favoritism would be allowed; class legislation was unconstitutional.[25] Paternalism, a most insidious sort of favoritism, was anathema.

In 1888, therefore, U.S. citizenship appeared to be a clear concept. There were exceptions, of course, such as Indians.[26] Moreover, distinctions between civil and political rights explained why female citizens could be treated differently in certain spheres.[27] Social rights constituted still another realm, a realm government could not enter.[28] Yet contemporary descriptions by late-nineteenth-century Americans, inextricably linked and often equated citizenship and self-sufficiency, manhood and individualism.

Despite a common assumption that Congress was almost moribund during the last quarter of the nineteenth century, Fuller and his colleagues often confronted claims involving federal legislation, enacted despite frequent congressional deadlocks produced by evenly matched, loyal party alignments, antiquated rules, and the waning of reform impulses following the panic of 1873 and the compromise of 1877. Still more legislative activity took place on the state level.[29] This increase in legislation combined with other factors to undermine the monochromatic vision of citizenship. Yet the idealized American citizen, able to care for himself, remained a pervasive image.

In 1889, Lord Bryce reported in the *American Commonwealth* that "so far as there can be said to be any theory on the subject in a land which gets on without theories, *laissez aller* is the orthodox and accepted doctrine in the sphere of Federal and State legislation."[30] Yet Bryce emphasized the total inaccuracy of this theory. He wrote, "Nevertheless the belief is groundless. The new democracies of America are just as eager for state interference as the democracy of England, and try their experiments with even more light-hearted promptitude."[31] Though in many respects Americans tolerated legislative interference with their personal autonomy more than did their English counterparts, Bryce observed that "few but lawyers and economists have yet become aware of it, and the lamentations with which old-fashioned English thinkers accompany the march of legislation are in America scarcely heard and wholly unheeded."[32] But

American judges were poised to listen, to hear, and to react to their own lamentations and to do so with authority and an American accent.

We now know that there was a large gap between lawyerly exhortations to avoid paternalism and the willingness of judges to resist legislative interventions on behalf of the citizenry. Moreover, the most striking pronouncements invalidating protective legislation were concentrated in state courts.[33] Recent scholarship suggests that even Justice Field occasionally rejected laissez-faire in the 1880s and 1890s and that Justice David Brewer was not such a totally doctrinaire fellow after all.[34] We also have begun to recognize that realist roots can be found even within the bedrock of high formalism; it also now appears that even a prophetic iconoclast such as Justice Oliver Wendell Holmes, Jr., had his formalistic movements.[35]

So many judges wrote so vigorously on the imminent danger of the loss of American individualism and the evils of rampant paternalism from the Gilded Age through the 1920s that it is hard to choose the best illustration. My favorite is a West Virginia Supreme Court decision, State v. Goodwill,[36] invalidating a state law that required mine and factory owners to pay workers in legal currency rather than scrip. This statutory interference with the poor man's patrimony, his right to choose how to contract for his own labor, was held to violate the "essential distinction between freedom and slavery; between liberty and oppression."[37] This preoccupation with slavery, combined with the assumption of a clear-cut binary choice between slavery and freedom, is typical of the period.[38] Moreover, according to the court's president, Judge Snyder, such "sumptuary legislation" had been "universally condemned" and recognized as "an attempt to degrade the intelligence, virtue, and manhood of the American laborer, and foist upon the people a paternal government of the most objectionable character, because it assumes that the employer is a knave, and the laborer an imbecile."[39] Such regulation interfered with the "natural law of supply and demand," Snyder asserted, and was an effort to have the government "do for its people what they can do for themselves."[40]

The U.S. Supreme Court never went quite as far as the West Virginia court in denouncing legislative efforts to protect the populace. Even the well-known statements by Justice Brewer, for example, who wrote, "The paternal theory of government is to me odious" and that "Edward Bellamy's Looking Backward was in fact nearer than a dream," tended to be in dissent.[41] The more dramatic exclamations by the justices usually were delivered in speeches off the bench.[42] But in the relatively obscure decisions I will consider, Brewer and his fellow justices did a great deal in their reasoning and their results to suggest that there is something to the stereotyped view of the Supreme Court as a bastion of laissez-faire ideology.[43]

Two forgotten 1890 decisions provide a good introduction to the Fuller Court's inconsistency between its proclamations and its actions concerning paternalism. In opinions written by Brewer, a unanimous Court upheld two convictions for desertion from the army. One case involved someone too young to enlist and the other a man too old. Brewer argued that a contract to join the army changed an individual's status and that his new status became irreversible.[44] In *In re Morrissey*, a habeas corpus petition alleged that a 17-year-old enlisted without his mother's consent, though her consent clearly was required by federal statute. Brewer reasoned that the statutory provision was "for the benefit of the parent" and that therefore "the statute simply gives no privilege to the minor."[45] In *In re Grimley*, Brewer reversed two lower courts that had granted habeas relief to a 40-year-old Irish immigrant who never actually served in the army and who enlisted without appropriate procedures but who still faced a six-month sentence for desertion.[46] Grimley was well over the statutory age maximum when he enlisted, and he had immediately changed his mind about the army in response to entreaties from his grief-stricken mother. Brewer answered with a revealing hypothetical from the formal law of contract he found "worthy of notice."[47] Suppose a "B," Brewer argued, who had lied about his identity in order to contract with "A," after A advertised for a "person of Anglo-Saxon descent."[48] It was obvious and analogous, said Brewer, that "where a party is *sui juris*, without any disability to enter into the new relation,"[49] his contract for enlistment became a one-way street, benefiting the government. Therefore neither B, who lied about his race in Brewer's hypothetical, nor poor old Grimley could revoke.

Once the parties agreed to a contract, iron legal rules assured enforcement. The *Grimley* and *Morrissey* decisions were not much noticed. Yet these interstitial pronouncements are illuminating and quite consistent with laissez-faire values even as they demonstrate the familiar but odd connection between reverence for individual autonomy and great deference accorded both to the objective legitimacy of legal rules and to the power of the military arm of the federal government.

Some of the most striking decisions of the Fuller Court comport with this formalistic approach. In upholding the exclusion of Chinese aliens, for example, despite obvious abrogation of treaty obligations and blatant procedural abuses, the Court explicitly accorded Congress unbounded power.[50] Similarly, Justice Brewer invoked the broadest kind of inherent federal power to meet the "duty to secure rights to all citizens" in validating President Cleveland's use of "the strong arm" of federal troops to put down the Pullman strike of 1894.[51] It was Justice Peckham who stretched inherent national power to the point that it supported the president's authority to condemn private property in order to preserve the Gettysburg battlefield.[52] And within three years of its restrictive decision in *United States v. E. C. Knight Co.*,[53] the Court referred to the notions of inherent power and obligation derived from morality and honor to sustain congressional power to pay price supports for sugar.[54]

The Court was far less bold in its construction of the Thirteenth Amendment and in its interpretation of federal power in statutes premised upon the enforcement section of that amendment. Explanations given by the Court pertain directly to consideration of whether protection inevitably involves disability.

PATERNAL CONSIDERATION: ACTION AND INACTION

Before I consider Thirteenth Amendment challenges to draconian enforcement of contract law in cases not explicitly concerned with race, several aspects of *Plessy v. Ferguson*[55] merit consideration. These generally are overlooked amid outrage at the equal protection language and holding in *Plessy* that legitimized deference to racial classifications.

Homer Plessy also attacked Louisiana's law separating the races on streetcars because, he claimed, that law imposed a badge of slavery forbidden by the Thirteenth Amendment. Rejecting his claim, Justice Henry B. Brown explained that any stigma involved was entirely in the eyes of the beholder. Brown also asserted that it was "too clear for argument" that the Thirteenth Amendment abolished nothing but slavery, bondage, and at least the "control of the labor and services of one man for the benefit of another, and the absence of a legal right to the disposal of his own person, property and services."[56] This definition of servitude might be expanded or contracted in future decisions. But it is noteworthy that even in *Plessy*, the Court appeared to concede that the Thirteenth Amendment could forbid at least some coercive labor contracts.

Moreover, in explaining why the Fourteenth Amendment's goal—"undoubtedly to enforce the absolute equality of the two races before the law"[57]—did not reach segregated public transportation, Brown may well have relished the opportunity to invoke a famous Massachusetts decision by Chief Justice Lemuel Shaw. Born in Massachusetts himself, Brown explained that *Roberts v. City of Boston*[58] came from a state "where the political rights of the colored race have been longest and most earnestly endorsed."[59] Yet Shaw had written:

But, when this great principle [of equal protection] comes to be applied to the actual and various conditions of persons in society, it will not warrant the assertion, that men and women are legally clothed with the same civil and political powers, and that children and adults are legally to have the same functions and be subject to the same treatment; but only that the rights of all, as they are settled and regulated by law, are *equally entitled to the paternal consideration and protection of the law for their maintenance and security.*[60]

It is likely that the *Plessy* majority neither detected any irony in, nor intended to affirm, Shaw's sentiment that the "rights of all" are "equally entitled to paternal consideration." Yet C. Vann Woodward may not have exaggerated when he termed the bridge between the opinions of Shaw and Brown the "most fascinating paradox in American jurisprudence."[61] For our purposes, that paradox connects Shaw's apparent endorsement of paternalism and Brown's abhorrence of the possible use of federal constitutional principles against folkways.

Robertson v. Baldwin: Protecting Sailors

Within a year of *Plessy*, in another case involving the Thirteenth Amendment, Brown again wrote for the Court over a vigorous dissent by John M. Harlan.

In *Robertson v. Baldwin*,[62] three white seamen challenged an 1872 federal statute that allowed them to be detained for deserting ship and for not following orders.[63] From the "somewhat meager"[64] record, it appeared that the men signed shipping orders for an overseas voyage of uncertain destination. When they abandoned ship, they were imprisoned for sixteen days by an Oregon justice of the peace until the *Arago* was again ready to sail. Then, when the trio refused an order to "turn," the three were charged with refusing to work and were imprisoned by a federal marshal in San Francisco.

Seeking release through habeas corpus, the seamen claimed that the two periods of confinement amounted to enforcement of involuntary servitude. The Court's holding was that the seamen, who voluntarily signed shipping orders, could not complain that their service had become involuntary. The Thirteenth Amendment did not interfere with an individual's freedom to "contract for the surrender of his personal liberty for a definite time and for a recognized purpose,"[65] even if it meant subordinating his will. Brown used a vast array of historical sources—a veritable tour de force of the worst kind of law office history—to prove that imprisonment was merely a modern example of the time-honored legal tradition of protecting sailors from themselves. Brown explained this ancient, abiding paternalistic commitment as follows:

Seamen are treated by Congress . . . as deficient in that full and intelligent responsibility for their acts which is accredited to ordinary adults, and as needing the protection of the law in the same sense in which minors and wards are entitled to the protection of their parents and guardians.[66]

In fact, Brown went so far as to assert that "the ancient characterization of seamen as 'wards of admiralty' is even more accurate now than it was formerly."[67]

Still, Brown did not reach the extreme position of Solicitor General Holmes Conrad, who argued that, like soldiers, seamen "cease to be independent, separate and distinct beings"[68] once they contract for service. They change their status, he asserted, and became mere "integers" and "parts of a machine."[69] Yet Brown chose to celebrate the 1872 amendments that added imprisonment to the 1790 Seaman's Act; he considered them provisions designed to protect seamen "as far as possible, against the consequences of their own ignorance and improvidence."[70]

In his scathing dissent, Harlan foresaw advertisements for fugitive seamen replicating those for fugitive slaves. He dismissed Brown's historical citations as products of earlier times "when no account was taken of man as man."[71] Harlan said the Thirteenth Amendment forbade any compulsion to serve another in private business. He agreed that seamen were generally ignorant and improvident but argued that this compelled increased solicitude by courts. Harlan sharply rejected the idea that protecting seamen could include the use of force to compel seamen to render personal service.[72]

Indian Wards

American Indians traditionally constituted a special case for paternalism. The crux of the reservation Indian problem was, according to Harvard Law School's James Bradley Thayer, that Indians were "A People without Law."[73]

In two *Atlantic Monthly* articles in 1891, Thayer provided a compelling review of abuses and misconceived attempts at Indian aid. He stressed that the federal government now owed an affirmative duty to the Indians, to the extent that the "mere neglect or refusal to act is itself action, and action of the worst kind."[74]

The Supreme Court had acknowledged the mess Thayer described even before Fuller arrived. In *United States v. Kagama* (1886), for example, Justice Gray emphasized the extreme dependence of Indian tribes on the federal government, the problem of local hostility, and the great extent to which the "very weakness and helplessness" of the Indians was itself "due to the course of dealing of the federal government with them."[75]

The Fuller and White courts wrestled and lost many bouts with the need to define the "duty of protection" endorsed by Thayer and Gray. Matters were complicated by the Dawes Severality Act of 1887, which was premised on the assumption that in their tribal units, the Indians lacked the "selfishness which is at the bottom of civilization."[76]

The Severalty Act attempted to use Congress's absolute control over Indian affairs to force individual property holding by breaking up the tribes and allotting their land to be held in trust by the federal government. It produced dozens of Supreme Court decisions further clouding the issue of Indian status. The Court often changed direction, in part because the justices struggled constantly to maintain a vision of completely separate spheres of state and federal sovereignty.[77]

The only Indian case I have found that raised a Thirteenth Amendment claim, however, was *United States v. Choctaw Nation*.[78] This strange controversy was the culmination of forty years of dispute among the federal government, several tribes, and their former black slaves. The Choctaw and Chickasaw joined the Confederate side in the Civil War. When the tribes signed treaties with the federal government in 1866, they agreed not only to free their slaves but also to give them the option of being adopted and thereby of sharing the rights of tribe members, including suffrage and 40 acres of land each. The United States was to hold $300,000 in trust and to subtract payments to freed slaves who opted to leave the reservations rather than to join the tribes.

The Choctaw themselves had been before the Court in 1886, arguing that a formal release they signed purportedly waiving federal treaty obligations that dated from Andrew Jackson's presidency could not be binding since the Choctaw signed under the duress of dire necessity. When plaintiffs' attorney Samuel Shellabarger cited several Supreme Court decisions to support the idea that, under such circumstances, legal formalities would yield to equitable considerations,[79] the federal government's brief responded that forcing the Indians to remove across the Mississippi in violation of the earlier agreement was not prompted by "lust of territory but a sincere desire to accomplish what was best for the Indian and the white man, by eliminating the disturbing element that *would* live in savagery, and planting it where it would be untrammeled by even the proximity of civilization, neither molesting nor being molested."[80]

In deciding that 1886 case, the Supreme Court noted that the relation of the federal government to the Choctaw was "that between a superior and inferior, whereby the latter is placed under the care and control of the former."[81] The United States owed Indians "care and protection." Accordingly, the Court abjured the "technical rules" that would use the release the Indians signed to defeat their claims and relied instead on "that larger reason which constitutes the spirit of the law of nations."[82]

In 1904, former black slaves and their descendants were before the Court, trying to hold the Choctaws to treaty obligations. The federal government took the side of the blacks but sought only to purchase land for them with the $300,000 and did not claim that the United States had fulfilled its part of the treaty.

In a brief opinion for a unanimous Court, Justice Joseph McKenna held that the tribes need not offer the adoption option. The Court readily agreed to the freedmen's claim that the Emancipation Proclamation and the Thirteenth Amendment freed them and gave them "all the rights of freedmen."[83] But, McKenna asked, "What is its consequence?"[84] The Court thought the obvious answer was "certainly not to invest the freedmen with any rights in the property, or to participate in the affairs, of their former owners."[85] Replying to the freedmen's fallback claim to the $300,000 trust fund, the Court stated that the fund was only for those freedmen who left the tribe, and none had done so. Although neither the Indians nor the United States had obeyed the treaty, the freedmen had no rights beyond formal emancipation from slavery.

This result seems to illustrate rule-boundedness run riot. It is almost a parody. Because no one followed the rules, the Court reasoned, the blacks who were least well off necessarily should be left in that position. No other rules could be found. If the freedmen wished a different result, they should have used the appropriate legal forms. As a constitutional matter, in the context of broken promises all around, the "declaration of universal freedom"[86] proclaimed by the Thirteenth Amendment was interpreted to mean freedom only from formal, coercive bondage.

THE PERILS OF FULL CITIZENSHIP: CONTRACTS AND PEONAGE

Black citizens soon received this message of a restrictive interpretation of the Thirteenth Amendment even more emphatically. Unlike Indians, who occupied a kind of never-never land as permanent wards of the government, blacks were formally full legal citizens. They were often told they should use democratic processes to change things if they wished, and they should not expect the Court to intervene.[87]

Despite decisions gutting Reconstruction statutes in the 1870s and 1880s and actions by Congress to repeal most surviving statutes in 1894, several criminal peonage statutes remained. Prosecutions based on these statutes, premised on Thirteenth Amendment power, suddenly sprang up around 1900 in the volatile southern political climate accompanying the rise of the single-party system. The story is told well elsewhere,[88] and I will mention only briefly the Supreme Court's manipulation of Thirteenth Amendment doctrine in 1905–1906, narrowing the criminal peonage statute to such a fine point that even had prosecutors been angelic, they could hardly dance their prosecutorial dances upon it.

In *Clyatt v. United States*,[89] the Court invalidated one of the few successful peonage prosecutions. Justice Brewer upset the conviction of a brutal white overseer in the southern Georgia and Florida turpentine farms. Although unwilling to accept the extreme states' rights construction of the Thirteenth Amendment advanced by Senator Augustus Bacon (D., Ga.) and Congressman William Brantley (D., Ga.) on behalf of the defendants, the Court refused to define peonage more broadly than as a "status or condition of compulsory service, based upon the indebtedness of the peon to the master."[90] Brewer emphasized that debt was the necessary "basal" condition.[91] Although one might contract to become a peon voluntarily, Brewer conceded, "a clear distinction exists between peonage and the voluntary performance of labor or rendering services in payment of a debt."[92] Justice Harlan, dissenting, found it "going very far" in a case "disclosing barbarities of the worst kind against these negroes"[93] to hold that the trial court erred in letting the case go to the jury.

Clyatt was a clear "go slow" message to the prosecutors, judges, and victims trying to reform the southern peonage system. Though the Supreme Court was unwilling to abrogate the Thirteenth Amendment entirely, as the construction proposed by Clyatt's lawyers had suggested, the call for restraint in Clyatt grew louder the following term in *Hodges v. United States*.[94]

Hodges and two codefendants were convicted and sentenced to the statutory maximum for their role in a mob effort to intimidate eight blacks into leaving their jobs at an Arkansas lumber mill. Brewer again wrote for the Court, but now he embraced a strong states' rights argument and merged it with the notion that the Thirteenth Amendment was "not an attempt to commit [blacks] to the care of the Nation."[95] Rejecting the argument that harassment of black workers was a badge or vestige of slavery, Brewer remanded them to Arkansas law for redress. To do otherwise, Brewer stated, would be to treat blacks as "wards of the Nation."[96] Such a paternalistic approach was rejected, he explained, because at the end of the Civil War, Congress decided to grant blacks citizenship on the assumption that "thereby in the long run their best interests would be subserved, they taking their chances with other citizens in the States where they should make their homes."[97]

This construction of the Civil War amendments was a stark proclamation of the "equal chance in the race of life" approach. It flowed naturally from the Court's distaste for national government intervention. It also reflected the Court's failure to take account of the brutal facts emerging from studies and muckraking articles about the labor system in the South. Once again Justice Harlan wrote in dissent to argue the inconsistency in the Court's announced belief in the liberty of contract. He pointed to the anomaly of ignoring the pleas for "national protection" by "millions of citizen-laborers of African descent,"[98] who were denied what he viewed as their right to earn a lawful living solely because of their race. This failure to protect, Harlan proclaimed, betrayed the Thirteenth Amendment promise, which "destroyed slavery and all its incidents and badges, and established freedom"[99] and had an "affirmative operation the moment it was adopted."[100]

The *Hodges* decision is less well known than *Clyatt* and the *Bailey v. Alabama*[101] decision that followed. But Hodges provides a clear demonstration of the paradox of paternalism. In the majority's view, to give blacks the special protection of national laws was to treat them as wards and, in the long run, to undermine their chances of successful competition with all other citizens. Notions of federalism entered the equation, of course, but the Court's central thrust was to sustain an ideal form of unified citizenship and to command formal equality for all. In opposing this position, Harlan took something of a realist's view of the social and political position of blacks. He claimed, in effect, that blacks could and should be treated as special. Ironically, Harlan's *Hodges* dissent also rested firmly on the very precedents that allowed the Court to "Lochnerize" on behalf of a particular judicial vision of freedom of contract.

Within the next few years, the Court's majorities showed some willingness to limit the *Lochner* approach. The best-known example was *Muller v. Oregon*,[102] upholding Oregon's limitation of the number of hours women could work in laundries. *Muller* is famous for the Court's nod toward the facts marshaled by Louis D. Brandeis and June Goldmark in a brief in defense of the statute, but it more recently has become something of a target in debates over sex discrimination. Justice Brewer's majority opinion rested on factual assumptions that women were naturally "at a disadvantage in the race for subsistence" and therefore "not upon an equality" with men.[103] To Brewer and the rest of the majority, it was natural to treat women paternalistically. Unlike blacks, women were not to be considered equals in life's natural struggles.

Muller's legally permissible paternalism by a state contrasted sharply with several contemporaneous holdings severely limiting the power of Congress to regulate employment relationships.[104] The Court also sent back to the lower court an attempt by a group of progressives, covertly backed by Booker T. Washington, to challenge Alabama's farm labor system.[105]

When this case, *Bailey v. Alabama*, returned to the Supreme Court in 1911, Bailey's claim of involuntary servitude directly posed the question of how far the Thirteenth Amendment might go to invalidate a contract that appeared to have been entered into voluntarily. In other words, did the federal Constitution restrict the power of a state to enforce contracts?

Bailey was portrayed as a "mere pawn" in the reformers' challenge to criminal convictions for breach of a year-long $12 per month labor contract. Ray Stannard Baker publicized the "unmistakable marks of ignorance, inertia, irresponsibility" in Bailey's "dull black face," yet Baker also celebrated Bailey's victory as "another bar . . . placed in the way of the strong white man who would take advantage of the weaker colored man."[106]

To Justice Hughes, who wrote for the majority in one of his first Supreme Court opinions, Alabama's presumption of criminal fraud in a breach of contract and its law limiting the defendant's ability to testify about his intent at the time he agreed to the contract furnished an "instrument of compulsion, particularly effective as against the poor and ignorant, its most likely victims."[107] Because the Thirteenth Amendment "was a charter of universal civil freedom for all persons, of whatever race, color or estate, under the flag,"[108] it invalidated Alabama's attempt to enforce labor contracts in this way. Hughes stated that the amendment prohibited all "control by which the personal service of one man is disposed of or coerced for another's benefit."[109]

Hughes began his opinion by insisting that the defendant's race was irrelevant, as was the fact that the contract was made in a southern state. Hughes also said he was unwilling to impute any oppressive intent to anyone in the case. Nevertheless, Alabama's enforcement scheme would make a barren thesis out of "freedom of labor upon which alone can enduring prosperity be based."[110] It was therefore invalid.

Holmes, who had not approved of earlier constitutional freedom of contract claims, saw the majority opinion as an encroachment on the power of states to enforce contracts effectively. "The Thirteenth Amendment does not outlaw contracts for labor,"[111] he proclaimed. In fact, Holmes suggested Alabama's scheme actually might aid the laborer, who would suffer because removing the enforcement mechanism would limit the terms of the bargain a laborer like Bailey could make. Holmes summarized his position as follows:

Breach of a legal contract without excuse is wrong conduct, even if the contract is for labor, and if a State adds to civil liability a criminal liability to fine, it simply intensifies the legal motive for doing right, it does not make the laborer a slave.[112]

He accused the majority of tacitly assuming that Alabama juries would be prejudiced. To the contrary, Holmes suggested, fair juries would sometimes acquit; it was perfectly appropriate for Alabama to leave ambiguous decisions to juries since "their experience as men of the world"[113] might have taught them that laborers frequently accept advances, work for part of the season, and then go off to other plantations seeking better wages.

In a sense, Hughes and Holmes agreed that individual freedom of contract was a paramount value. Their vigorous debate was over the permissible degree of government intervention.[114] Hughes viewed the Thirteenth Amendment as an "overdrive," so that both government and individual power over another individual were limited by it. Holmes was much more the formalist, willing to suppose that Alabama juries would be fair and that deference was due the legislature. Hughes adopted a pose of not looking behind the formal categories of the law, but he could not avoid seeing "poor and ignorant farm workers"[115] in need of the Court's protection, no matter what contracts they might have signed. In a sense, while alleging belief in freedom of labor, Hughes joined Ray Stannard Baker in a directly paternalistic effort to ensure that the Constitution would protect farm laborers from themselves, at least insofar as they signed year-long contracts from which no real escape was possible. Holmes rejected such paternalism and argued that economics explained how Alabama's enforcement scheme actually could benefit farm laborers.

The Court soon extended its *Bailey* holding to the pervasive, vicious criminal surety system. *United States v. Reynolds*[116] was a carefully arranged test prosecution that challenged an Alabama law allowing employers to pay the fines of people convicted of crimes and then to keep them working until fines and costs were repaid. Alabama defended the system as a humane alternative to the chain gang. The state also alleged the added benefit of leaving the convict free to choose for himself whether he wanted to take part.[117]

The Supreme Court did not find these humanitarian arguments convincing. In fact, Justice William Day noted for a unanimous Court that the "convict is kept chained to an ever-turning wheel of servitude."[118] Because the convict's service was owed to private parties and not to the state, the Thirteenth Amendment applied. In a revealing concurrence, Holmes repeated his objections to the *Bailey* decision but went on to say: "But impulsive people with little intelligence or foresight may be expected to lay hold of anything that affords a relief from present pain even though it will cause greater trouble by and by."[119] Given this willingness to generalize about an unspecific but obvious class of people unable to endure pain or delay gratification adequately, in his view, Holmes could agree that the "inevitable" and "contemplated" outcome of the Alabama laws should be invalidated.[120]

Even the unanimous *Reynolds* decision demonstrated that it was difficult for the Court to determine when an individual's freedom to contract might actually be so constricted as to allow intervention to regulate that freedom. Within a year, the Court extended the *Adair* decision and the Lochner approach to the states in *Coppage v. Kansas*,[121] invalidating Kansas's ban on antiunion, yellow dog labor contracts. Freedom of contract remained sufficiently vital to disallow intervention in labor-management affairs, particularly when the state's policy suggested redistribution of wealth or power. Legislation would be struck down as paternalistic when it was perceived to interfere overly with equality of exploitation.

THE THIRTEENTH AMENDMENT TAKES A HOLIDAY

Thirteenth Amendment challenges to involuntary servitude reached the Court several more times while White was chief justice. In the first two cases, individuals challenged traditional forms of forced labor. But the Court had little difficulty in affirming Florida's power to use its criminal law to force people who were unable to hire substitutes to work on road crews.[122] Then, against a background of war fever and anti-German hysteria, the Court disposed of a Thirteenth Amendment challenge to the World War I draft in a single paragraph; White scoffed at the idea of constitutional doubt about the government's power to compel military service.[123]

At the close of the Fuller-White era, it was fitting that property owners were the final litigants to invoke the Thirteenth Amendment. They did so in a broad attack on post–World War I rent control provisions in New York City.[124] The landlords failed to convince the Court that rent control—and the requirement that they supply heat and water without being able to raise the rent—constituted a badge or incident of servitude.

In majority opinions in two companion cases,[125] Justice Holmes noted that emergency housing shortages were a "publicly notorious and almost world-wide fact." Holmes's attention to facts differed from his focus in *Bailey* perhaps, as some suggested, because he had begun to fall under the influence of his colleague, Justice Louis Brandeis, and to heed Brandeis's fact-focused approach.[126] In the rent control cases, the facts allowed Holmes to defer to legislative restrictions on the ability of landlords to make the contracts they chose in the housing market. Holmes's opinions evoked bitter, rather personal dissents. Four justices joined McKenna's warning to Holmes and the rest of the majority that they were opening the way for "socialism, or some form of socialism," which would destroy "personal rights and the purposeful encouragement of individual incentive and energy."[127]

Although not involving Thirteenth Amendment claims, *Hammer v. Dagenhart*[128] and *Adkins v. Children's Hospital*[129] provide an illuminating coda from the early Taft years. In *Hammer v. Dagenhart*, the Court decided that the Federal Child Labor Act of 1916 impinged upon the sovereignty of the states and thereby violated the Tenth Amendment; the 5–4 majority also found the act to be an unconstitutional extension of Congress's commerce power. To the majority, there was a "right to thus employ child labor"[130]—and an apparent corollary right of a child to be employed, here invoked by Dagenhart as next friend for two of his sons under age 16. Congress did not have the power to regulate despite the view that "all will admit," as Justice Day put it, that "there should be limitations upon the right to employ children in mines and factories in the interest of their own and the public welfare."[131]

Concern and care for the child had to remain exclusively with the states and the parents to whom states might delegate authority.[132] Work even in mines and factories was beyond Congress's constitutional ken. If paternalism toward children was to be allowed, it must flow from the proper authorities. For the dissenters, Holmes pointed to the majority's inconsistency in allowing Congress to regulate oleomargarine, lottery tickets, the so-called white slave trade, and strong drink but not child labor.[133]

During the early Taft years, avoiding paternalism still meant invalidation of employment contract regulations.[134] But now there was an added wrinkle. Striking down a District of Columbia law establishing minimum wages for women, Justice George Sutherland claimed that the civil disability of women had reached the ''vanishing point'' after passage of the Nineteenth Amendment.[135] Women should no longer receive special care and protection but should compete as equals. Holmes, now in his eighties, disagreed: ''It will take more than the nineteenth amendment to convince me that there are no differences between men and women, or that the legislature cannot take those differences into account.''[136]

By 1923, the Court no longer relegated women to what the justices saw as their natural God-given place.[137] Like blacks forty years earlier, women were now proclaimed to be full citizens. They had achieved sui juris legal status. The Court claimed that intermeddling through a minimum wage requirement would violate the constitutional presumption that each and every individual enjoys freedom of contract.

Hammer v. Dagenhart and the *Adkins* decisions show that the Court had managed to complete a full circle. Just as 17-year-olds could enlist in the army without the parental consent required by statute, so parents could send minors to the cotton mills while congressional attempts to intervene were held unconstitutional. Avoidance of paternalism permitted the justices to pick and choose who would be protected and to what degree, according to their own lights.

The indeterminacy of the paternalism concept created a basic paradox of paternalism during the years Fuller and White were the chief justices. The Court enthusiastically thrust itself into the role of the ultimate paternalist. Lacking any coherent theory to confine their discretion, the justices simply assumed the role of fathers who knew best.

CONCLUSIONS

After World War I, the Supreme Court was poised to join or even to lead the country in its quest for a return to normalcy. Had the justices paused to assess the status of paternalism when Taft joined them in 1921, they would have seen that earlier constitutional efforts to confine and control the threat were inconsistent and largely unavailing. The federal judiciary had not succeeded in its effort, as Brooks Adams put it, ''to dislocate any comprehensive body of legislation whose effect would be to change the social status.''[138] But protecting individuals and the nation from the dangers of debilitating legislative protection was not a cause to be abandoned lightly, and the Taft Court tried to stem the tide.

The mask covering the direct connection between halting paternalism and maintaining the economic and social status quo slipped a bit, however. Holmes even suggested in his *Coppage* dissent that the Constitution would not forbid a state to ''establish the equality of position between the parties in which liberty of contract begins.''[139] Thus Holmes suggested that state intervention could precede individual contract decisions. This odor of redistribution probably provoked some of the most vehement fulminations against paternalism by the *Coppage* and *Adkins* majorities. After all, if any constitutional doctrine seemed settled during the prior half-century, it was the impermissibility of redistribution by government.[140]

The conflation of paternalism and redistribution is significant. Today we may have some sense that politics near the turn of the century was actually the politics of redistribution[141] and that the state and federal governments have played redistributive roles throughout U.S. history.[142] Yet there is probably no more basic strand of ideology—in a country without much of an ideological tradition—than unexamined enthusiasm for individualism and self-help.

If the Fuller and White courts provoked criticism at times and even threats of reprisals,[143] the justices also tapped into a fundamental American theme when they set out to choose who was a permissible subject for protection and what legislative initiatives were acceptable. Richard Hofstadter said in *The Age of Reform*:

One of the primary tests of the mood of a society at any given time is whether its comfortable people tend to identify, psychologically, with the power and achievements of the very successful or with the needs and sufferings of the underprivileged. In a large and striking measure the Progressive agitations turned the human sympathies of the people downward rather than upward in the social scale.[144]

The Supreme Court from 1888 to 1921 reacted by assuming the role of guardian against expression of such sympathies in law.

Deciding when to permit paternalism certainly is not an easy task. It can be difficult and sometimes impossible to distinguish between providing for people and deciding for them. Yet promiscuous use of the pejorative *paternalism* interferes with any possibility of creating structures for, and providing analysis of, crucial distinctions. The Court's struggle to identify and patrol paternalism, employing a priori categorizations and legal or scientific ideals allegedly deduced from first principles, became a juggling act that was hard to sustain while performing the ''giddy trapeze act'' of constitutional law.[145]

Some paternalism goes with any judge's territory, of course, and more is attached to the judicial icons at the Supreme Court. But the Fuller and White courts used the threat of paternalism to arrogate an unusual degree of authority to themselves. The justices set out to cleave the popular will from the popular whim, as James Russell Lowell once phrased the distinction.[146] But the boundary they sought to establish to contain paternalism provided the justices with a kind of constitutional accordion. They never approached a coherent theory of how to classify litigants or when it was appropriate to defer to legislative judgments.

Instead the justices attempted to be the ultimate guardians of all Americans and American values.

It may be a "very bad lawyer who supposes that manipulability and infinite manipulability are the same thing,"[147] but my point is not that a number of justices during this period could probably be called very bad lawyers. Rather it is that the justices' efforts to deploy legal doctrine to contain paternalism provided particularly effective protective coloration for the interposition of their own values. Legal values, in turn, both reflected and helped to form the views of powerful contemporaries.

Through the lens of antipaternalism, those victimized in societal struggle had only themselves to blame. Losers belonged in their places if winners could designate their status as fitting or natural. By seeking to constitutionalize what was seen as scientific and necessary, the justices acted not only in paradoxical fashion but with a fashionable scienticism that now often seems tragic as well. Aggressive efforts to maintain a binary constitutional distinction between admirable autonomy and insidious paternalism characterized the Gilded Age through the time of Harding and Coolidge. We may have learned the lessons of the past so well that we are able to repeat mistakes almost exactly.

NOTES

1. A. Dicey, Lectures on Law and Public Opinion in England During the Nineteenth Century 150n.1 (1905). Dicey thought this point "elementary" but "worth insisting upon." Carol Weisbrod of the University of Connecticut School of Law first alerted me to this passage. The nexus between law, public opinion, and the relative protection of the flag and the Constitution as they traveled the globe was obvious to Peter Finley Dunne. Indeed, his most famous saying was, "No matter whether th' constitution follows th' flag or not, th' Supreme Court follows th' iliction returns." F. Dunne, "The Supreme Court Decisions," in E. Ellis, ed., Mr. Dooley at His Best 77 (1938). But long after San Juan Hill and Manila Bay, the vexing issue of how much protection the flag, the Constitution, or some combination thereof should provide individuals and corporations overseas still confused U.S. Supreme Court justices, as well as the rest of the population. This subject is not one I wish to explore here.

For recent work considering Blackstone's great influence in the United States, see, e.g., R. Ferguson, Law and Letters in American Culture 15 (1985) ("the Commentaries rank second only to the Bible as literary and intellectual influence on the history of American institutions"); K. Newmyer, Supreme Court Justice Joseph Story 40–43, 243–46 (1985); R. Cover, Justice Accused: Antislavery and the Judicial Process 16 (1975); Nolan, "Sir William Blackstone and the New American Republic: A Study of Intellectual Impact," 51 N.Y.U.L. Rev. 731 (1976). For general consideration of A. V. Dicey, see R. Cosgrove, The Rule of Law: Albert V. Dicey, Victorian Jurist (1980), and a provocative review, Sugarman, "The Legal Boundaries of Liberty: Dicey, Liberalism and Legal Science," 46 Modern L. Rev. 102 (1983).

2. Hollinger, Comments on Papers by Sharlin and Wall in Symposium on Spencer, Scientism and American Constitutional Law, 33 Annals of Science 475, 476 (1976).

3. The recent debate about terminology, and particularly about social Darwinism

and the influence of Herbert Spencer, is largely the result of revisionist attacks on R. Hofstadter, Social Darwinism in American Thought (1944). Examples of that attack include J. F. Wall, Andrew Carnegie (1970); R. Bannister, Social Darwinism: Science and Myth in Anglo-American Social Thought (1979), and the Symposium, supra note 2. I am not fully persuaded by arguments such as that by Wall about what conclusions properly may be drawn from the paucity of explicit citations to Spencer, particularly when antipaternalism could carry much of the social Darwinist load, as it did, for example, in the brief for appellants in Lochner v. New York, 198 U.S. 45 (1905), quoted by Wall at 471. For a good compendium with useful introductory essays, see R. J. Wilson, ed., Darwinism and the American Intellectual (1967).

4. Quoted in an excellent book, R. J. Wilson, In Quest of Community: Social Philosophy in the United States, 1860–1920 56 (1968). For similar ideas about the thought of Holmes and Langdell, see Gordon, Holmes' Common Law as Legal and Social Science, 10 Hofstra L. Rev. 719, 22–23 (1982) (tendency of the age "to treat the world as a hard object gradually being discovered by means of the suppression of human subjectivity"); Grey, Langdell's Orthodoxy, 45 U. Pitt. L. Rev. 1 (1983) (impact of analogy to geometry).

5. R. McCloskey, The American Supreme Court 105 (1960). Among the best additional earlier sources for this view, see S. Fine, Laissez-faire and the General-Welfare State (1956); C. Jacobs, Law Writers and the Courts: The Influence of Thomas M. Cooley, Christopher G. Tiedeman, and John F. Dillon upon American Constitutional Law (1954); R. McCloskey, American Conservatism in the Age of Enterprise (1951); Hofstadter, supra note 3; B. Twiss, Lawyers and the Constitution: How Laissez-Faire came to the Supreme Court (1942); E. Corwin, The Twilight of the Supreme Court (1934); M. Josephson, The Robber Barons (1934); Lerner, The Supreme Court and American Capitalism, 42 Yale L.J. 669 (1933).

Standouts within the recent work refining or redefining our understanding of the legal history of the period are McCurdy, Justice Field and the Jurisprudence of Government-Business Relations: Some Parameters of Laissez-Faire Constitutionalism, 1863–1897, 61 J. Am. Hist. 970 (1975); Benedict, Laissez-Faire and Liberty: A Re-Evaluation of the Meaning and Origins of Laissez-Faire Constitutionalism, 3 L. & Hist. Rev. 293 (1985); R. Semonche, Charting the Future: The Supreme Court Responds to a Changing Society (1978). For an impressive overview of the era, see A. Bickel & B. Schmidt, Jr., History of the Supreme Court of the United States: The Judiciary and Responsible Government (1984).

Willard Hurst and his oeuvre blazed the legal history trail for these and many other issues. Although this chapter certainly does not show it adequately, particularly since it concentrates on doctrinal developments in Supreme Court decisions, I am personally very much in Willard's and Frances's debt. In addition to many other kindnesses, they allowed my family and me to use their home—and Willard's office—during the University of Wisconsin Legal History Workshop in the summer of 1982 while I worked on this chapter.

6. Quoted in Nore, Charles A. Beard's Act of Faith: Context and Contest, 66 J. Am. Hist. 850 (1980). The best treatment of Beard and others of his generation in terms of the common intellectual enemy they fought still is M. White, Social Thought in America: The Revolt against Formalism (1949).

7. For a helpful historiographic overview, see Rodgers, In Search of Progressivism, 10 Rev. Am. Hist. 113 (1982). See also R. Wiebe, The Search for Order, 1877–1920 (1967).

8. G. Gilmore, The Ages of American Law 60 (1977).

9. Lochner v. New York, 198 U.S. 45 (1905).

10. See, e.g., Ely, The Wages of Crying Wolf: A Comment on Roe v. Wade, 82 Yale L.J. 920, 944 (1973). (Ely actually uses "Lochnering," but I find "Lochnerizing" more felicitous.)

11. The best-known exception prior to Lochner was Holden v. Hardy, 169 U.S. 366 (1898), which allowed Utah to limit to 10 hours the maximum miners could work per day for reasons of health and safety. Less well known are several other decisions in which the Court announced, for example, "It is within the undoubted power [of Congress] to restrain some individuals from some contracts." The author of this statement was Justice David Brewer, writing for a unanimous Court in Frisbie v. United States, 157 U.S. 160, 165 (1895). The decision upheld a criminal conviction imposed on a lawyer for charging more than the statutory maximum allowed for processing a widow's pension under the Dependent Pension Act of 1890. See also Holmes's statement in Minnesota Iron Co. v. Kline, 199 U.S. 593, 598 (1905) ("There is no doubt that [freedom of contract] may be limited where there are visible reasons for public policy for the limitation."); Cantwell v. Missouri, 199 U.S. 602 (1905). Decisions also permitted states to forbid or severely restrict access to cigarettes, liquor, and oleomargarine; see, e.g., Austin v. Tennessee, 179 U.S. 343 (1900); James Clark Distilling Co. v. Western Maryland Ry. Co., 242 U.S. 311 (1917); Powell v. Pennsylvania, 127 U.S. 678 (1888). Muller v. Oregon, 208 U.S. 412 (1908) and Bunting v. Oregon, 243 U.S. 426 (1917) are additional well-known exceptions to the traditional understanding of the Lochner doctrine; these decisions allowed states to act with explicit paternalism toward women. See generally Currie, The Constitution in the Supreme Court: The Protection of Economic Interests, 1889–1910, 52 U. Chi. L. Rev. 324 (1985).

12. Laissez-faire itself is not a concept that is easily defined. See L. Robbins, The Theory of Economic Policy (1952); Woodard, Reality and Social Reform: The Transition from Laissez-Faire to the Welfare State, 72 Yale L.J. 286 (1962). As with social Darwinism and formalism, whose heyday laissez-faire is often thought to have shared, much of the definition must rely on context.

13. Gordon, Legal Thought and Legal Practice in the Age of American Enterprise, 1870–1920, in Professions and Professional Ideologies in America, 1730–1940 (Stone & Geison eds. 1983); See generally L. Beth, The Development of the American Constitution, 1877–1917 (1971); T. McGraw, Prophets of Regulation (1985); Kennedy, Form and Substance in Private Law Adjudication, 89 Harv. L. Rev. 1685 (1976).

14. Warren's articles reporting the results of his survey of 560 Supreme Court decisions from 1888 to 1911 bore such titles as "The Progressiveness of the United States Supreme Court" and "A Bulwark to the State Police Power," 13 Colum. L. Rev. 294, 667 (1913). In his famous two-volume history of the Supreme Court, C. Warren, The Supreme Court in United States History 742–44 (1926), Warren updated his survey to include such decisions as Adair and Coppage, but he held firm to his conclusion. Warren's sampling technique is subject to some criticism—for example, police power decisions were not the only source of restrictive constitutional holdings, as developments in doctrinal categories such as contract clause and commerce clause make clear—but his point is too often overlooked. Lochnerizing did not really arrive until after World War I. For a handy scorecard of that doctrine's impact during the 1920s, see F. Frankfurter, Mr. Justice Holmes and the Supreme Court (1938).

15. William Jennings Bryan's attack on the federal judiciary during the tumultuous presidential campaign of 1896, as well as Theodore Roosevelt's vehement appeal for

popular recall of state judicial decisions in the 1912 campaign indicate that capable politicians believed their attacks on judicial decisions might create popular campaign issues. The fact that these presidential candidates lost does not prove popular support for their judicial targets; it is impossible to measure a national obsession with precision. Stagner, The Recall of Judicial Decisions and the Due Process Debate, 24 Am. J. Legal Hist. 257 (1980). The same journal issue also contains interesting related articles, Pratt, Rhetorical Styles on the Fuller Court, at 189 and Goetsch, The Future of Legal Formalism, at 257.

16. The pathbreaking work is E. Genovese, Roll, Jordan, Roll (1974), and it is criticized in J. Oakes, The Ruling Race (1982). See, e.g., William McFeely, Yankee Stepfather (1968), in which McFeely pursues the theme in the context of the Freedmen's Bureau; H. Belz, A New Birth of Freedom (1976) and H. Belz, Reconstructing the Union (1966), considering the tension between paternalism and individualism in congressional goals as the Civil War ended. See also J. Hermann, The Pursuit of a Dream (1981), a fascinating chronicle of an Owenite experiment on a Mississippi plantation, owned by Jefferson Davis's brother, who sold it after the Civil War to the former slaves who had worked the fields and cotton gins. For important recent considerations of paternalism moving beyond slavery and its immediate aftermath, see, e.g., J. McPherson, The Abolitionist Legacy (1975); D. Montgomery, Beyond Equality (1967). For a useful study of English varieties, see D. Roberts, Paternalism in Early Victorian England (1979). Cf. R. Sennett, Authority (1980).

17. J. M. Barrie's Peter Pan was first performed in London in 1904. The portrait of Wendy as housewife, who believes that "Father knows best," is particularly striking. But that is another story.

18. W. King, Melville W. Fuller 120 (1950). Senator George F. Edmunds (R., Vt.) led the opposition to Fuller from his base as chairman of the Senate Judiciary Committee; he was able to discover actions by Fuller during the Civil War that smacked of Copperhead sentiments. Nevertheless, Fuller was confirmed by a 41–20 vote. See generally id. at 114–24.

19. Id. at 114, quoting the Philadelphia press. For a somewhat similar description of White, see R. Highsaw, Edward Douglass White: Defender of the Conservative Faith (1981).

20. King, supra note 18, at 90.

21. For example, The Nation in 1887 praised President Cleveland for his "firm and pronounced stand against paternalism in government" in his refusal to allow federal drought and flood relief, and for his veto of what The Nation dubbed the "Pauper Pension Bill." 44 The Nation, Mar. 10, 1887, at 202. Cleveland had given the country the important lesson that " 'though the people support the government, the Government should not support the people.' " Id. See generally M. Keller, Affairs of State (1977); R. H. Williams, Years of Decision (1978).

22. Compare, e.g., Blyew v. United States, 80 U.S. (13 Wall.) 581 (1872); United States v. Reese, 92 U.S. 214 (1876); United States v. Cruikshank, 92 U.S. 542 (1876); United States v. Harris, 106 U.S. 699 (1883) with Strauder v. West Virginia, 100 U.S. 303 (1879); Virginia v. Rives, 100 U.S. 313 (1879); Ex parte Virginia, 100 U.S. 339 (1879). The Court was somewhat more willing to allow government intervention in matters concerning the franchise. See, e.g., Ex parte Yarborough, 110 U.S. 651 (1884).

23. 109 U.S. 3, 25 (1883).

24. Santa Clara County v. S. Pac. R.R. Co., 118 U.S. 394 (1886) (dictum); Pembina

Mining Co. v. Pennsylvania, 125 U.S. 181 (1888) (holding that corporation was a person for purposes of Fourteenth Amendment).

25. See, e.g., Missouri v. Lewis, 101 U.S. 22 (1879); Barbier v. Connolly, 113 U.S. 27 (1885). For a useful treatment of the implications of this theme, see Kay, The Equal Protection Clause in the Supreme Court, 1873–1903, 29 Buffalo L. Rev. 667 (1980). Its ramifications in the realm of due process are somewhat better known. See generally C. Jacobs, supra note 5.

26. Elk v. Williams, 112 U.S. 94 (1884).

27. See, e.g., Minor v. Happersett, 88 U.S. (21 Wall.) 162 (1875); Bradwell v. State, 83 U.S. (15 Wall.) 130 (1872).

28. Civil Rights Cases, 109 U.S. 3, 24 (1883), in which the Supreme Court declared that "it would be running the slavery argument into the ground" to hold that the Thirteenth Amendment guaranteed nondiscriminatory practices in public theaters, hotels, and the like.

29. See, e.g., Beth, supra note 13; D. Rothman, Politics and Power (1966); R. Williams, supra note 21, M. Keller, supra note 21.

30. J. Bryce, 2 American Commonwealth 408 (1889).

31. Id. at 409. Bryce supplied charts and summaries of "recent legislation tending to extol state intervention and the scope of the penal law" to prove that Americans spoke one way and acted quite another concerning government intervention.

32. Id. at 410.

33. See generally C. Jacobs, supra note 5; Pound, Liberty of Contract, 18 Yale L.J. 454 (1909).

34. Field was the "doyen of conservatives on the postwar Court," according to M. Keller, supra note 21, at 366, but even Field has been "rehabilitated" somewhat—if one favors government intervention—in McCurdy, Justice Field and the Jurisprudence of Government-Business Relations: Some Parameters of Laissez-Faire Constitutionalism, 1863–1897, 61 J. Am. Hist. 970 (1975). His nephew, Justice Brewer, also has had recent defenders. See, e.g., J. Semonche, Charting the Future 168–79, 244–45 (1978); Garner, Justice Brewer and Substantive Due Process: A Conservative Court Revisited, 18 Vand. L. Rev. 615 (1965). Useful additional recent studies of the period include W. Nelson, The Roots of American Bureaucracy, 1830–1900 (1982); Currie, supra note 11; and Pratt, supra note 15.

35. See, e.g., Hamilton, On Dating Mr. Justice Holmes, 9 U. Chi. L. Rev. 1, 10, 15, 26–9 (1941); Rogat, Mr. Justice Holmes: A Dissenting Opinion, 15 Stan. L. Rev. 3, 254 (1962–63) and Rogat & O'Fallon, Mr. Justice Holmes: A Dissenting Opinion—The Speech Cases, 36 Stan. L. Rev. 1349 (1984); Touster, Holmes a Hundred Years Ago: The Common Law and Legal Theory, 10 Hofstra L. Rev. 673 (1982); Gordon, Holmes' Common Law as Legal and Social Science, 10 Hofstra L. Rev. 719 (1982); G. Gilmore, supra note 8, at 48–56. See also Belz, The Constitution in the Gilded Age: The Beginnings of Constitutional Realism in American Scholarship, 13 Am. J. Legal Hist. 110 (1969).

36. State v. Goodwill, 33 W. Va. 179 (1889).

37. Id at 183.

38. For example, Eugene V. Debs constantly instructed workers that they actually were wage slaves, perhaps not as well off as slaves had been in the South. See, e.g., B. Brommel, Eugene V. Debs 49, 61–63, 80 (1978). Similarly, Upton Sinclair was commissioned to do a study of wage slavery in the meatpacking industry, resulting in The

Jungle (1906). For similar concern about slavery, from a very different perspective, see generally A. Paul, Conservative Crisis and the Rule of Law: Attitudes of Bar and Bench, 1887–1895 (1960). In this way, the rhetoric of the period was reminiscent of the tone of the American Revolution. See B. Bailyn, The Ideological Origins of the American Revolution (1967).

39. State v. Goodwill, 33 W. Va. 179, 186 (1889). To illustrate "universal condemnation," Snyder relied on Godcharles v. Wigeman, 113 Pa. 431 (1886), which found Pennsylvania's similar statute to be "utterly unconstitutional and void" since it was "an insulting attempt to put the laborer under a legislative tutelage, which is not only degrading to his manhood, but subversive of his rights as a citizen of the United States." Snyder also cited Millett v. Illinois, 117 Ill. 294 (1886), which invalidated legislation requiring owners to weigh coal fairly and pay miners accordingly. Snyder could have cited many other contemporary decisions. See generally Twiss, supra note 5.

40. Id. at 184.

41. Both statements by Justice Brewer were in his dissent in Budd v. New York 143 U.S. 517, 551 (1892). Brewer also insisted that New York went too far in regulating prices at a grain elevator because "the utmost possible liberty to the individual and the fullest protection to him and his property is both the limitation and duty of government." Id. at 551. Rufus Peckham, who was soon to join the U.S. Supreme Court, had much the same thing to say for the New York Court of Appeals in the Budd case.

42. See, e.g., the speeches by Field, Brewer and Brown disussed in A. Paul, supra note 38 at 63–64, 70–72, 84–85. See also John Chipman Gray's attack on paternalism and socialism, which Gray saw exemplified in the spendthrift trust, discussed in Alexander, The Dead Hand and the Law of Trusts in the Nineteenth Century, 37 Stan. L. Rev. 1189, 1244–47 (1985).

43. Charles Warren found overwhelming evidence that Lochner was atypical. Warren, The Progressiveness of the United States Supreme Court, 13 Colum. L. Rev. 294, 295 (1913). See supra, note 14. For a very different view, see Pound, Law in Books and Law in Action, 44 Am. L. Rev. 12 (1910).

44. This idea of status created by contract evokes feudalism and rather starkly reverses Sir Henry Maine's famous aphorism. H. Maine, Ancient Law 165 (5th ed. 1873).

45. In re Morrissey, 137 U.S. 157, 199 (1890). William Howard Taft signed the briefs as U.S. solicitor general.

46. In re Grimley, 137 U.S. 147 (1890).

47. Id. at 150.

48. Id. at 151.

49. Id. at 153.

50. Congress first acted to exclude the Chinese in 1882. Its power to do so was upheld in Chae Chan Ping v. United States, 130 U.S. 581 (1889). The Court accorded Congress unqualified discretion in upholding the Geary Act of May 5, 1892 in Fong Yue Ting v. United States, 149 U.S. 698 (1893). Brewer, Field, and Fuller dissented. Brewer's dissent, while showing little sympathy for the "obnoxious Chinese," is a good example of his penchant for arguing that questions of degree provided an impermissible basis for legislation. Id. at 742. But see United States v. Wong Kim Ark, 169 U.S. 649 (1898). See generally R. McClellan, The Heathen Chinese (1970); McClain, The Chinese Struggle for Civil Rights in 19th-Century America: The Unusual Case of Baldwin v. Franks, 3 L. Hist. Rev. 349 (1985).

51. In re Debs, 158 U.S. 564, 586, 582 (1895). The position ultimately vindicated

in the Debs case was that of George Pullman, whose relations with his workers in his town of Pullman, Illinois, may have made him the foremost paternalist of the day.

52. United States v. Gettysburg Electric Ry., 160 U.S. 688 (1896).

53. 156 U.S. 1 (1895). As constitutional law students still learn, the Court attempted to draw an impossible line between manufacturing and commerce and thereby determined that Congress could not reach the sugar trust, though it controlled 98 percent of the nation's sugar.

54. United States v. Realty Co., 163 U.S. 427 (1896).

55. 163 U.S. 537 (1896).

56. Id. at 542.

57. Id. at 544.

58. Id., quoting 5 Cush. 198, 209–10 (1849).

59. Id.

60. Id. (emphasis added). For a discussion of the Roberts case, see L. Levy, The Law of the Commonwealth and Chief Justice Shaw 109–17 (1957). The positive flavor of Shaw's reference to "paternal consideration and protection of the law" had been transmuted over the ensuing half-century. By 1896, paternalism was anathema. In private law, however, remnants of the old affirmative aspects of paternal consideration survived. A good and revealing example appears in a fairly typical summation of the Law of Persons by Brigadier General Norman L. Lieber, son of the first famous American jurisdprudent, Francis Lieber, in The Supreme Court on the Military Status, 31 Am. L. Rev. 342, 353 (1897). Lieber wrote: "The *status* of a person is his legal position or condition. . . . The term is chiefly applied to persons under disability, or persons who have some peculiar condition which prevents the general law from applying to them in the same way as it does to ordinary persons. The question of status is of importance in jurisprudence, because it is generally treated as a basis for the classification of law, according as it applies to ordinary persons (general law, normal law, law of things), or to persons having a status, *i.e.*, a disability or peculiar legal condition, such as infants, married women, lunatics, convicts, bankrupts, aliens, public officers, etc. (particular law, abnormal law, law of persons)."

61. Woodward, The Case of the Louisiana Traveler, in J. Garraty, ed., Quarrels That Have Shaped the Constitution 145, 155 (1975).

62. 165 U.S. 275 (1897).

63. Shipping Commissioners' Act of 1872, 17 Stat. 243.

64. 165 U.S. at 276 (1897).

65. Id. at 280.

66. Id. at 287. In the course of his historic essay, Brown drew from the ancient Rhodians through the Rules of Oleron promulgated during the reign of Henry III to French, German, and Dutch law. What he omitted, however, was that the then-current law of England apparently would not have permitted the imprisonment at issue. Additionally the U.S. law from 1790 to 1872 also made no such provision. Finally, one of the essential preconditions in many of his examples—knowledge of the duration and destination of the voyage—was not present in Robertson v. Baldwin.

67. Id. at 287.

68. Brief for Appellee, at 10, 165 U.S. 275 (1897).

69. Id.

70. 165 U.S. at 293 (1897).

71. Id. at 303.

72. By the end of 1898, Congress had adopted Harlan's views in the White Act, which eliminated all imprisonment for desertion, except for a one-month maximum for desertion in foreign ports, not vigorously opposed by the sailors' unions, and regulated the seaman's diet and the contract allotment system with great specificity. 55th Congress, 3d Sess., 30 Stat. 755 (1898). I have benefited a great deal from an excellent paper by Ronnie Sussmann about Robertson v. Baldwin and earlier cases involving sailors and their "care" (unpublished manuscript, 1982).

73. This is the title of two articles Thayer wrote in Atlantic Monthly, Oct., Nov. 1891, at 540, 676. But see, e.g., K. Llewellyn & F. A. Hoebel, The Cheyenne Way (1941); Talton v. Mayes, 163 U.S. 376 (1896); Santa Clara Pueblo v. Martinez, 436 U.S. 49 (1978).

74. Id. at 678.

75. 118 U.S. 375, 383–84 (1886). In Kagama, protection concerned federal jurisdiction over seven major crimes, when committed on Indian reservations.

76. Dawes is quoted in A. Debo, And Still the Waters Run 21–22 (1940). Upon returning from a visit to the Cherokees in 1886, Dawes noted that there was not a pauper in the nation, and the nation owed no debts. They had schools and hospitals. "Yet the defect of the system was apparent. . . . There is no enterprise to make your home any better than that of your neighbors."

77. Perhaps the most revealing decision concerning the Severalty Act was an opinion written by Justice Brewer, In re Heff, 197 U.S. 488 (1905). Brewer used the Tenth Amendment to hold that Congress could not regulate the sale of liquor to a former member of the Kickapoo tribe who was now an allottee. He stated that Congress "is under no constitutional obligation to perpetually continue the relationship of guardian and ward. It may at any time abandon its guardianship and leave the ward to assume and be subject to all the privileges and burdens of one sui juris. And it is for Congress to determine when and how that relationship of guardianship shall be abandoned." Id. at 499. See generally R. Barch & J. Henderson, The Road: Indian Tribes and Political Liberty (1980); W. Washburn, Red Man's Land/White Man's Law (1970); D. Littlefield, The Cherokee Freedman (1978). I benefited a great deal from an excellent paper by Despena Lee Fillios on Heff and related matters (unpublished manuscript, 1980).

78. United States v. Choctaw Nation, 193 U.S. 115 (1904).

79. Brief for Appellant at 88–99, 119 U.S. 1 (1886). The cases ranged from Russell v. Southard, 51 U.S. (12 How.) 139 (1851) to Graffam v. Burgess, 117 U.S. 180 (1886).

80. Brief for Appellee at 4, 119 U.S. 1 (1886). See generally id. at 2–10 for astonishing statements about General Jackson's knowledge of and solicitude for the Indians and the general theme that they were lucky not to have been massacred so they should not complain. See also M. Rogin, Fathers and Children (1975).

81. 119 U.S. 1, 28 (1886).

82. Id. The Court held that a Senate award to Indians as compensation for land taken by the federal government was not conclusive but would be given prima facie effect to establish the validity of Indian claims in the Court of Claims, authorized by an 1881 statute. This seems one of the rare occasions when even a credible claim could be made that a Great Spirit of any description sided with the Indians in court during this period.

83. 193 U.S. 115, 124 (1904).

84. Id.

85. Id.

86. Civil Rights Cases, 109 U.S. 3, 20–21 (1883).

87. See, e.g., Williams v. Mississippi, 170 U.S. 213 (1898); Brownfield v. S. Carolina, 189 U.S. 426 (1903) (Holmes' first opinion on the U.S. Supreme Court); Giles v. Harris, 189 U.S. 475 (1903), in which Holmes told the black plaintiffs complaining of disfranchisement that "relief from a great political wrong, if done . . . must be given by [the people of the State] or by the legislative and political department of the government of the United States." Id. at 488.

88. For peonage, see, e.g., P. Daniel, The Shadow of Slavery (1972); D. Novak, The Wheel of Servitude (1978); Schmidt, Principle and Prejudice: The Supreme Court and Race in the Progressive Era. Part 2: The Peonage Cases, 82 Colum. L. Rev. 646 (1982). For southern politics, see, e.g., J. Kousser, The Shaping of Southern Politics, 1880–1910 (1974); S. Hackney, Populism to Progressivism in Alabama (1969); C. Woodward, The Strange Career of Jim Crow (2d rev. ed., 1966).

89. 197 U.S. 207 (1905).

90. Id. at 215.

91. Id.

92. Id.

93. Id. at 233.

94. 203 U.S. 1 (1906).

95. Id. at 16. Brewer reasoned that since the Thirteenth Amendment reached all persons and since Chinese laborers now had to carry certificates as free Negroes did during slavery, the Thirteenth Amendment could not affect wrongs to persons not shown in the record to be slaves or the descendants of slaves. State law was said to be the place to go to seek remedies.

96. Id. at 20.

97. Id.

98. Id. at 37. This time, Harlan was joined in dissent by Day.

99. Id. at 27.

100. Id. at 29.

101. 219 U.S. 219 (1911).

102. 208 U.S. 412 (1908).

103. Id. at 421.

104. See, e.g., Lawlor v. Lowe (Danbury Hatters' Case), 208 U.S. 274 (1908); Adair v. United States, 208 U.S. 161 (1908); Employers' Liability Cases, 207 U.S. 463 (1908).

105. Bailey v. Alabama, 211 U.S. 452 (1908). Holmes, for the majority over dissents by Harlan and Day, rejected attempts to "take a short cut" to get the case before the U.S. Supreme Court. Id. at 455.

106. Baker, A Pawn in the Struggle for Freedom, 72 Am. Mag. 608, 610 (1911). See also the article celebrating the victory in the New York Age, Jan. 19, 1911, but also describing Bailey as a "cipher" who was "last heard from slinging hash at the clubhouse, caring not which way the winds of the court blew, so they robbed him not of his good meals and freedom to break contracts whenever he listed."

107. 219 U.S. 219, 245 (1911).

108. Id. at 241.

109. Id.

110. Id. at 245.

111. Id. at 246.

112. Id. This example of Holmes expostulating about "wrong conduct" is striking; it contrasts starkly with Holmes's position in *The Common Law* (1881) and with his

characteristic enthusiasm for the utility of life's struggles. See, e.g., The Soldier's Faith in M. Howe, ed., The Occasional Speeches of Justice Oliver Wendell Homes 73 (1962) and sources cited supra notes 35 and 88.

113. Id. at 248.

114. For a provocative discussion, see Schmidt, supra note 88.

115. 219 U.S. 219 (1911).

116. 235 U.S. 133 (1914).

117. See Schmidt, supra note 88, at 691–702.

118. 235 U.S. at 146–47 (1914).

119. Id. at 150.

120. Id.

121. Coppage v. Kansas, 236 U.S. 1 (1915). As Brandeis put it in The Living Law, 10 Ill. L. Rev. 461 (1916), "In the *Coppage* Case, the Supreme Court showed the potency of mental prepossessions."

122. Butler v. Perry, 240 U.S. 328 (1916). Justice McReynolds emphasized the long tradition of mandatory road work. He explained the intention of the Thirteenth Amendment: "The great purpose in view was liberty under the protection of effective government, not the destruction of the latter by depriving it of essential powers." Id. at 333. Therefore, McReynolds explained for the unanimous Court, the Thirteenth Amendment certainly did not "interdict enforcement of those duties which individuals owe to the state, such as service in the army, militia, on the jury, etc." Id. The person objecting to mandatory road work was apparently white, but it had long been clear that Thirteenth Amendment protections were not limited by race. In fact, one of the test cases in Hodges involved a white convict; the Court also indicated that the Civil Rights Act of 1866, premised on the Congress's Thirteenth Amendment power, could reach a politically motivated prosecution in a bitter battle among white citizens in Kentucky. Kentucky v. Powers, 201 U.S. 1 (1906).

123. Selective Service Cases, 245 U.S. 366 (1918). The Court found that the involuntary servitude challenge to the draft was "refuted by its mere statement." Id. at 390.

124. Marcus Brown Holding Co. v. Feldman, 256 U.S. 170 (1921).

125. Marcus Brown Holding Co. v. Feldman, 256 U.S. 170 (1921) (New York City); Block v. Hirsch, 256 U.S. 135 (1917) (Washington, D.C.).

126. See, e.g., S. Konefsky, The Legacy of Holmes and Brandeis (1956); but see Letter from Oliver Wendell Holmes to Sir Frederick Pollock (May 16, 1919), reprinted in 2 Holmes-Pollock Letters 13 (M. Howe ed. 1941): "I hate facts. I always say the chief end of man is to form general propositions—adding that no general proposition is worth a damn. Of course a general proposition is simply a string for the facts and I have little doubt that it would be good for my immortal soul to plunge into them, good also for the performance of my duties, but I shrink from the base—or rather I hate to give up the chance to read this and that, that a gentleman should read before he dies." See generally Hamilton, On Dating Mr. Justice Holmes, 9 U. Chi. L. Rev. 1, 24 (1941).

127. Block v. Hirsch, 256 U.S. 135, 161–163 (1921). The dissenters bemoaned the demise of the Constitution, id. at 160, 163, and proclaimed that Fifth Amendment prohibitions were being violated, though "they are as absolute as axioms. A contract existing, its obligation is impregnable." Id. at 163–64. By 1924, even Holmes was convinced that the District of Columbia had gone too far in proclaiming that the World War I emergency still applied; Chasleton Corp. v. Sinclair, 264 U.S. 543 (1924). He invalidated this extension of the rent control scheme. By then, however, not only was

Taft chief justice, but President Harding had remade the Court with three additional appointments. It was the Taft Court that produced what was then a record high batting average of invalidated statutes, as well as embracing and expanding precedents that were to be invoked to strike down New Deal legislation in the early 1930s. For surveys of the carnage, see E. Corwin, supra note 5; F. Frankfurter, supra note 14.

128. 247 U.S. 251 (1918).

129. 261 U.S. 525 (1923).

130. 247 U.S. at 273.

131. Id. at 275.

132. See generally M. Keller, supra note 21, at 461–72. Keller quotes Ernst Freund, for example, stating that parental authority came to be "power in trust . . . the authority to control the child is not the natural right of the parents; it emanates from the State, and is an exercise of police power." E. Freund, Police Power 248 (1904). But Robert Wiebe makes the point that "if humanitarian progressivism had a central theme, it was the child." Wiebe, supra note 7, at 169 (1967).

133. 247 U.S. 251, 278–80 (1918).

134. See, e.g., Wolff Packing Co. v. Court of Industrial Relations, 262 U.S. 522 (1923); Wolff Packing Co. v. Industrial Court, 267 U.S. 552 (1925) and discussion in F. Frankfurter, supra note 14; Brown, Due Process of Law, Police Power and the Supreme Court, 40 Harv. L. Rev. 943 (1927).

135. Adkins v. Children's Hospital, 261 U.S. 525 (1923).

136. Id. at 569–70. Justice Taft's discomfort in his dissent, joined by Justice Sanford, id. at 562, is revealing. Taft clearly seemed to favor the result reached by the majority but recognized that the precedents pointed the other way. He wrote, "I have always supposed that the Lochner Case was thus overruled sub silentio" since the Court had begun "laboriously pricking out a line" between the police power and liberty. Id. at 564, 562.

137. Compare Adkins with, e.g., MacKenzie v. Hare, 239 U.S. 299 (1915), in which the Court upheld a woman's loss of U.S. citizenship when she married a foreigner. McKenna wrote for the Court: "The identity of husband and wife is an ancient principle of our jurisprudence. It was neither accidental nor arbitrary and worked in many instances for her protection." Id. at 311. He continued: "There has been, it is true, much relaxation of it but in its retention as in its origin it is determined by their intimate relation and unity of interest, and this relation and unity may make it of public concern in many instances to merge their identity and give dominance to the husband." Id. at 311. See also In re Lockwood, 154 U.S. 116 (1894); Bradwell v. State, 83 U.S. (16 Wall.) 130 (1872).

138. B. Adams, The Theory of Social Revolutions 218 (1913).

139. Coppage v. Kansas, 236 U.S. 1, 27 (1915).

140. The usual first citation for the proposition is Loan Ass'n v. Topeka, 87 U.S. (20 Wall.) 655, 662–63 (1875), but the statement was repeated constantly during the Fuller and White era.

141. McCormick, The Party Period and Public Policy: An Exploratory Hypothesis, 66 J. Am. Hist. 279 (1979).

142. See, e.g., Scheiber, Property Law, Expropriation, and Resource Allocation by Government: The United States, 1789–1910, 33 J. Econ. Hist. 232 (1973); Gates, An Overview of American Land Policy, 50 Agri. Hist. 213 (1976); M. Horwitz, The Trans-

formation of American Law, 1780–1860 (1977); O. Handlin & M. Handlin, Commonwealth (1948); L. Hartz, Economic Policy and Democratic Thought (1948).

143. For example, the Democratic party included anti-Court planks in its 1896 and 1900 platforms, and Theodore Roosevelt triggered a movement to recall or restrain the justices in 1912.

144. R. Hofstadter, The Age of Reform 243–44 (1955).

145. Llewellyn, The Constitution as an Institution, 34 Colum. L. Rev. 1, 14n.28 (1934).

146. This was another favorite judicial phrase during the period. It probably originated in a "happy phrase" by James Russell Lowell, quoted in C. Warren, 2 The Supreme Court in United States History 751 (1926).

147. J. Ely, Democracy and Distrust 112 (1980).

III. Further Policy and Performance Consequences

8

THE CORPORATION AND ANTITRUST LAW POLICY: DOUBLE STANDARDS

David Dale Martin

The antitrust policy of the United States is rooted in the ideology of individual freedom. Americans have tenaciously retained the myth of competitive private enterprise with representative democracy in spite of the emergence of the modern corporate state. Their ability to retain the forms of individualism amid collectivism in substance is due in large measure to the corporate form of business organization. By treating the corporation as a person, in both law and economic theory, Americans have been able to retain not only the old legal relations of property and contract among free people but also the classical theoretical structure that explains and justifies capitalism. Large corporate organizations govern internally through hierarchy while relating to other corporations as if they were persons in a decentralized society. Economics looks primarily at the external relations, treating the firm as an optimizing entity without regard to whether it is a single proprietor or a multinational complex of corporations. Thus the corporation has been a mechanism through which the U.S. economy and the whole society has been transformed radically without revolution. Legal developments have provided more protection of the corporation than from the corporation.

For the past century, antitrust law has been used as a conservative policy instrument to slow down the apparently inexorable change from individualism to collectivism. The very name antitrust implies opposition to the movement toward combination of small firms into big business. This movement began in the 1880s with the perversion of the trust device to unite many small corporations under common control and continued at the turn of the century under the sanction of newly liberalized general incorporation laws, particularly those of New Jersey.[1] The trusts were transformed into holding companies under corporate charters that no longer imposed significant constraints on the degree of centralization of control of economic activity. The Sherman Act of 1890 was an attempt by Congress to counter the revolutionary combination movement. Thus from the beginning, the federal antitrust law policy conflicted with a policy favoring combination implicit in state incorporation statutes. This chapter focuses on this policy conflict, examining both its roots in the nation's first century under the Constitution and its development in the century following the *Santa Clara* case.[2]

The 1886 Supreme Court decision in *Santa Clara* recognized the status of a business corporation as a person within the meaning of that word as used in the Fourteenth Amendment's provision prohibiting a state from denying any person equal protection of the laws. The precedent set was most important as an assertion of jurisdiction by the Court to review any state government attempts to regulate, tax, or otherwise constrain corporations. For example, it provided the basis for declaring unconstitutional an Illinois antitrust statute that exempted agricultural products.[3] Perhaps more important was the indirect effect this concept had in the development of federal antitrust law. By treating a combination of two or more persons associated in corporate form as a single entity incapable of conspiring or agreeing, the Court has adopted a double standard. Loosely knit combinations are prohibited from doing what closely knit combinations in corporate form are permitted to do: centralize decision making on such matters as price, output, investment, and allocation of customers.

The double standard was not inevitable. Ironically, the basis of the *Santa Clara* decision was that the fact of incorporation should not shield the incorporating persons from the protection of the Fourteenth Amendment. Yet the corporate veil turned out to shield such persons from the prohibitions on combination in restraint of trade adopted to protect the public generally. The Court looked through the corporation to protect rights but not to enforce the duties to behave independently.

The Sherman Act itself was partially to blame. Section 8 of the statute says:

That the word "person" or "persons," wherever used in this act, shall be deemed to include corporations and associations existing under or authorized by the laws of either the United States, the laws of any of the Territories, the laws of any State, or the laws of any foreign country.[4]

The word *person* was used in the very important section 2 of the act, which provides that "every person who shall monopolize, or attempt to monopolize, or combine or conspire with any other person or persons, to monopolize . . . shall be deemed guilty."[5] To give effect to this section, as worded, it was necessary to define person to include a corporation. The drafters of the section, of course, might have said "every person or corporation." The intent seems clear, however. Treating the corporation as a person was to have strengthened the prohibition against monopolizing. Section 1 of the Sherman Act, however, presents a different problem. It provides that "every contract, combination in the form of trust or otherwise, or conspiracy, in restraint of trade or commerce among the several States, or with foreign nations, is declared to be illegal."[6] At the time the Sherman Act was enacted in 1890, the trust was the obvious problem, but the holding company charter was not unknown.[7] Congress had the foresight to use the phrase "combination in the form of trust *or otherwise*," but it did not explicitly state that a corporation could be treated as a combination of persons as well as a person. Congress attempted to cover all the bases by using the common law doctrines of both restraint of trade and conspiracy to monopolize, but in so doing it left very much leeway to the courts in giving specific content to the general language of the statute. Before examining the Court's treatment of combinations in corporate form, let us look at the roots of the *Santa Clara* doctrine of the corporation as a person.

THE *SANTA CLARA* CASE

The Supreme Court opinion in the *Santa Clara* case provides no justification at all for the crucial holding. Chief Justice Waite simply announced from the bench:

The court does not wish to hear argument on the question whether the provision in the Fourteenth Amendment to the Constitution, which forbids a State to deny to any person within its jurisdiction the equal protection of the laws, applies to these corporations. We are all of the opinion that it does.[8]

We must look, therefore, at the circuit court opinion for the arguments and precedents that underlay such unanimity. The circuit court opinion was written by Supreme Court Justice Stephen L. Field sitting with the lower court, as was common a century ago.[9] In his opinion, Justice Field focused not on whether the corporation is a person but on whether the natural persons who comprise the corporation are to be denied the protection of the amendment merely because they associate themselves together under a corporate charter from the state. His argument was that the corporate cloak should not be used as a barrier to natural persons' rights. He said:

In this state [corporations] are formed under general laws. By complying with certain prescribed forms any five persons may thus associate themselves. In that sense corporations are creatures of the state; they could not exist independently of the law, and the law may, of course, prescribe any conditions, not prohibited by the constitution of the United States, upon which they may be formed and continued. But the members do not, because of such association, lose their rights to protection, and equality of protection. They continue, notwithstanding, to possess the same right to life and liberty as before, and also to their property, except as they may have stipulated otherwise. As members of the association of the artificial body, the intangible thing, called by a name given by themselves—their interests, it is true, are undivided, and constitute only a right during the continuance of the corporation to participate in its dividends, and, on its dissolution, to a proportionate share of its assets; but it is property, nevertheless, and the courts will protect it, as they will any other property, from injury or spoliation.

. . . Whatever advances the prosperity or wealth of the corporation, advances proportionately the prosperity and business of the corporators, otherwise no one would be benefited. It is impossible to conceive of a corporation suffering an injury or reaping a benefit except through its members. The legal entity, the metaphysical being, that is called a corporation, cannot feel either. So, therefore, whenever a provision of the constitution or of a law guaranties to persons protection in their property, or affords to them the means for its protection, or prohibits injurious legislation affecting it, the benefits of the provision of law are extended to corporations; not to the name under which different persons are united, but to the individuals composing the union. The courts will always look through the name to see and protect those whom the name represents.[10]

Justice Field cited a number of precedents for this treatment of the persons who make up a corporation. For example, he quoted Justice Marshall in *Bank of the United States v. Deveaux*, who said:

Aliens, or citizens of different states, are not less susceptible of these apprehensions, nor can they be supposed to be less the objects of constitutional provision, because they are allowed to sue by a corporate name. That name, indeed, cannot be an alien or a citizen, but the persons whom it represents may be the one or the other, and the controversy is in fact and in law between these persons suing in their corporate character, by their corporate name, for a corporate right, and the individual against whom the suit may be instituted.[11]

Field also cited another early case in which the rights of a corporation under the 1783 treaty of peace that ended the Revolutionary War were at issue. Article 6 of the treaty provided that there should be "no further confiscation made, nor any prosecutions commenced, against any person or persons for or by reason of the part which he or they may have taken in the present war, and that no person shall on that account suffer any future loss or damage, either in his person, liberty, or property." Vermont attempted to confiscate and distribute the property of an English corporation.[12] Field said that the "Supreme court looked with undimmed vision through the legal entity, the artificial creation of the state, and saw the living human beings whom it represented and protected them under their corporate name."[13]

Without citing any specific cases, Justice Field also relied on the earlier interpretations of the Fifth Amendment's due process clause:

This is a limitation upon the federal government similar to that which exists in the constitution of several of the states against their own legislative bodies; and the term "person" thus used has always been held, either by tacit assent or express adjudication, whenever the question has arisen, to extend, so far as property is concerned, to corporations, because to protect them from spoliation is to protect the corporators also.

The Fourteenth Amendment extends in this respect the same prohibition to the states that the Fifth Amendment did to the federal government—"Nor shall any state deprive any person of life, liberty, or property without due process of law"—and it adds to the inhibition, "nor deny to any person within its jurisdiction the equal protection of the laws." By every canon of construction known to the jurisprudence of the country, the same meaning must be given to the term *person* in the latter provision as in the former. Surely these great constitutional provisions, which have been, not inaptly, termed a new Magna Charta, cannot be made to read as counsel contend,

"nor shall any state deprive any person of life, liberty, or property without due process of law, unless he be associated with others in a corporation, nor deny to any person within its jurisdiction the equal protection of the laws, unless he be a member of a corporation." How petty and narrow would provisions thus limited appear in the fundamental law of a great people.[14]

Justice Field then went on to reveal his own value judgment that the growing use of the corporate ownership of property was good and should not be discouraged by the law. He said:

Indeed, the aggregate wealth of all the trading, commercial, manufacturing, mining, shipping, transportation, and other companies engaged in business, or formed for religious, educational, or scientific purposes, amounts to billions upon billions of dollars; and yet all this vast property which keeps our industries flourishing, and furnishes employment, comforts, and luxuries to all classes, and thus promotes civilization and progress, is lifted, according to the argument of counsel, out of the protection of the constitutional guaranties, by reason of the incorporation of the companies; that is, because the persons composing them—amounting in the aggregate to nearly half the entire population of the country—have united themselves in that form under the law for the convenience of business. If the property for that reason is exempted from the protection of one constitutional guaranty, it must be from all such guaranties. If, because of it, the property can be subjected to unequal and arbitrary impositions, it may for the same reason be taken from its owners without due process of law, and taken by the state for public use without just compensation. If the position be sound, it follows that corporations hold all their property, and the right to its use and enjoyment, at the will of the state; that it may be invaded, seized, and the companies despoiled at the state's pleasure. It need hardly be said that there would be little security in the possession of property held by such a tenure, and of course little incentive to its acquisition and improvement.

But in truth the state possesses no such arbitrary power over the property of corporations. When allowed to acquire and own property, they must be treated as owners, with all the rights incident to ownership. They have a constitutional right to be so treated. Whatever power the state may possess in granting or in amending their charters, it cannot withdraw their property from the guaranties of the federal constitution.[15]

Because Justice Field not only wrote the circuit court opinion but also was one of the members of the Supreme Court that considered the case on appeal, it is quite possible that he played a role in the Court's decision to refuse even to hear arguments on the issue. The Supreme Court, however, has always tended to come down on the side of retaining its own jurisdiction. By granting the corporation the constitutional protections afforded to natural persons, the Court made itself into what John R. Commons called the "first authoritative faculty of political economy in the world's history."[16] The *Santa Clara* decision was certainly not the beginning of that role.[17] Aside from those few cases cited explicitly by Field, a number of other cases afforded the Court the opportunity to consider the nature of the corporation.

As early as 1804, in *Head v. Providence Insurance Co.*, the Court defined a corporation as the "mere creature of the act to which it owes its existence" and said, "It may correctly be said to be precisely what the incorporating act has made it, to derive all its powers from that act, and to be capable of exerting its faculties only in the manner which that act authorizes."[18] The next case was the 1809 *Bank of the United States v. Deveaux*, cited by Justice Field, in which the Court claimed jurisdiction under the diversity of citizenship clause of the Constitution. While denying citizenship status to the corporation, the Court reached through the corporate entity to the citizens of which it was composed.[19] The Court defined the corporation as "a mere creature of law, invisible, intangible, and incorporeal."[20]

Article I, section 10 of the Constitution prohibits any state from making "any law impairing the obligation of contracts." In 1819 in the well-known *Dartmouth College* case, also cited by Field against the argument that states can treat corporations differently from natural persons, the Supreme Court held the charter granted by King George to the founders of the college to be a contract protected from modifications made by the New Hampshire legislature in spite of the successful revolt of the king's colony from his jurisdiction. That ruling served to increase the power of the Court over the states. In addition Chief Justice Marshall gave an explicit definition of a corporation that was consistent with the 1804 *Head v. Providence Insurance Co.* case. He said:

A corporation is an artificial being, invisible, intangible, and existing only in contemplation of law. Being the mere creature of law, it possesses only those properties which the charter of its creation confers upon it, either expressly, or as incidental to its very existence. These are such as are supposed best calculated to effect the object for which it was created.[21]

Statutory as well as constitutional language has given rise to a Supreme Court definition of a corporation. In 1826 a defendant was convicted under a statute making illegal the destruction of a vessel "with intent or design to prejudice any person or persons that hath underwritten, . . . any policy or policies of insurance thereon."[22] In holding the corporation to be a person under this statute, the Court cited an English case and said, "Where the word used is, 'no person shall, . . . this extends as well to persons politic and incorporate, as to natural persons whatsoever.' "[23]

In 1830 a charter was strictly construed, and the Court ruled that a tax levied on a bank did not impair a contract because the charter granted no exemption from taxation. In this case the Court refused to give the corporate person any privileges not expressly granted, saying:

The great object of an incorporation is to bestow the character and properties of individuality on a collective and changing body of men. This capacity is always given to such a body. Any privileges which may exempt it from the burthens common to individuals, do not flow necessarily from the charter, but must be expressed in it, or they do not exist.[24]

In another case, the treatment of the corporation as a person also went against the interests of the corporation. In *Beaston v. Farmers' Bank* in 1838, the Court cited *Amedy* and held a corporation to be a person for purposes of a tax garnishment priority statute.[25]

In 1839 the Court decided that a corporation chartered in one state could make a contract with an out-of-state resident only because authority to do so was included in its charter.[26] On the nature of the corporation, the Court said:

It is very true, that a corporation can have no legal existence out of the boundaries of the sovereignty by which it is created. It exists only in contemplation of law, and by force of the law; and where that law ceases to operate, and is no longer obligatory, the corporation can have no existence. It must dwell in the place of its creation, and cannot migrate to another sovereignty.[27]

An 1840 case involved the right of a New York corporation to own land in Pennsylvania. The Court held that the corporation could own the land and in its reasoning dealt not only with the rights of the states to withhold the sanctioning of acts by out-of-state corporations but also with limitations on such states' rights imposed by the Constitution. The Court cited *Earle* and said:

A corporation is considered an artificial being, existing only in contemplation of law; and being a mere creature of the law, it possesses only those properties which the charter of its creation confers upon it, either expressly, or as incidental to its very existence. That corporations created by statute must depend for their powers and the mode of exercising them, upon the true construction of the statute. A corporation can have no legal existence out of the sovereignty by which it is created, as it exists only in contemplation of law, and by force of the law; and that when that law ceases to operate, and is no longer obligatory, the corporation can have no existence. It must dwell in the place of its creation, and cannot migrate to another sovereignty; but although it must live and have its being in that state only, yet it does not follow, that its existence there will not be recognised in other places; and its residence in one state creates no insuperable objection to its power of contracting in another. The corporation must show that the law of its creation gave it authority to make such contracts; yet, as in the case of a natural person, it is not necessary that it should actually exist in the sovereignty in which the contract is made. It is sufficient, that its existence as an artificial person in the state of its creation, is acknowledged and recognised by the state or nation where the dealing takes place; and that it is permitted by the laws of that place to exercise there the powers with which it is endowed. Every power, however, which a corporation exercises in another state, depends for its validity upon the laws of the sovereignty in which it is exercised; and a corporation can make no valid contract, without the sanction, express or implied, of such sovereignty; unless a case should be presented in which the right claimed by the corporation should appear to be secured by the constitution of the United States.[28]

Thus in 1840 the Supreme Court laid out clearly the role of the chartering state, other states, and the Supreme Court itself in the regulation of the emerging business corporations. It was the principle stated here that made the *Santa Clara* ruling so important to later attempts by states to regulate their own as well as foreign corporations. The Court from the beginning took it upon itself to oversee state regulation of corporations and generally used its asserted power to further the interests of the corporations and their managers and owners rather than to protect the public from the combination of human persons in corporate form. An analogous oversight power with respect to congressional regulation of interstate commerce is evident in the Court's interpretation of the Sherman Act, which also furthered the trend toward incorporation and centralization of control of economic activity.

THE DOUBLE STANDARD IN ANTITRUST POLICY

The first test of the Sherman Act came in 1895 in the *E. C. Knight* case.[29] Chief Justice Fuller gave the opinion of the Court.[30] The unanimity that prevailed in *Santa Clara* was broken. This time Justice Harlan dissented. The policy issue had to do with whether a combination in the form of a New Jersey holding company was a combination in the form of trust or otherwise in restraint of trade or commerce among the states. By its acquisition of the E. C. Knight Company and several other companies in Pennsylvania, the American Sugar Refining Company had acquired control of plants accounting for at least 90 percent of the sugar refining capacity in the United States. The question whether a corporation is a person was not directly raised. Instead the decision rested on interpretation of the commerce clause of the Constitution. The effect, however, was to give federal sanction to New Jersey's legalization of the trust in holding company form under a corporate charter. The Supreme Court asserted its right to overrule the attempt by Congress to outlaw the trust in any form.

The Court might have considered the holding company to be a combination in restraint of trade, looking through the corporate veil to the persons making it up—the incorporators. Or it might have treated the holding company as a person that had monopolized a part of commerce among the several states. The complaint alleged both. Before the acquisition in March 1892, the four acquired companies, operating independently of each other in competition with the American Sugar Refining Company, produced 33 percent of the sugar refined in the United States. The combination included all the sugar refiners in the United States except Revere of Boston that produced only 2 percent, according to the complaint.[31] The trial court found that ''about ten percent of the sugar refined and sold in the United States is refined in other refineries than those controlled by the American Sugar Refining Co.'' and that ''the object in purchasing the Philadelphia refineries was to obtain a greater influence or more perfect control over the business of refining and selling sugar in this country.''[32] Yet the trial court dismissed the bill, holding "that the facts did not show a contract, combination, or conspiracy to restrain trade or monopolize trade or commerce 'among the several States or with foreign nations.' ''[33] The circuit court of appeals affirmed the dismissal decree.[34]

Chief Justice Fuller passed over several other arguments made in defense of the combination to reach the interstate commerce issue, saying:

> In the view which we take of the case, we need not discuss whether because the tentacles which drew the outlying refineries into the dominant corporation were separately put out, therefore there was no combination to monopolize; or, because, according to political economists, aggregations of capital may reduce prices, therefore the objection to concentration of power is relieved; or, because others were theoretically left free to go into the business of refining sugar, and the original stockholders of the Philadelphia refineries after becoming stockholders of the American Company might go into competition with themselves, or, parting with that stock, might set up again for themselves, therefore no objectionable restraint was imposed.
>
> The fundamental question is, whether conceding that the existence of a monopoly in manufacture is established by the evidence, that monopoly can be directly suppressed under the act of Congress in the mode attempted by this bill.[35]

That question was answered in the negative. Manufacturing is not commerce, said the Court. "Commerce succeeds to manufacture, and is not a part of it."[36] Yet there was more to the Court's reasoning than this simple distinction. The underlying question was whether, under the Constitution, the states or the federal government should deal with the monopoly problem. Chief Justice Fuller said:

> The relief of the citizens of each State from the burden of monopoly and the evils resulting from the restraint of trade among such citizens was left with the States to deal with, and this court has recognized their possession of that power even to the extent of holding that an employment or business carried on by private individuals, when it becomes a matter of such public interest and importance as to create a common charge or burden upon the citizen; in other words, when it becomes a practical monopoly, to which the citizen is compelled to resort and by means of which a tribute can be exacted from the community, is subject to regulation by state legislative power.[37]

This passage seems to be a veiled reference to *Munn v. Illinois*. If New Jersey does not wish to prevent the sugar "trust" in its general incorporation law or Pennsylvania does not wish to exercise its power to refuse a New Jersey corporation the right to acquire the stock of Pennsylvania sugar refineries, then Illinois or any other state could regulate the price of sugar to protect its citizens from the monopoly power of the combination. Yet it seems quite likely that this same Court would have stricken down such regulation if the refineries were located out of state. The next sentence says: "On the other hand, the power of Congress to regulate commerce among the several States is also exclusive. . . .

That which belongs to commerce is within the jurisdiction of the United States, but that which does not belong to commerce is within the jurisdiction of the police power of the State.''[38]

Fuller's opinion elaborates at length on this distinction. Implicit in his reasoning is the conclusion that public-utility-type regulation of prices by the federal government, as in the case of railroads, would be the only constitutional way to protect the sugar trade from unlawful restraints and monopolies. He said:

> The argument is that the power to control the manufacture of refined sugar is a monopoly over a necessary of life, to the enjoyment of which by a large part of the population of the United States interstate commerce is indispensable, and that, therefore, the general government in the exercise of the power to regulate commerce may repress such monopoly directly and set aside the instruments which have created it. But this argument cannot be confined to necessaries of life merely, and must include all articles of general consumption. Doubtless the power to control the manufacture of a given thing involves in a certain sense the control of its disposition, but this is a secondary and not the primary sense; and although the exercise of that power may result in bringing the operation of commerce into play, it does not control it, and affects it only incidentally and indirectly. Commerce succeeds to manufacture, and is not a part of it. The power to regulate commerce is the power to prescribe the rule by which commerce shall be governed, and is a power independent of the power to suppress monopoly. But it may operate in repression of monopoly whenever that comes within the rules by which commerce is governed or whenever the transaction is itself a monopoly of commerce. . . .
>
> It will be perceived how far-reaching the proposition is that the power of dealing with a monopoly directly may be exercised by the general government whenever interstate or international commerce may be ultimately affected. The regulation of commerce applies to the subjects of commerce and not to matters of internal police. Contracts to buy, sell, or exchange goods to be transported among the several States, the transportation and its instrumentalities, and articles bought, sold, or exchanged for the purposes of such transit among the States, or put in the way of transit, may be regulated, but this is because they form part of interstate trade or commerce. The fact that an article is manufactured for export to another State does not of itself make it an article of interstate commerce, and the intent of the manufacturer does not determine the time when the article or produce passes from the control of the State and belongs to commerce.[39]

If the Congress had followed the *E. C. Knight* case with railroad-type regulation of the price of sugar refined in one state and sold in another, the Court, as in the case of railroad rate regulation, would have asserted its power to be the ultimate arbiter of the reasonableness of the sugar prices set by the government.

The majority opinion in *E. C. Knight*, like the *Santa Clara* ruling, was not manufactured out of whole cloth. Fuller was able to cite a number of precedents making the same distinction between manufacturing and commerce and between the role of the states and of the federal government. In *Coe v. Errol*, the Court had allowed New Hampshire to tax logs intended for but not yet actually exported to Maine.[40] In *Kidd v. Pearson*, the Court had allowed a state to prohibit manufacture of liquor even though it was intended for sale out of state.[41] In other cases, the Court had stricken down state regulation that interfered with actual commerce among the states. Yet Justice Harlan found grounds for dissent.

With respect to Fuller's citation of precedents for the distinction between commerce and manufacturing, Harlan cited several cases in which commerce had been held to include purchase, sale, and exchange of commodities as well as transportation and to extend to "all of the external concerns of the nation, and to those internal concerns which affect the States generally."[42] He said:

> In *Kidd* v. *Pearson*, 128 U.S. 1, 20, it was said that "the buying and selling, and the transportation incidental thereto constitute commerce." Interstate commerce does not, therefore, consist in transportation simply. It includes the purchase and sale of articles that are intended to be transported from one State to another—every species of commercial intercourse among the States and with foreign nations.[43]

To Harlan the fundamental question in the case was what is an unlawful restraint of trade. The Sherman Act, in Harlan's view, clearly made a combination in restraint of trade illegal no matter what its form. He cited a number of state cases defining restraint of trade by combinations of various sorts, including holding company acquisition of stock in competing companies, and then said:

> This extended reference to adjudged cases relating to unlawful restraints upon the interior traffic of a State has been made for the purpose of showing that a combination such as that organized under the name of the American Sugar Refining Company has been uniformly held by the courts of the States to be against public policy and illegal because of its necessary tendency to impose improper restraints upon trade. And such, I take it, would be the judgment of any Circuit Court of the United States in a case between parties in which it became necessary to determine the question. The judgments of the state courts rest upon general principles of law, and not necessarily upon statutory provisions expressly condemning restraints of trade imposed by or resulting from combinations. Of course, in view of the authorities, it will not be doubted that it would be competent for a State, under the power to regulate its domestic commerce and for the purpose of protecting its people against fraud and injustice, to make it a public offense punishable by fine and imprisonment, for individuals or corporations to make contracts, form combinations, or engage in conspiracies, which unduly restrain trade or commerce carried on within its limits, and also to authorize the institution of proceedings for the purpose of annuling contracts of that character, as well as of preventing or restraining such combinations and conspiracies.
> But there is a trade among the several States which is distinct from that carried on within the territorial limits of a State. The regulation and control of the former is committed by the national Constitution to Congress . . .
> It is the Constitution, the supreme law of the land, which invests Congress with power to protect commerce among the States against burdens and exactions arising from unlawful restraints by whatever authority imposed. Surely a right secured or granted by that instrument is under the protection of the government which that instrument creates.[44]

Harlan made the interesting point that the constitutional prohibition against state interference with interstate commerce should apply equally to combinations of corporations or individuals, saying:

If the national power is competent to repress *State* action in restraint of interstate trade as it may be, involved in purchases of refined sugar to be transported from one State to another State, surely it ought to be deemed sufficient to prevent unlawful restraints attempted to be imposed by combinations of corporations or individuals upon those identical purchases; otherwise, illegal combinations of corporations or individuals may— so far as national power and interstate commerce are concerned—do, with impunity, what no State can do.[45]

Harlan concluded:

While the opinion of the court in this case does not declare the act of 1890 to be unconstitutional, it defeats the main object for which it was passed. For it is, in effect, held that the statute would be unconstitutional if interpreted as embracing such unlawful restraints upon the purchasing of goods in one State to be carried to another State as necessarily arise from the existence of combinations formed for the purpose and with the effect, not only of monopolizing the ownership of all such goods in every part of the country, but of controlling the prices for them in all the States. This view of the scope of the act leaves the public, so far as national power is concerned, entirely at the mercy of combinations which arbitrarily control the prices of articles purchased to be transported from one State to another State. I cannot assent to that view.[46]

Harlan's dissent represents much more than a difference from the majority over the meaning of the commerce clause of the Constitution. It represents a fundamentally different evaluation of public policy with respect to the degree of centralization of control of economic activity. Harlan's failure to dissent in the *Santa Clara* case can be explained by the basis of that holding in the rights of individuals to constitutional protections in spite of the corporate veil. He was just as willing to reach through that corporate veil to hold individuals to proper standards of conduct in the interest of protecting trade and commerce from unlawful restraints and monopolies. The majority of the Court simply held a different set of values, or perhaps only Harlan perceived the implications of the tremendous change taking place through the rise of the corporation.

The effect of the *E. C. Knight* decision was to remove all legal impediments to combination of all the firms in any industry. The great merger movement was the immediate result. Between 1896 and 1904, when the *Northern Securities* case at least partially overturned *E. C. Knight*, the twentieth-century pattern of oligopoly was accomplished without interference from the federal antitrust laws. Most of today's blue chip corporations are rooted in that period.[47] The Supreme Court not only permitted combinations in corporate form but also encouraged such closely knit combinations by its decision in the *Addyston Pipe and Steel* case, in which a cartel arrangement among a number of manufacturing companies was held to violate the Sherman Act.[48] Herein lies the double standard. In fact, the pipe companies actually merged together between the circuit court of appeals' decision in 1898 and the Supreme Court's ruling a year later.

This first great merger movement was fundamentally different from the various waves of merger activity that followed in later years because the resulting combines were, in most cases, many times larger than the combining companies. For example, in 1901 the United States Steel corporation combined some 180 formerly independent companies under the control of a single holding company.

The states that wished to resist this revolutionary change were powerless to do anything effective to stop it. If they had tried to deny the right of New Jersey corporations to do interstate business in their state, they would have run afoul of the prohibition against states interfering in interstate commerce. In 1900 the Supreme Court ruled that Texas could revoke the permit to do intrastate business in Texas of the Waters-Pierce Oil Company without denying it due process of law but only because the Texas court had limited the decree to intrastate business.[49] The Waters-Pierce Oil Company was a Missouri corporation that had joined the Standard Oil trust. The Texas action had a negligible effect on that trust, which converted itself into the Standard Oil Company of New Jersey and operated undisturbed by state actions until 1911.

Policy clearly had to be made on the federal level, and federal policy was made by a Supreme Court that was willing and able to give legal sanction to this transformation of American society, in spite of a deep concern about concentration of economic power at the grass-roots level. Congress, however, did not take these developments lying down. In 1898, soon after the great merger movement began, Congress created the Industrial Commission, a temporary agency empowered to "collate information and to consider and recommend legislation to meet the problems presented by labor, agriculture, and capital."[50]

The Industrial Commission consisted of ten members of Congress and nine persons appointed by the president. In its nineteen reports, it made public a wealth of information on the structure of the U.S. economy and made a number of recommendations for legislation by state and federal governments. As a result, in 1903 Congress took three important actions designed to bring the trusts under public control. In that year Congress created the Antitrust Division in the Department of Justice and the Bureau of Corporations in the Department of Commerce and Labor. It also enacted the Expediting Act to give priority in the district courts to civil antitrust cases brought by the attorney general and to provide for direct appeal of such cases to the Supreme Court, bypassing the circuit courts of appeal. The Bureau of Corporations, which was converted into the Federal Trade Commission in 1914, was an important part of Teddy Roosevelt's trust-busting efforts. Building on the work of the Industrial Commission, it investigated several manufacturing industries, including tobacco and petroleum, and laid the basis for several important Sherman Act cases.

Meanwhile in 1904 the Supreme Court, for the first time since *E. C. Knight* in 1895, had an opportunity to apply the Sherman Act to a New Jersey holding company.[51] In the intervening years four justices had been replaced. Field, Gray, Shiras, and Jackson had left the Court, replaced by Peckham, McKenna, Holmes, and Day. The case involved a combination of two railroad corporations through an exchange of stock with the Northern Securities Company, which was created for that purpose. The Court ruled 5 to 4 that the corporation constituted a combination in restraint of trade and ordered the acquired companies neither to pay it dividends nor allow it to vote the acquired stocks, thereby forcing it to dissolve.

The company argued that it was a person, which could not be deprived of its property without due process of law. Because this combination was of railroad companies, the question whether manufacturing is commerce was not an issue. Yet White and Fuller, who had been in the majority in *E. C. Knight*, still found grounds for allowing the combination. They were joined in dissent by Peckham and Holmes. Brewer and Brown, who had voted with Fuller in *E. C. Knight*, this time joined Harlan, McKenna, and Day in condemning the combination, although Brewer wrote a separate concurring opinion. Harlan wrote the opinion of the Court.[52] Illegal purpose and intent were inferred from the elimination of competition between the previously competing railroads, and every such restraint was held to be unlawful. The Court relied on the precedent set in *United States v. Trans-Missouri Freight Association*, even through the combination in *Northern Securities* was accomplished as a closely knit combination in which the combining companies lost their autonomy completely and the *Trans-Missouri* case involved a loosely knit, cartel arrangement to fix prices jointly.[53]

At this point, the double standard appeared to be eliminated, and the great turn-of-the-century merger movement came to an end.[54] The state of antitrust policy remained uncertain, however, until the 1911 landmark decisions in two cases involving manufacturing corporations.[55] In both cases the combinations were held to be in restraint of trade and ordered dissolved. The victory for the trust-busters was lessened by two important features of the cases. The remedies were superficial since the Court allowed a simple spinoff that left a community of interest. The stock in the thirty-three corporations owned by Standard Oil of New Jersey was divested to the owners of Standard Oil of New Jersey stock on a pro rata basis, leaving control of all of them in the hands of John D. Rockefeller and his associates. Second, the Court for the first time laid down the rule of reason, over the dissent of Justice Harlan. The Supreme Court by this ruling assured itself of the opportunity to continue to be the "authoritative faculty of political economy" in future cases of closely knit combination.

The full effect of the rule of reason was felt in 1920 when the U.S. Steel Company's control of two-thirds of the steel industry was sanctioned.[56] Bigness was not badness, and combination in corporate form was judged by a different standard from agreements among separate companies. That the difference in treatment of closely and loosely knit combinations had not been eliminated by the rule of reason was made clear in *Trenton Potteries* in 1927 when the Court held price fixing to be per se unlawful for any substantial part of trade or commerce.[57]

The double standard was partially removed for a few years by the Warren Court's interpretation of section 7 of the Clayton Act.[58] In the 1962 *Brown Shoe* case, the Court applied a much more stringent standard of illegality and held a merger of Brown Shoe and the Kinney Shoe Company to be unlawful because of a reasonable probability that it would substantially lessen competition in some lines of commerce. Until the Reagan administration greatly relaxed antitrust enforcement in the 1980s, the antitrust policy on new closely knit combinations was brought very close to the policy on loosely knit, cartel-like arrangements. Except for the Warren Court's order forcing du Pont to divest itself of long-held General Motors stock, however, the permissive policy remained in effect for closely knit combinations created in earlier days.[59] If the *Brown Shoe* policy had prevailed in 1895, the great merger movement could not have occurred.

Commerce was primarily local in character at the beginning of the nineteenth century. As the means of transport improved and commerce became predominantly interstate in character, competition increased. The law of corporations, the antitrust policy, and the Supreme Court's interpretation of the Constitution all served to facilitate the rise of large national corporations. In the twentieth century, the trend toward corporate concentration in the United States has continued, while the giant corporations have become transnational. As competition has increased for a share of the U.S. market by foreign producers, the call has arisen anew for relaxation of the antitrust policy "to allow American companies to compete with foreign competitors."[60] The secretary of commerce has recently called for the outright repeal of section 7 of the Clayton Act.[61] Joint ventures and stockholding links have become common between U.S. and Japanese automobile companies. The new turn of the century may well bring a radical transformation of world industry structure but this time without any higher-level government in being to undertake social control of the anational corporations.

THE INTRAENTERPRISE CONSPIRACY QUESTION

Apart from the question whether a merger creates as much restraint of trade as a loosely knit agreement among the merging firms, the double standard enters into antitrust policy in another way that warrants consideration. Anticompetitive behavior or predatory practices come under antitrust scrutiny. Section 2 of the Sherman Act makes it unlawful for a person to monopolize. With the rule of reason, the standard of illegality for monopolization is the same as that for a closely knit combination in restraint of trade. If the corporation's size and market power falls short of this standard, under which, for example, U.S. Steel was acquitted in 1920 and Alcoa was found guilty in 1945, it still may run afoul of the antitrust laws if it conspires either to restrain trade or to monopolize. For such collusive behavior, the standard is relatively strict, with some offenses having come to be considered per se violations and others requiring application of a rule of reason. But section 2 of the Sherman Act also makes it unlawful for a single person to attempt to monopolize. The standard used for judging attempts to monopolize by one person is more permissive than that used for the same behavior with the same economic effects when engaged in by two or more persons.[62]

To prove that one person alone has attempted to monopolize, the plaintiff must prove a dangerous probability of success.[63] Most firms have less market power than that required by the dangerous probability of success test, and yet they do have many ways of behaving anticompetitively without the collaboration of a second person. Therein lies the double standard. It has given rise over the years to many attempts, particularly by private plaintiffs, to find more than one actor within the structure of a single firm, but success has become increasingly difficult.

Several Supreme Court opinions have given some support to plaintiffs, and in the lower courts the holdings have varied among the various circuits. In 1984, however, the Supreme Court reversed the Seventh Circuit Court of Appeals and held that as a matter of law, a parent company and its wholly owned subsidiary are incapable of conspiring.[64] Thus the concept of the artificial person has been extended explicitly to groups of corporations.

The case involved predatory practices by Copperweld Corporation to deter entry of a competitor, Independence Tube Corporation. Copperweld had acquired Regal Tube Company as a wholly owned subsidiary. The former president of Regal, David Grohne, formed Independence Tube Corporation to compete with Copperweld in the steel tubing business. Independence ordered a tubing mill from the Yoder Company. Copperweld sent letters to firms with which Mr. Grohne attempted to deal, including banks, prospective suppliers, and customers, and real estate firms expressing its concern about Grohne's entering the market in competition with Regal. After receiving Copperweld's letter, Yoder voided the order from Independence, delaying its entry into the tube market by nine months. Independence brought suit alleging a conspiracy among Copperweld, Regal, and Yoder. The jury found a conspiracy between Copperweld and Regal, but it found Yoder not to be part of the conspiracy.

The Seventh Circuit Court based its decision on a 1968 Supreme Court decision in which the most lenient standard of proof had been laid down.[65] In *Perma Life Mufflers, Inc. v. International Parts Corp.*, the Court said:

But since respondents Midas and International availed themselves of the privilege of doing business through separate corporations, the fact of common ownership could not save them from any of the obligations that the law imposes on separate entities.[66]

The Court had earlier sustained an allegation of conspiracy among related corporations in four cases. In 1947 in *United States v. Yellow Cab Co.*, the Court said:

[An unreasonable restraint] may result as readily from a conspiracy among those who are affiliated or integrated under common ownership as from a conspiracy among those who are otherwise independent. . . . The corporate interrelationships of the conspirators, in other words, are not determinative of the applicability of the Sherman Act. That statute is aimed at substance rather than form.[67]

The case involved the Checker Cab Manufacturing Company, its president, and five affiliated corporations.

The following year in *Schine Chain Theatres v. United States*, the Court said:

The concerted action of the parent company, its subsidiaries, and the named officers and directors in that endeavor was a conspiracy which was not immunized by the fact that the members were closely affiliated rather than independent.[68]

In this case the Court included natural persons who were agents of the corporations in its finding. In later years, the lower courts generally distinguished between a corporate agent and an outside contractor and between an individual acting in his corporate capacity and that same individual acting in his private interests.[69]

A second case involved two commonly owned subsidiaries of Joseph E. Seagram and Sons, Inc. The subsidiaries were charged with conspiring with each other in refusing to deal with a wholesaler who refused to follow pricing policies of the manufacturer. The Supreme Court said:

This suggestion [that two wholly owned subsidiaries cannot conspire] runs counter to our past decisions that common ownership and control does not liberate corporations from the impact of the antitrust laws. This rule is especially applicable where, as here, the respondents hold themselves out as competitive.[70]

The third case involved a market-sharing arrangement among three interrelated firms. Timken Roller Bearing Company owned 30 percent of the stocks of an English corporation, and the two firms had a joint venture in France in which Timken owned a half-interest.[71] The Court repeated the Kiefer-Stewart doctrine, saying "The fact that there is common ownership or control of the contracting corporation does not liberate them from the impact of the antitrust laws."[72]

Thus, the 1984 *Copperweld* case appears to be a significant change in public policy that gives even more privilege to business firms using the corporate form of organization. They are now free not only to combine under the protections of a single corporate charter but also to divide their operations into a number of separate corporations and still be considered a single entity incapable as a matter of law of conspiring. The *Copperweld* case involved a wholly owned subsidiary. Whether this new doctrine will be extended to less than wholly owned subsidiaries remains to be seen, but the logic of the Court indicates that it will be. The next step would be extension to a corporation and any other corporations over which it has control with less than 100 percent voting rights. Such a development would open the door to a withering away of the per se rules against price fixing as corporations take an equity position in competitors as is becoming common in the world automobile industry.

THE CONFLICT OF VALUES

The course of U.S. history can be viewed as a continuing conflict between the forces of centralization versus the forces of decentralization—that is, between groups and individuals as the basic units of society and between hierarchies and markets as the organizational features of the economy. Some would have us believe that the outcome of this continuing struggle is determined by natural laws discovered by economic science—that the answer to the question how much centralization is optimal is objectively determinable.[73] In my view this basic policy issue arises from the differences in values, and it goes back far in history.[74] Some people are Tories, and some are not. At the time of the Declaration of Independence, the pendulum had swung far over in the direction of an individualistic political philosophy, and the American Revolution set off a struggle against imperialism that has continued to this day throughout the world. The adoption of the Constitution with its creation of the Supreme Court and the presidency was the beginning, however, of a swing in the other direction in the United States. The Supreme Court has played a crucial role as part of the mechanism of conflict resolution. Except for a few brief interludes, from the days of John Marshall to those of Warren Burger, the Court has come down on the side of centralization of control of the economy by encouraging the development of ever larger corporate hierarchies. From time to time, however, the Court has included and occasionally been dominated by individual justices with a deep-seated commitment to individualism. When the antitrust issue is seen in this light, it is easy to understand why such defenders of civil liberties of individuals as John Marshall Harlan, Louis Brandeis, Hugo Black, William O. Douglas, and Earl Warren were also the strongest opponents of corporate dominance of U.S. society.[75] Black and Douglas even attempted to overturn the *Santa Clara* holding that the corporation is a person for purposes of the Fourteenth Amendment.

In 1938 just before Douglas joined the Court, Hugo Black wrote a dissenting opinion on the question in *Connecticut General Life Insurance Co. v. Johnson, Treasurer of California.*[76] In 1949 Douglas, with Black concurring, made another attempt to overturn the *Santa Clara* ruling.[77] Each served a third of a century on the Court and consistently supported strong antitrust policies. Only in the brief Warren years were they able to form a majority on most antitrust issues, but they apparently found no occasions again to try to overturn *Santa Clara*.

In the Connecticut General case, the Court, in an opinion by Justice Harlan Stone, held that the due process clause prohibited California from taxing business carried on in Connecticut to reinsure insurance policies written in California. Black considered the tax on the reinsurance business to be a legitimate condition the state could impose on the corporation for the privilege granted to do business in California. He cited Brandeis's dissent in *Liggett Co. v. Lee*.[78] Brandeis had stopped short of claiming that the Fourteenth Amendment did not apply to corporations but instead rested his argument on whether the plaintiff had in fact been denied equal protection and due process. Black went much further:

I do not believe the word ''person'' in the Fourteenth Amendment includes corporations. ''The doctrine of stare decisis, however appropriate and even necessary at times, has only a limited application in the field of constitutional law.'' This Court has many times changed its interpretations of the Constitution when the conclusion was reached that an improper construction had been adopted. Only recently the case of *West Coast Hotel Co. v. Parrish*, 300 U.S. 379, expressly overruled a previous interpretation of the Fourteenth Amendment which had long blocked state minimum wage legislation. . . .

Neither the history nor the language of the Fourteenth Amendment justifies the belief that corporations are included within its protection. . . .

Certainly, when the Fourteenth Amendment was submitted for approval, the people were not told that the states of the South were to be denied their normal relationship with the Federal Government unless they ratified an amendment granting new and revolutionary rights to corporations. . . .

The history of the Amendment proves that the people were told that its purpose was to protect weak and helpless human beings and were not told that it was intended to remove corporations in any fashion from the control of state governments. The Fourteenth Amendment followed the freedom of a race from slavery. Justice Swayne said in the *Slaughter House Cases, supra*, that ''by 'any person' was meant *all* persons within the jurisdiction of the State. No distinction is intimated on account of race or color.'' Corporations have neither race nor color. He knew the Amendment was intended to protect the life, liberty and property of *human* beings.

The language of the Amendment itself does not support the theory that it was passed for the benefit of corporations.[79]

Black went on to show the various instances in which the amendment itself uses the word *person* in the context of human persons capable of such things as life, naturalization, citizenship, representation, and even membership in Congress and never applied to corporations. He went on to say:

Both Congress and the people were familiar with the meaning of the word ''corporation'' at the time the Fourteenth Amendment was submitted and adopted. The judicial inclusion of the word ''corporation'' in the Fourteenth Amendment has had a revolutionary effect on our form of government. The states did not adopt the Amendment with knowledge of its sweeping meaning under its present construction. No section of the Amendment gave notice to the people that, if adopted, it would subject every state law and municipal ordinance, affecting corporations, (and all administrative actions under them) to censorship of the United States courts. No word in all this Amendment gave any hint that its adoption would deprive the states of their long recognized power to regulate corporations.[80]

Citing the *Slaughter House Cases*[81] and a 1912 study of the consequences of the amendment,[82] Black said:

This Amendment sought to prevent discrimination by the states against classes or races. We are aware of this from words spoken in this Court within five years after its adoption, when the people and the courts were personally familiar with the historical background of the Amendment. "We doubt very much whether any action of a State not directed by way of discrimination against the Negroes as a class, or on account of their race, will ever be held to come within the purview of this provision." Yet, of the cases in this Court in which the Fourteenth Amendment was applied during the first fifty years after its adoption, less than one-half of one percent invoked it in protection of the Negro race, and more than fifty percent asked that its benefits be extended to corporations.[83]

One of the cases Black cited in his demonstration that the words *life* and *liberty* do not apply to corporations was *Western Turf Association v. Greenburg.*[84] In that case John Marshall Harlan, writing for a unanimous Court, accepted the *Santa Clara* precedent as far as property was concerned but held that all corporations were equally treated by the statute in question. On other claims of the plaintiff, Harlan said:

Of still less merit is the suggestion that the statute abridges the rights and privileges of citizens; for a corporation cannot be deemed a citizen within the meaning of the clause of the Constitution of the United States which protects the privileges and immunities of citizens of the United States against being abridged or impaired by the law of a state. The same observation may be made as to the contention that the statute deprives the defendant of its liberty without due process of law; for, liberty guaranteed by the Fourteenth Amendment against deprivation without due process of law is the liberty of natural, not artificial, persons. *Northwestern Life Insurance Co.* v. *Riggs*, 203 U.S. 243. Does the statute deprive the defendant of any property right without due process of law? We answer this question in the negative.[85]

In the *Northwestern Life* case, Harlan also wrote for a unanimous Court, saying:

As the present statute is applicable alike to all life insurance companies doing business in Missouri, after its enactment, there is no reason for saying that it denies the equal protection of the laws. Equally without foundation is the contention that the statute, if enforced, will be inconsistent with the liberty guaranteed by the Fourteenth Amendment. The liberty referred to in that Amendment is the liberty of natural, not artificial persons. Nor in any true, constitutional sense does the Missouri statute deprive life insurance companies doing business in that State of a right of property. This is too plain for discussion.[86]

Justice Harlan, in both *Western Turf* and in *Northwestern Life*, supported the right of a state to regulate corporations so as to protect the rights of individuals. Although he accepted the *Santa Clara* doctrine, he interpreted the facts so as not to exert the Court's power to overrule the state. These two opinions, along with the opinion in *Northern Securities*, were written during a brief period in which Harlan's egalitarian values were shared by a majority of the Court.

Hugo Black seems to have been consistent in his support of civil liberties, but he was not consistent in his interpretations of the Fourteenth Amendment. In writing for the Court in *Bridges v. California*,[87] with Justice Douglas joining, Justice Black accepted the 1925 Gitlow doctrine[88] that the liberty protected by the Fourteenth Amendment includes the freedom of speech and of the press protected by the Fifth Amendment. But Black went further than Gitlow. He implicitly applied that doctrine not only to the individual, Harry Bridges, but to the Times Mirror Corporation. Both had been held in contempt by a California state court. Black made no explicit reference to the question whether the corporation was a person in this context. That question was not a point of contention in the case.

In 1949 in *Wheeling Steel Corporation v. Glander*, Justice Robert Jackson wrote the opinion of the Court striking down an Ohio tax statute on the grounds that it denied the corporations equal protection of the laws.[89] The statute levied a tax on intangibles that exempted Ohio corporations. In his opinion of the Court, Jackson implicitly assumed, without discussion, that the equal protection clause of the Fourteenth Amendment protects corporations as well as natural persons, but he also wrote a second, concurring opinion in response to Douglas's dissent explaining why he made the assumption in the Court opinion. He pointed out that the Court had consistently held the protection to apply to corporations since *Santa Clara* in 1886 and that the doctrine had been challenged only once, by Black in *Connecticut General*. Jackson then cited several cases in which Douglas or Black had written the Court's opinion without intimating any doubt on the question, including the *Bridges* case.[90]

In his dissenting opinion, with Black concurring, Douglas conceded that implicit in all the Court's decisions since 1886 was the treatment of the corporation as a person within the equal protection clause. Douglas repeated much of the argument made by Black in *Connecticut General*. He said, "One hesitates to overrule cases even in the constitutional field that are of old vintage. But that has never been a deterrent heretofore and should not be now."[91] He then cited five cases in which the Court had overruled earlier cases ranging from forty-two to ninety-five years standing.

CONCLUSIONS

The bicentenary of the adoption of the Constitution is approaching, along with the centenary of the *Santa Clara* case and the Sherman Act. It seems very unlikely that the Supreme Court will reverse the trend toward the corporate state. Even if the Court were to reverse such longstanding precedents and treat the corporation as a group of human persons, the patterns of relations among persons and things have evolved so far in the direction of collectivism that the Court alone probably could not effect a revolution toward individualism. But the Court might nudge the pendulum in the other direction. The law is the master institution.

Corporations do govern in a very real sense. Concentration of control of economic activity in the hands of relatively few giant transnational corporations is as much a threat to democracy as centralization of political governmental powers, if not more so, since the latter follows from the former. The relations between government and business are crucial. For at least forty years, the policy debate in the United States has been so completely dominated by the threat to democracy from Marxian and Soviet expansion that we have lost sight of the threat from fascism, which is the end result of the trend toward corporativism.

NOTES

1. See Corporations, in Dictionary of American History (1976); and Liggett Co. v. Lee, 288 U.S. 517, 548–69 (1933) (Brandeis, J., dissenting). New Jersey was the first state to allow intercorporate stockholding generally. Act of April 4, 1888, ch. 269, 1888 N. J. Laws 385; Act of April 17, 1888, ch. 295, 1888 N. J. Laws 445; Act of March 14, 1893, ch. 171, 1893 N. J. Laws 301.

2. County of Santa Clara v. S. Pac. R. R. Co., 118 U.S. 394 (1886).

3. Connolly v. Union Sewer Pipe Co., 184 U.S. 540 (1902).

4. 26 Stat. 209, ch. 647 (1890).

5. 15 U.S.C. § 2 (1976).

6. 15 U.S.C. § 1. The section also contains another sentence: "Every person who shall make any contract or engage in any combination or conspiracy declared to be illegal shall be deemed guilty of a felony."

7. Brandeis, supra note 1, at 556 n. 32, says about the holding corporation: "Although unconditional power was not conferred until the Act of 1893, supra, it had been the practice of corporations formed in New Jersey to purchase the shares of other corporations. ...In no other state had there been a provision permitting the formation of holding companies, although by special act, notably in Pennsylvania, a few such companies had been formed."

8. See supra note 2, 118 U.S. 394, 396.

9. County of Santa Clara v. S. Pac. R. R. Co., 18 Fed. 385. (1883). Seven cases were combined on appeal from state courts. They involved two counties and the state of California claiming unpaid taxes levied on three railroad corporations. The railroads claimed the tax assessments were discriminatory in violation of the Fourteenth Amendment.

10. Id. at 402–3.

11. 9 U.S. (5 Cranch) 61, 87 (1809).

12. Society for the Propagation of the Gospel in Foreign Parts v. Town of New Haven, 21 U.S. (8 Wheat.) 464 (1823).

13. 18 F. at 404.

14. Id. at 404.

15. Id. at 405.

16. J. Commons, Legal Foundations of Capitalism 7 (1924).

17. See A. Miller, The Modern Corporate State (1976).

18. 6 U.S. (2 Cranch) 127, 166 (1804). On the basis of this definition, the Court held to be binding on an insurance company a settlement negotiated through the mail by the company's broker even though the settlement differed from the provisions in the policy.

19. 13 U.S. (9 Cranch) 61, 89 (1809).

20. Id. at 87.

21. Dartmouth College v. Woodward, 17 U.S. (4 Wheat.) 518, 636 (1819).

22. United States v. Amedy, 24 U.S. (11 Wheat.) 391 (1826).

23. Id.

24. The Providence Bank v. Billings, 29 U.S. (4 Pet.) 514, 562 (1830).

25. 37 U.S. (12 Pet.) 102, 135 (1838).

26. Bank of Augusta v. Earle, 38 U.S. (13 Pet.) 584 (1839).

27. Id. at 588.

28. Runyan v. Costes, 39 U.S. (14 Pet.) 122, 129 (1840).

29. United States v. E. C. Knight Co., 156 U.S. 1 (1895).

30. He was joined by Field, Gray, Brewer, Brown, Shiras, and White. Howell E. Jackson did not participate.

31. 156 U.S. at 3.

32. Id. at 6.

33. Id., quoting from 60 F. 306.

34. 60 F. 934.

35. 156 U.S. at 10–11.

36. Id. at 12.

37. Id. at 12.

38. Id. at 11–12.

39. Id. at 12–13.

40. 116 U.S. 517.

41. 128 U.S. 1, 21–22.

42. 156 U.S. at 21–22, citing Gibbons v. Ogden, 22 U.S. (9 Wheat.) 1, County of Mobile v. Kinkaid, 102 U.S. 691, 702, and Gloucester Ferry Co. v. Pennsylvania, 114 U.S. 196, 203.

43. 156 U.S. at 22.

44. Id. at 32–33.

45. Id. at 38.

46. Id. at 42–43.

47. For an excellent brief discussion of this revolutionary change in industrial organization in the United States, see P. Homan, Trusts, Early Development, in Encyclopaedia of the Social Sciences. Also see D. Martin, Mergers and the Clayton Act (1959) and the works cited therein.

48. United States v. Addyston Pipe and Steel Co., 175 U.S. 211 (1899).

49. Waters-Pierce Oil Co. v. State of Texas, 177 U.S. 28 (1900).

50. Final Report of the Industrial Commission, H. R. Doc. No. 380, 57th Cong., 1st. Sess. 7 (1902).

51. Northern Securities Company v. United States, 193 U.S. 197 (1904).

52. White wrote a dissenting opinion in which Fuller, Peckham, and Holmes joined, and Holmes wrote a dissenting opinion in which Fuller, Peckham, and White joined.

53. 166 U.S. 290 (1897).

54. In my judgment, the purely coincidental timing of these important legal developments at the end of a century in our Gregorian calendar has contributed greatly to the myth that small business goes with the old century with its archaic technology and the rise of big business in the new century goes along with twentieth-century technology. One wonders whether the twenty-first century will also bring new myths in its wake.

55. Standard Oil Co. v. United States, 221 U.S. 1 (1911); United States v. American Tobacco Co., 221 U.S. 106 (1911).

56. United States v. U.S. Steel Corporation, 251 U.S. 417 (1920).

57. United States v. Trenton Potteries Co., 273 U.S. 392 (1927).

58. For an account of the failure of the holding company provisions of the 1914 Clayton Act in preventing mergers, see D. Martin, Mergers and the Clayton Act (1959). For an account of the Warren Court's interpretation of the Celler-Kefauver Amendment to section 7 of the Clayton Act, see Martin, The Brown Shoe Case and the New Antimerger Policy, 53 Am. Econ. Rev. 340–58 (1963), and Brown Shoe v. United States, 370 U.S. 294 (1962).

59. United States v. du Pont, 353 U.S. 586 (1957). This case was brought in 1949 before the Celler-Kefauver amendment was enacted, but the Court in 1957 was probably affected by the 1950 statement of policy by the Congress.

60. See D. Martin, The Role of Antitrust in the Industrial Policy of the United States, in Policies for Industrial Growth in a Competitive World, Joint Economic Committee, 98th Cong., 2d Sess. (1984).

61. Wall St. J., Feb. 26, 1985, at 60, and Oct. 15, 1985, at 30.

62. For an excellent discussion of this point, see J. Gardner, Policing Single Firm Anticompetitive Behavior in Light of Copperweld Corp. v. Independence Tube Co., Ind. L. Rev (forthcoming). Also see Handler and Smart, The Present Status of the Intracorporate Conspiracy Doctrine, 3 Cardozo L. Rev. 23 (1981).

63. National Commission for the Review of the Antitrust Laws and Procedures, Report to the President and the Attorney General, 145 (1979).

64. Copperweld Corp. v. Independence Tube Corp., 104 S. Ct. 2731 (1984).

65. 392 U.S. 134 (1968).

66. Id. at 141–42.

67. 332 U.S. 218, 227 (1947).

68. 334 U.S. 110, 116 (1948).

69. See Gardner, supra note 62.

70. Keifer-Stewart Co. v. Joseph E. Seagram & Sons, Inc., 340 U.S. 211, 215 (1951).

71. Timken Roller Bearing Co. v. United States, 341 U.S. 593 (1951).

72. Id. at 598.

73. Such a view seems to be implicit in both O. Williamson, Markets and Hierarchies: Analysis and Antitrust Implications (1975), and R. Bork, The Antitrust Paradox: A Policy at War with Itself (1978).

74. See Van Cise, Religion and Antitrust, 23 Antitrust Bulletin (1978).

75. John Marshall Harlan not only dissented in E. C. Knight and Standard Oil, but also in the Civil Rights cases and Plessy v. Ferguson. He should not be confused with his grandson and namesake, who was appointed by President Eisenhower and often dissented in the Warren years.

76. 303 U.S. 77 (1938).

77. Wheeling Steel Corporation v. Glander, 337 U.S. 562 (1949).

78. 288 U.S. at 546.

79. 303 U.S. at 85–87.

80. Id. at 89.

81. 83 U.S. (16 Wall). 36, (1873).

82. C. Collins, The Fourteenth Amendment and the States (1912).

83. 303 U.S. at 89–90.

84. 204 U.S. 359 (1907).

85. Id. at 363.

86. 203 U.S. at 255.

87. 314 U.S. 252.

88. Gitlow v. New York, 268 U.S. 652 (1925).

89. 337 U.S. 562 (1949).

90. Other cases included: Ry. Express Agency v. New York, 336 U.S. 106; Ott v. Mississippi Barge Line, 336 U.S. 169; Illinois Central R.R. Co. v. Minnesota, 309 U.S. 157; Lincoln Life Ins. Co. v. Read, 325 U.S. 673; Queenside Hills Co. v. Saxl, 328 U.S. 80; in all of which the corporations lost the case, and Bridges v. California, 314 U.S. 252 and Pennekamp v. Florida, 328 U.S. 331, in which the corporations won their claims.

91. 337 U.S. at 580.

9

BIGNESS AND SOCIAL EFFICIENCY: A CASE STUDY OF THE U.S. AUTO INDUSTRY

WALTER ADAMS AND JAMES W. BROCK

"The emergence of Big Business . . . as a social reality during the past fifty years is the most important event in the recent social history of the Western world," Peter F. Drucker asserted in 1946. "It is even possible that to future generations the world wars of our time will seem to have been an incident in the rise of big-business society just as to many historians the Napoleonic wars have come to appear incidental to the industrial revolution."[1]

Statistics corroborating this claim are not in serious dispute. The rise to preeminence of a small number of gigantic corporations, and the aggregate concentration of control of economic activity they embody, were traced as long ago as 1932 by Berle and Means in their classic, *The Modern Corporation and Private Property*.[2] Today the largest 200 industrial firms in the United States collectively account for more than 60 percent of total U.S. industrial assets; the share of the largest 0.2 percent of them stands at 73 percent.[3] Measured in terms of revenues received, corporate giants like Exxon, General Motors, and IBM tower above individual states. Their value product exceeds that of most nations of the world.

Yet it is a glaring intellectual anomaly that economists have generally declined the challenge of assaying the parameters of corporate bigness and size-based economic power. The profession has exhibited extraordinary ingenuity in attempting to rationalize industrial giantism. It has concocted an abstruse lexicon of economies of scale, economies of "scope," deterministic dictates of technical progress and research and development, "synergy," and minimization of "transactions costs." In sharp contrast and despite a monumental revolution in industrial organization over the past century, the economists' conception of power—defined as the capacity to influence price in a particular market—has remained remarkably unchanged, unidimensional, and, in all, anemic and innocuous. As Kurt Rothschild puts it: "If we look at the main run of economic theory . . . we find that it is characterized by a strange lack of power considerations. More or less homogeneous units—firms and households—move in more or less given technological and market conditions and try to improve their lot *within the constraints of these conditions*. This model has been explored in great detail

[and] important insights into the working of the market mechanism have been gained.'' But, Rothschild points out, ''that people use power to alter the mechanism itself; that uneven power may greatly influence the outcome of market operations; that people may strive for economic power as much as for economic wealth; these facts have largely been neglected.''[4]

Modest reflection suggests that, in a market society, at least two types of economic power attach to disproportionately large firm size and, further, that such power comprises considerably more than a mere ability to influence the price of mousetraps.

First, disproportionate firm size and high aggregate concentration of control over economic activity in relatively few hands strongly suggest that corporate giantism is increasingly displacing the competitive market as society's primary instrument for planning and resource allocation. Size gives rise to private planning power, and, beyond some threshold, disproportionate size marks a transfer of society's planning and resource allocation functions into the hands of corporate giants. For example, conservative business historian Alfred D. Chandler posits the central economic fact of post–Civil War America to be that the ''modern business enterprise took the place of market mechanisms in coordinating the activities of the economy and allocating its resources. . . . As modern business enterprise acquired functions hitherto carried out by the market, it became the most powerful institution in the American economy and its managers the most influential group of decision makers''—a phenomenon Chandler tellingly characterizes the ''visible hand.''[5] To John Kenneth Galbraith, the quest for planning power and its exercise are the animus of the modern industrial economy. Size, he says, is the predicate for planning and planning the essence of power: ''The most obvious requirement of effective planning is large size. This . . . allows the firm to accept market uncertainty where it cannot be eliminated; to eliminate markets on which otherwise it would be excessively dependent; [and] to control other markets in which it buys and sells.'' In a graphic passage, he points to the automobile industry, arguing that the ''size of General Motors is in the service not of monopoly or the economies of scale but of planning. And for this planning—control of supply, control of demand, provision of capital, minimization of risk—there is no clear upper limit to the desirable size. It could be that the bigger the better. The corporate form accommodates to this need. Quite clearly it allows the firm to be very, very large.''[6]

Indeed, it is ironic that while mainstream economics has ignored the private planning power derived from corporate giantism, apostles of bigness have been quite sensitive to it and have sought to turn it into a defense of the larger corporation. According to Peter Drucker, an ''important advantage of bigness is that it enables the business enterprise to have a policy and to have a special policy-making body which is sufficiently removed from the actual day-to-day problems *to take the long view, and to take into account the relationship between the organization and society.*''[7] Similarly a former president of Exxon contends that the ''large enterprise has the means, capabilities, and experience to perform large-scale economic tasks in a socially responsible manner when given the opportunity and flexibility to do so."[8] For these reasons, a former chairman of Dow Chemical admonishes us to "cast aside our outmoded notions of size and our fear of bigness."[9]

Second, in a democratic society, corporate giantism would seem to give rise to a further kind of power, a type of power that buttresses private planning power and renders it more potent. With disproportionate economic size comes disproportionate influence on government policy making in the political arena. This second dimension of size-based power would seem capable of being exerted in at least two ways. On the one hand, the giant corporation is potentially able to mobilize massive political resources—finances, employees, executives, unions, subcontractors, suppliers, mayors and governors, Democrats and Republicans—in lobbying for government policies that bolster private planning power and vouchsafe its ends. These variously might include protection from foreign competition (tariffs, quotas, voluntary import restraints), privileged tax dispensations, or, in the extreme, government subsidies and bailouts. On the other hand but by the same token, the giant corporation is singularly situated to obstruct public policy through the threat of shutdowns, mass layoffs, and unemployment—in short, economic catastrophe. Henry C. Simons alluded to this threat of bigness long ago. In a modern "economy of intricate division of labor," he warned, "every large organized group is in a position at any time to disrupt or to stop the whole flow of social income; and the system must soon break down if groups persist in exercising that power or if they must continuously be bribed to forgo its disastrous exercise."[10] Bigness thus would seem to possess by virtue of disporportionate size the power to engage in economic extortion on a grand scale and the discretion to deploy this influence either in conjunction with or as a supplement to its private planning power.

We shall explore these dimensions of size-based power with reference to the U.S. automobile industry, which, because of its structure and the size of the firms that have long dominated it, is a suitable case study. The analysis will put to one side the economically subsidiary issues of whether giant firms produce at lowest unit cost (production efficiency) or whether they are peculiarly adept at promoting technical progress (innovation efficiency).[11] Rather, the analysis will proceed from the perspective of social efficiency. We shall frame the analysis by asking the following interrelated questions: How is size-based power exercised by the auto giants? To what ends is it directed? With what consequences? For whom? And most important, with what assurance that the objects of this power necessarily will be in accordance with society's best interest—that they necessarily will represent that use of resources which achieves (in J. M. Clark's terminology) the "lowest terms of ultimate expenditure and sacrifice" for the community?[12] This perspective of social efficiency is most appropriate to an examination of size-based power; it asks whether corporate giants do what, from the public interest in rational resource allocation, should not be done at all.

THE AUTOMOBILE INDUSTRY: SIZE AND STRUCTURE

The U.S. automobile industry is a powerful triopoly of firms of truly Brob-dignagian proportions. The Big Three producers—General Motors, Ford, and Chrysler—respectively rank as the second, fourth, and fourteenth largest industrial corporations in the United States. They are the world's third, fifth, and twenty-second largest manufacturers.[13] Collectively, they directly employ 1.2 million workers and have $162.9 billion in sales, assets of $100 billion, and combined net income of $10.8 billion in 1984.

Traditionally, the Big Three have accounted for 90 percent or more of U.S. automobile production and, until recently, controlled an approximately equivalent share of U.S. auto sales. General Motors (GM) has long dominated the field, accounting for a larger share of the market than the remainder of the industry combined. As described by one Detroit executive, "General Motors is the kind of institution whose like doesn't exist elsewhere in Western civilization. It is America's Japan."[14]

The automobile triopolists are integrated horizontally, vertically, internationally, and conglomerately. They assemble motor vehicles in a multitude of locations across the country. They fabricate a variety of automotive parts and components in scores of plants. They are integrated internationally, ranking among the largest motor vehicle manufacturers in a myriad of nations around the globe, and are enmeshed in an intricate web of joint venture and joint production agreements with the world's other leading motor vehicle manufacturers. They are diversified, especially GM, which until recently controlled the production of 75 percent of U.S. city and intercity buses, 100 percent of U.S. passenger locomotives, and 80 percent of U.S. freight locomotives.[15] Finally, the Big Three recently have made a number of large conglomerate acquisitions: GM expended $2.5 billion to acquire Electronic Data Systems (EDS) in 1984 and outbid Ford in 1985 to acquire Hughes Aircraft Company (a leading defense contractor) for $5 billion. Chrysler has disclosed plans to acquire Gulfstream Aerospace ($636.5 million) and credit operations of E. F. Hutton ($125 million). Ford has disclosed plans to buy the First Nationwide Financial Corporation (the nation's ninth largest savings and loan association) for $493 million. Here then is an industry featuring size on a massive scale.[16]

BIGNESS, POWER, AND SOCIAL EFFICIENCY

What is the nature of the size-based power wielded by GM and the other auto giants, and how is it exerted? What kind of private planning does the industry engage in? How have the allied powers to influence government policy making been brought to bear? Is it automatically the case (as former GM chairman and Secretary of Defense Charles Wilson once said) that what is good for GM is good for the rest of the country? Has corporate giantism comported itself in a manner conducive to an optimal utilization of society's scarce resources? Has it served to facilitate a rational resolution of pressing national problems, or, instead, has it acted to create or compound them? In short, to what extent has bigness in autos promoted social efficiency? The record is revealing in such problem areas as urban congestion, pollution, automotive safety, and automotive fuel consumption and energy depletion.

Urban Congestion

A variety of different modes of transportation are available for moving people within densely settled urban areas, including mass transit railways and trolleys, gasoline-powered buses, and private passenger cars. Social efficiency in this context, then, calls for the combination of these modes best able to transport large numbers of people quickly, comfortably, at low cost, and with a minimum requirement of scarce urban land and space.

In actuality, urban transportation systems in the United States are overwhelmingly dominated by the private automobile—a mix that, objectively, represents in many respects the least socially efficient urban transport system. As summarized by urban expert Wilfred Owen, the preponderance of private automobiles results in "congestion, pollution, and a growing sense of frustration. Where all-out efforts have been made to accommodate the car, the streets are still congested, commuting is increasingly difficult, urban aesthetics have suffered, and the quality of life has been eroded. In an automotive age, cities have become the negation of communities—a setting for machines instead of people. The automobile has taken over, and motorist and nonmotorist alike are caught up in the congestion, and everyone is a victim of the damaging side effects of the conflict between the car and the community."[17] Or, as former Transportation Secretary Alan Boyd once observed, the description of a city under siege would differ little from that of a contemporary large U.S. city at rush hour.[18]

The predominance of the private passenger car, and its adverse impact on urban communities, are not accidental. Nor is it due solely to the play of free market forces passively responding to the command of consumer preference. Instead, the automobile industry, and GM in particular, have played a decisive role in planning an urban transportation system best suited to its private—as opposed to the public—interest.

As the nation's dominant producer of buses as well as automobiles, GM understood at an early date that if urban railways could be eliminated as a viable competitive option, the sales of its buses could be vastly expanded. And if transit systems using buses could subsequently be made to decline or fail, a huge market would open up for additional sales of private automobiles. Anything that reduced the attractiveness of mass urban transportation—its speed, cleanliness, or reliability—would be perceived as a desirable trend from GM's private perspective—adverse public consequences for urban congestion to the contrary notwithstanding.

According to the findings of a federal court (sustaining a conviction for criminal conspiracy to violate the nation's antitrust laws),[19] GM was instrumental in organizing National City Lines, an operating company that engineered the demise of forty-six electric mass transit systems in forty-five cities in sixteen states. Through its National City Lines subsidiary, GM and its coconspirators (a tire producer and an oil company) gained control of urban rail transit systems, quite literally destroyed them, and replaced them with GM buses.

The impact of GM's planning in San Francisco has been described by the city's former mayor, Joseph L. Alioto. According to Alioto, the Key System, which once linked San Francisco to Oakland and other communities of the East Bay region,

operated 180 electric street cars and 50 sleek, fumeless, electric passenger trains across a right-of-way on the lower deck of the San Francisco-Oakland Bay Bridge. . . . In 1946, National City Lines, a holding company organized and financed by General Motors, acquired the controlling interest in Key's parent company. A scant two days later, GM's newly acquired transit company announced that street cars would be replaced by buses. The buses, a fleet of 200 vehicles, were purchased during the next two years from GM.[20]

With respect to Los Angeles, Bradford Snell offers the following assessment:

Thirty-five years ago Los Angeles was a beautiful city of lush palm trees, fragrant orange groves and ocean-clean air. It was served then by the world's largest electric railway network. In the late 1930's General Motors and allied highway interests acquired the local transit companies, scrapped their pollution-free electric trains, tore down their power transmission lines, ripped up their tracks, and placed GM buses on already congested Los Angeles streets. The noisy, foul-smelling buses turned earlier patrons of the high-speed rail system away from public transit and, in effect, sold millions of private automobiles. Largely as a result, this city is today an ecological wasteland: the palm trees are dying of petro-chemical smog; the orange groves have been paved over by 300 miles of freeways; the air is a septic tank into which 4 million cars, half of them built by General Motors, pump 13,000 tons of pollutants daily.[21]

To buttress its planning power further and additionally secure its private ends, GM president Alfred Sloan organized the National Highway Users Conference (NHUC) in 1932 "to combine representatives of the Nation's auto, oil, and tire industries in a common front against competing transportation interests."[22] The organization's announced objectives were dedication of gasoline taxes solely to highway purposes and development of a continuing program of highway construction. Its 2,800 lobbying groups have persuaded more than forty states to create trust funds, and NHUC has deployed its political influence again and again to defeat efforts to use highway trust funds for rapid transit or railway improvement. In effect, NHUC became a perpetual motion machine to promote automobiles.[23]

In the field of urban congestion, then, size does give rise to private planning power, planning power can be bolstered by influence exerted in the political arena, and the exercise of size-based power can have devastating consequences. Although it would be foolish to claim that "streetcars disappeared *only* because General Motors was seeking a market for its buses," it is clear that GM was not a passive bystander observing the natural evolution of market forces.[24] Thus, after examining the historical record, transportation expert George Smerk concludes that street "railways and trolley bus operations, even if better suited to traffic needs and the public interest, were doomed in favor of the vehicles and material produced by the [National City Lines] conspirators."[25]

Smog and Automotive Air Pollution

By the early 1960s, the typical U.S. automobile spewed approximately 1 ton of pollutants per year into the nation's atmosphere, and motor vehicles accounted for an estimated 60 percent of all air pollution.[26] Initially an acute problem in southern California, automotive air pollution soon reached epidemic proportions and afflicted every major metropolitan area in the country. Here, too, however, size-based power was hardly conducive to a triumph of social efficiency.

At first, the auto industry denied the existence of the problem—human sensory perceptions and the industry's own internal research results to the contrary notwithstanding.[27] "Waste vapors are dissipated in the atmosphere quickly and do not present an air-pollution problem," Ford Motor Company assured Los Angeles County supervisors in 1953. "The fine automotive powerplants which modern-day engineers design do not 'smoke.' "[28]

Later, as automotive air pollution worsened and as national concern about the problem increased, the Big Three colluded to eliminate rivalry among themselves in the development and commercialization of pollution control technology. In an antitrust suit filed in 1969 (which the industry did not contest), the Justice Department found that the auto giants "conspired not to compete in research, development, manufacture, and installation of [pollution] control devices, and did all in their power to delay such research, development, manufacturing, and installation." Specifically, they ignored promising inventions, refused to purchase pollution controls developed by others, delayed installing smog controls already available and known to them, and at times disciplined individual members of the cartel whose team loyalty flagged temporarily. "Since the industry was fortified from the beginning of the program with the agreement among its members not to take competitive advantage over each other," the Justice Department concluded, "all auto manufacturers were able through the years to stall, delay, impede and retard research, development, production and installation of motor vehicle air pollution control equipment."[29]

In the 1970s, under intense government pressure, the industry hastily seized on the catalytic converter as a pollution control device, an approach that the prestigious National Academy of Sciences characterized as the "most disadvantageous with respect to first cost, fuel economy, maintainability, and durability." The academy's scientists were less than impressed with the industry's planning performance: "It is unfortunate that the automobile industry did not seriously undertake such a [pollution control] program on its own volition until it was subjected to governmental pressure. A relatively modest investment, over the past decade, in developmental programs related to emission control could have precluded the crisis that now prevails in the industry and the nation. The current crash programs of the major manufacturers," the academy concluded, "have turned out to be expensive and, in retrospect, not well planned."[30]

Automotive Safety

"In 1965," a congressional committee reported, "49,000 persons lost their lives in highway accidents, 1,500,000 suffered disabling injuries, and an equal number suffered non-disabling injuries. Economic costs of highway accidents which can be tabulated for the same year aggregated $8.5 billion. Since the introduction of the automobile in the United States, more Americans have lost their lives from highway accidents than all the combat deaths suffered by America in all our wars."[31] In the same year, the secretary of health, education and welfare described automobile accidents as "one of the great national problems in medicine and national health"; he pointed out that auto accidents "are the first cause of death in age groups 1 to 35 years, and the fourth cause of death across the board. . . . Accident victims occupy more general hospital beds than heart disease and cancer patients combined."[32]

Although a variety of factors (road design, weather conditions, reckless and drunk driving) affect automotive safety, it is incontrovertible that the design of the automobile itself plays a major role in the carnage on the nation's roads and highways. The power of corporate giantism in this field is notable in at least five respects.

First, and most significant, bigness largely absolved itself of any safety responsibility. As GM president Alfred Sloan once candidly confided, "It is not my responsibility to sell safety glass."[33]

Second, the industry seemed casually indifferent to the safety tragedy. Patents awarded to the auto giants in the 1920s and 1930s for such safety features as padded dashboards and collapsible steering wheels were shelved for decades until their incorporation in cars was mandated by government decree.[34] The industry also ignored safety research reports: "Regrettably," *Automotive News* remarked in 1965, "the companies are making little use" of research results made available to them by university automotive crash research programs.[35]

Third, automobiles became progressively more dangerous in design over the post–World War II era. In a comparative analysis conducted in 1955, for example, Cornell researchers found that "when injury producing accidents occur, occupants of 1950–54 cars are injured more often than occupants of 1940–49 cars. Further, there is a statistically significant increase in the frequency of fatality among the occupants of 'newer' cars."[36] A decade later, the Senate Commerce Committee "was presented with graphic evidence that the interior design of many 1966 model cars reveal interiors bristling with rigid tubes, angles, knobs, sharp instruments, and heavy metal of small radius of curvature. . . . The committee was likewise made aware of the substantial needless hazards to pedestrians presented by external fins, ornamental protrusions, sharp edges, stylistically angled bumpers."[37] And in 1983, *Wall Street Journal* readers learned of GM's efforts "to persuade the federal government that it isn't dangerous for a car's rear-wheel axle to fall off."[38]

Fourth, the industry insisted that safety should be optional, supplied in response to consumer demand and preference (or the lack thereof). Yet it steadfastly refused to make available the safety information essential to informed, rational consumer decision making. As one expert explained:

The industry has actively cultivated a consumer ignorance about safety by promoting a concept of an automobile that stressed style, ride, and performance. While eager to tell the potential customer about the rated horsepower, acceleration capability and kinds of interior decor, the automaker will not tell him, even if he demands it, such important facts about the safety of the cars as: brake stopping ability, tire skid and blowout resistance, roof collapse strength, door latch and door hinge strength, the dash panel's and windshields cushioning ability, the amount of rearward displacement of the steering wheel and shaft under a forward crash into a fixed barrier, the side and roof crash resistance of the vehicle and the seat anchorage strength. These technical values can all be given in quite precise terms against clearly expressed criteria. Since the auto makers boast about their instrumented crash testing, they must have the answers. But they will fight to the end to deny their publication for the motoring public—notwithstanding the fact that nearly half of all cars will be involved, sometime in their use, in an injury-producing collision.[39]

At the same time, some safety features such as seatbelts were deliberately made more expensive and troublesome to install and until recently were rarely advertised or merchandised.[40] The industry spent hundreds of millions of dollars extolling raw horsepower and rocket acceleration and then (disingenuously) pleaded that "safety doesn't sell"—despite evidence to the contrary.[41]

Fifth, although the Department of Transportation has estimated that equipping all cars with air bags would save at least 9,000 lives and prevent hundreds of thousands of serious injuries, GM has, according to a senior vice-president of the Insurance Institute for Highway Safety (IIHS), "pursued a policy of withholding that technology from the public, encouraging delay of federal passive restraint requirements, and discouraging consumer interest in the handful of air bag–equipped cars it produced in the mid–1970s."[42] It has done this despite a GM survey (subsequently suppressed for eight years) revealing that between 40 and 50 percent of the customers surveyed by the firm would pay some significant amount for air bag protection; despite a 1985 IIHS poll showing that 52 percent of those polled were in favor of "requiring car manufacturers to equip new cars with airbags even if airbags cost $350"; despite the conclusion of two former GM officials that air bags for front-seat occupants should cost about $148 per car, not $225 or $335 as the auto companies have claimed; and despite a 1981 benefit-cost analysis conducted by economist William Nordhaus that found the present value of benefits in reduced injury and death as a result of air bags to be double the cost of equipping all new cars with such devices.[43] As the *Wall Street Journal* found, the air bag "received no wholehearted promotion" by GM, and "the company and its dealers actively discouraged [air bag] sales."[44] Indeed, in 1983 the U.S. Supreme Court observed that the industry had "waged the regulatory equivalent of war against air bags for a decade" a war that the industry thus far seems to have waged successfully.[45]

With respect to automotive safety, the guideposts for bigness were perhaps most bluntly set forth by Alfred Sloan: "I feel that General Motors should not adopt safety glass for its cars," he once explained. "I can only see competition being forced into the same position. Our gain would be purely a temporary one and the net result would be that both competition and ourselves would have reduced the return on our capital and the public would have obtained still more value per dollar expended."[46]

Fuel Consumption and the Small Car

Because U.S. passenger cars consume 80 billion gallons of gasoline annually, the fuel efficiency (or inefficiency) of the Big Three's automobiles importantly affects petroleum consumption and the nation's dependence on volatile foreign energy supplies. Automotive fuel consumption thus exerts a not insubstantial influence on the nation's economic security and the urgency, as well as eventual success, of national energy policy. For these reasons, fuel economy provides a further test of bigness and social efficiency in the auto industry. The Big Three's now familiar lackluster performance in this field paints a less than flattering picture of size and power with regard to the industry's own interest and the national interest. It is significant in at least five respects.

First, the Big Three traditionally considered neither the fuel efficiency of their products nor limited petroleum supplies to be a matter of serious concern. They ignored warnings of impending fuel shortages, even when voiced by responsible officials within the industry itself.[47] When the general manager of GM's Buick division was asked in 1958 what steps his division was taking in the area of fuel efficiency, he flippantly replied: "Oh, we're helping the gas companies, the same as our competitors."[48] Later, only months before the first OPEC oil embargo in 1973, GM's chairman suggested nuclear power plants as an important means for resolving the nation's energy "question." One month before the overthrow of the shah of Iran in 1979 and the onset of the nation's second energy crisis is six years, GM assured the public that automotive "fuel economy standards are not necessary and they are not good for America."[49] The auto giants seemed uninterested in innovations (including alternative powerplants) capable of improving fuel economy. A parade of inventors, scientists, and engineers testified to the auto giants' indifference during congressional hearings conducted in 1973. "I was assured in the first meetings with the Big Four in Detroit that what they would like to do with this is put it into a 20 or 30-year development program," said one. "I told them I would rather do it next year in Japan, and I meant that very seriously."[50]

Second, as a result of the industry's nonchalance, the fuel efficiency of U.S. automobiles steadily worsened from 1958 to 1973. The principal cause was the increasingly bloated size and weight of the cars the industry elected to produce in its race for styling supremacy.[51] For example, "in 1958 the [Chevrolet] Impala weighed 4000 pounds and ran at an efficiency of 12.1 mpg; by 1973 the size of the Impala . . . ballooned to 5500 lbs. with an efficiency of only 8.5 mpg."[52] A team of economists estimated that styling rivalry artificially inflated automobile gasoline consumption by more than 18 billion gallons between 1950 and 1960.[53] Attesting to the industry's less than brilliant display of planning wizardry, *Fortune* later pointed out that had the government not imposed fuel economy standards on the industry, "the auto companies, especially Chrysler, might have been even less prepared than they were for the . . . swing in customer preferences to small cars."[54]

Third, the Big Three's studied refusal to develop the small, inexpensive, and fuel-efficient segment of the market exacerbated the nation's serious petroleum problems. Indeed, in conjuction with the giants' generally nonchalant attitude, it eventually proved catastrophic for the automakers (and the vast industrial complex dependent upon them) when, in the wake of successive gasoline shortages and skyrocketing fuel prices, the American market was swamped with fuel-efficient imports.

As early as the 1940s, the United Auto Workers urged Detroit to build a small, fuel-efficient car, citing an opinion survey conducted by the Society of Automotive Engineers that revealed that 60 percent of the public favored this type of automobile.[55] Later, a committee of the National Academy of Engineering found that a secular shift in consumer preferences toward small cars "was evident long before OPEC quadrupled the price of crude oil. From 1967 to 1972, for example, the large-car share fell from 71.5 to 57.8 percent, with most of the decline coming from the standard group. At the same time the share of subcompacts more than doubled to reach 22 percent." Contrary to the industry's protestations, the academy observed that this long-term evolution in demand toward small cars did not occur overnight but instead "reflected fundamental demographic trends (increased suburbanization, shifts in the age structure, changes in female labor force participation) and the growth of multicar families."[56]

Rather than recognizing this evolution in consumer demand, anticipating it, or astutely reacting to it, planning by the Big Three was directed toward ignoring consumer demand and the market, avoiding competition in small cars, and thereby protecting what the domestic oligopoly perceived as being its best collective short-run profits.

The Big Three did not seriously undertake to manufacture and market small, fuel-efficient cars until the 1970s, at least in the U.S. market,[57] and only then in the face of energy crises, government-mandated fuel economy standards, and the onslaught of foreign competition. Attempts were occasionally made to meet successive import surges—for example, with the appearance of the compact car in the late 1950s and the subcompacts of the 1960s. But these efforts were, at best, halfhearted and dilatory. In 1962, for example, Ford cancelled the planned introduction of its Cardinal, featuring a front-mounted four-cylinder engine and front-wheel drive, a compact car quite similar to the X-cars, Escort, and Omni of the 1980s.[58] The Big Three generally, and GM in particular, persisted in their delusion that the small, fuel-efficient car was an aberration.[59]

This delusion was reinforced by the concentrated structure of the industry and their oligopolistic efforts to protect group profits. According to industry expert Lawrence J. White, GM, Ford, and Chrysler each seemed to recognize that vigorous entry into small cars by any one of them would trigger entry into the field by the others. Further, each firm seemed to believe that the demand for small cars was not large enough to permit profits acceptable to the group if all of them should enter this segment of the market. "Twice, one or two of the Big Three pulled back from plunging ahead with a small car when the market did not look large enough for all three. . . . A sizable niche might well have been carved out at the bottom of the market by a Big Three producer in 1950, or again, with a 'subcompact' in 1962 or 1963. Room-for-all considerations, how-ever, appeared to rule this out."[60] Buttressing this room-for-all outlook was the apparent desire by each of the Big Three to protect their above-average profits in large cars by withholding the small car as an inexpensive substitute.[61]

Fourth, the full social ramifications of the industry's private planning appeared with a vengeance in the 1970s, when the nation was convulsed by oil shortages, gasoline crises, and mile-long service station lines, a torrent of small, fuel-efficient cars imported from abroad, record losses, and layoffs in automobiles, which reverberated throughout U.S. industry, and the financial collapse of Chrysler (at the time, the nation's tenth largest industrial firm).

Fifth, in the 1980s, confronted with the consequences of their private planning, the Big Three provided an abject demonstration of the power politics of corporate giantism in action. By stressing the important place of automobile manufacturing at the core of the U.S. industrial economy, they successfully manipulated the state to obtain government favors and privileges.

On the one hand, the companies joined with the United Auto Workers to mobilize an all-out assault on government—the International Trade Commission, the Congress, the president—in order to restrain the importation of the fuel-efficient foreign cars that consumers found so attractive. Extending the calculus of catastrophe that earlier had succeeded in obtaining a government bailout of Chrysler, the automotive industrial-labor complex detailed the industry's dire straits and argued that the state of the entire national economy was inextricably bound up with the economic health of the Big Three auto companies. The problems of the industry "are serious indeed," a Ford vice-president told Con-gress in 1981: "Some 2,100 domestic dealerships have closed their doors; some

140 domestic supplier plants have closed as well, auto unemployment remains at unacceptable levels—185,000 auto production workers are on permanent layoff status; and import levels for 1980 were a record high—a 26.5 percent share versus 15 percent in the mid–1970s.'' But, he stressed, ''A lot more is at stake than the health of auto companies alone. Autos account for one out of twelve U.S. manufacturing jobs, a quarter of U.S. steel production and over half of U.S. rubber production. This industry is such a vital part of the U.S. economy,'' he said in clinching the argument, ''it should be clear that we can't have a healthy U.S. economy without a healthy U.S. auto industry.''[62] Against the backdrop of a general recession on the verge of becoming a full-blown depression, and the specter of upcoming congressional elections, the industry's not-so-subtle efforts at economic extortion succeeded in obtaining government-imposed restraints on fuel-efficient Japanese imports—an outcome ultimately attributable to the industry's own delinquent performance. The cost to the public has not been insignificant. In addition to the generalized economic trauma of fuel shortages and layoffs inflicted by the industry on the nation, the import restraints obtained by the auto companies—formally in place from 1981 to the spring of 1985—are estimated to have cost American car buyers as much as $15 billion in the aggregate as a result of artificially inflated car prices.[63]

On the other hand, after utilizing the breathing space of import restraints to forge a spate of joint small car ventures with their Japanese and newly emerging South Korean rivals and apparently in preparation for abandoning small car production to foreign countries, GM and Ford have recently succeeded in obtaining an easing of government fuel economy standards, again in rather blatantly extortionate fashion. Unless these standards are relaxed, GM warned Congress in May 1985, ''full-line manufacturers face the prospect of restricting product availability,'' which, a GM vice-president pointedly noted for Congress's benefit, ''translates to plant closings, job losses and lower economic growth.''[64] The impact if the government refused the Big Two's demands, Ford echoed, could be ''severe''[65]—this despite evidence that the fines imposed on auto companies for failing to meet government mileage standards would amount to less than 1 percent of the suggested retail prices of the least fuel-efficient cars; despite the fact that even the industry-oriented National Highway Traffic Safety Administration (NHTSA) concedes that the manufacturers ''influence demand [for large fuel-efficient cars] through their marketing and pricing strategies''; and despite the fact that an easing of the fuel economy standard could well cost U.S. jobs by leaving domestic manufacturers free to pursue their plans to import more small cars from abroad instead of producing them in the United States.[66] Nevertheless, the GM and Ford threats were crowned with success in October 1985 when NHTSA relaxed automotive fuel economy standards in accordance with the demands of the two largest producers. In a now-familiar refrain, NHTSA cited ''adverse economic consequences, including job losses in the tens of thousands in the auto industry, if the standard was not lowered.''[67]

CONCLUSION

The most important conclusions to be drawn from this analysis are fourfold.

First, corporate giantism does have economic consequences, and the economic power that flows from disproportionate size is in fact more potent and polymorphic than the mere ability to influence price in an isolated market. The economic power of giantism includes the capacity to exert inordinate influence on society-wide planning, control, and allocation of resources. It also comprises an affiliated capacity to exercise disproportionate pressure on the state in order to reinforce private planning power or, alternatively, as a means for avoiding the consequences of private planning and for shifting the costs of such planning to the public.

Second, corporate giantism is basically incompatible with a society steeped in the belief that the only legitimate power is accountable power. The power of bigness includes the discretion to operate outside the accountability mechanism of checks and balances presumed to be provided by the market. The automobile industry is not unique.[68] The power derived from bigness is, at bottom, irresponsible power, wielded with no effective guarantee that its objectives and consequences necessarily will be socially efficient and in the public interest. Nor, it is important to recognize, is import competition an answer to the accountability problem, when corporate giants are able to manipulate the state in order to neutralize foreign competition through tariffs, quotas, voluntary restraints, and the like. Indeed, as Henry Simons long ago warned, the very sovereignty of the state is called into question when corporations are big enough to challenge public policy making by threatening shutdowns and economic catastrophe.

Third, and for these reasons, efforts to rationalize the prevailing industrial power structure by defenders of bigness and advocates of laissez-faire, particularly those by the Chicago school and its ideological devotees, are unconvincing. Corporate conscience and a refined sense of social responsibility are scarcely credible protectors of the public interest. Neither can social efficiency meaningfully be equated, as the Chicago school would have it, with "aggregate consumer willingness to pay for goods and services." For example, Richard Posner argues that social efficiency is "determined by the willingness to pay, and the only way in which willingness to pay can be determined with certainty is by actually observing a voluntary transaction. Where resources are shifted pursuant to a voluntary transaction, we can be reasonably confident the shift involves a net increase in efficiency. The transaction would not have occurred if both parties had not expected it to make them better off. This implies that the resources transferred are more valuable in their new owner's hands."[69]

The fatal defect in this line of reasoning is that it conveniently ignores corporate giantism and its capacity to control the options from which consumers are permitted to choose. It fails to recognize that "voluntary" choice within the confines of a restricted range of alternatives does not signify a socially optimal outcome. This is especially the case when bigness can plan to deny consumers and society the freedom to choose (for example) urban rail transport, the freedom to choose nonpolluting, safe, and fuel-efficient automobiles, and when bigness can manipulate government to validate and legitimize its private ends. Given the economic reality of corporate giantism, such Chicago school scholasticism is nothing more than an assertion that "whatever is, is right," when in fact a different configuration of size and power would result in a wholly different array of consumer options and choices and therefore an entirely different pattern of resource allocation.[70]

Fourth, if we are correct, then corporate giantism and aggregate concentration quite properly are valid economic concerns for public policy. Perhaps public policy ought not cheerfully applaud mega-merger mania, as is currently the case, when the theoretical underpinnings for doing so are rooted in the erroneous proposition that bigness is benign. Perhaps public policy ought not permit consolidations between the nation's largest corporations on the highly dubious ground that these mergers and acquisitions seldom involve direct competitors and, hence, presumably pose no economic problems.[71] As our study shows, mergers of epic and unprecedented scale and, more important, the vast power concentrates created thereby, pose a far greater threat than the potential lessening of competition in particular markets, the erosion of production and innovation efficiency, or the monumental squandering of scarce resources on futile paper entrepreneurialism when they are so desperately needed to reindustrialize U.S. industry with world-class plants and products.[72] At a minimum, prudence would dictate that policy makers abjure admonitions by those, like the former assistant attorney general for antitrust, William F. Baxter, who soothingly assure us that "there is nothing written in the sky that says that the world would not be a perfectly satisfying place if there were only 100 companies, provided each had 1 percent of every product and service market."[73]

Instead, in the centenary year of *Santa Clara*, public policy might well be better informed by recalling Justice Brandeis's warning of a half-century ago: "Businesses may become as harmful to the community by excessive size, as by monopoly or the commonly recognized restraints of trade," he wrote. "If the State should conclude that bigness . . . menaces the public welfare, it might prohibit the excessive size or extent of that business as it prohibits excessive size or weight in motor trucks or excessive height in the buildings of a city."[74] Juxtaposed against the collectivist anthropomorphism of Santa Clara and in the light of the available evidence, limiting merger-induced giantism in order to effectuate the competitive market as a decentralized mechanism of power control seems an eminently conservative step.

NOTES

1. P. Drucker, Concept of the Corporation 9 (1946).
2. A. Berle & G. Means, The Modern Corporation and Private Property (1932).

3. W. Mueller, The Celler-Kefauver Act: The First 27 Years, H.R. Doc. No. 243, 96th Cong., 1st Sess. 76 (1980).

4. Power in Economics 7 (K. Rothschild ed. 1971).

5. A. Chandler, The Visible Hand 1 (1977).

6. J. Galbraith, The New Industrial State 74, 76 (2d ed. rev. 1971). This point did not escape V. I. Lenin. "Where there are trusts," he observed in 1918, "it is already too late to speak of the absence of planning."

7. P. Drucker, supra note 1, at 226–27 (emphasis added).

8. R. Meyer, The Role of Big Business in Achieving National Goals, in Economics: Mainstream Readings and Radical Critiques 81 (D. Mermelstein ed. 3d ed. 1976).

9. Carl Gerstacker, The Structure of the Corporation, address prepared for the White House Conference on the Industrial World Ahead, Washington, D.C., February 7–9, 1972, quoted in R. Barnet & R. Muller, Global Reach 37 (1974).

10. H. Simons, Economic Policy for a Free Society 122 (1948).

11. For an examination of production and innovation efficiency in automobile production, see W. Adams & J. Brock, "The Automobile Industry," in The Structure of American Industry (W. Adams ed. 7th ed. 1986). For an analysis of these aspects of economic efficiency in industry generally, see W. Adams & J. Brock, The Bigness Complex (1986).

12. J. Clark, Social Control of Business 133 (2d ed. 1939).

13. Fortune, April 29, 1985, at 266; Aug. 19, 1985, at 179.

14. J. Kraft, Annals of Industry, New Yorker, May 5, 1980, at 140.

15. The Industrial Reorganization Act: Hearings on S. 1167 Before the Senate Subcomm. on Antitrust and Monopoly, part 4A, 93d Cong., 2d Sess. A–26, A–39 (1974) (submission of Bradford C. Snell).

16. A more detailed discussion of the industry's structure can be found in "The Automobile Industry," supra note 11.

17. W. Owen, The Accessible City 1 (1972).

18. Quoted in H. Leavitt, Superhighway-Superhoax 13 (1970). John Burby provides the following illustrative calculations: "Traffic in downtown New York, which in 1906 crept along behind horses at an average speed of 11.5 miles an hour, was by 1966 creeping along at 8.5 miles an hour behind the most powerful engines Detroit could mass-produce." J. Burby, The Great American Motion Sickness 4 (1971).

19. United States v. Nat'l City Lines, 186 F.2d 562 (7th Cir. 1951).

20. Industrial Reorganization Act Hearings, supra note 15, part 3, at 1,810.

21. Id., part 4A, at A–2-A–3.

22. Id., at A–44.

23. See Federal Trade Commission, Report on the Motor Vehicle Industry (1939); H. Leavitt, supra note 18; B. Kelly, The Pavers and the Paved (1971); W. Owen, supra note 17.

24. See General Motors; reply to Snell, Industrial Reorganization Act Hearings, supra note 15, at A–126-A–127 (emphasis added).

25. G. Smerk, Urban Transportation 50 (1965).

26. L. White, The Automobile Industry since 1945 228–29 (1971).

27. "GM has been cognizant of the exhaust gas problem for many years," the firm's technical director confided in 1953, "and the research laboratories of GM have been responsible for the discovery of much of the basic information on exhaust gas that is available today on the subject." Quoted in Automotive Research and Development and

Fuel Economy: Hearings before the Senate Comm. on Commerce, 93d Cong., 1st Sess. 619 (1973). Internal memoranda indicate that GM had been sufficiently concerned about automotive air pollution to begin researching it as early as 1938. See "Smog Control Antitrust Case," 117 Cong. Rec. 15,626–27 (1971).

28. Air Pollution—1967 (Automotive Air Pollution): Hearings before the Senate Subcomm. on Air and Water Pollution, part 1, 90th Cong., 1st Sess. 158 (1967).

29. "Smog Control Antitrust Case," supra note 27, at 15,627 and 15,633.

30. National Academy of Sciences, Report by the Committee on Motor Vehicle Emissions (1973), reprinted in 119 Cong. Rec. 5,831, at 5,832 and 5,849 (1973).

31. Senate Comm. on Commerce, National Traffic and Motor Vehicle Safety Act of 1966, S. Rep. No. 1301, 89th Cong., 2d Sess. 2–3 (1966).

32. Federal Role in Traffic Safety: Hearings before the Senate Subcomm. on Executive Reorganization, part 1, 89th Cong., 1st Sess. 214 (1965).

33. Planning, Regulation, and Competition: Automobile Industry—1968: Hearings Before the Senate Select Comm. on Small Business, 90th Cong., 2d Sess. 968 (1968). Senator Abraham Ribicoff (D., Conn.) was astounded by the auto giants' efforts to procure for themselves a peculiarly privileged position of irresponsibility: "What is an automobile manufacturer's responsibility to produce a safe car: If he wants to? Do we ask an airplane manufacturer if he wants to produce a safe airplane? Do we ask the person who produces a locomotive or a train whether he wants a safe train? Do we ask the person who drives a truck or a bus does he want a safe truck, does he want a safe bus? Do we ask the man who builds a ship to carry passengers whether he wants a safe ship?

"You are talking about an item that last year killed 48,000 people. You are talking about an item which injured 3.5 million Americans. You are talking about an item that involved $8 billion in property damage.

"So it is not a question of does a person want to. What is the responsibility of the automobile manufacturer for putting in safety features in an automobile? Is it a question of selling him safety or do you have a responsibility of producing a safe car with safety items?" Federal Role in Traffic Safety Hearings, supra note 32, part 2, at 829–30.

34. Federal Role in Traffic Safety Hearings, supra note 32, part 3, at 1,319–21; R. Nader, Unsafe at Any Speed 92–93 (1965).

35. Quoted in R. Nader, supra note 34, at 142.

36. Id., at 134.

37. S. Rep. No. 1301, supra note 31, at 3.

38. Wall St. J., March 8, 1983, at 44.

39. Federal Role in Traffic Safety Hearings, supra note 32, part 3, at 1,279.

40. L. White, supra note 26, at 241.

41. In his study of the industry, John Jerome found that Ford could not meet the unexpectedly strong consumer demand for safety options offered in some of its 1956 car models. J. Jerome, The Death of the Automobile 273 (1972). Yet Ford abruptly cancelled the safety package the same year it was offered—perhaps, some suggest, because of pressure exerted by General Motors. See L. Iacocca, Iacocca 296 (1984). Ford also remained silent after discovering (through its own internal testing) the dangerous design of GM's infamous Corvair. Ford's reticence appears to have been motivated in part by a desire to maintain cordial relations with its dominant rival. See E. Cray, Chrome Colossus 409 (1980). For charges of tacit collusion in the provision of seat belts, see Federal Role in Traffic Safety Hearings, supra note 32, part 3, at 1,302.

42. Motor Vehicle Safety and the Marketplace: Hearings before the Senate Subcomm. on Surface Transportation, 99th Cong., 1st Sess. 71 (1983).

43. Id., at 71–76; United Services Automobile Association, Aide Mag. Summer 1985, at 13–14; Nordhaus study cited in P. Passell, What's Holding Back Air Bags? N. Y. Times Mag., Dec. 18, 1983, at 75.

44. Wall St. J., Nov. 11, 1976, at 1.

45. Motor Vehicle Manufacturers Association v. State Farm Mutual, 103 S. Ct. 2856, 2870 (1983).

46. Quoted in Planning, Regulation, and Competition Hearings, supra note 33, at 967.

47. Jacob E. Goldman, director of Ford's science laboratory, warned the industry in 1956: "If there is any industrial area in the U.S. where an important new idea is absolutely necessary for survival, it is in the automobile industry. The oil prospects for the world are so very dim that this largest of all American industries must have an important, inspired breakthrough sometime within the next 25 years." Quoted in S. Melman, Profits without Production 41 (1983).

48. Quoted in J. Keats, The Insolent Chariots 14 (1958).

49. Automotive Research and Development Hearings, supra note 27, at 564; E. Cray, supra note 41, at 524.

50. Automotive Research and Development Hearings, supra note 27, at 70.

51. In part, this decline was attributable to the installation of automotive air pollution controls in the 1970s. But the industry's delinquency on the smog control front compounded and aggravated the pollution-fuel economy trade-off.

52. Automotive Research and Development Hearings, supra note 27, at 424.

53. Fisher, Griliches, & Kaysen, The Costs of Automobile Model Changes Since 1949, 70 J. Pol. Econ. 433 (1962).

54. Fortune, Oct. 22, 1979, at 48.

55. Blumberg, Snarling Cars, New Republic, Jan. 23, 1983, at 12.

56. National Academy of Engineering, The Competitive Status of the U.S. Auto Industry 20, 70 (1982).

57. A small, lightweight car GM developed was marketed in Australia in 1948 by a GM subsidiary; Ford's light car appeared the same year as the French Ford Vedette. See White, The American Automobile Industry and the Small Car, 1945–1970, 20 J. Indus. Econ. 181 (1972).

58. National Academy of Engineering, supra note 56, at 70.

59. "Of all Detroit auto makers," Fortune reported, "G.M. has been the most scoffingly skeptical of the prospects of the small car in the U.S. market. If G.M. has said it once, it's said it ten thousand times: 'A good used car is the answer to the American public's need for cheap transportation.' " Fortune, August 1957, at 105.

60. White, supra note 57, at 191.

61. "In this behavior, the Big Three definitely recognized their mutual interdependence, since in the absence of retaliation by rivals a single firm contemplating the production of a small car should have expected to gain more profits from stealing the dissatisfied customers from other firms than he would lose from dissatisfied customers of his own large cars. . . . But the Big Three mutually contemplating a small car could only see lost profits from reduced sales of large cars." Id., at 180.

62. Issues Relating to the Domestic Auto Industry: Hearings before the Senate Subcomm. On International Trade, part 1, 97th Cong., 1st Sess. 133 (1981). For a detailed analysis of coalescing power and the industrial-labor complexes in autos and other major

U.S. industries, see Adams & Brock, Tacit Vertical Collusion and the Labor-Industrial Complex, 62 Neb. L. Rev. 621 (1983).

63. International Trade Commission, A Review of Recent Developments in the U.S. Automobile Industry, Including an Assessment of the Japanese Voluntary Restraint Agreements (1985). See also Crandall, Import Quotas and the Automobile Industry: The Costs of Protectionism, Brookings Rev. Summer 1984.

64. Statement of General Motors Corporation, submitted to the Senate Subcomm. on Energy Regulation and Conservation, May 14, 1985, at 1.

65. Statement of Ford Motor Company, submitted to the Senate Subcomm. on Energy Regulation and Conservation, May 14, 1985, at 2.

66. Statement of Clarence M. Ditlow, Director, Center for Auto Safety, Before the Senate Subcomm. on Energy Regulation and Conservation, May 14, 1985, at 9; Statement of Diane K. Steed, Administrator, National Highway Traffic Safety Administration, before the Senate Subcomm. on Energy Regulation and Conservation, May 14, 1985, at 3.

67. N. Y. Times, Oct. 2, 1985, at 11.

68. See The Bigness Complex, supra note 11.

69. R. Posner, Economic Analysis of Law 11 (1977).

70. Elaborate studies purporting to show that corporate giants operate more efficiently (either because their profits are high, or their unit-costs are low) scarcely close the debate regarding the economic desirability of bigness when corporate giants may do well something that, from the public interest, should not be done at all (such as producing large, polluting, and fuel-wasting motor vehicles).

71. Evidence that large conglomerate mergers and acquisitions involving firms operating in unrelated markets and industries can have anticompetitive consequences is documented in Mueller, Conglomerates: A Non-Industry, in The Structure of American Industry, supra note 11.

72. See The Bigness Complex, supra note 11.

73. Dun's Rev., August 1981, at 38.

74. Liggett Co. v. Lee, 288 U.S. 517 (1932) (Brandeis, J., dissenting).

IV. The Corporation as Private Government: Democratizing Policy Implications

10

CORPORATIONS AND OUR TWO CONSTITUTIONS

ARTHUR S. MILLER

Is the Constitution a polished but empty political shell destined to screen
and disguise the most arbitrary private governments, more dangerous than
other tyrannies because totally anonymous, totally irresponsible, and refined
to such a point as to deny their own existence? It has been said of the Devil
that he played his neatest trick when he persuaded western man that the
Devil does not exist. Is constitutionalism *plus* freedom of private associations
the latest and most refined trick of age-old enemies of justice and liberty
who went underground and persuaded mankind that they cannot possibly be
tyrants for the simple and conclusive reason that they are not governments?
—Alexander Pekelis[1]

To most American commentators, including the justices of the Supreme Court,
the concept of constitutionalism has two facets: it is a limitation on governmental
powers, and government consists only of the organs of the formal constitution
(as compared with those of what will be called the secret constitution). No room
is left for other forms of governance, however important they may in fact be to
the citizenry. This is true even though perceptive observers since the turn of the
twentieth century have called attention to a system of private governments that
exists in the United States. This chapter argues that the failure of the Supreme
Court to recognize the obvious—the governing power of giant corporations—
has distorted the development of constitutional law for a century. A false dichotomy between public and private pervades the theory and practice of American
constitutionalism. It is further contended that this was no happenstance: the
Supreme Court knew what it was doing when it called the business corporation
a constitutional person in 1886 and in fact wanted to do it.

The consequences are multiple and significant. First, the corporations have
not only been permitted to grow unchecked by little more than minimal restraints;
they have been actively encouraged to do so. As such, they are the chosen
instruments of U.S. public economic policy. Second, the notion of obligation
that is central to the concept of personhood for the individual has no place for

the artificial persons called corporations. Third, and of most importance, the rise of the giant corporations during the past century has been the principal influence in the creation of a second—the secret—constitution. Corporations, at least those of giant size, are private governments and should be recognized as such. Their power and influence, both externally in the national political order and internally in the so-called corporate community, make them a true form of governance. Their actions, accordingly, make up a large part of the institutions of America's secret constitution.

The size and strength of the corporate behemoths require no restatement here. They are truisms. Attention, rather, will focus on the existence of our bifurcated constitutional order and on the fact that under neither constitution do corporations have obligations or duties of a constitutional dimension. (I speak of the corporation in shorthand terms, as if it were a thing, which most assuredly it is not. Corporations are collectivities, which can act only through humans—corporate managers.)

That the justices of the Supreme Court knew precisely what they were doing when Chief Justice Waite told counsel in the *Santa Clara* case that they did not want to hear argument on the question of whether the corporation was a constitutional person, because they were all agreed that it was, admits of no doubt. They did it, they wanted to do it, and they thereby fundamentally altered the Fourteenth Amendment generally and the due process clauses specifically. Waite's assertion was a necessary prelude to the invention of substantive due process by the Court. And it should be considered in connection with the Court's decision in the *Civil Rights Cases* (1883)[2] that congressional power to regulate discrimination in inns and other private enterprises was barred by another invention: the state action doctrine.

The Constitution, it is often said, runs against governments only. This means that some sort of official action by an institution of the formal constitution must be involved in some way. "State action" is the label employed to indicate that much of American life is insulated from formal constitutional constraints. The doctrine is thus more important than the *Santa Clara* decision and its aftermath. There is no a priori reason for the decision in the *Civil Rights Cases*; the state action requirement for triggering constitutional restraints is essentially an arbitrary differentiation, one that with the other Supreme Court decisions shows that the Supreme Court is an arm of corporate capitalism.

By no means were these decisions, or such supporting ones as *Smyth v. Ames* (in which the Court in effect guaranteed profits to businesses governmentally regulated because they were "affected with a public interest"),[3] mere fortuities. All but the willfully myopic have come to realize, as the revelations in the Pentagon Papers clearly showed, that those in positions of power usually, perhaps always, know what they are doing, at least in the short run, and in fact want to do it. They may not be able to predict all or even most of the long-term consequences of their actions, and surely they are not able fully to control the flow of events. Nonetheless they do proceed from certain philosophies and have rather clear objectives in mind. *Santa Clara*, accordingly, is best seen as one of a clutch of decisions in which the Supreme Court was a willing ally of the property-owning class in the United States—those that Alexander Hamilton called "the rich and well-born" in the Constitutional Convention of 1787.

Less than a decade before *Santa Clara*, the Court told a corporation being regulated by Illinois that it did not have a judicial—a constitutional—remedy.[4] The complainant was told to go to the Illinois legislature and try to get the statutes changed. The meaning is simple and starkly clear. An amendment, the Fourteenth, that presumably was promulgated to aid the freed slaves was transmogrified into one that primarily aided the business corporations. Should there be any doubt about that, one should consider only the substantive due process decisions, of which *Lochner v. New York*[5] is the leading exemplar, that the Supreme Court began to render in the late nineteenth century (the process lasted until 1937). The state action doctrine added to corporate privilege, rendering the firms immune from constitutional norms. The justices almost without exception favored the economic class whence they came. Only in such aberrations as *Muller v. Oregon*[6] did they see matters differently. Justice Samuel J. Miller, far from a wild-eyed liberal, knew what his colleagues were up to. He wailed in an off-bench speech, "It is vain to contend with judges who have been at the bar for forty years the advocates of railroad companies, and all the forms of associated capital, when they are called upon to decide cases where such interests are in contest. All their training, all their feelings are from the start in favor of those who need no such influence."[7]

The Supreme Court did not stop with the *Santa Clara, Civil Rights Cases, Lochner* line of decisions. It neatly rewrote the Sherman antitrust law and legitimized the use of federal troops in the Pullman strike.[8] Violence was condoned when employed by those in power but savagely repressed when used by the nascent trade union movement. The point is so well known that it need not be labored. A statement by William Howard Taft, then a federal judge, sums up the situation: "When the Pullman strike in 1894 stopped trains and the mail, Judge William Howard Taft, far from a ferocious man, wrote to his wife, 'It will be necessary to kill some of the mob before the trouble can be stayed. They have killed only six . . . as yet. This is hardly enough to make an impression.' "[9] This was class war, something not prevented by any organ of the formal constitution, which must be taken to mean that the "rich and well-born" agreed with Taft. No part of public government, save an occasional legislature, intervened in behalf of those lowest in the social pecking order. Blacks, for example, found themselves in a de facto caste system. The working class became the butt of adverse action, either under the operation of the legal system generally or through the use of condoned violence (both by private groups and the public armed forces and police). When they had the temerity to take the rhetoric of democracy seriously, they were the targets of adversity from what Alexis de Tocqueville called the "manufacturing aristocracy" of America, which he said was one of the "harshest" the world had seen.[10]

There thus can be no doubt that the Supreme Court and the other organs of public government generally were minions of those who controlled the institutions of America's secret constitution. This was not a latter-day aberration. It had been so since the beginnings. And it is so today. As Martin Shapiro has cogently argued,[11] courts are part of the "governing coalition" of the nation, seldom if ever out of phase with those who control the levers of power in the United States, and as John Griffith has observed: "The judiciary in any modern industrial society, however composed, under whatever economic system, is an essential part of the system of government and . . . its function may be described as underpinning the stability of that system and as protecting that system from attack by resisting attempts to change it."[12] To the extent that the United States has an elitist government, judges, always taken from that nebulous group called the establishment, are in basic agreement with its values and preferences. This will become clearer when it is perceived that the United States is governed by two constitutions: the formal document of 1787, plus its amendments and the patina of interpretation that has developed since 1789, and a secret, unwritten fundamental law.

The doctrinal trilogy of state action, corporate personhood, and substantive due process provides the basis for maintaining that the secret constitution exists and likely is more important than the formal. I do not, however, wish to imply that this development, as revolutionary as it was, came as a constitutional volcanic explosion. The secret constitution, in one form or another, has always been with us; its roots lie deep in American history, and, indeed, in pre-Revolutionary history.

CONSTITUTIONAL DUALISM

Why does the public-private distinction endure? Morton Horwitz traces it to Chief Justice Marshall's opinion in the *Dartmouth College* case.[13] Likely, he is correct. Surely he is accurate when he observed that the growth of corporate giantism has eliminated the socioeconomic basis for the distinction. I believe, however, that it should be acknowledged that a close relationship has always existed between government and business in the United States. This relationship is not recognized in the standard texts on constitutional law, mainly because most of it was never litigated. Since U.S. constitutionalism is in large part considered to be constitutional law rather than the political theory that it really is, little is studied in law schools about the constitutional aspects of the government-business interface. This failure has persisted because of the well-nigh infinite capacity of the human mind for self-delusion. As Hans Vaihinger observed, "I called this work The Philosophy of 'As if' because it seemed to me to express more convincingly than any other possible title what I wanted to say, namely, that 'As if,' i.e., appearance, the consciously false, plays an enormous part in science, in world-philosophies, and in life."[14]

But there is much more. Two propositions are advanced. First, the pertinent and indispensable question to be asked about any public policy, including judicial policy, is cui bono? Who benefits from it? It is clear that the beneficiaries of the trilogy of doctrines were, and still are, the moneyed and the propertied. These are the people (mostly men) who exercise effective control in the United States over significant public policies. They are, in Robert Merton's terminology,[15] both the manifest and the latent beneficiaries. Second, this means that a second—an unwritten—constitution exists. It is called a secret constitution because it is generally not recognized in formal law, though its activities and institutions are plain for all who would see.

About the same time as the doctrinal trilogy became law, Woodrow Wilson maintained that the "constitution in operation is a very different thing from the constitution of the books,"[16] and Walter Bagehot, writing about the English constitution, said:

There are two great objects which every constitution must attain to be successful, which every old and celebrated one must have wonderfully achieved: every constitution must first *gain* authority, and then *use* authority; it must first win the loyalty and confidence of mankind, and then employ that homage in the work of government.[17]

Therefore, he observed, every constitution has "*dignified*" parts that "excite and preserve the reverence of the population" and "*efficient*" parts, by which "it, in fact, works and rules."[18]

We thus have known—at least, should have known, although there is little cognizance of the fact in the enormous literature on American constitutionalism— for at least a century that a system of constitutional dualism exists in the United States. The institutions of the formal constitution—the document of 1787, as amended and interpreted—are well known; they are the "dignified" parts of American constitutionalism that enable public officers to gain authority. It, however, takes a mental leap to see the contours of the secret constitution, the "efficient" parts by which government actually works.

What, then, is the secret constitution? No comprehensive analysis of it may be found in the literature, but enough is known to make some general statements. The discussion can begin with the assumption, which requires no proof because it is beyond argument, that all human groups up to and including the nation-state itself are oligarchically ruled. The United States is not exempt from that generalization. No useful purpose is served by calling it a democracy, for it is not now, was not in the past, and shows no likelihood of being a democracy— however that nebulous word is defined (more than 200 definitions have been identified). To call any government democratic is always a confusing piece of propaganda. It confuses doctrine with theory. We may—perhaps, should—wish the democratic element in government to be increased, but it still is only one element when it is government at all. Of course, as Bernard Crick has written, "American writers can still be found in abundance who are simply naive democrats";[19] and further, "democracy, in its clearest historical and sociological sense, is simply a characteristic of modern governments both free and unfree.''[20] In sum, all governments must be based on consent. The United States has always had an elitist form of government; or to give it its full due, the United States is governed by a type of "democratic elitism."[21] This is not to say that the United States has a closed, authoritarian society. Under the formal constitution, it is anything but that, but it is to say that the institutions of the secret constitution have marked antidemocratic, authoritarian tendencies.

All governments have certain functions and exercise social control. Public government's functions are twofold: internal order and external security. But private governments also have the function of internal order and even at times of external security. The institutions of both types of government routinely interact, so much so that in Phillippe Schmitter's terminology, a form of "societal corporatism"[22] has become evident in the United States.

Certain definitional matters remain. Social control refers to those processes, whether planned or unplanned, by which individuals are persuaded or compelled to conform to the values of groups. It operates on three levels: group over group, and group over its members, and individuals over other persons. It can be coercive, as in the sanctions of the criminal law, but usually it takes more subtle forms, such as the socializing functions of public education and the mass media. The purpose is to "bring about conformity, solidarity, and continuity of a particular group or society."[23] Social control can be either formal, as in the application of the positive law, or informal, as in the insidious pressures of the invisible but nonetheless existent conventions of society (or, indeed, of the inchoate law of the corporate community).

The purpose of internal order is to suppress defection and to divert discontent into innocuous channels. The ruling or governing class (the elites) of any societal entity must perforce have several techniques available by which its privileged position can be protected and solidified. One is to pretend that everyone benefits, or can benefit, from the operations of the U.S. political economy. This is accomplished by employment of cosmetic gains in the formal constitution accompanied by a tacit commitment to continuing economic growth and a rhetoric that extols popular sovereignty. More specifically, the pretense in the United States is that everyone has equality of opportunity, but there is no desire by those in power for equality of condition.

Another technique worth mention here is repression, which is the ultimate device employed. Still another has been described by B. F. Skinner:

A government may prevent defection by making life more interesting—by providing bread and circuses and by encouraging sports, gambling, the use of alcohol and other drugs, and various kinds of sexual behavior, where the effect is to keep people within the reach of aversive sanctions. The Goncourt brothers noted the rise of pornography in the France of their day: "Pornographic literature," they wrote, "serves as a Bas-Empire, one tames a people as one tames a lion, by masturbation."[24]

What is often called the permissive society came into being in the United States in the post–World War II period for definite reasons and specific aims.[25] It was and still is a means of mass mental masturbation by many of the people.

The secret constitution, may be compared to what Nathan Leites called the "operational code,"[26] a concept adopted by Michael Reisman and Justice Richard Neely of the West Virginia Supreme Court.[27] However labeled, it consists of the informal understandings and conventions governing what occurs in fact in societal and governmental affairs. The secret constitution should not be confused with what some call the living constitution, in essence a label to describe the ways in which the formal constitution has been progressively updated since 1789 as different exigencies confronted succeeding generations of Americans. Don K. Price has called attention to "America's Unwritten Constitution"[28] in a preliminary probe into one segment of the secret constitution: the actual decision-making processes within the legislative and executive branches of the national government.

Michael Reisman's subtle analysis of bribery in social affairs distinguished between what he calls the myth system and the operational code (he calls these the *jurisprudence publique* and *jurisprudence confidentielle* of the constitutional order). He explains:

Jurisprudence confidentielle is never expressed openly. High government lawyers and private practitioners who may advise the elite will be privy to secret agreements that they interpret; pleadings and arbitrations, sometimes rendered by judges of public courts acting in their private capacity, will be suppressed by agreement of the parties; opinions rendered for corporations will be kept confidential; and vast amounts of legal material in the public sector will be classified. None of this *jurisprudence confidentielle* will be expressed by these same practitioners in the *jurisprudence publique*. . . . The *jurisprudence publique* is not a sham, for it may apply to some events and to certain groups; given the curious and almost sacramental role of generative logic in legal scholarship, *jurisprudence publique* can always be presented as a complete system of thought. But since it represents only a part of what is going on, it is inadequate as an explanatory or predictive tool.[29]

Reisman comes rather close to what I have in mind by the term the *secret constitution*, which refers to the invisible but nonetheless existent set of rules by which Americans are actually governed. The important question is this: Who gets what, when, how, and in what circumstances? By no means can the question be answered by reference to the formal constitution only.

Finally, Robert Michels's "iron law of oligarchy" is accepted as an accurate shorthand label for the American constitutional order. "Who says organization says oligarchy," said Michels.[30] So it is. Save perhaps in precivilizational times, there is no evidence that any nation or any group has ever been ruled other than oligarchically. Representative democracy in the United States, if that term means anything, at best signifies that the people are able to choose their formal rulers. They have no role at all in the selection of those who rule under the secret constitution—for example, corporate managers. The further meaning is that the

United States has always been a class, even a caste, society, despite the myth to the contrary. The moneyed and propertied have always been on top of the social and political pecking orders, and there has always been an underclass.

Implicit in the foregoing is one relevant fact and one distinction. The fact is that no society in human history has ever been able to exist without power being exercised by someone or some group. It is the irreducible core of any system of governance or any group's behavior. Power is the key concept of constitutionalism: it is the ability or capacity to make decisions affecting the values of others, the ability or capacity to impose deprivations and to bestow rewards so as to control the behavior of others. As Franz Neumann once wrote, "No greater disservice has been rendered to political science than the statement that the liberal state was a 'weak' state. It was precisely as strong as it needed to be in the circumstances. It acquired substantial colonial empires, waged wars, held down internal disorders, and stabilized itself over long periods of time."[31]

The distinction is that those who wield formal authority should always be distinguished from those who exercise effective control over societal decisions. The former label refers to those vested with the trappings of officiality—national, state, and local. Their decisions are the fodder of the many public law courses that dominate law school curricula. Effective control is another matter. Those who wield it operate in the institutions of the secret constitution. Price defines this constitution as the "fixed political customs that have developed without formal constitutional amendment, but have been authorized by statute or frozen, at least temporarily, in tradition."[32] Consider, for example, the notorious "iron triangles" (or "issue networks") that exist in Washington, D.C.—the means by which much public policy is actually made.[33] An iron triangle consists of the industry or other group being regulated or affected by legislation, the relevant administrative agency, and the congressional committee(s) having jurisdiction over the agency (and thus the industry). The military-industrial complex is by far the most prominent triangle, but many others exist. The principal function of the corporate body called Congress is to endorse the decisions of the iron triangles, which are reached by a complex system of bargaining among the three principal participants. As Jacques Ellul observed, "The organs of representative democracy no longer have any purpose than to endorse decisions prepared by experts and pressure groups."[34] Effective control, accordingly, resides in those who influence or direct the flow of triangle decisions. All too often, as John Kenneth Galbraith has remarked, the fox (the industry supposedly regulated) is in charge of the chicken coop.[35]

The suggestion is not that a sharp line always exists between formal authority and effective control. The two classes of decision makers at times meet and merge, although it remains true that those who exercise effective control prefer to operate through surrogates. For example, Senators Lyndon Johnson, Robert Kerr, and Russell Long in effect were representatives of the oil industry. This is not a new development; it has always been so. The Supreme Court has in general been a willing arm of corporate capitalism; it has made property rights highest in the hierarchy of rights protected against government intervention. And when the two classes do merge, their decisions are from time to time constitutionalized by the Court. This is not to say that the justices speak in terms of the merger of myth and operational code. To the contrary, as Justice Neely has remarked, judges never speak in such terms. This leads Neely to assert that "most of what appears in legal opinions on constitutional law cannot be given or received with a straight face."[36] The justices of the Supreme Court are, of course, sentient beings and as such know about the operation of the secret constitution. But they stoutly refuse to acknowledge its existence. They seem to follow the advice of Socrates: "Our rulers will find a considerable dose of falsehood and deceit necessary for the good of their subjects."[37] This, of course, is Machiavellianism pure and simple.

In essence, we have in the United States a fictional separation of economy and polity. The two governments, public and private, routinely interact, so much so that an indigenous version of the corporate state is the best way to describe the constitutional order. Economy and polity are complementary processes. The need, accordingly, is to recognize the actual governing power of corporations and to perceive that it is employed in conjunction with the willing cooperation of public officials. Among other things, this contributes to distortion of the public dialogue that supposedly is the hallmark of constitutional democracies. As Mark Kesselman has observed:

> The hidden face of power is exercised not so much by the suppression of specific issues from the political agenda as by the exclusion of the most fundamental matters of public concern from the political sphere. To ignore the limited scope of public decision-making and to consider political arrangements democratic under these conditions is akin to accepting that democracy exists in the fifth-grade classroom because the youngsters select class officers.[38]

Distortion of the dialogue over fundamental matters of public concern is aided by—indeed, probably could not be accomplished without—the willingness of the giant corporations that control the mass media to further the values and preferences of corporate capitalism. The major media have three basic functions: make a profit for their owners, sell consumers goods through advertising, and help to socialize the populace to make the people accept what the leaders of the secret constitution want.[39] They thus are propaganda arms of the officers of both of the American constitutions. Possibly, corporate managers believe their own rhetoric and systematically repress the idea that they in fact are governing; this, however, is doubtful, for surely they are fully aware of their actual power, however much they want it hidden from the populace.

SOCIAL CONTROL UNDER THE DUAL CONSTITUTIONS

A primary duty of government is to ensure internal order. This is accomplished in the United States (and elsewhere) by a variety of means. Each is important, both because they are designed to achieve the same ends and because they often show the close interaction of public and private power.

First, the ability of the citizenry to think clearly and take active part in public debates is deformed by the educational system and the media. Academia propagates servile ideologies and a bias toward conformity and the civil religion of nationalism and patriotism. Julien Benda was accurate when he wrote fifty years ago about the "treason of the intellectuals";[40] there is far too little independent thought or detachment among the professoriate, many of whom are all too willing to become toadies of corporate wealth. The media have already been mentioned. They contribute to the inability of citizens to think responsibly by "systematic distortion of thought. Most journalists are shallowly educated, bound to the intellectual conventions of those with whom they deal, and, in temper, *arrivistes*."[41]

Second is what I have elsewhere called the Principle of Minimal Satisfaction of Human Needs,[42] by which is meant that those in power—mainly, in effective control but also those with formal authority—extend just that amount of gains to the discontented and disadvantaged to siphon off any desire to work for change in the system. All of U.S. history provides evidence of the employment of the principle. A brief summary will suffice to illustrate the point. Edmund Morgan has shown that as far back as the Jamestown colony (1607–1699), indentured servants, the principal work force, were treated badly, physically abused, and even worked to death.[43] Finally they rebelled. "Out of that experience the Virginia gentry learned that in order to keep the peace they had to give other whites the right to own property, and by that act, the privilege to vote."[44] Simultaneously, however, black workers were denied the right to own property or to exercise their civil rights. The law was used to help one group (whites) and to abuse another (blacks). Law was twisted in Jamestown, in what likely was the first example in the United States of where the legal system is used by those in power to further their own ends. By no means was it the last time. The power structure has always known what to do to preserve its position.

The Constitutional Convention of 1787 is another example. The document, when drafted, was a bundle of compromises. The dominant note of the conclave was stated by Alexander Hamilton:

All communities divide themselves into the few and the many. The first are the rich and well-born, the other the mass of the people. The voice of the people has been said to be the voice of God; and however generally this maxim has been believed and quoted, it is not true in fact. The people are turbulent and changing; they seldom judge or determine right. Give therefore to the first class a distinct permanent share in the government.[45]

The "permanent share" then was to permit only white, male property owners to vote, to insulate both the presidency and the Senate from direct election, and (implicitly) to establish the predominance of the Supreme Court in questions of constitutional interpretation.

The institutions of the formal constitution were thus dominated by members of the institutions of the secret constitution. The sops thrown to Hamilton's masses were the House of Representatives, which was to be elected biennially by the people (the so-called Great Compromise), and the principle of federalism, which supposedly established dual sovereignties. Popular discontent was sufficiently diluted to enable the formal constitution to be ratified.

Next came the Bill of Rights, speedily enacted into constitutional amendment to diffuse discontent with the new constitution among people who were not deluded by Hamilton's specious argument in Federalist No. 84 that the formal document was itself a bill of rights. Part of the price paid for ratification of the constitution was the Bill of Rights, which promised that reasons of freedom and liberty would, at least in the letter, prevail over reasons of state.

That the propertied elite were the chief beneficiaries of the new governmental system cannot be doubted. There was, however, enough flexibility in the federal system, accompanied by the far more important fact of the untapped wealth of the new nation, to convince small property owners and middle-class mechanics and farmers to favor the formal constitution. These people provided a social basis of support for the elite. They were "buffers against the blacks, the Indians, the very poor whites."[46] Thus the elite were able to keep control "with a minimum of coercion, a maximum of law—all made palatable by the fanfare of patriotism and unity."[47] Not all was sweetness and light, however. The Whiskey Rebellion in Pennsylvania in 1794, preceded by Shays's Rebellion in Massachusetts in 1786, terrified the propertied elite. (Both were quickly smashed by use of violence.) The constitution as drafted was, in sum, a counterrevolution to the principles of the Declaration of Independence. It was a means of social control—in the interests of the moneyed and propertied. National public policies, both judicial and legislative, quickly made that evident in the early nineteenth century. In *Fletcher v. Peck*[48] the Supreme Court, speaking through Chief Justice Marshall, made up some law and legitimized a gigantic land fraud perpetrated by some leading public figures, including members of Congress and federal judges. And Congress with a fit of unparalleled generosity gave away most of the "commons"—the publicly owned riches of the nation—to a favored few.[49] The *Fletcher* decision is the first important instance of a core principle of the secret constitution: the many shall not be allowed to do to the few what the few had done to the many.

At the end of the nineteenth century, still another example of the Principle of Minimal Satisfaction may be perceived. Simultaneously with the rise of corporate gigantism, the trade union movement began to blossom, together with the Granger movement and populism. The economy had become a zero-sum game with the closure of the frontier. Something had to be done to satisfy the rising demands of the working class. Two avenues were taken: savage repression and the Progressive movement. Progressivism, which came into fruition with the coming of a regulatory interventionist public government, was ostensibly to help those who most needed it. But that was not to be, although many historians today still repeat it as a fact; the revisionists such as Gabriel Kolko, James Weinstein, and R. Jeffrey Lustig[50] know better. They have demonstrated that progressivism was taken over by corporate capitalism and turned to its ends. Woodrow Wilson[51] was the philosopher for the business class, and a railroad lawyer named Richard Olney, who was to become President Cleveland's attorney general, showed the way. Counseled Olney to a president of the railroad who was distressed about formation of the Interstate Commerce Commission (ICC): do not try to get it declared unconstitutional (although with a complaisant Supreme Court, that probably would have occurred); rather, use it. In that way, the public's clamor for regulation would be satisfied without undue harm to the companies.[52]

That is precisely what happened. The ICC, an institution of the formal constitution, was dominated by officials who were surrogates of the institutions of the secret constitution. The fox early entered the chicken coop. The business class had it both ways: they were at once able to allay working-class discontent, while the ICC and other regulatory agencies were able to eliminate many of the excesses of what they considered to be cut-throat competition. A neat trick, that, all the more so when a similar public-private interaction took place during the Great Depression and President Franklin Roosevelt's New Deal. The economy had broken down. Something had to be done—by government, for the business community was morally and intellectually bankrupt. The ruling elites were like the storied Bourbons: they had learned nothing and forgotten nothing. Or as George Orwell commented about Great Britain, "Whether the British ruling class was wicked or merely stupid is one of the most difficult questions of our time, and at certain moments a very important question."[53] That observation applied to the United States after the Great Crash. In other words, those who exercised effective control under America's secret constitution were too stupid to realize that FDR's New Deal measures were actually pro-business. As Paul Conkin has written:

> The enemies of the New Deal were wrong. They should have been friends. Security was a prime concern of the insecure thirties. It cut across all classes. Businessmen, by their policies, desperately sought it in lowered corporate debts and tried to get government to practice the same austerity. Even when ragged and ill-housed, workers opened savings accounts. The New Deal . . . underwrote a vast apparatus of security. But the meager benefits of Social Security were insignificant in comparison to the building system of security for large, established businesses. . . . The New Deal tried to frame institutions to protect capitalism from major business cycles and began in an unclear sort of way to underwrite continuous economic growth and sustained profits.[54]

In net, the "liberal" measures of FDR did not transmute the American system. No real redistribution of power or wealth occurred. Corporate capitalism survived and, with the coming of World War II, flourished. The National Recovery Act (NRA) of 1933 enacted a form of corporatism into law. When it was declared unconstitutional (on other grounds), the formal system the NRA established continued in the secret constitution. The many trade associations now head-quartered in Washington, D.C., are a direct consequence and have helped to keep corporatism, American style, alive.

Roosevelt thus may be said to have saved the businessman from his own stupidity and shortsightedness. New Deal programs also served as a safety valve; they diluted public discontent over the manifest shortcomings of an economy that had rendered too many people ill fed, ill housed, and ill clothed. The confusion among the business elite was matched by a like confusion among members of the lower classes, who saw in FDR a savior and the New Deal a way out of the morass into which they had sunk.

But if the New Deal, when finally validated by the Supreme Court, was far from revolutionary in that basic configurations of social power were not altered, it nonetheless marked a sea change in America's formal constitutional history. New public policy directions were followed, though the old order was left intact. The net total was a classic example of the Principle of Minimal Satisfaction. Property, wealth, and privilege were still highest among protected constitutional values but seemed to give way to improvement in the protection of human rights. Reality belied the appearance. New Deal programs did not solve festering economic problems, such as unemployment. At least 6 million were unemployed as late as 1941.[55] What got the nation out of the depression was precisely what has kept it from truly serious economic distress since: a war economy. This is pure Keynesian economics written into public policy—but with a military face. The manifest beneficiaries of the New Deal were those in the working classes who had suffered most in past economic reverses. The latent and more lasting beneficiaries were members of the capital-owning class, who had always ben-efited most from the constitutional system.

When those in effective control of the American polity enact measures that accord some gains to the lower classes, it should not be thought that they are acting altruistically. To the contrary, use of the principle is perceived as a preferred means of buying off social unhappiness that might erupt into social turmoil. By helping others, the officers of the secret constitution help themselves. This is neither morality nor altruism; it is simply common sense.

Not that common sense was always followed. Far from it. Perhaps the first resort of those in actual power when dissent and discontent began to boil over is violent repression. Judge Taft was quoted above: his was a classic utterance of the few who would do to the many—to the "mob"—what they feared the many might do to them. Shays's Rebellion in 1786 struck a note of lasting terror among the moneyed and propertied. They used the state—the institutions of the formal constitution—to protect themselves.

Consider in this connection the situation of the post–Civil War period, when the economy began to become a zero-sum game. The riches of an expanding nation had been seized or given away, fully exploited by their new owners. The business class had always been in effective control of politics since the beginning.

But new groups began to emerge and to demand larger shares of material goods. With new technologies not yet greatly increasing the productivity of labor, the economic pie was essentially static.

When new groups—farmers, workers, and others—demanded larger shares, there was little play in the social joints to enable their demands to be met while still maintaining the social status quo. The reaction of those with effective control was immediate and brutal. Dissent was savagely suppressed, usually with the police and the army working in conjunction with the private armies of the corporations (often the Pinkertons). Indians were killed or consigned to reservations in barren lands. Newly freed blacks found that they had exchanged the legal bonds of slavery for the de facto and equally onerous bonds of peonage. Their labor was needed, but their freedom was denied them. Law and the legal system, dominated by institutions of the secret constitution, were openly employed to further the interests of corporate capitalism. Oliver Wendell Holmes knew this in 1873, writing that the idea that law was neutral, impartially imposed by judges, "presupposes an identity of interests between different parts of a community which does not exist in fact." Holmes claimed that not only was there no unity in law as a whole but that there was a lack of unity at the social level that eventually was translated into law. Holmes believed that, as with Plato's Thrasymachus, judicial decisions represented the interests of the stronger in society. As he put it, "Whatever body may possess the supreme power for the moment is certain to have interests inconsistent with others which have competed unsuccessfully. The more powerful interests must be more or less reflected in legislation [and court decisions]; which, like every other device of man or beast, must tend in the long run to aid the survival of the fittest."[56] This example of social Darwinism was reflected not only in constitutional decisions but in such private law doctrines as assumption of risk and contributory negligence through which industrial workers had to suffer the dreadful costs of the new factory system. Gianfranco Poggi has summed up the implications: "Under capitalism the economy does not operate within the social sphere simply as one 'factor' among and coordinate with others; rather, it imperiously subordinates or otherwise reduces the independent significance of all other factors, including religion, the family, the status system, education, technology, science, and the arts."[57]

Robert Justin Goldstein has exhaustively demonstrated that political repression is one of the dark holes of American scholarship.[58] This was particularly true of the growing trade union movement after the Civil War: "From approximately 1873 . . . until 1937 . . . American labor suffered governmental repression that was probably as severe or more severe than that suffered by any labor movement in any other Western industrialized democracy. According to the foremost historians of American labor violence, the U.S. has had the 'bloodiest and most violent labor history of any industrial nation in the world.' "[59] Business and government elites cooperated closely together, employing such devices as the company town, private police squads, detectives, the deputization of private police, the manipulation of governmental police agencies, the revival of the criminal conspiracy doctrine against union activity, and the labor injunction. There was both a widespread use of private resources to achieve public ends (law and order) and the use of public resources (the police and the army) to further private ends.[60]

The moneyed and propertied were terrified and convinced themselves that workers were inherently criminal. Even so-called liberal reformers joined the hue and cry:

Liberal reformers became deathly afraid of the poor and the unfortunate, afraid that the underprivileged masses would rise up and strike down property and all that was decent and respectable in life. . . . Liberals claimed to detest the crude businessman who ran most of the giant corporations in postwar America. Yet they ultimately became staunch supporters of these same men; for, no matter how corrupt or unscrupulous or cruel a businessman was in his daily affairs, he stood for property. . . . For all their vaunted concern for the individual, liberal reformers readily and repeatedly set aside human rights whenever the rights of property came under attack. Much as they deplored outbursts of human passion and pleaded for reasoned solutions to human problems, most liberals agreed that the only sure method of dealing with violence among strikers was to shoot the offenders. . . . But with dogged consistency [they] opposed meaningful proposals to provide workers with the means, the opportunity and the incentive to acquire good taste and enlightenment.[61]

Political repression, then, has always been a fact of American life. The Supreme Court has dutifully gone along, as witness its 8–1 decision in *United States v. O'Brien* (1968)[62] sustaining a savage sentence imposed on a young man for publicly burning his draft card as a protest against the Vietnam War. The Court has never upheld the exercise of civil liberties when important societal matters (important as seen through the eyes of the establishment) are considered to be at stake. The dominant political coalition at the time of the *O'Brien* decision wanted "to put a stop to this particular form of antiwar protest, which they deemed extraordinarily contemptible and vicious—even treasonous—at a time when American troops were engaged in combat."[63] It is worth noting that all three branches of the federal government—Congress in passing the law, the executive in prosecuting O'Brien, and the Court for upholding his sentence to jail—failed to live up to the spirit and perhaps the letter of the formal constitution.

All of this is not to say that the United States is on a par with totalitarian governments. But it is to say that when governing elites consider it necessary, violence is used domestically and abroad—with the actual beneficiaries being those who have always profited most from the American constitutional order: the moneyed and the propertied.[64] Social control comes in a variety of guises; whatever technique is used, it consists of cooperative action between the officers of public government (the formal constitution) and private government (the secret constitution). The concentration here has been on the function of the giant corporations as the most important of the decentralized private groups of the nation. But others exist—farmers' leagues, veterans' legions, trade unions—and much of what has been said about corporations can to some extent be said about the others. Nonetheless, it is the corporate juggernaut that overshadows the rest— and to a marked extent public government itself. This may accurately be labeled as the dark side of the American constitutional order.

EMERGENT CORPORATISM AND CONSTITUTIONAL OBLIGATIONS

I have suggested that the institutions of the formal and the secret constitutions routinely interact. On the national level, this is particularly to be seen in the pervasive operation of the iron triangles of the policy-making process. The drift of American constitutionalism is definitely in the direction of an indigenous form of corporatism. This is neither capitalism nor socialism but the third great "ism" of contemporary politics. Not mentioned in the formal constitution or its amendments, the emergent system got its constitutional imprimatur in the state action doctrine invented by the Supreme Court after the Civil War.

I do not mean to imply that the corporate state, American style, burst forth full panoplied and is widely recognized as such. The *Santa Clara* decision solidified what had been implicit in the *Civil Rights Cases*: that there was a distinction in formal constitutional law between public and private. The state action doctrine may be inevitably incoherent, as Michael Phillips has argued,[65] but it nevertheless has all the appearances of being as settled as any express part of the formal constitution. Only by penetrating into the intricacies of the informalities of the secret constitution can it be seen that, as Schmitter observed, societal corporatism is imbedded in the political system: "Societal corporatism appears to be the concomitant, if not ineluctable, component of the postliberal, advanced capitalist, organized democratic welfare state."[66] The modern state and modern interest groups—corporations principally but others too—seek each other out. Andrew Shonfield showed in his magisterial *Modern Capitalism* that the state seeks to foster maximum employment, promote economic growth, curb inflation, smooth out business cycles, regulate conditions of work, help alleviate individual economic and social risks, and resolve labor disputes. This he calls corporatist: "The major interest groups are brought together and encouraged to conclude a series of bargains about their future behaviour, which will have the effect of moving economic events along the desired path."[67]

The development poses enormous theoretical problems. If corporations do exercise governing power, however invisible it may be, and since they are constitutional persons, the crucial question of defining their constitutional rights and duties immediately emerges. This is not the time or place to essay a full explication of the question; it will be enough to point out some general principles.

First, as a constitutional person, a corporation has the power—the legal right— to hold and convey property, to enter into contracts, and to sue and be sued. All of this is of great importance. Of even more importance is the second principle: a corporation can invoke the formal constitution when it considers its rights to be transgressed by the state. A corporation has the protection of the due process and equal protection clauses and even before 1886 could trigger Congress's constitutional authority (via the judiciary) to regulate commerce so as to stave off adverse regulation by a state. (The reach of *Barron v. Baltimore*, confining application of the Bill of Rights to the federal government, did not extend to the affirmative powers of Congress—as witness *Gibbons v. Ogden*.)[68] More recently, corporations have been accorded freedom of expression (First Amendment) rights on nonbusiness public issues and are protected against unreasonable searches and seizures (Fourth Amendment).

Protection from the state has been, however, a one-way street. Third, no concomitant corporate constitutional duties are owed to the nation. A natural person has certain constitutional obligations. Despite the Thirteenth Amendment's prohibition of involuntary servitude, he or she can be compelled to serve on juries and, of more significance, fight and even to die for the state.

Fourth, the time surely has come—it is long overdue—to think seriously about the need for imposing analogous constitutional duties on giant corporations. Robert Dahl has outlined some reasons for this development:

By its decisions, the large corporation may: Cause death, injury, disease, and severe physical pain, e.g., by decisions resulting in pollution, poor design, inadequate quality control, plant safety, working conditions, etc.;

Impose severe deprivations of income, well-being, and effective personal freedom, e.g., by decisions on hiring and firing, employment practices, plant locations, etc.;

Exercise influence, power, control, and even coercion over employees, suppliers, and others by manipulating expectations of rewards and deprivations, e.g., by advertising propaganda, promotions, and demotions, not to mention possible illegal practices.[69]

Although it is often said that the state is characterized by having a monopoly on the legitimate use of violence, surely the corporate decisions Dahl summarizes inflict violence—and do so lawfully (legitimately). This is yet another reason to call their activities part of the secret constitution and reason enough for the populace to be able to cry *haro!*—as Adolf Berle suggested—against the giant corporations.[70]

Chief Justice Marshall's views in *Dartmouth College* have been rendered obsolete, as has the unjustified public-private distinction central to the state action doctrine. Giant corporations are states within a state—constitutionally autonomous entities free to go their own way unfettered by the limitations of the formal constitution. They are also of the state because of their close interlocks with public governance. They are even more: they are outside the state, for most large corporations have become transnational. Their governing power is neither constitutionally legitimate (under the formal constitution) nor accountable. Corporate managers do not generally have to answer in another place for their activities. This, in any nation that trumpets it is a democracy, is not—indeed, cannot be—justified. As Mark V. Nadel has observed:

We would not countenance a totally nonelected self-perpetuating oligarchy in government merely because many of the policies of that oligarchy were beneficent. Corporations also make public policy. When they do so, however, there is not even the formal accountability to the public that we have in government. The task for scholars and the public alike is to assess the amount of public policy that is privately made and to formulate ways of limiting such policy-making power—or at least of making it more accountable.[71]

In short, how can corporate power that is necessary be made as tolerable and decent as possible? If we assume that giant corporations are here to stay for at least the foreseeable future, the problem is essentially one of devising ways to impose constitutional obligations on corporate giants. Leon Duguit said it well: "Any system of public law can be vital only so far as it is based on a given sanction to the following rules: First, the holders of power cannot do certain things; second, there are certain things they must do."[72]

Constitutional duty or obligation has a dual face: limitations on power and the "must do" aspect. This is not a semantic quiddity. Most of American constitutional history has emphasized the "cannot do" aspect of governmental power. Nonetheless, during the past few decades, there are some indications that the Supreme Court, as well as other courts, have begun to think in terms of duty to act.[73] The ready example is the many legislative reapportionment decisions, in some of which judges ordered legislatures to act on pain of having the court act if legislators failed in their duty. As Abram Chayes has said, adjudication has often tended to become "problem-solving" rather than "dispute-settling."[74]

Constitutional obligation has generally been perceived as the duty of the individual to the state. "The great problem of political theory, especially for a period of over two centuries after the Reformation, was to explain how any man, born 'free and equal,' could be rightfully under the domain of any other man."[75] But what about the constitutional obligations of the state? If the state is defined to include the apparatuses of both public and private governance, we should inquire into the obligations of both.

What, then, can be said about the concept of obligation in the American system of two constitutions? Several propositions may be advanced in outline form:

1. A distinction must be made between the "is" and the "ought."

2. The "is" may be divided: (1) the two governments and their obligations are complementary; (2) the principal obligation of public government has been to follow Lockean principles of the protection of property; and (3) government in the United States has always followed Machiavellian principles, mainly as stated in *The Discourses* but also in *The Prince*.[76] Each of these cuts against the grain of orthodox constitutional theory—even the second: many believe that the formal constitution is— or has been—interpreted in ways that make property rights less in importance to other rights. But that simply is not so.

3. The "ought" of American constitutionalism is the furtherance of human needs and human deserts.[77] This, again, is contrary to the orthodoxy.

If the state is Janus like—facing toward both the obviously public and the supposedly private—the governments of the two constitutions should have dual responsibilities or obligations. That they do not is obvious.

What should be done? I suggest two things. First, we as humans have a right, at least in the ideal, to satisfaction of those human needs that human action can reasonably be expected to satisfy. Second, we as humans do not have a right to satisfaction of needs that the environment, broadly defined, will not accommodate. This looks toward the necessity for major constitutional revision. The basic question is this: Were the formal constitution to be rewritten today, what would—what should—be put in it? In answering that question, three other questions must be addressed: What type of society do Americans want? And what type of governmental apparatus would be best suited to achieve it? What is the environment in which the future constitution must exist and operate? How can the indubitable governing power of the institutions of the secret constitution be curbed and channeled?[78]

I have attempted to invite attention to a more sophisticated view of American constitutionalism than that which is usually portrayed. Much that has been said has, concededly, been too terse and conclusory. But that could not be avoided. It remains only to say that the Supreme Court has in the past decade continued its systematic protection of corporate privilege. What the *Santa Clara* and *Civil Rights Cases* started takes on modern garb in *Buckley v. Valeo, First National Bank v. Bellotti*, and *Federal Election Commission v. National Conservative Political Action Committee*.[79] The net effect of these decisions is to constitutionalize Jesse Unruh's mordant quip, "Money is the mother's milk of politics." The Court has now legitimized oligarchical control of electoral campaigns. What has been a feature of the secret constitution is part of the formal constitution as well. "Is money speech?" Judge J. Skelly Wright once asked.[80] Indeed it is, say the Justices of the Supreme Court.

NOTES

1. A. Pekelis, Private Governments and the Federal Constitution, in Law and Social Action 91, 97–98 (M. Konvitz ed. 1950) (collection of essays).

2. 109 U.S. 3 (1883).

3. 169 U.S. 466 (1898).

4. Munn v. Illinois, 94 U.S. 113 (1877).

5. 198 U.S. 45 (1905).

6. 208 U.S. 412 (1908).

7. Quoted in C. Fairman, Mr. Justice Miller and the Supreme Court 374 (1939).

8. See In re Debs, 158 U.S. 564 (1895). On antitrust, see chapter 3 to this book.

9. Quoted in B. Tuchman, The Proud Tower 478 (1966) (pagination from paperback edition).

10. Quoted in L. Berg, H. Hahn, & J. Schmidhauser, Corruption in the American Political System 11 (1976).

11. M. Shapiro, Courts: A Comparative and Political Analysis (1981).

12. J. Griffith, The Politics of the Judiciary 213 (1977).

13. 4. Wheat. 518 (1819).

14. H. Vaihinger, The Philosophy of "As If": A System of Theoretical, Practical and Religious Fictions of Mankind xli (2d English ed., C. Ogden trans. 1935).

15. R. Merton, Social Theory and Social Structure 115–22 (rev. ed. 1968).

16. W. Wilson, Congressional Government 9–10 (2d ed. 1885).

17. W. Bagehot, The English Constitution 61 (1867) (pagination from 1963 paperback ed.).

18. Id.

19. B. Crick, In Defence of Politics 69 (1962) (revised paperback ed. 1964).

20. Id., at 73.

21. See P. Bachrach, The Theory of Democratic Elitism: A Critique (1967); T. Dye & L. Zeigler, The Irony of Democracy 112 (1970). P. Burch, Elites in American History: The New Deal to the Carter Administration 388 (1980) concludes: "Great family wealth, as well as corporate wealth, has long exercised more influence in American government than has generally been realized. In fact, if anything, this is an understatement. For . . . it would be more accurate to say that, regardless of its changing form, America has always been dominated by some form of wealth."

22. Schmitter, Still the Century of Corporatism? 36 Rev. Pol. 85 (1974). See Panitch, The Development of Corporatism in Liberal Democracies, 10 Comp. Pol. Stud. 61 (1977).

23. J. Roucek, Social Control 7 (2d ed. 1956).

24. B. Skinner, Beyond Freedom and Dignity 34 (1971).

25. For discussion, see Miller, Social Justice and the Warren Court: A Preliminary Examination, 11 Pepperdine L. Rev. 473 (1984); Miller, Pretense and Our Two Constitutions, 54 Geo. Wash. L. Rev. 375 (1986).

26. N. Leites, The Operational Code of the Politburo (1951). See George, The Operational Code: A Neglected Approach to the Study of Political Leaders and Decision-making, 13 Int'l Stud. Q. 190 (1969).

27. W. Reisman, Folded Lies: Bribery, Crusades, and Reforms (1979); R. Neely, How Courts Govern America (1981).

28. D. Price, America's Unwritten Constitution: Science, Religion, and Political Responsibility (1983), discussed in Miller, Myth and Reality in American Constitutionalism, 63 Texas L. Rev. 181 (1984).

29. Reisman, supra note 27, at 12–13.

30. R. Michels, Political Parties (1915).

31. F. Neumann, The Democratic and the Authoritarian State 8 (1957).

32. D. Price, supra note 28, at 9.

33. Compare id., at 93 with D. Cater, Power in Washington 17 (1964) and Heclo, Issue Networks and the Executive Establishment, in The New American Political System 87 (A. King ed. 1978). See also G. Adams, The Iron Triangle (1981).

34. J. Ellul, The Political Illusion 138 (K. Kellen trans. 1967).

35. Quoted in The Economy as a System of Power vi–vii (W. Samuels ed. 1979) (the passage comes from Professor Samuels's introduction).

36. R. Neely, supra note 27, at 19.

37. Plato, Republic, Book V. See also R. Neely, supra note 27, at 13–14, concluding (p. 14): "All branches of government lie, and so do judges."

38. Kesselman, The Conflictual Evolution of American Political Science: From Apologetic Pluralism to Trilateralism and Marxism, in Public Values & Private Power in American Politics 34, 57 (J. Greenstone ed. 1982).

39. See M. Schramm, Mass Communications, cited in N. Chomsky, For Reasons of State 95, 205 (1973); Bethell, The Myth of an Adversary Press, Harper's Magazine, Jan. 1977 (The mass media "can best be understood as departments of the federal bureaucracy"). See also P. Knightley, The First Casualty (1976).

40. J. Benda, The Treason of the Intellectuals (1928).

41. Birnbaum, Letter to a European Friend, 74 Yale Rev. 47, 54 (1984).

42. Miller, Pretense and Our Two Constitutions (54 Geo. Wash. L. Rev. 375 (1986).

43. E. Morgan, American Slavery, American Freedom: The Ordeal of Colonial Virginia 3–107 (1975).

44. Lamar, The First American West: Jamestown, 1607–1699, 74 Yale Rev. 64, 75 (1984).

45. 1 Records of the Federal Convention (M. Farrand ed. 1927), quoted in M. Parenti, Democracy for the Few (3d ed. 1977).

46. H. Zinn, A People's History of the United States 98–99 (1980).

47. Id., at 99. See generally J. Diggins, The Lost Soul of American Politics: Virtue, Self-Interest, and the Foundations of Liberalism (1984).

48. 6 Cranch 87 (1810).

49. See M. Josephson, The Robber Barons 52 (1934); R. Lustig, Corporate Liberalism: The Origins of Modern American Political Theory 95 (1982).

50. G. Kolko, The Triumph of Conservatism (1963); J. Weinstein, The Corporate Ideal in the Liberal State: 1900–1918 (1968); R. Lustig, supra note 49.

51. See the several essays in A New History of Leviathan: Essays on the Rise of the American Corporate State (R. Radosh & M. Rothbard eds. 1972), particularly that of Martin Sklar.

52. Olney is quoted in L. Jaffe, Judicial Control of Administrative Action 11 (1966).

53. Quoted in Hitchens, Anthony Wedgwood Benn: Can He Put England Together Again? Mother Jones, Nov. 1981, at 14.

54. P. Conkin, The New Deal 74–75 (1967). See Bernstein, The New Deal: The Conservative Achievements of Liberal Reform, in Towards A New Past 264–65 (B. Bernstein ed. 1968).

55. See W. Leuchtenberg, Franklin D. Roosevelt and the New Deal 336, 346–47 (1963). Some put the figure higher. See L. Peikoff, The Ominous Parallels 295 (1982): "At the end of the thirties there were still ten million people unemployed, about two-thirds of the number without jobs in 1932."

56. Holmes, The Gas-Stokers' Strike, 7 Am. L. Rev. 582 (1873). For discussion of Holmes's comment, see Tushnet, Truth, Justice and the American Way: An Interpretation of Public Law Scholarship in the Seventies, 57 Texas L. Rev. 1307 (1979).

57. G. Poggi, The Development of the Modern State: A Sociological Introduction 120–21 (1978).

58. R. Goldstein, Political Repression in Modern America from 1870 to the Present (1978).

59. Id., at 3.

60. Id. See also J. Cooper, The Army and Civil Disorder (1980).

61. J. Sproat, "The Best Men": Liberal Reformers in the Gilded Age 227, 235, 277 (1971).

62. 391 U.S. 367 (1968).

63. Alfange, Free Speech and Symbolic Conduct: The Draft-Card Burning Case, 1968 Sup. Ct. Rev. 115.

64. For a classic statement of how violence has been employed to protect corporate interests abroad, see the statement by General Smedley Butler, former commandant of the marines, quoted in S. Lens, The Forging of the American Empire 270–71 (1971).

65. Phillips, The Inevitable Incoherence of Modern State Action Doctrine, 28 St. Louis Univ. L. J. 683 (1984). Charles Black called it a "conceptual disaster area" in Black, "State Action," Equal Protection, and California's Proposition 14, 81 Harv. L. Rev. 69, 95 (1967).

66. Schmitter, supra note 22.

67. A. Shonfield, Modern Capitalism 231 (1965).

68. Barron v. Baltimore, 7 Pet. 243 (1833); Gibbons v. Ogden, 9 Wheat. 1 (1824).

69. Dahl, A Prelude to Corporate Reform, 1 Bus. & Soc'y Rev. 18 (1972).

70. A. Berle, The 20th Century Capitalist Revolution (1954). "The 'Haro' cry was . . . the recognized means of appeal to the conscience of feudal power. . . . It is probably one of the origins of the British law of equity." Id., at 62. It may seem to be a far cry from feudal lords to corporate management. But it is not so far when it is perceived, as it should be, that giant corporations are units of neofeudalism.

71. Nadel, The Hidden Dimension of Public Policy: Private Governments and the Policy-Making Process, 37 J. Pol. 3, 34 (1975).

72. L. Duguit, Law in the Modern State 26 (H. Laski trans. 1919).

73. For preliminary discussion, see Miller, Toward a Concept of Constitutional Duty, in A. Miller, Social Change and Fundamental Law: America's Evolving Constitution 129–78 (1979).

74. Chayes, The Role of the Judge in Public Law Litigation, 89 Harv. L. Rev. 4 (1976).

75. Pennock, Introduction, in NOMOS XII: Political and Legal Obligation xiii, xiv (J. Pennock & J. Chapman eds. 1970).

76. See Miller, Reason of State and the Emergent Constitution of Control, 64 Minn. L. Rev. 585 (1980).

77. Miller, Taking Needs Seriously: Observations on the Necessity for Constitutional Change, 41 Wash. & Lee L. Rev. 1243 (1984).

78. Discussed in id., at 1274–77; and in A. Miller, *The Secret Constitution and the Need for Constitutional Change* (work in progress).

79. 424 U.S. 1 (1976); 435 U.S. 765 (1978); 105 S. Ct. 1459 (1985).

80. See Wright, Politics and the Constitution: Is Money Speech? 85 Yale L. J. 1001 (1976); Wright, Money and the Pollution of Politics: Is the First Amendment an Obstacle to Political Equality? 82 Colum. L. Rev. 609 (1982). Both articles are reprinted in J. Wright, On Courts and Democracy: Selected Nonjudicial Writings of J. Skelly Wright (A. Miller ed. 1984).

11

TOWARD MORE COMPETITIVE DIVERSITY IN A MARKET-CONCENTRATED ECONOMY

SAMUEL M. LOESCHER

When, some four or five generations ago, freedom of private enterprise was first systematically advocated as the ideal basis of an economic system, . . . the grant of a corporate charter was then universally regarded as the grant of a special privilege potentially dangerous to society, and it was therefore then assumed as a matter of course that such grants would be made only sparingly and would then be jealously circumscribed in each instance, by restrictions as to permitted size, nature and range of activities.
—J. Viner, The Short View and Long View in Economic Policy (Presidential Address, American Economic Association, Dec. 27, 1939) in The Long View and the Short 120 (J. Viner, ed., 1958).

The general conclusion is that the legal and institutional permissions of capitalism imply a self-organizing process leading to persistently increasing concentration in the absence of special fiscal handicaps imposed on larger firms.
—R. Maris and D. Mueller, The Corporation and Competition, 18 J. Econ. Lit. 32, 50 (1980).

The initiation of a megaconglomerate merger movement during 1981, crowned by the acquisitions by du Pont and U.S. Steel of Conoco and Marathon Oil, respectively, revived concerns about the level of aggregate corporate concentration in the U.S. economy. Concerns have only intensified during the following years of merger mania, which saw takeovers as Getty, Gulf Oil, General Foods, and the announcement of a plan by General Electric to take over RCA during 1986. Important horizontal mergers have been effectively prohibited since *Brown Shoe*[1] in 1962, notwithstanding some dubious approvals of mergers in import-sensitive industries. Debate continues as to whether the magnitude of conglomerate mergers during the two decades ending in 1980 made up for the falloff in horizontal mergers, so that aggregate corporate concentration continued to increase[2] or was merely prevented from declining.[3]

Little debate exists that merger mania between 1981 and 1985 has substantially increased the share of industrial assets controlled by the largest 200 corporations, but the Federal Trade Commission under the Reagan administration has ceased collecting data that would allow official confirmation. No debate exists, however, as to the multifold rise in aggregate corporate concentration during the sweep of the twentieth century. One of the most recent estimates suggests that the share in U.S. manufacturing assets held by the 200 largest manufacturing corporations rose three times—from about 20 percent to 60 percent— between 1900 and 1980.[4] By contrast, the market concentration, or oligopoly, problem has appeared to stabilize during the twentieth century. The share of manufacturing, as measured by value-added, coming from industries in which the largest four firms produce at least a majority of the output continues around the substantial 30 percent inherited from the raging horizontal merger decade of the 1890s.[5]

DIVERSE COMPETITION VERSUS RIVALROUS COMPETITION

Those concerned with aggregate corporate concentration have not sufficiently spelled out how such concentration relates to competition. Concerns with increased aggregate corporate concentration, in contrast with average market concentration, have not primarily focused upon its weakening of the behavior of rivalrous competition and that behavior's constraint upon contrived scarcity in particular markets.[6] Attention has properly been directed at theoretical tendencies of aggregate concentration to strengthen the financial bases of market entrenchment and to weaken other dimensions of potential competition over the long run.[7] But, holding constant the degree of static competition and strategic behavior, varying degrees of dynamic competition will be functionally related to the number of research-oriented participants engaged in independent experimentation. Product market structures congruent with given static patterns of rivalrous competition (most notably varying patterns of conglomerateness) are concurrently consistent with a strengthened or weakened structure of diverse competition. Greater diversity in crucial choices increases potentials for variegated experimentation, which is so important for the healthy functioning of a dynamic economy and democratic society.[8]

Preservation of a structure of diverse competition was undoubtedly one of the purposes leading to the adoption of the Sherman Act. Populists and pragmatists, in reaction to William Graham Sumner's social Darwinism, were especially interested in purposeful governmental intervention in the economic environment in order to preserve substantial decentralization. Such decentralization was deemed conducive to both rich experimentation in the development of managerial progress, as well as to federalist-like protections to democracy in its challenge from the plutocracy of corporations and captains of the trusts.[9] Indeed, the extensive oratory directed at "kingly prerogatives" during the congressional debates on the Sherman Act[10] were directed exclusively to a threatening diminution of socioeconomic diversity in the process of competition.

The stricture against restraint of trade in section 1 of the Sherman Act, whether pursuant to either loose or close combinations, could have been treated either as restraints upon the free price levels of rivalrous competition or restraints upon the enriched experimentation of diverse competition. In the instance of industrial pools, rings, and trade associations, the opting for restraint of trade as the restriction of rivalrous competition was clearly the appropriate standard in developing a per se rule against collusive practices that fix prices.[11] Such collaborative behavior lacks social offsets to redeem its output-restricting effects. In the instance of close combination (mergers), where balancing of the allegedly substantial efficiency offsets would have to be weighed, the appropriate standard for restraint of trade should have been, I believe, the combined effect upon both rivalrous competition and diverse competition. The supplementary evaluated weakening of diverse competition could frequently have been deemed sufficient to ascertain unreasonable restraint of trade in a horizontal merger in instances where the injury to rivalrous competition was otherwise found to be outbalanced by the promise of substantial efficiencies of combination. Other things equal, the larger the absolute size of the merger, the more readily would the magnitude of injury to diverse competition offset any shortfall in the magnitude of injury to rivalrous competition, in weighing the social costs over the promised benefits of close combinations. Adding the effect on diverse competition in evaluating close combinations would have achieved substantially more, however, than incremental protection of society's interest in maintaining relevant market structures conducive to price competition. It also would have gone substantially further in protecting society's interest in maintaining market economy structures conducive to commercial experimentation and democratic pluralism. Specifically, sizable conglomerate and vertical mergers would have become subject to examination. Furthermore, many huge horizontal mergers of the past twenty years, such as those in crude petroleum and coal reserves[12] where markets are huge, would also have come under examination, notwithstanding corporate shares of relevant markets deemed to be either too small to affect price or at least too small substantially to affect price. (Ironically, the per se test of tampering with prices for evaluating restraint of rivalry by loose combination has itself apparently been tampered with, or tempered, in the case of close combination.)[13]

The authors of the Sherman Act accepted limited amounts of corporate centralization, and indeed expected more, in the interest of conferring sufficient corporate power to management to obtain nondebatable economies of scale. Hence, Congress was implicitly resigned to accepting the legitimacy of some occasional industrial concentration within what today we would call relevant markets through horizontal mergers.[14] The promised benefits of efficiencies, however, had to more than compensate for the combined costs of the relaxation of rivalrous competition to constrain the levels of costs and prices and the weakened structure of diverse competition to preserve a healthy potential for managerial experimentation and political pluralism. Some rule of reason to allow for possible substantial impacts on efficiency was clearly implicit in the intent of Congress to apply section 1's strictures against restraint of trade to close combinations. In turn, mere absolute size of a merged corporation would indeed be irrelevant to balancing efficiency effects against reductions in the behavior of rivalrous competition. But absolute size would become central in balancing alleged gains of substantial efficiency against the evaluated sacrifices in the structure of diverse competition. Absolute size was also anticipated by that Congress to grow somewhat in order to gain economies from emerging technology and organization. Even if Congress foresaw much small business succumbing inevitably in fair competition to the economies of scale of their larger rivals in manufacturing, Congress could not foresee as inevitable extensive vertical, and especially conglomerate, integration. Substantial economies of scale were not perceived to arise from such ventures. The Sherman Act debates suggest that Congress was prepared to burden corporate leaders to justify to society the inherent substantiality of the alleged economies when arranging huge vertically and conglomerately organized corporations—at the diminution of diverse competition.

A socioeconomic-political purpose was clearly embraced in the passage of the Sherman Act.[15] There was indeed a deep nostalgic regret for the passing of the pastoral-yeoman Jeffersonianism. But most of Congress realistically accepted the coming of industrial centralism. More important, spokesmen revealed a vague, but hopeful, possibility of a new kind of industrial-managerial Jeffersonianism with an emphasis on experimentalism and pluralism, if no longer on character and atomism. Their vision was of an industrial-managerial Jeffersonianism holding within it the potentiality to accommodate innovatively to rapid changes and to declining agricultural self-employment and rising corporate employment. Indeed, theirs was a living charter of freedom that would permit reformist social critics during the period of the Temporary National Economic Committee 50 years later, to speak to the distinction between merely medium versus big business and today, almost one-hundred years later, to speak to the distinction between merely big versus megabusiness within the top 50, 100, or 200 on the Fortune 500.

Both market concentration and aggregate concentration substantially increased during the Sherman Act's first decade because of nonenforcement against horizontal mergers. The principal damage, however, was done to rivalrous competition. During the twentieth century, both the Sherman Act and antimerger sections of the Clayton acts of 1914 and 1950 have been employed so to unwind and deter sufficient horizontal mergers so that further weakening in the average level of rivalrous competition has been halted. By contrast, conglomerate and vertical growth, both internal and by acquisition, has so increased over the past eighty-five years as to weaken diverse competition substantially. Importantly, imaginative lines of research during the past twenty-five years suggest that no

significant corporate economies are associated with most of the twentieth century's relative growth of the corporate giants.

THE LAW OF PROPORTIONATE GROWTH

Substantial stochastic modeling of Gibrat's law of proportionate growth has
been undertaken,[16] especially by managerial-economy-oriented economists.
These begin with Herbert Simon (and J. Bonini)[17] in 1958 and continue through
Robin Maris and Dennis Mueller's[18] review article of 1980. These simple models
all show that mere random variation around specified rates of growth for business—even firms subject to constant returns to scale (above some minimum size)
and to the costs of growth—will generate increasing overall levels of concentration in the economy, which simulate observed experience remarkably well.
More sophisticated models, which allow for both new entries and absorptions
by merger, do an even better job of aping the trends of aggregate concentration
actually experienced in the economy.

The studies lend themselves to no simplistic conclusions of outdated social
Darwinism. Indeed the premises of the model suggest that firms that rise to the
top of the Fortune 500 have been selected solely by chance. Chance in like
manner explains extensions, whether by acquisition or otherwise. The premise
of constant returns (about a minimum size) suggests, as did Herbert Simon[19] in
1958, that society might feel free to employ (fiscally neutral) special taxing
instruments to reverse the contemporary levels of aggregate concentration to
some lower level judged more desirable. But if corporate responses to such fiscal
deterrents were directed toward shrinking size by shedding their conglomerateness in order to preserve their strength of oligopolistic power, no increases would
ensue in rivalrous competition.[20] No important purpose would be served unless
less aggregate corporate concentration does contribute importantly, as I contend
it does, to competitive diversity for managerial experimentation and democratic
pluralism.

ECONOMIC AND POLITICAL DIMENSIONS OF
COMPETITIVE DIVERSITY

Diversity in competition, with its enriched potential for managerial experimentation, is particularly important in three domains of socioeconomic activity
to help reverse the slowdown in productivity growth that has plagued highly
organized economies for about twenty years:[21] (1) errors of commission in investment decision; (2) errors of omission in research, development, and innovation decisions; and (3) errors in imagination of the personnel administration
of potentially creative professionals.

Societies of citizens are no less risk averse than typical citizen investors who
minimize risk by diversifying their investment portfolios.[22] Societies of citizens

are prepared to trade off some average expected gain in return for minimizing the dangers of excessive uniformity of corporate investment decisions that can turn sour. Even under the strongest of competitive pricing conditions—and no less under conditions of oligopolistic market power—corporate managements are bestowed with enormous "choice,"[23] "discretionary authority,"[24] or "power"[25] when it comes to making investment decisions with respect to process design, production design, and productive location. Judgmental elements inevitably arise in assessing forecasts of cost and benefit associated with alternative investment options. If most managerial decision makers happen to make the choice that turns out to be a serious error, a substantial drag can be placed on real growth in the economy. Three dramatic illustrations of conformity in commitment to what have proved to become major bloopers may be drawn from U.S. industrial experience since World War II: the overcommitment to obsolescing open-hearth furnaces by the steel industry during the 1950s; the overcommitment of the automobile industry to the engineering of model changes of oversized fuel-extravagant vehicles begun in the 1950s and continued into the 1970s; and the siting of excess capacity-laden nuclear power plants unduly close to metropolitan areas, begun in the 1960s and continued into the 1970s.

Undue shrinkage of the experimental centers of managerial initiative in committing large investment expenditures is probably even more serious to society with respect to finding the best than in avoiding the bad. The competitive structure of diversity, as much economy-wide as by industry, appears to be far more important when it comes to investing in research, development, and innovation. Here the elements of uncertainty are even greater. The potentialities are magnified by variety in the perceptions of management as to the relative future payoff of alternative choices, and thus are magnified societal shortfalls from failing to experiment earlier with an exploratory route that generates a surprising payoff.[26] Real economic growth can be substantially accelerated by increasing the probability of an early openness to the development of a new, unconventional, and widely perceived as dubious idea, such as xerography,[27] which itself was previously rejected for developmental support by twenty-some corporations possessing the technical and financial resources for investment in a long shot.

Third, diversity in imaginative styles of employment relations may become an element in restoring high rates to productivity gain in the U.S. economy. Professionals and technicians are becoming an increasing fraction of the American, and corporate, labor force. Highly educated persons with unique mixes of talents, training, and experience are not readily welcomed, let alone appreciated, by routine staffs in the bureaucracy of personnel departments. (Appreciation will be even less should the talented professional or technician happen also to possess non-job-related eccentric sex, artistic, religious, or political persuasions.) Yet a hospitable climate for experimentation with ideas is too important an element in the work environment to be confined to academia. Competitive diversity in the structure of corporate organization will increase the probability for the more creatively inclined to find their way into industry, remain stimulated there, and contribute to regenerating an innovative economy. Greater professional creativity within corporate industry should accelerate development of cost-effective technology in responding to social regulation and the rising relative shortage of resources.[28]

Diversity in competition is even more important for the preservation of political pluralism and the continuation of democratic experimentation. Corporate-plutocracy, or corpocracy for short, seeks to preserve the status quo and traditional prerogatives of corporate management from the experimental challenges of democracy.[29]

CORPORATE POLITICAL ACTION COMMITTEES AND THE BUSINESS ROUNDTABLE

During the last fifteen years, the power of aggregate corporate concentration has been greatly enhanced through its lobbying success in winning legislative approval of corporate political action committees (whose financial largesse tripled that of labor during the 1980 elections) and through its organizational skill in creating the Business Roundtable of chief executive officers (CEOs).[30] The organization of captains of the largest corporations in the United States represents most of the Fortune 100 industries, plus a scattering of heads of the largest utilities, banks, insurance companies, mass retailers, and transporters. Cumulative revenues of the Roundtable corporations are equal to about half the nation's GNP.

The Roundtable is designed to lobby exclusively on transindustry rather than industry-specific issues.[31] In this it matches the interests of aggregate corporate concentration. Prior associations and coalitions of corporations would focus upon such industry-specific issues as tariffs or subsidies or excise taxes, on which issues unconcentrated industries could frequently lobby as well as, or better than, the concentrated. The Business Roundtable, by contrast, focuses on truly broad economic issues of concern to all megacorporations concurrently. The Roundtable emphasizes federal budgetary policies (with respect to general tax and expenditure issues), income policies, labor legislation, social regulation (with respect to environment, health, safety, antidiscrimination, pensions, and consumers), and antitrust.

Selecting fitness for survival by tests of profitability and growth rates may not only fail to select the good but may actually contribute to socially dysfunctional selection. As long as the magnitude of externality damages continues at high levels and as long as truth continues in Thomas Nixon Carver's perception that the impersonality of giant corporations encourages both pervasive temptations to irresponsibility and opportunistic inclinations to sacrifice even private long-run profitability to the short-run bottom line of profitability,[32] Thorstein Veblen's bête noir, "business" may prosper at the social expense of "industry."[33] Yet even if the wedge between private and social performance is no bigger for greater than for lesser-sized business, aggregate corporate concentration may still render social misallocation by wounding pluralism in public choice. The growth-biased preference functions of the CEOs of the Business Roundtable are likely to succeed in their challenge to social regulation and thus hold gains in environmental conservation to levels substantially below the trade-off that the average citizen would prefer.[34]

The most notable legislative successes in the short history of the Business Roundtable have come in defeating the consumer protection agency (proposed as a modestly funded public interest law firm of consumer advocates), the labor law reform bill, and *Illinois Brick*,[35] an important antitrust issue in the domain of rivalrous antitrust involving restoration of the right to consumers to engage in class action price-fixing suits against manufacturers who sell only indirectly to consumers.[36] (Such consumer suits against the tacit delivered price-fixing system of producer goods industries could otherwise have become endemic should the Supreme Court have endorsed during 1981–1982 the path-breaking class action victory against tacit collusion to employ a basing-point system in *Southern Plywood*.)[37] Currently the Business Roundtable seeks to raise the risks to plaintiffs' class action litigation by changing the ancient law of contribution.[38] The Business Roundtable has not had to contend with any proposals tailored along lines of Senator Gary Hart's (D., Colo.) proposed industrial reorganization act, designed to streamline the process of horizontal dissolution, so as to reestablish market structures conducive to rivalrous competition.[39]

DIVERSE COMPETITION AS A CONTRIBUTOR TO RIVALROUS COMPETITION

Fundamental reform of antitrust in the traditional domain of market deconcentration, for the purpose of increasing rivalrous competition's tendency to undermine price stability, could contribute substantially to the reindustrialization of the United States without the inegalitarian contortions of Reagonomics. Increased price competition can pressure oligopolized industries to gain control over costs. It will immediately tend to squeeze out X-efficiency and thereby tend to restore total factor productivity to levels attainable with existing technology, shrink the socially nonproductive use of resources associated with redistributive and self-cancelling nonprice marketing competitive behavior, and constrain noncompetitive wage and salary compensations—and thereby counter stagflationary tendencies and the adoption of periodic deflationary macroeconomic policies designed to deal with stagflation.

But aggregate corporate concentration tends toward a political structure of corpocracy. Moreover, corpocracy's power has been newly amplified, through corporate political action committees and the Business Roundtable, to undermine political democracy. Persons could scarcely hope to organize directly against Hart's proposed industrial reorganization act.[40] Hart's proposal was designed to increase specifically the behavior of rivalrous competition by deconcentrating the structures of individual product markets.

The corporacy problem would have to be overcome, however, before product markets could be restructured so as to make price competition widespread. I have elsewhere argued that effective fragmentation of corpocracy might require a populist-oriented citizen campaign directed toward getting enacted a progressive corporate value-added tax.[41] A rising marginal tax in accordance with corporate size would create incentives automatically to encourage divisional spinoffs by corporations. Such a campaign, in effect, would be directed at restoring the competition of diversity in the interest of rehabilitating political pluralism and democratic experimentation. Following the abatement of the political muscle of corpocracy, strengths and weaknesses of the industrial reorganization act's approaches to horizontal dissolution and enhanced behavioral competition could at least be entertained by open congressional debates upon the merits.

The carte blanche state chartering grants offered first by New Jersey's holding corporation law, almost comtemporaneously with the passage of the Sherman Act, offered to corporations the freedom to grow by acquisition to unlimited size throughout the world. To correct this flaw in our practice of federalism, supplementary federal incorporation might be required for the largest U.S. corporations. Harlan Blake has suggested that the "most politically potent approach to the concentration would be to bring under close scrutiny, for possible deconcentration, in rank order of their sales, the largest 20, 50, or 200 firms in the economy."[42] For reasons that I have detailed elsewhere, I would much prefer on grounds of efficacy, expediency, and efficiency my own recently proposed progressive corporate value-added tax,[43] a proposal made fiscally neutral by combining progressivity into the negative as well as positive direction. Again for reasons elsewhere detailed, I also prefer a fiscally neutral progressive tax on value-added to a comparable tax on either corporate net income or assets, as proposed separately by Julian Simon[44] and Robin Maris,[45] in order to restore the socioeconomic diversity dimension of competition surrendered in the carte blanche grants of corporate charters.

Collateral research that I have undertaken suggests that the waves of conglomerate mergers, which have so much contributed toward the growth in aggregate concentration during the past twenty-five years, have subtracted from the dynamic efficiency of innovation far more than they may have contributed to static efficiency through increases in economies of scale and displacements of inferior management.[46] Responses to intimidation of takeover fears by managements of corporations with periodic undervaluations on the stock market have undoubtedly accentuated short-run profit goals that had already been tilted in that direction as bureaucratic tendencies toward simplistic evaluation of managerial performance increased with the size of enterprise. Trustees of pension funds, which together own a decisive majority of stock in virtually all of the Standard and Poor 500, have recently rallied collective dissatisfaction with corporate management.[47] The trustees are now beginning to attribute to such managerial failures a substantial responsibility for the slowdown in growth in both productivity and stock market indexes in the United States during the past twenty-five years.[48]

Should the pension fund trustees begin to use their collective power to nominate, elect, and instruct the directors of leading corporations to turn executive incentive systems sharply in the direction of long-term compensations,[49] managers would lose their appetite for both friendly and unfriendly takeovers acquired at super-premium market prices. Merger mania would be brought to a screeching halt. Furthermore, if reforms are made in incentive systems that propel managerial motivation toward long-run profitability, the research, developmental, and general experimental orientation of corporate management will be strengthened. Therefore the immediate economy-wide setbacks to static efficiency that could come from the adoption of public tax policies geared toward encouraging corporate deconcentration through deconglomerating spinoffs would all the more be expected to be offset by gains to dynamic efficiency if pension-fund-engineered reforms in managerial incentives were available to interact synergistically with socially engineered enrichments to diverse competition.

NOTES

1. Brown Shoe Co. v. United States, 370 U.S. 294 (1962).

2. Willard F. Mueller is assembling data that show a substantial rise in the share of total assets of all nonfinancial corporations held by the two hundred largest.

3. L. White, Reforming Regulation 198–210 (1981) and The Merger Wave: Is It a Problem? Wall St. J., December 11, 1981. The value-added in manufacturing measure on which White principally relies, however, excludes the petroleum industry (which is classified as part of mining).

4. Maris & Mueller, The Corporation, Competition, and the Invisible Hand, 18 J. Econ. Lit. 32, 33 (1980).

5. See, e.g., F. Scherer, Industrial Market Structure and Economic Performance, 67–80 (1980).

6. See, e.g., P. Steiner, Mergers (1975).

7. See, E.g., Blake, Conglomerate Mergers and the Antitrust Laws, 73 Colum. L. Rev. 555 (1973), and Mueller, Conglomerates: A "Nonindustry," in The Structure of American Industry, 442–481 (W. Adams, ed., 5th ed. 1977).

8. See Brodley, Potential Competition Mergers: A Structural Synthesis, 87 Yale L.J., 1, 33 (1977) (on "nonefficiency values").

9. See H. Thorelli, The Federal Antitrust Policy: Origins of an American Tradition (1954), and R. Hofstadter, Social Darwinism in American Thought (1944).

10. See 21 Cong. Rec., Mar. 21, 24, 1890, 3:2456–62, 2597–2616.

11. Restraint of trade was interpreted as restriction upon rivalrous competition in United States v. Trans-Missouri Freight Ass'n, 166 U.S. 290 (1897), United States v. Joint Traffic Ass'n, 171 U.S. 505 (1898), and United States v. Addyston Pipe and Steel Co., 85 F.297 (1899). In neither of the first major merger cases—Northern Securities Co. v. United States, 193 U.S. 197 (1904), or Standard Oil Co. of New Jersey v. United States,

221 U.S. 1 (1911)—was restraint of trade explicitly expanded beyond the concept of rivalrous competition to embrace diverse competition. Yet in neither case was it restrictively defined as rivalrous competition. The close combination in each instance involved consolidating perpetually in a holding company corporations that were not at the time in rivalrous competition with each other because of their already majority ownership and control by a few common owners. The Supreme Court chose to find the offense of close combination in the long run (indeed "perpetual") suppression of the potentiality for rivalrous competition. See Loescher, A Sherman Act Precedent for the Application of Antitrust Legislation to Conglomerate Mergers, in Industrial Organization and Economic Development: In Honor of Edward S. Mason, 154–215 (J. Markham and G. Papanek eds. 1970). In a more recent paper, I contend that government counsel in the 1911 Standard Oil litigation indeed implicitly urged the Court to add the equivalent of diverse competition (for citizen, as distinct from mere consumer, protection) in evaluating section 1 violations involving the merger of giant corporations. See Rehabilitation of the Concept of Potential Competition for the Deconcentration of Conglomerate Mergers, mimeo., presented at the Third Annual Middlebury College Conference on Industrial Organization and Public Policy, April 18, 1981.

12. The recent rejection under antitrust of Mobil Oil's acquisition of Marathon turned upon regional refining, pipeline, and gasoline markets. But the concept of protecting diverse competition from megamergers would have sufficed to thwart this merger had the sole market been crude oil reserves. In like manner, this standard of diverse mergers would have disallowed mergers over the past two decades between such major oil companies as Atlantic-Richfield-Sinclair, Sohio-British Petroleum, Sun Oil-Sunray DX and Union Oil-Pure Oil, as well as Texaco-Getty and Socal-Gulf.

13. See, for example, on the matter of horizontal mergers, R. Posner, Antitrust Law: An Economic Perspective (1976), and R. Bork, The Antitrust Paradox (1978).

14. See Cong. Rec., supra note 10.

15. Pitofsky, The Political Content of Antitrust, 127 U. Pa. L. Rev. 165 (1979).

16. See Scherer, supra note 5, at 145–150.

17. Simon & Bonini, The Size Distribution of Business Firms, 48 Am. Econ. Rev. 607 (1958).

18. Maris and Mueller, supra note 4.

19. Supra note 17 at 616.

20. See Loescher, Limiting Corporate Power, 13 J. Econ. Lit. 557 (1979).

21. L. Thurow in The Zero-Sum Society (1980) speaks to the highly organizational nature of society in contributing to economic doldrums for the final third of the twentieth century, but he believes the antitrust movement to be obsolete. By contrast, Hayes & Abernathy, in Managing Our Way to Economic Decline, Harv. Bus. Rev., July-Aug. 1980, at 66–77, find much of our problem in the overly organized financial management of giant corporations.

22. Risk aversion is the basis of modern theories of investment management, embracing the premise underlying the line of research that led to a Nobel Prize for James Tobin. See Samuelson, 1981 Nobel Prize in Economics, Science, Oct. 30, 1981, at 520–22.

23. See Kaysen, The Corporation: How Much Power? What Scope? in The Corporation in Modern Society 85, 91–94 (E. Mason ed. 1959).

24. See D. Dewey, The New Learning: One Man's View, in Industrial Concentration: The New Learning, 1–14 (Goldschmidt, Mann, & Weston eds. 1974).

25. See Simons, Economic Policy for a Free Society, 52, 124, 247–7 1948).

26. "Surely the economic world, as it exists, is marked by considerable uncertainty at any time regarding the best designs for particular products, what kinds of products consumers want most, the most efficient techniques for producing various products and services, etc. In such situations one wants a considerable amount of experimenting going on in the economic systems, and market competition is to a considerable extent associated with just that experimentation. Some firms will bet right, being either smart or lucky, and others will bet wrong, and the former will tend to grow and prosper and the latter put under serious pressure to do better or get out of business." R. Nelson, Commentary, 154 in The Economics of Firm Size, Market Structure and Social Performance (Siegfried ed. 1980). See also R. Nelson, Assessing Private Enterprise: An Exegesis of Tangled Doctrine, 12 Bell J. Econ. 93, 104–9 (1981).

27. See testimony of Daniel V. De Simone in Senate Subcommittee on Antitrust and Monopoly, Economic Concentration (1965) (Part 3, Concentration, Invention, Innovation, 1091–93). IBM and Eastman Kodak were both among the corporations that rejected an invitation to develop Chester Carlson's xerography.

28. See W. Scott and D. Hart, Organizational America (1979).

29. R. Lindblom, Politics and Markets, 170–220 (1977), and his Commentary in Siegfried, supra note 26, at 319–24.

30. See Merry and Hunt, The Company Line: Business Lobby Gains Power, As It Rides Antigovernment Tide, It Uses Sophisticated Means to Marshall Grass Roots, Wall St. J., May 17, 1978; Business Lobbying Threat to the Consumer Interest, Consumer Reports, Sept. 1978, at 526–31; D. Vogel, Business's New Class Struggle, Nation, Dec. 15, 1978, at 609, 625–28; M. Green and A. Buschbaum, The Corporate Lobbies (1980); McQuaid, Big Business and Public Policy in Contemporary United States, 20 Q. Rev. Econ. & Bus. 57–68 (1980); and Miller, The Political Danger of New Mega-Corporations, Wall St. J., Aug. 20, 1981.

31. See Vogel, Businessmen Unite, Wall St. J., Jan. 14, 1980, and McQuaid, The Roundtable: Getting Results in Washington, Harv. Bus. Rev., May-June 1981, at 114–23.

32. See T. N. Carver, Essays in Social Justice (1915), esp. ch. 13, The Question of Monopoly, which, in fact, is primarily about the joint stock corporation and giant size. See also Loescher, Corporate Giantism, Degradation of the Plane of Competition, and Countervailance, 8 J. Econ. Issues 329–51 (1974).

33. See T. Veblen, The Theory of Business Enterprise (1904) and Absentee Ownership (1923).

34. See M. Green and N. Waitzman, Business War on the Law: An Analysis of the Benefits of Federal Health/Safety Enforcement (1979).

35. Illinois Brick Co. v. Illinois, 431 U.S. 720 (1977).

36. See Harris and Sullivan, Passing on Monopoly Overcharge: A Comprehensive Policy Analysis, 128 U. Pa. L. Rev. (1978) 268, and Congress Dawdles over Right to Sue, Consumer Reports, Feb. 1980, at 128.

37. See Loescher, Economic Collusion, Civil Conspiracy, and Treble Damage Deterrents: The Sherman Act Breakthrough with Southern Plywood, 20 Q. Rev. Econ. & Bus. 6 (1980).

38. See R. Taylor, Bill That Would Cut Price-Fixers' Liability Stirs Up a Lobbying War, Charges of Bailout, Wall St. J., Oct. 14, 1981.

39. See Industrial Concentration: The New Learning, supra note 24, at 444–48 (for

the text of the industrial reorganization act) and at 339–426 (for an extensive discussion of this and earlier deconcentration proposals).

40. See H. Blake, Legislative Proposals for Industrial Concentration, in Industrial Concentration: The New Learning, supra note 24, at 340–59.

41. Loescher, Limiting Corporate Power, 13 J. Econ. Issues 557 (1979) and The Political Economy of Consumer Protection, mimeo., a paper presented at the Midwest Economic Association meetings, Louisville, Ky., April 3, 1981.

42. H. Blake, supra note 40 at 360.

43. Loescher, Limiting Corporate Power, supra note 41.

44. Simon, Antitrust and the "Size" Problem: The "Graduated" Corporate Income Tax as an Anti-Bigness Device, 6 Antitrust L. & Econ. Rev. 53 (1972).

45. R. Maris, The Theory and Future of the Corporate Economy and Society, 144–149 (1979).

46. Loescher, Bureaucratic Measurement, Shuttling Stock Shares, and Shortened Time Horizons: Implications for Economic Growth, 24 Q. Rev. Econ. & Bus. 10 (1984), and Accelerating the Rate of Technological Progress in a World of Changing Comparative Advantage: The Case for Reform in Corporate Governance, Distinguished Scholar Lecture, Indianapolis, Oct. 11, 1985, forthcoming in 1985 Proceedings of the Indiana Academy of the Social Sciences, (1986).

47. D. Vise, Institutional Investors Join Forces for Clout, Washington Post, April 12, 1985, Sunday Business Section, p. 1.

48. I addressed the Council of Institutional Investors on Oct. 29, 1985 in Atlanta, on the topic Reforming Corporate Governance, Productivity and the Standard and Poor 500.

49. See my Pension Funds as Corporate Control, Midwest Economic Association, Chicago, March 21, 1986.

12

MORAL AND CRIMINAL RESPONSIBILITY AND CORPORATE PERSONS

Martin Benjamin and Daniel A. Bronstein

Should corporate legal persons be subject to the same legal protections and penalties as human persons? Certainly the due process clause of the Constitution applies equally to both. Other protections, however, are not as clear. Are corporations entitled to protections of the Fourth Amendment?[1] To protection against self-incrimination?[2] To the attorney-client privilege?[3] Such cases suggest the need for an analysis of the concept of corporate persons. The extent to which legal persons can logically be held to the same conditions of moral and criminal responsibility as human persons can shed light on the legal and constitutional protections to which they might be entitled.

Although the concepts and categories of ethics may be applied to the conduct of corporations, there are important differences between the values and principles underlying corporate behavior and those underlying the actions of most individuals. Whereas the former are invariably teleological or based on furthering one or another basic overall goal, the latter usually include a number of nonteleological elements. As individuals, we are often concerned with integrity, autonomy, and responsibility even when they cannot be shown to futher a basic goal such as overall happiness. We regard them as important and valuable in themselves and not simply as means to some other more basic ends. But a preoccupation with integrity, autonomy, and responsibility for their own sakes is morally questionable when ascribed to corporations or corporate persons.

As formal organizations, corporations are "planned units, deliberately structured for the purpose of attaining specific goals."[4] All activities of such organizations are determined by the extent to which they contribute to the realizations of particular goals. Thus decision making by a member of an organization, qua member, is determined and constrained by the organization's structure and purpose. As John Ladd has put it:

When the official decides for the organization, his aim is (or should be) to implement the objectives of the organization *impersonally*, as it were. The decisions are made for the organization, with a view to its objectives and not on the basis of the personal interests or convictions of the individual official who makes the decision. This is the theory of organizational decision-making.[5]

Therefore the conduct of a person within an organization is, as member of the organization, constrained by his or her particular role within it. The ethically right thing to do as a member of the organization is what is required by one's role; and one's role will be more or less fully determined by the organization's goals, its structure, and the prevailing circumstances.

As formal organizations, business corporations are distinguished by their particular goals, which include maximization of profits, growth, and survival. Providing goods and services is a means to this end. The following statement from the board of directors of the 3M Company is exemplary in this regard: "The objective of the 3M Company is to produce quality goods and services that are useful and needed by the public, acceptable to the public, and in the best interests of the global economy—and thereby to earn a profit which is essential to the perpetuation of the useful role of the company."[6] These goals provide the raison d'être and ultimate ethical values of the 3M Company. Other things have ethical value only insofar as they are instrumental in furthering the ultimate goals. It is thus that honesty and keeping one's word in one's dealing with other members of the organization takes on considerable importance. Without them, overall efficiency and the realization of overall goals would be severely compromised.

But to one inside an organization, honesty and keeping one's word in one's dealings with outsiders will be important only if they come under the heading of what Ladd calls "limiting operating conditions":

These are conditions that set the upper limits to an organization's operations, e.g., the scarcity of resources, of equipment, of trained personnel, legal restrictions, factors involving employee morale. Such conditions must be taken into account *as data*, so to speak, in organizational decision-making and planning. In this respect information about them is on a par logically with other information and planning utilized in decision-making, e.g., cost-benefit computations.[7]

If, for example, a number of individuals (outsiders or even insiders) believe that a company's aggressively marketing infant formula in third world countries is morally wrong, the company is unlikely to be moved by moral arguments alone as long as what it is doing remains profitable. But if those opposed to the company's practice organize a highly effective boycott of the company's products, their moral views will soon enter into the company's deliberations indirectly as limiting operating conditions. They can, at this point, no more be ignored than a prohibitive increase in the costs of certain raw materials. They are acknowledged not as normative conditions but rather as factual constraints on the realization of the company's goals.

Similarly, if dishonesty with customers is likely to drive them away, a company's representatives ought to be honest—but not because honesty is of intrinsic value or importance. Rather it will be that honesty is the best policy for achieving the overall goal. "It is," as Ladd has pointed out, "fatuous to expect an industrial organization to go out of its way to avoid polluting the atmosphere or to refrain from making napalm bombs or to desist from wire-tapping on purely [noninstrumental] moral grounds. Such actions would be [from the standpoint of the logic of organizational behavior] irrational."[8]

Thus honesty, integrity, sympathy, charity, autonomy, respect for the moral and legal rights of others, and so on, which are often valued for their own sake by individuals as individuals, have no intrinsic values for corporations or other formal organizations.[9] And insofar as they remain true to their organizational roles, bureaucrats and "organization men [and women]" will take notice of these notions only as limiting operating conditions. Moral or legal considerations will be given serious consideration only insofar as it is necessary to do so to further the organization's basic goals. Unenforced or unenforceable legal rights, for example, will carry no weight with a corporation as such, but actual or threatened legal coercion cannot, from an organizational standpoint, rationally be ignored.

The basic principle of the criminal common law is that of *malum in se*, things that are "wrong in and of themselves."[10] This immediately demonstrates a fundamental conflict. If corporations are by their nature end- or goal-directed legal persons, how can they acknowledge acts as wrong in and of themselves? If corporations are incapable of recognizing *malum in se*, is it possible to hold one criminally responsible for acts that if performed by a human person would result in criminal liability?

For a long time, the law has avoided this problem by the simple expedient of not attempting to hold corporations liable for *malum in se* crimes but only for malum prohibitum crimes. Malum prohibitum crimes are acts that are "wrong because they are forbidden."[11] There is no difficulty in holding corporations responsible for such acts, since the dictates of a legal code are among the considerations (limiting operating conditions) that goal-directed entities must consider in attempting to achieve their aims.[12]

Violations of the antitrust laws are the classic types of criminal cases for corporations. Other types of criminal violations that have been traditionally charged against corporations are violating governmentally mandated standards of workplace safety, antidiscrimination requirements, or environmental protection regulations; bribery of public officials; fraud; and misappropriation of property. None of these is a *malum in se* crime, although many of them require scienter, and it is important to keep the two concepts separate.

Scienter is the need to show that a defendant knew or should have known that the act committed was of the type forbidden by the statute allegedly violated.[13] In the corporate setting, the main problem of scienter is showing that the corporate agent who committed the allegedly illegal act was at a high enough level in the corporate hierarchy that his or her actions can be imputed to the corporation under the traditional agency doctrine of respondeat superior. Innumerable courts, agencies, practicing attorneys, and scholars have wrestled with this problem for many years,[14] but it is not the type of fundamental philosophical issue we are considering here. It should also be made clear that we are not discussing the question of whether a corporate agent, of whatever hierarchical level, can be criminally prosecuted for acts taken on behalf of the corporation. There has been a recent flurry of interest in this subject among lawyers, courts, and commentators, and it is an important issue to criminologists concerned with securing corporate compliance with the laws.[15] Nevertheless, it is not the issue we are discussing.

The classic *malum in se* crimes are those specified in the Ten Commandments. Merely stating this should illustrate the problem. Can a corporation, as such, violate the Ten Commandments? Of particular interest in the light of some recent attempts to prosecute corporations for homicide is the question of the Fifth Commandment, "Thou shalt not kill." It would be very difficult, after all, to picture a corporation being prosecuted for, say, adultery.

The first case of this type to achieve widespread public attention was the attempt to prosecute the Ford Motor Company for manslaughter as the result of alleged negligent or reckless decision making concerning the safety engineering of the Pinto vehicle.[16] Although the defendant corporation and its officers were found innocent after trial, the case can serve as an exemplar for our purposes. In essence, the prosecution in this case attempted to show that the corporation had produced and distributed a vehicle that was known to be defective at the time of production and sale and that even after a great deal of additional information accumulated regarding the nature of the problems, the corporation took no action to correct them. The obvious noncorporate analogy would be the prosecution of a person who was driving a car with brakes known to be faulty, who does not have them repaired because it would cost too much, and who kills someone when the brakes eventually fail and the car does not stop in time. Such cases involving individuals are prosecuted and won regularly.

If, as we have argued, corporations have no concept of inherent right and wrong because they are exclusively goal-directed legal persons, can they be convicted in cases of this type, and what purpose would be served by such a conviction? Remember that we are talking only about the corporate entity itself— not its managers, agents, and owners who, as human persons, can be held to interpersonal standards of moral and legal responsiblity. It is very difficult to argue for holding goal-directed entities to interpersonal standards; in fact, we do not believe it can be done.

Perhaps we can make a utilitarian argument for convicting corporations of such crimes. The argument would be that of deterrence; conviction and punishment would deter other corporations from taking similar actions under similar circumstances. An individual convicted of homicide for knowingly driving with faulty brakes could be sentenced to jail or fined. What, however, could have been done to Ford Motor Company had it been found guilty in the Pinto case? By the very nature of corporations, it could only have been fined; one cannot incarcerate a corporation. Were the charge a capital one, punishable by death, it would be possible to impose a similar penalty on a corporation; it could have its charter revoked so that it ceased to exist.[17] There appears to be no middle ground for corporations; they can only be fined or "executed." Thus even on utilitarian grounds, there is a clear distinction between legal and human persons.

Moreover, there appears to be considerable evidence that deterrence does not work on corporations, even if, arguably, it works on individuals (a currently controversial subject). The newspapers regularly report on corporations being convicted of malum prohibitum crimes and fined in consequence.[18] The penalties imposed do not appear to discourage other corporations from engaging in similar acts. The possibility of being discovered and the potential magnitude of the fine merely become more data to be included in the analysis of limiting conditions. The dispute about the deterrent effect of the death penalty on human persons is bitter and complicated; the potential deterrent effect of a death penalty for legal persons raises even more unresolved issues.

The fact is that corporations cannot be treated as persons under the criminal law despite the concept of legal personhood. Corporations are entirely goal directed in their nature and outlook; persons in ordinary morality and the criminal law are not. Thus it is inappropriate to extend to corporations many of the legal and constitutional protections enjoyed by human persons. In this area, both lawyers and philosophers will continue to face many unresolved problems in attempting to reconcile the fiction of legal persons with the logic of corporate behavior.

NOTES

1. Compare United States v. Morton Salt Co., 338 U.S. 632, 70 S. Ct. 357, 94 L. Ed. 401 (1950) with General Motors Leasing Corp. v. United States, 429 U.S. 338, 97 S. Ct. 619, 50 L. Ed. 2d 530 (1976).

2. First Nat'l Bank of Boston v. Bellotti, 435 U.S. 765, 98 S. Ct. 1407, 55 L. Ed. 2d 707 (1978).

3. Upjohn Co. v. United States, 449 U.S. 383, 101 S. Ct. 677, 66 L. Ed. 2d 584 (1981).

4. A. Etzioni, Modern Organizations 4 (1964).

5. Ladd, Morality and the Ideal of Rationality in Formal Organizations, 54 (4) The Monist 492 (1970).

6. Quoted in French, Corporate Moral Agency, Tom L. Beauchamp and Norman E. Bowie, eds. Ethical Theory in Business 184 (1979).

7. Ladd, supra note 5, at 498.

8. Ladd, supra note 5, at 507.

9. Conflicts between the demands of the comparitively simple, single-minded morality of organizational roles, on the one hand, and the more complex demands of individual or personal morality, on the other, are all too frequent in the modern world. To identify fully with one's roles in various organizations is to become alienated from oneself as an autonomous, responsible moral agent. But to eschew all institutional and organizational affiliation is to alienate oneself from social and political life and participation in large-

scale efforts that often promise to better the human condition. This difficult and important topic, however, lies beyond our present concern.

10. "An act or case involving illegality from the very nature of the transaction." Black's Law Dict. (5th ed. 1983).

11. "An act which is not inherently immoral but becomes so because its commission is expressly forbidden." Id.

12. Virtually all crimes, whether malum in se or malum prohibitum are now statutory and thus must be taken into account as "limiting operating conditions." Nevertheless, there remains a distinction both in law (degree or proof of mens rea, the "evil intent") and in the degree of public opprobrium they carry.

13. See, e.g., United States v. Corbin Farm Services, 444 F. Supp. 510 (E.D. Cal. 1978).

14. Kraackman, Corporate Liability Strategies and the Costs of Legal Controls, 93 Yale L.J. 857 (1984); Brickey, Corporate Criminal Liability: A Primer for Corporate Counsel, 40 Bus. L. 129 (1984); Joseph DiMento, Getting Compliance (ms in process, 1984); Alan F. Westin, Whistle Blowing! Loyalty and Dissent in the Corporation (1981).

15. Rodella, Corporate Liability for Homicide: Has the Fiction Been Extended Too Far? 4 J. Law & Comm. 95 (1984); Note, "Putting Polluters in Jail," 20 Land & Water L. Rev. 93 (1985); Shipp, Can a Corporation Commit Murder? N.Y. Times, May 19, 1985, Sec. E, at 2; and many of the items in note 14, supra.

16. Miller, Ford Acquitted in Pinto Trial, Wall St. J., Mar. 14, 1980, at 5; Stuart, "Ford Auto Company Cleared in 3 Deaths," N.Y. Times, Mar. 14, 1980, at 1.

17. This would require changes in the corporation laws of most of the states, which do not now have criminal forfeiture provisions, and such changes might themselves result in constitutional challenges. However, the license of a foreign state corporation to do business in the state of conviction could probably be revoked (pursuant to an appropriate statute) without major constitutional challenge.

18. Ralph Nader, "America's Crime without Criminals," N.Y. Times, May 19, 1985, Sec. F, at 3; William Safire, "On Sutton and Hutton," N.Y. Times, May 9, 1985, Sec. A, at 31.

13

PROFIT SHARING AND ESOPs: IMPROVED INCENTIVES AND EQUITY

William A. Lovett

Historians agree that the industrial and corporate revolutions unleashed a flood of new output and wealth for modern societies. Few challenge that overall benefits, improved prosperity, and well-being followed. But the problem of how to best organize this productive revolution and share its proceeds among managers, workers, property owners, and society at large remains controversial among economists and law reformers. Ideological conflict continues between many successful enterpreneurs and capitalists, the middle classes, poorer workers and farmers, and competing social reformers—communists, socialists, fabians, liberal progressives, trade unionists, populist agrarians, progressive taxers, social insurers, fascist corporatists, and adherents of conservative laissez-faire.

Until recent years, profit sharing and employee stock ownership, a major alternative for more humane, equitable organization of the corporate production process, had been greatly neglected. But with increasing momentum, spurred by stronger competitive challenges from Japan, East Asia, and other new industrial nations, U.S. industry is turning to this neglected opportunity. Old steel towns facing shutdown, overextended airlines needing retrenchment, high-tech electronics outfits, aggressive defense contractors in Silicon Valley, textile operations, retailers and service firms, new airline entrants, and many other enterprises have sought in profit-sharing and/or employee stock ownership plans (ESOP) arrangements a way to improve productivity, save plants or jobs, and raise incomes over the long run for participants.

During the last decade, nearly 7,000 U.S. companies set up ESOP plans to share ownership with their employees. Included are airlines, steel mills, restaurants, retail merchandising chains, trucking firms, engineering and high-tech companies, textile manufacturers, newspapers, and magazines. Some 10 million employees now are enrolled in ESOPs (or PAYSOPs). Some 367,000 additional profit-sharing plans are established, with perhaps 22 million employees having access to some form of collaboration in earnings. Among the distinguished list of company names are Eastern, Pan Am, Weirton Steel, Wheeling-Pittsburg Steel, GM, Ford, Uniroyal, *New York Daily News*, and the *Milwaukee Journal*.

Other names include Dan River Mills, People Express and Republic Airlines, U.S. Sugar, Interstate Motor Express, Hyatt Roller Bearings, Janco (aerospace components), Rural Metro (fire protection), W. L. Gore Associates, Lowe's Home Improvement Stores, and Eaker's (home improvement stores). Longer-established profit-sharing plans have included Sears Roebuck, Eastman Kodak, Procter & Gamble, Safeway, Winn Dixie, Chase Manhattan, and Standard Oil of California.[1]

Participation levels vary substantially. Many ownership and profit-sharing plans are restricted to the company's stock and marketing fortunes. Others enjoy more diversification. In a small percentage of ESOPs, the employees are sole owners. More commonly, the employee involvement is a minority of equity ownership and/or claims on profits, ranging from a substantial chunk to a modest slice. But in recent years, the trend is clearly upward, with broadening interest among business people and the public at large.[2]

How the trend to greater employee stock ownership and more profit sharing should be shaped will be resolved in the coming years. But the roster of endorsements is now diverse—Ronald Reagan, Ted Kennedy, the New York Stock Exchange, U.S. Chamber of Commerce, House Democrats, Russell Long, and the Pope.[3] Polls of the general public also show strong support.[4]

This chapter explores the recent trend, and tries to explain why profit sharing and ESOPs developed belatedly in the modern industrial revolution. It concludes by suggesting how a greatly enlarged opportunity for profit sharing and employee stock ownership could be properly exploited.

TRADITIONAL ECONOMIC CONTROVERSIES AND RENEWED INTEREST IN PROFIT SHARING AND EMPLOYEE STOCK OWNERSHIP

Under most traditional arrangements for teamwork enterprise, the business-person or entrepreneur took contractual responsibility for delivering goods and services, received the purchase prices paid by consumers, and absorbed the residual profits (or losses). When additional labor was employed beyond the entrepreneur's immediate household (apart from servants, apprentices, or slaves), this outside labor was priced according to prevailing market wages or local custom. When entrepreneurs began putting out more work into other local families or assembling workers into early factories, these customary patterns of contracting for labor continued. And as the modern industrial corporation slowly emerged as the most important, large-scale employer of labor, their workers were similarly paid. Standard hourly, daily, or periodic wages became the norm, with perhaps some piece-rate bonuses, incentive compensation, or other premiums attached to the base wage. Hence, it has become necessary to think of profits as the normal reward or wage for enterprise; standard wages appropriate to the area, skill, or rank for working employees; and market rents for landlords and other leasing property owners.[5]

Profits became extremely generous, however, which gradually aroused social criticism. When corporations mobilized vast amounts of capital, employed great numbers of workers, and exploited innovative profit potential or restricted competition or mobility in the marketplace, these residual profit rewards might become very large and perhaps excessive. For leading entrepreneurs, their profits and capital accumulation often vastly exceeded incomes and wealth for ordinary working families. And where "exploitation" occurred—that is, monopolistic market positions with artificially fattened profit margins or monopsonistic buying power with artificially reduced wages or harsh working conditions—profits could become even more controversial and often justify some corrective adjustment.[6]

Remedies for excess enrichment, disproportionate wealth accumulation, unfairness in the marketplace, and various forms of maldistribution have been among the most important issues in modern political economy. These controversies gradually became more intense during the nineteenth century, and especially since the Russian bolshevik revolution in 1917, and the rise of Marxist-Leninist ideology and its challenge to Romanist–Common law patterns of capitalist corporate enterprise.[7] Included among the policy alternatives are (1) antitrust, public utility, and public enterprise regulation to limit excessive prices or unfair practices; (2) collective bargaining and labor unions to offset undue bargaining power for employers; (3) progressive taxes and social insurance to correct maldistribution and provide desirable services; (4) broader access to good education; (5) worker participation in management or codetermination schemes; (6) socialized ownership or control of the corporate capitalist sector (or some portions of it); (7) land reform, deconcentration measures, and/or small business–farmer assistance programs that offset tendencies toward excessive scale in enterprise; and (8) profit sharing and ESOPs that subdivide the ownership interests more equitably in larger corporations and allow workers a direct share in the residual profits and the gains of enterprise in some form or another.[8]

Much of the politics in modern industrial society for the last century has revolved around the relative emphasis to be given these alternative remedies for market failure and undue wealth accumulation and the best blend of institutions and incentives for economic growth, fairness, and overall well-being.[9] The most conservative free market analysts see less need, in general, for any correctives. But many liberals, populists, and socialists favor more of these reforms. And yet a long-standing controversy has been the social efficiency of such reforms in each of the eight major channels for corrective action. In other words, what is the best blend of these corrective reforms, and how far, if at all, should each channel be utilized?

In the United States, the most important reform channels in the Progressive–New Deal era have been (1) antitrust and regulation, (2) collective bargaining and unions, (3) progressive taxes and social insurance, (4) broader access to higher education, and (7) small farm–business aid in one form or another.[10] In Western Europe channels 2 through 7 have received more attention, while in Japan limited antitrust and public regulation, paternalistic company unions,

strong educational efforts, post–World War II land reform and extensive protection to farmers and small business, together with generous annual bonuses,
lifetime employment in many companies, and strong economic growth have
proved a successful combination.[11] Most recently in the United States, a shift
of emphasis may be in progress, with a decline in some of the older Progressive–
New Deal reform efforts, except broad access to higher education and greater
new stress on profit sharing, ESOPs, and a better tradition of teamwork for a
high-tech-style worker-management collaboration.[12]

Questions naturally arise. To what extent is profit sharing and employee stock
ownership feasible and desirable? From what resources should these new flows
of profit and stockholding be drawn? From existing wages and salary reductions?
From existing management and shareholder earnings and profits? To what extent
should dilution of existing stockholder wealth be enforced for profit sharing and
ESOPs? How much tax subsidy should be involved? How rapidly should these
changes be phased in? What level of worker profit sharing and employee stock
ownership is desirable over the long run? How much extra incentive and how
large an economic growth dividend may develop from enlarged profit sharing
and ESOPs? And why has the potential for employee stock ownership been
neglected so long? This chapter will try to resolve these questions and explain
the intriguing potential for further reform in this area.

Recently profit sharing and ESOPs have received more favorable attention,
and the Reagan administration's emphasis on supply-side incentives, reduced
tax loads, and greater profit retention by enterprise make this channel of reform
more interesting and important.[13] If free market energies, incentives, and profits
enjoy more latitude and the majority of working lives are caught up within profit-
making enterprises (large and small corporations), it follows that setting the
terms for sharing in this enlarged profitability becomes crucial. Not surprisingly,
there is a surge of new literature and proposals for more worker profit sharing
and employee stock ownership.[14] Most strikingly, President Reagan's Commission on Industrial Competitiveness provides strong language in this direction:

"*Labor and management must recognize common interests*. If American business is to
increase productivity and improve the quality of its products—both key to greater com-
petitivess—labor and management must cooperate more effectively. The traditional adversarial relationship may no longer serve the best interests of both parties and the public.
Increasing competitive pressures from abroad coupled with slow growth and new technology at home—now create a new impetus to work more cooperatively.

"Although great strides have been made over the last decade toward increased cooperation in some industries, teamwork remains the exception rather than the rule. In a
discouraging comparison to our strongest competitor, only 9 percent of American workers
felt they would benefit directly from the increased productivity of their companies, while
a similar survey of Japanese workers showed that 93 percent felt they would benefit from
such improvements." *Global Competition: The New Reality*, The Report of The President's Commission on Industrial Competitiveness, Vol. 1, Jan., 1985, at 31. . . .
Recommendations [among others]

Forge new understandings between labor and management. This urgent call to action in the area of human resources is one that cannot be legislated. Labor and management are in the same boat—one that is being rocked by a storm of new competitive challenges. Americans must embark on a new era of trust and cooperation.

For management, that means disclosure of relevant information and a willingness to share prosperity as well as austerity. For labor, that means responsiveness to a firm's basic goals and flexibility in taking on new challenges. For both labor and management, trust can only be built by a commitment to equity, consistency, candor, and problemsolving.

Strengthen incentive programs that increase employee motivation. Compensation plans such as gain-sharing link employee compensation to performance and allow employees to share in the success that their efforts make possible. Employee stock purchase programs help create a sense of "ownership" that is both literal and figurative. To make the use of incentive stock options a better motivational tool, the tax code should be amended to avoid the immediate taxation of options and thus encourage long-term ownership. Changes are also needed to allow employees to exercise their options in any order they choose." *Ibid.*, at pp. 34–35.

This high-quality commission comprised seventeen industrial leaders, four bankers, five academics, several union leaders, and a few lawyers and reflects enlightened business thinking.

REASONS FOR MODEST PREVIOUS USE OF WORKER PROFIT SHARING AND EMPLOYEE STOCK OWNERSHIP

To appreciate fully the neglected potential for worker profit sharing and ESOPs, we must understand the historical reasons why other approaches received priority. Not only did capitalists and employers resist sharing for the most part by giving up their profits and stockholdings, but most labor parties and unions sought other remedies and techniques for redressing grievances, redistribution, and improving their economic position. Only recently, and especially in the United States, do circumstances combine (including relative weakness in the labor union movement and its political vitality) to allow a strong effort for greater profit sharing and ESOPs.

New Lands, Colonies, and Agrarian Movements

It is helpful to retrace the earlier history of political and economic liberalism in the eighteenth and nineteenth centuries and to appreciate their idealistic aspirations for common people. The American and French revolutions, along with their progeny in Europe, Latin America, and elsewhere, emphasized political rights, personal liberty for most people, the end of feudal privileges, and soon thereafter universal suffrage. Economic well-being for most families was presumed to follow.

Substantial agrarian redistribution often followed as well. The infant United

States, for example, drove out many Tory landowners, and the new lands opened up on its expanding western frontier provided massive new economic opportunities, farmlands, ranches, towns, and cities for another 150 years or more.[15] Cheap frontier land provided a way to absorb excess labor and millions of immigrants. And the Civil War added further momentum by breaking up some of the southern plantations through hard times in the Reconstruction period.[16] The French Revolution also achieved considerable agrarian redistribution and broadened considerably its peasant and other landowning classes.[17] Liberalism on the U.S. and French models implied populist broadening of landownership in other countries, although achievements in this direction were often more limited than the new American Republic or Revolutionary France.[18]

Even the British Empire provided significant new economic opportunities and landowning potential in the colonies, especially Canada, Australia, New Zealand, and South Africa, along with military, government, and business careers in India and other parts of the imperial network.[19] This colonial safety valve was provided in significant degree for France, the Netherlands, and Portugal, while substantial emigration to the Americas was important for Norway, Sweden, Switzerland, Germany, Italy, and, to some extent, Spain and the Austrian Empire. Latecomers to European colonial expansion in Africa were Germany, Italy, and Belgium, joined by Japan in East Asia in the twentieth century, with hopes along similar lines.

In many of these countries, the social problems and strains of agricultural labor surplus and increased low wage factory employment were eased by new lands, colonial expansion, and/or, in a few situations, agrarian reforms. Accordingly this delayed somewhat and softened, at least in many countries, the reaction to harshness or exploitation in growing factory labor markets. And to the extent agriculture, smaller towns, and rural areas remained the larger portion of a nation's people, populist or agrarian political movements were often the most important response to growing industrial wealth and financial power. From this viewpoint, dominated by traditional farmer outlooks and small business interests, favorable laws and regulation, easier money and credit, broader state education, antitrust policies, public utility controls, and, perhaps, progressive taxes on high wealth classes seemed logical remedies. U.S. history strongly reflected this perspective in the later nineteenth and early twentieth centuries, including Progressive politics and legislation between 1887 and 1914.[20]

Different Political-Economic Objectives for Trade Unions

Trade unions normally sought increased wages and improved working conditions as economic objectives.[21] With respect to political goals, the recognition and legalization of unions and collective bargaining, suffrage for workers (regardless of property owned), and subsequently social insurance programs (sickness and disability protection, old age pensions, and unemployment compensation) were top priorities.[22] Because employers and capitalists generally resisted unions and collective bargaining until after World War II, the prospects for collaboration over profit sharing were quite limited until recently.[23] Much of the profit sharing and employee stock ownership that did emerge, in fact, was offered by paternalistic employers, sometimes as part of a strategy to inhibit adversarial trade unions.[24] But most profit sharing and ESOPs were confined, until lately, to higher-level executives, and were designed in part to help reduce high progressive income tax burdens in these brackets.[25]

Trade Union Goals in the United States

Early U.S. trade unions were concerned with self-preservation, often had broad political goals, and generally did not achieve wide enough representation to affect market wages seriously.[26] The failure of the more politically oriented Knights of Labor in the 1880s left Sam Gompers and the American Federation of Labor (AFL) as the dominant type of unionism in the United States.[27] Gompers strongly believed in business-style representation, seeking better wages and working conditions for skilled craftsmen from many employers.[28] This strategy did not lend itself to accepting compensation through modest stock ownership or unreliable shares in profits.[29] This outlook became a strongly entrenched tradition in U.S. labor bargaining, such that labor regularly sought higher wages, improved conditions, and, since World War II, increasingly generous fringe benefits (including pensions, health insurance, and group life coverage). Management and profits were left to the companies, although increased profitability normally brought higher union wage and fringe benefit demands in the years after World War II.[30]

Ultimately, however, the trend to more generous pension benefits led unions to have more interest in the investment resources needed to support these commitments. When a number of company pension plans failed through insufficient funding and widespread complaints developed about late vesting practices, organized labor supported the Employment Retirement and Income Security Act of 1974 (ERISA), which greatly improved pension funding and brought earlier, more reliable vesting.[31] (Part of the pressure for ERISA also came from complaints against corrupt union trusteeship in some pension funds.) The most interesting feature in ERISA, though, was the gradual process by which major new financial liabilities were phased in over a twelve-year period.[32] Although everyone realized that many employers and companies could not bear the abrupt burden of bringing pension funding up to desired levels overnight, a gradual buildup over twelve years could achieve this result gracefully.[33] This precedent is significant for possible major enlargements of employee stock ownership, which could be gradually expanded over an extended period in somewhat similar fashion.

More recently, a number of unions also have accepted stock ownership in conjunction with efforts to save companies and jobs under distress, with serious need of retrenchment and labor cost reduction, so that some employees at least could retain work and incomes.[34] In some of these situations, part of the reasoning behind teamwork reorganizations is the hope that stronger productivity will come through employee stockholding and involvement as equity owners. This leads many to ask whether a broader trend to employee stock ownership and/or profit sharing finally may be coming to the United States and perhaps other countries.[35] The Commission on Industrial Competitiveness clearly encouraged this trend, though it remains to be seen what kind of new emphasis may be placed on these reforms by labor, business, and the Congress.

Social Democratic Unionism in Other Western Countries

Trade and labor unions had a different history in most other Western countries.[36] Unionism was generally more political, somewhat socialist in ideology, heavily interested in government policies and social insurance, and somewhat less preoccupied with market-style bargaining for wages, working conditions, and fringe benefits. In some of these countries, such as Britain, Netherlands, Belgium, the Scandinavian countries, France, and even West Germany, trade unions became, and still are, a stronger force in politics with a larger share of the labor force than in the United States. In Southern Europe, trade unions have become significant more recently in Italy, Portugal, Spain, and Greece. Trade unions were also traditionally strong in Australia and New Zealand, though to a lesser extent in Canada.

In many of these countries, profit sharing and employee stock ownership has been used occasionally, but the more socialistic ideologies of their unions and social democratic political parties generally inhibit workers from taking equity, stockholding, or profit-sharing interests. Managers and capitalists may be more resistant to worker stock ownership as well due to a long tradition of polarized, adversarial relations in politics. More common as a reformist aspiration in Western Europe is codetermination, worker participation in management boards, and tripartite collaboration of government-labor-industry representatives for industrial policies.

In principle, however, the teamwork ethic, improved cooperation, and higher productivity that may come from substantial employee stock ownership and profit sharing could work in most of the Western democracies. It seems more likely though, that other Western nations will follow the United States, rather than lead, in this area of institutional development, at least in the near future.

Japanese and Other East Asian Work Incentives and Arrangements

Feudalism in Japan lasted longer, with more centralized discipline, throughout the Tokugawa era (1600–1868) and into the modernizing Meiji period (1868–1912), than in Western Europe. Yet in the first third of this century, liberal ideology and institutions, limited parliamentary democracy, and later some weak trade unions and mild socialist dissidence did come to Japan in a modest way and took partial root. Then militarist governments and imperial expansionism took over in the early 1930s and largely suppressed most liberal political institutions. But war with China (1937–1945), the United States, Britain, and Netherlands (1941–1945) brought disastrous defeat and mild U.S. occupation. During this stage, reconstruction efforts significantly improved upon previous arrangements, and an unusually successful industrial growth machine got underway.

Land reform, deconcentration measures, broadened access to education, rapid economic growth and full employment policies, and largely company-style unions emerged in the postwar era. Gradually increased growth performance became reliable, at least for most of the stronger companies, and a pattern of liberal annual bonuses, lifetime employment, and shared benefits in improved productivity became widely established. Although a few areas of older, more socialist-style unionism remain, the predominant tradition of worker-company relations in Japan today is increasingly studied by foreign observers as worthy of some emulation. This tradition seems to have some real elements of de facto profit sharing, and explicit employee stock ownership plans have become more popular lately as well.[37]

In other East Asian growth countries, most notably South Korea, Taiwan, Hong Kong, and Singapore in the last twenty to thirty years, increasing confidence in shared benefits from improved productivity has been operating too. But these nations came from relative poverty right after World War II, without a comparable prewar base of industrial and commercial development. Although some elements of gain sharing in expanded prosperity are institutionalized, this has not been carried so far as in more affluent and more high-technology-oriented Japan. And yet a basic trick is similar. Rapidly sustained economic growth and increased productivity tend to enable the sharing of prosperity without necessarily institutionalizing this into formalized profit sharing or ESOP plans.[38]

Dramatic industrial progress in Japan and East Asia demonstrate the value of discipline, high savings, the work ethic, and the benefits of teamwork. Mutual confidence in sharing the benefits of an expanding pie of production is a constructive incentive and tends to promote morale and productivity.

Marxist-Leninist and Communist Labor Policies

A basic claim of Marxist economics is that private enterprise contracts for employment tend to be inherently exploitative. The capitalist entrepreneur's normal profit is condemned as surplus value that exceeds a legitimate wage for managerial services, and the capitalist property owner's rent is denounced as the accumulated result of previous exploitation from workers. The Marxian remedy for exploitation and excessive rewards to the capitalist class has been to convert most productive capital, land, and resources into social ownership. Thus, socialist managers should replace capitalists, and rewards would be shared more equitably according to the proper value of labor in the productive process.[39]

Once capitalist property (the fruits of previous exploitation) is socialized, workers are supposed to collaborate harmoniously in healthy teamwork, and conflicts are to be eliminated in a new socialist fraternalism. Under socialism, adversarial trade unions are no longer desirable (as a means to resist capitalist oppression), and worker organizations become integrated into the productive discipline of a socialist society. In practice, however, most communist societies have found difficulty in sustaining work incentives, overcoming centralized bureaucratic inefficiency, and maximizing consumer welfare. In many respects, critics insist that bolshevik revolutions merely substituted a new class of Communist party and technocratic elites for the older capitalist and professional classes and that centralized state bureaucracy can be as oppressive (especially with police-state repression) as the more highly unequal capitalist societies, with badly distributed wealth and opportunites.[40]

Within some communist countries, including Yugoslavia, to some extent Hungary, and more recently, the People's Republic of China since the early 1980s, considerable decentralization has occurred.[41] For certain idealistic socialists, even greater latitude for divergent success in worker-owned enterprises is desirable, thus implying some scope for profit sharing within each competing socialist enterprise. But most communist governments have limited closely the potential for such profit sharing and enforce significant taxation, capital budgeting, and borrowing discipline on their socialist enterprise. And socialist enterprises are normally enmeshed in the state planning process, subject to significant accountability and regulatory supervision.

Ultimately, the differences between socialist enterprises and capitalist corporations could be substantially lessened if profit sharing were employed extensively for the benefit of employees. At issue might remain the precise profit distribution formula, base pay scales for employees and managers, and the extent to which private and socialist banking, pension fund, and other investment intermediaries might receive interest and equity-risk capital compensation, and be allowed a share of the enterprise or corporate profits.

OPPORTUNITY FOR SPREAD OF PROFIT SHARING AND EMPLOYEE STOCK OWNERSHIP

A great opportunity exists for broader profit sharing and employee stock ownership in the 1980s and 1990s. Advanced Western nations realize their economies need rejuvenations.[42] East Asian and other new industrial countries are expanding their challenge of exports, higher-quality production, with a wider network of international marketing and investment.[43] In these circumstances, more incentives and flexibility will be helpful. Considerable middle-class affluence already had been accumulated, and the younger generation wants more personal fulfillment and income growth potential.[44] Older trade union tactics and working-class mentality seem rather outdated, and a shift toward more economic conservatism and individualism has been underway.[45] And yet this new emphasis for sharing in the capital accumulation process could be disillusioned if the great bulk of prospective corporate stock ownership and profit opportunities are enjoyed by a small minority of high-wealth families and relatively few executives.

A crossroads has been reached in which more even wealth sharing, higher morale, and stronger productivity could emerge in the corporate sector. On the other hand, if this increased eagerness to participate in broader ownership of corporate enterprise is frustrated, the large majority of salary and wage employees could find their economic lot declining. Tough competition from low wage countries abroad, continued high structural unemployment, heavy trade deficits, and gradual devaluation of currencies could limit and constrain real wage levels.[46] As recent tax relief for high wealth families, corporate shareholders, individual retirement accounts (IRAs), Keoghs, pension plans, and other tax sheltering opportunities in real estate, international trade and overseas investment continue, the broad middle class would benefit significantly from a bigger slice of the action.[47] How to engineer this evolutionary change as constructively as possible is an important question.

Some trend toward more profit sharing and employee stock ownership is already underway. More companies are offering profit sharing and ESOPs, with a widening in the ranks of employees offered stock option and bonus pension plans.[48] More families are accumulating capital through real estate, IRAs, Keoghs, double incomes, and side-line businesses.[49] Life insurance companies and agencies are more aggressively exploiting investment counseling as traditional markets adjust to greater competition and cheaper group rate rivalry.[50]

But a real breakthrough toward general profit sharing and enlarged worker shareholding probably will require stronger government encouragement. Mandatory ESOPs and/or profit sharing under appropriate guidelines, over a fifteen to twenty-year period, following the precedent and phase-in formula of The Employee Retirement Income Security Act of 1974 (ERISA) would be a logical path, and this could be supported by a broad alliance of business, corporate, labor union, middle class, and idealistic reform interest.[51]

Economic Potential and Limits for Profit Sharing and Employee Stock Ownership

The pie of production in free enterprise countries is divided into wages to employees and managers, interest paid to debt holders (including financial intermediaries, depositors, and shareholders), returns to property and resource owners, and profits to entrepreneurs and equity shareholders. In the United States, such incomes break down roughly as follows (table 1).

Wages and salaries took roughly 76 to 80 percent of national income in 1982 (depending how broadly we define employee compensation).[52] (This year was selected as the most recent with complete data. Although business profits were down somewhat with recession in 1982, interest rates were above normal that year. To provide more typical profits and business cash flow estimates, three to four-year averages have been used.)

Increased profit sharing and employee stock ownership might alter slightly these allocations. More important, to the extent stronger incentives, better morale, and higher productivity result, the pie of production should increase over time with greater efficiency and economic growth. As long as the transition to

Table 1

Labor Compensation, Wages and Salaries, Capital Stock, Profits, National Income and Gross National Product, 1982.

Billions of Dollars

```
Wages and Salaries (all industries)
        102, 315,000 employees x $18,488  =    $ 1,892b.

Total Compensation (including executive bonuses
   and contributions to pensions, soc. security)
        102, 315,000 employees x $21,907  =    $ 2,248b.

Unemployed              10,700,000
Total Labor Force      113,000,000

Total Fixed Capital Stock                       $ 5,296b.
     (non-residential, all industries)
Profits (estimated - 10% on capital stock)        529.6b.
Corporate Capital Funds Flow
     (non-farm, non-financial, av. 1980-83)       358.9b.
Profits (reported tax data, av. 1979-81, all
     corporations, partnerships, proprietorships)  307.3b.

Personal Income                                 $ 2,585b.

National Income  1/                             $ 2,487b.

Gross National Product 1/                       $ 3,069b.
```

Source: Statistical Abstract of the U.S., 1985,
         Bureau of the Census, U.S. Dept. Commerce

1/   The main differences between GNP and National Income are
     that the latter is reduced by depreciation or "capital
     consumption" allowances in the business sector [$395b. in
     1982], and by indirect business taxes (sales and property
     taxes) and other non-tax liabilities of business $259b. in
     1982].

greatly increased employee stock ownership is slow, however, the dilution of present (short-run) ownership interests, stock values, and profitability would be minimal. On the other hand, if most employees have confidence in their enlarged equity ownership interests over the longer run, this should significantly improve morale and efficiency, provided that a guaranteed commitment toward greatly enlarged employee stock ownership and profit sharing is established under a reliable schedule.[53]

Two factors influence the productivity dividend from general profit sharing and/or employee stock ownership.

The first is the extent of alienation, lack of care, slovenliness, and reduced productivity in existing companies. Productivity problems are commonplace in larger organizations, big companies, and/or plants and are aggravated by adversarial unionism. But many nonunion companies suffer similar problems, with latent potential for collective bargaining and union-style grievance representation.

More wisely managed, friendly, and collaborative companies may have fewer of these problems, although an instinct for job preservation and not working too hard is widespread in sizable organizations (and often tolerated by supervisors, who do not want their budgets or crews reduced). Also, small business enterprise normally has fewer of these productivity problems and offers more modest social output dividends from profit sharing in this way. And yet even for many small businesses, work intensity and sharpness is increasd by allocating some of the profits to journeymen workers (for example, partnerships in law firms, adequate splits for real estate brokers, commissions for salespeople, or franchise profit sharing in restaurants and retailing).[54]

The second factor is the extent to which work efforts, productivity, and sharpness of employees affect the profitability of companies and organizations. In most industrial and/or marketing activities, profitability is strongly linked to productivity and quality of work efforts. But external problems like the business cycle, low wage foreign competition, foreign government subsidies, inferior product development or design, or weak engineering can negatively affect profits and even bring entrepreneurial failure. Therefore, although profit sharing can positively affect output in most business and industrial sectors (especially in larger companies, plants, or establishments), success cannot be guaranteed. This means bonuses, profits, or generous stock options should not be assured; they are available only in good times.

National macroeconomic, industrial, and trade policies will significantly improve profit prospects sharing and overall growth (for example, Japanese prosperity since the early 1950s versus stop-go sluggishness in the United Kingdom or, more recently, the United States). Broader participation in profits and employee stock ownership also changes considerably the political climate for national policies. As more people enjoy a direct stake in industrial profitability and economic growth, this goal should become more predominant in politics. Unfortunately countries that suffer more adversarial, splinter group infighting tend to lack overall incentives for growth and general prosperity policies. Divisiveness can be increased when many elements in the labor force fail to share adequately in economic growth.[55]

Employment implications are interesting from greater profit sharing and more wage flexibility. Some writers have argued recently (as did neo-classical economics in the Great Depression) that greater wage flexibility and profit sharing will bring fuller employment.[56] This claim is more controversial. Although a considerable wage reduction trend might bring greater employment in countries suffering substantial structural unemployment, this is not what most profit sharing or ESOP enthusiasts have in mind. The main claims for greater profit sharing and ESOPs are greater incentives, increased productivity, and more output. This should bring larger employment eventually through expanded economic activity over the longer run. But in many respects, widespread profit sharing, employee stock ownership, and greater concern for productivity will bring stronger leaness discipline, and reduce the short-run demand for marginal, less productive employees.[57] It is true, however, that some wage flexibility over the business-trade cycle would ease difficulties for some companies in distress.

But the more widespread desire of many companies in the United States lately is wage-cost retrenchment.[58] Most of U.S. manufacturing is suffering from increased import penetration, reduced exports, an overvalued dollar, excessive interest rates, and a massive trade deficit. In some situations recently, profit sharing and ESOPs have been sold to workers as a means for job saving and plant survival.[59] But the economic premise of such deals is primarily a hope for greater productivity. Leaner staffs and pruning of excess workers are normally considered part of this increased productivity therapy. Consequently, although widespread profit sharing and ESOP usage should increase long-run social output, efficiency, and ultimate prosperity, there is little hope for significantly increased employment levels in the short run from these reforms.

The scope for greatly increased profit sharing and employee stock ownership will vary considerably among industries.[60] (See table 2.) The greatest potential for a social productivity dividend from profit sharing and ESOPs probably lies in manufacturing, where large companies and plants are most important. Mining and other extractive industries also offer substantial potential for the same reasons. In service sectors (retail and wholesale trade, finance, insurance, real estate, transport, public utilities, and other services), there may be less scope for expanded profit sharing and ESOPs, at least initially. In most of these sectors, small business is more significant. And in public utilities, there might be limitations of custom or regulation.[61] Nonetheless, for the economy as a whole, at least 30 million U.S. employees could be included in such formalized arrangements. Since a large part of the Gross National Product is generated in these parts of the economy, the potential for productivity gains is substantial.[62]

Just how much the ultimate employee share of profits and equity stockholding should be depends on the capital intensity of the company and industries. A reasonable norm for substantial incentives might be a third for the low and moderately capital-intensive industries, and a quarter for the most highly capital intensive.[63] It makes sense for the worker share to be somewhat reduced where capital equipment is relatively more important in the production process. But the labor or worker share should always be big enough to provide a sufficient stake and incentive in the enterprise and its success.

Spread over fifteen to twenty years, the cost of this amount of capital (one-quarter or one-third of the outstanding equity in corporations) is not too expensive a burden. This outlay can be comfortably carried with regular contributions by employees (out of wages) and existing company owners (present shareholders). (See table 3.)

Cost of the stock or equity for workers can be divided equally between employee wages and the employer company. This represents a modest cut in direct wage income (more than offset by employee increases in wealth through stock value accumulation) and a modest apparent squeeze in company profits. But this "loss" in profits to the company would be more than offset by increased pro-

Table 2
Estimated Potential for ESOP and Profit-Sharing Plan Participation

	Net Value Added to National Income, 1982	Employees 1982 (thousands)	ESOP and Profit Sharing Potential (% employees) 1/
Agriculture Forestry, Fisheries	$ 69.6b.	3,751	10%
(Farms)	(61.5b.)		
Mining, Extractive	45.5b.	1,028	50%
Construction	107.8b.	5,756	15%
Manufacturing	549.6b.	20,286	60%
Transportation (Rail, Local, Trucking, Air)	83.3b.	3,103	25%
Communications	59.3b.	1,420	25%
Electric, gas, utilities	57.7b.	1,020	10%
Retail and Wholesale Trade	358.9b.	20,758	35%
Finance, Insurance, Real Estate (includes rental)	355.1b.	6,270	30%
Services	387.0b.	30,090	25%
Government and Public Enterprise	364.1b.	4,710	---
	----------	---------	----------
National Income (less rest of world contribution)	$2,386.9b. ($48.0b.)	99,526,000 civilian employees	30,000,000 Employees (ESOP and Profit-Sharing plan potential 2/

Source: Statistical Abstract of the U.S., 1985
         Bureau of the Census, U.S. Department of Commerce

1/ Estimated by author. 2/ Expanded participation beyond
                              present levels.

ductivity and enlarged profits because employees will work harder, produce more, and increase their efficiency and innovation. In most company situations, the increased productivity dividend should exceed the contribution by the company to the profit sharing or ESOP plan. (In table 3 annual company contributions to employee stock purchases would normally total less than 10 percent of annual profits, which easily should be offset by greater productivity and efficiency.)[64]

The government should encourage expanded profit sharing and ESOPs by allowing the annual contributions by workers and companies to be tax sheltered.[65]

Table 3
Illustrative Cash Flow—Transitional Company Expenses for Substantial Employee Ownership

	"Low" Capital	"Moderate" Capital	"High" Capital
Present Capitalization	$ .45b Equity .3b Debt	$.75b Equity .60b Debt	$1.25b Equity 1.0 Debt
Present Annual Sales	$1b Sales	$1b Sales	$1b Sales
Present Annual Profit (12% on Equity)	$50m Profit	$100m Profit	$150m Profit
Annual Contribution to Purchases Stock for Workers (15-20 year plan)	$8-10m	$12-16m	$15-20m
		[annual contributions divided equally between employees and employer company]	
Ultimate Workers' Equity Capital	$150m	$250m	$300m

For convenience, these amounts could be flowed directly into each employee's IRA. Thus, individual employees could select their own stock management or trustee.[66] Alternatively, the employee stock might be held collectively for employees by a trustee, perhaps even a labor union or other representative entity, properly supervised by government agencies under fiduciary standards.[67] Ultimately employees should be given the right of decision as to the best trustee and portfolio manager.[68] Employees could diversify out of their own company's stock (at least after several years) through self-managed IRA accounts or pooled investment accounts managed by professional mutual funds, banks, or other financial institutions.[69]

This kind of profit sharing and employee stock ownership would help transform the mentality and wealth formation prospects for a growing proportion of families. As substantial profit sharing and ESOPs become the norm for larger employers, this prospect and its substantial tax-saving advantages (through IRAs) will spread to smaller businesses. Eventually the initial beachhead for profit sharing and ESOPs will expand more substantially throughout the economy. Although profit sharing would not become universal (a significant part of small business is probably too ephemeral and informal for such arrangements, and government normally would not generate profits), ESOPs and profit sharing could become predominant in the private sector.[70]

This changing outlook and new shared responsibility for enterprise profits will transform labor-management relations and the role of trade unions. Unions will now take on supervision, oversight, and trusteeship roles for their member-employees as stockholders. The growing interest of workers in protecting their stock investments and values will provide more muscle to stockholder democracy. As employees of companies become a substantial block of shareholders, this will promote more attention to employee interests and their lives on the part of the management.[71]

Not only will worker productivity increase through better incentives, but management, officers, and boards of directors should become more responsive to the "corporate" team as a whole. Real collaboration and shared interests will be enforced that go beyond present employee relations propaganda.[72]

More discipline and healthy limitations will be placed on irresponsible corporate raiding, questionable tender offers, greenmail, and other recent games of the stock takeover market.[73] Constructive discipline and limits will be placed upon job flight and branch plant relocations to low wage countries. The bulk of employees would be brought into decision making about job relocations more responsibly under profit sharing, ESOP, and related teamwork arrangements.[74]

For all these reasons—enlarged profits, higher worker incomes, increased national productivity, more equitable distrubution of capital wealth, improved teamwork and morale, and more constructive, healthier labor-management relations—it seems evident that profit sharing and ESOPs should be implemented.[75] These benefits are mutually reinforcing and tend to snowball together. Established patterns of social insurance contribution (one half from employees, and half from employer companies), together with ERISA's multiyear funding plan for pension liabilities, provide good precedents and guidelines. And the rapid spread of IRA and Keogh plan fund management, together with mutual and other pension fund arrangements, offer ample choice to employees (under proper fiduciary standards) for responsible handling of employee stock holdings. The time is ripe for profit sharing and ESOPs, and larger employer companies should lead the way under new federal legislation for this purpose.

Problems of Political Implementation

Despite the broad benefits from widespread profit sharing and ESOPs, active leadership and a reasonable coalescence of political forces is needed to implement this reform. Ideally this reform could achieve bipartisan consensus during the later 1980s. U.S. economic recovery seems sluggish and incomplete, world trade rivalry and competitive pressures are worsening, and measures to improve productivity should be welcomed.

The most enlightened, progressive-minded business leaders are now ready for this idea. The Commission on Industrial Competitiveness has urged strongly the need for better teamwork, more collaboration, and the desirability of profit sharing and/or ESOPs. The current question is political leadership in Congress and the executive branch and how much push should come from legislation and the tax system.

Broader profit sharing and ESOPs should be politically popular at this juncture. Most families and employees, many companies, financial managers (mutual funds, banks and other depository institutions), and the national economy will be beneficiaries. Politicians and presidential candidates seeking proposals to improve the economy should be in support.

The opposition should be largely inertia and normal resistance to new ideas. But some of the more selfish, old-fashioned, and antiworker business leaders may be expected to resist such reforms. This bloc within the employer class has often fought improvements in wages, benefits, and working conditions and wants to keep any concessions to an absolute minimum. We might expect a considerable part of the union hierarchy and establishment to resist profit sharing and stock ownership, fearing that it could reduce employee resistance to employers, undermine solidarity, and perhaps weaken unionism. More enlightened union leaders would respond, however, by welcoming a new element of leverage—stock ownership for workers—in a climate of reduced worker interest in traditional unionism. But many union stalwarts might oppose more collaborative worker-management relations, just as narrow-minded business conservatives may resist this concept.

Still another strand of opposition will come from socialists and Marxists, who seek to subvert capitalism and replace it with social ownership and control. Healthier teamwork, profit sharing, and improved industrial relations are not their objectives—until the forces of socialism take control of the government. If profit sharing and ESOPs should improve social morale, broaden capitalist participation, and strengthen these economies, the ultimate prospects for socialism or communism are reduced substantially. Such attitudes are understandable but should receive little sympathy from those with more faith in free enterprise or, at least, broader confidence in a predominantly free market economy.

Whether Democratic and Republican politicians will embrace profit sharing and ESOPs more widely remains to be seen. The potential is clear, and the subject has aroused great interest among journalists, academics, and many businesspeople. Support will come more from the center, moderate conservatives, and moderate liberals. In many respects, however, the historical opportunity may be unique today.[76] As sluggishness is widespread in U.S. industry, a strong shot in the arm, with improved productivity and renewed teamwork, definitely is wanted for the later 1980s.

NOTES

An extensive literature on profit sharing and ESOPs is cited within this chapter. Further background data may be obtained from the Profit Sharing Research Foundation (PSRF), Evanston, Illinois, and the National Center for Employee Ownership, Arlington, Virginia.

1. Hoerr, "Why Labor and Management Are Both Buying Profit-Sharing," Bus. Wk., Jan. 10, 1983, at 84; Morrisson, When Employees Get a Piece of the Action: Stock Ownership Is Raising Productivity and Profits, Nation's Bus., Dec. 1983, at 20–24; Rosen, Next Step: Worker Ownership? Commonweal, Aug. 10, 1984, at 434–36; and Corey Rosen, Katherine Klein, & Karen Young, Employee Ownership in America: The Equity Solution (1986).

These estimates for ESOP participation and some form of profit-sharing opportunity involve considerable overlap and double counting. Some profit-sharing participants are also in limited plans (mainly for executives and higher employees).

2. Ibid. See also sources cited in notes 14, 35, and 59 infra at 435.

3. Rosen, supra note 1, at 435.

4. Ibid.

5. Classical and neoclassical economists since Adam Smith divided society's output into the three categories of wages, rent, and profit. See Adam Smith, Wealth of Nations 51–52 (Modern Library ed. 1776); Joseph Schumpeter, History of Economic Analysis, esp. Pt. 2, chap. 5, 6 (1954); Henry W. Spiegel, The Growth of Economic Thought, esp. chap. 11 (1971).

6. See, for example, John Kenneth Galbraith, Affluent Society, chaps. 6, 7 (1958); C. Wright Mills, The Marxists (1962); J. Schumpeter, supra note 5, chaps. 19–21; Allan Gruchy, Modern Economic Thought: The American Contribution, chaps. 2, 3 (1947); William Lovett, Economics, Law and Governance chaps. 5–8 (1976); Jan Pen, Income Distribution: Facts, Theories, Policies (1971).

7. Ibid. See also George H. Sabine, A History of Political Theory chaps. 33–36 (3d ed. 1961); Rene David & David Brierley, Major Legal Systems in the World Today pt. 2 (1968); John Hazard, Communists and Their Law (1969); Wolfgang Friedmann, Law in a Changing Society chaps. 3, 8, 9 (2d ed. 1972).

8. For summaries of these alternative policy approaches, see Friedmann, supra note 7; Lovett, supra note 6; David & Brierley, supra note 7; Clair Wilcox and William G. Shepherd, Public Policies toward Business (5th ed. 1975); Andrew Shonfield, Modern Capitalism: The Changing Balance of Public and Private Power (1969).

For more recent controversy on the desirable scope of government intervention and its effectiveness in correcting shortcomings of the marketplace, see Milton & Rose Friedman, Free to Choose (1980); George Gilder, Wealth and Poverty (1981); Bruce Bartlett, Reaganomics: Supply-Side Economics in Action (1981); Lester Thurow, The Zero Sum Solution (1986); Robert Lekachman, Greed Is Not Enough (1982); Wallace Peterson, Our Overloaded Economy (1982); D. Bell & I. Kristol, The Crisis in Economic Theory (1981); William Lovett, Inflation and Politics: Fiscal, Monetary, and Wage-Price Discipline (1982); Herbert Stein, Presidential Economics (1984); Martin Feldstein, The American Economy in Transition (1980); David Calleo, The Imperious Economy (1982); John Oliver Wilson, The Power Economy; Building an Economy That Works (1985); Chalmers Johnson, ed., The Industrial Policy Debate (1984); Kevin Phillips, Staying on Top: The Business Case for a National Industrial Policy (1984); William Lovett, Competitive Industrial Policies and the World Bazaar, Staff Report, Subcommittee on Economic Stabilization, Committee on Banking, Finance and Urban Affairs, House of Representatives, 98th Cong., 2d Sess., Nov. 1984; Robert Baldwin & Anne Kreuger, The Structure and Evolution of Recent U.S. Trade Policy (1984); and John Culbertson, International Trade and Future of the West (1984).

9. Ibid.

10. See, particularly, Wilcox & Shepherd, Milton Friedman, Gilder, Bartlett, Thurow, Lekachman, Peterson, Stein, Feldstein, Calleo, Johnson, Phillips, Baldwin & Krueger, supra note 8. In addition, see standard U.S. histories, such as John Hicks, The Federal Union (3d Ed. 1952) and The American Nation (2d ed., 1947); or John Garraty, The American Nation, (1983), together with leading bibliographies and histories of the Frank-

lin Roosevelt, Truman, Eisenhower, Kennedy, Johnson, and Nixon administrations and the more recent literature on the Ford, Carter, and Reagan administrations.

11. See, for example, W. Friedman, David & Brierley, Shonfield, and more recently, comparative economic system texts, such as John Elliot, William Loucks, and J. Weldon Hoot, and more specific economic and governmental histories on the various European countries, such as those cited by Lovett, Inflation and Politics (supra note 8, esp. Ch. 5 notes 4–6, and 30–33), and by Lovett, Competitive Industrial Policies, supra note 8, in his bibliography.

12. See, for example, Lovett, Inflation and Politics, supra note 4, together with Milton Friedman, Gilder, Bartlett, Stein, Wilson, Phillips, and Culberston, supra note 4. See also the Urban Institute series on Reagan administration policies, particularly L. M. Salamon & M. S. Lund, eds., The Reagan Presidency and the Governing of America (1984), C. F. Stone & I. V. Sawhill, Economic Policy in the Reagan Years (1984); G. C. Eads & Michael Fix, The Reagan Regulatory Strategy (1984); and J. L. Palmer & I. V. Sawhill, The Reagan Experiment (1982).

13. See, especially, Gilder & Bartlett, supra note 4, together with the Urban Institute studies, supra note 8, and the report of President Reagan's Commission on Industrial Competitiveness, Global Competition: The New Reality, January 1985.

14. See, for example, J. Hoerr, Why Labor and Management Are Both Buying Profit Sharing, Bus. Wk., Jan. 10, 1983; An ESOP Fable, Time, Mar. 28 (1983); J. Egerton, Workers Take over the Store, N.Y. Times Mag., Sept. 11, 1983; Labich, A Steel Town Tries to Save Itself, Fortune, April 18, 1983; J. Batchelder & R. Rizzo, ESOP's, TRA-SOP's, PAYSOP's and Other Employee Stock Ownership Plans (1982); G. Latta, Profit Sharing and Stock Ownerhip, Savings, and Asset Formation Plans in the Western World (1979); and Martin Weitzman, The Share Economy (1984). See also, for literature on the complementary approach toward stronger employee participation, John Simmons & William Mares, Working Together: Employee Participation in Action (1985); Peter Brannen, Authority and Participation in Industry (1983). In addition, see sources cited notes 35 and 59 infra. For an earlier review based upon data from the early 1950s, see Schotta, The Distribution of Profit-Sharing Plans: An Analysis, 30 S. Econ. J. 49 (1963).

15. See Hicks & Garraty, supra note 6, together with Herman E. Kroos, American Economic Development (1966); Lance E. Davis, American Economic Growth, An Economist's History of the U.S. (1963); Seymour E. Harris, American Economic History (1961); Harold Faulkner, American Economic History (1935); Edward C. Kirkland, American Economic History since 1860, (1971); and William Greenleaf, American Economic Development since 1860 (1968). For more specific historical background on labor union growth, see Joseph G. Rayback, A History of American Labor (1966); Charles O. Gregory, Labor and the Law (2d ed. 1961); Richard L. Rowan, ed., Readings in Labor Economics and Labor Relations (3d ed. 1976); and Herbert R. Northrup & Gordon F. Bloom, Government and Labor: The Role of Government in Union-Management Relations (1963).

16. See Hicks & Garraty, supra note 4, together with Georges E. B. Clemenceau, American Reconstruction, 1865–70, (1928); E. Merton Coulter, The South during Reconstruction, 1865–1877, vol. 8, and C. Vann Woodward, Origins of the New South, 1877–1913, vol. 9, in the series, A History of the South (1971). See, particularly, the latter bibliography on agriculture, at 591–96.

17. See Pierre Gaxotte, Histoire des Français vol. 2 (1951); Christian & Arlette Ambrosi, La France, 1870–1981 (3d ed. 1981); François Caron, An Economic History of

Modern France (1979); S. Herbert, The Fall of Feudalism in France (1921); Herbert Heaton, Economic History of Europe, at 428–39, (Rev. ed. 1948); and, more generally, R. Ergang, Europe, From the Renaissance to Waterloo (1954).

18. See, generally, Heaton, supra note 17; Walter P. Hall & William S. Davis, The Course of Europe since Waterloo (3d ed. 1951); and Hubert Herring, A History of Latin America (3d ed. 1968).

An important echo of later nineteenth-century agrarian populism was the land reform and redistribution movement in development economics after World War II, and even currently, in some countries. See, for example, a leading advocate, Edmundo Flores, The Economics of Land Reform, Paper for Eighth FAO Conference, Vina del Mar, March 1965; Progress in Land Reform, United Nations, Department of Economic Affairs (1954); and Benjamin Higgins, Economic Development, at 450–54 (Rev. ed. 1968). Most experts on East Asian economic development stress the significant contribution of land reform to Japan, South Korea, and Taiwan after World War II. (See sources on East Asian development cited by Lovett, Inflation and Politics, supra note 4, esp. notes 4, 46, and 47. Latin America has had widespread controversy and efforts, but less progress, on the whole, except for the Mexican Revolution (1910–1940). Proponents for land reform as redistribution policy often emphasize the ancient Hebrew custom of reallocating land after every fifty years. See Spiegel, supra note 5 at 5, 58, 564.

19. See, for example, Hall & Davis, supra note 18 together with James Truslow Adams, Empire on the Seven Seas, The British Empire, 1884–1939 (1940); W. T. Easterbrook & Hugh L. J. Aitken, Canadian Economic History (1961); Mary Quayle Innis, An Economic History of Canada (1948); T. R. H. Davenport, South Africa: A Modern History (1977); Cornelius William De Kiewiet, A History of South Africa, Social and Economic (1943); Monica Wilson & Leonard Thompson, The Oxford History of South Africa (1969); and Winston S. Churchill, A History of the English Speaking Peoples, vol. 4, esp. chaps. 6, 7, The Migration of Peoples: Canada and South Africa; Australia and New Zealand (1958). See also Brian Fitzpatrick, The Australian People, 1788–1945 (1981), and W. H. Oliver & B. R. Williams, The Oxford History of New Zealand (1981).

20. See, for example, Hicks, supra note 10; Garrety, supra note 10; and Kroos, Harris, Faulkner, Greenleaf, Rayback, Gregory, and Northrup & Bloom, supra note 15, together with Wilcox and Shepherd cited note 8 supra.

21. See Hicks, supra note 10; Ergang, supra note 17; Heaton, supra note 17; Rayback, supra note 15; together with John R. Commons, ed., Trade Unionism and Labor Problems (2d ser. 1921); David McCord Wright, ed., The Impact of the Union, Eight Economic Theorists Evaluate the Labor Movement, Conference, May 12–13, 1950 (1966); Richard Perlman, ed., Wage Determination: Market or Power Forces? (1964); Rowan, supra note 15, esp. pts. 4, 5; and Lloyd Reynolds, Labor Economics and Labor Relations (6th ed. 1974).

22. Ibid.

23. Ibid. Special attention should be given to Geoffrey W. Latta, Profit Sharing, Employee Stock Ownership, Savings, and Asset Formation Plans in the Western World, Multinational Industrial Relations Series no. 5, (1979), a survey of the uneven, limited progress toward profit sharing in the United States and Western Europe by the later 1970s. For earlier, thoughtful literature, see Nicholas P. Gilman, Profit Sharing between Employer and Employee (1891), and his subsequent, A Dividend to Labor (1899); National Industrial Conference Board, Practical Experience with Profit Sharing in Industrial Establishments, Research Rep. no. 29, June 1920; and Gorton James, et al., Profit Sharing

and Stock Ownership for Employees (1926). It would be fair to say that serious interest in profit sharing began with the late nineteenth century. This increased some until the Great Depression, when widespread slump, unemployment, and stronger unionism greatly reduced interest in profit sharing. Some revival of interest occurred during the 1950s and beyond, prompted by a desire for broader sharing in stock ownership and prosperity. See, for example, Louis O. Kelso & Mortimer Adler, The Capitalist Manifesto (1958); Charles Barek, There's More to ESOP Than Meets the Eye: After 20 Years Louis Kelso Finally Got His Employee Stock Ownership Plan into Law, Fortune, Mar. 16, 1976, at 128. Greater interest emerged recently, when unions were weakening, and concern for slowed productivity became widespread.

24. Ibid. Until recent years most of the support for profit sharing and ESOPs (benefiting employees generally) came from a limited range of idealistic employers and observers of industrial relations. Employers favored such profit sharing and/or employee stock ownership to promote better morale, teamwork, and thrift among employees. Educating workers to better attitudes was a common goal, and discouraging unions was seen as advantageous. Experimentation was frequent but not widespread, and serious depressions greatly reduced profit-sharing plans. See particularly James et al., supra note 23.

25. While many employers had doubts about extending profit sharing and stock ownership to the generality of employees, most business corporations now routinely use stock option and bonus plans to encourage ownership and shelter higher incomes from taxes for executives and leaders. This trend was emerging in the 1920s but became widespread with higher income tax rates in World War II and subsequently. See, for example, William Lovett, Banking and Financial Institutions Law, esp. chap. 7 (1984). See also Latta, supra note 14; Batchelder & Rizzo, supra note 14; Munnell, cited note 31 infra.

26. See, particularly, Hicks, Rayback, Gregory, Rowan, Northrop, and Bloom, supra note 15, plus Reynolds, supra note 21.

27. Ibid.

28. Ibid.

29. In a celebrated remark, Sam Gompers said (1916) of profit sharing: "This proposition has never been seriously considered by the organizations of labor. I desire to say further that it has come under my observation that some employers who have inaugurated systems of so-called profit sharing have pared down the wages of their employees so that the combined sharing of profits and their wages did not equal the wages of other companies in the same line of industry. What we are especially interested in more than profit sharing is a fair living wage, reasonable hours and fair conditions of employment." See Latta, supra note 23, at 15.

30. See, generally, sources cited supra note 26.

31. See Lovett, Banking and Financial Institutions Law, supra note 25, chap. 7; J. L. Treynor, P. J. Regan, & W. W. Priest, The Financial Reality of Pension Funding under ERISA (1976); Alicia Munnell, The Economics of Private Pensions (1982); Danger: Pension Perils Ahead, Time, Sept. 24, 1979, at 68–70.

32. See Munnell, supra note 31, at 130–58.

33. A further grace period was allowed of up to another ten years for companies suffering some financial distress and up to forty years was allowed to fund obligations related to prior serivce. Ibid. For appropriate transition and grace period for mandatory profit sharing and ESOPs, see text and notes 42–51 infra. In general, a fifteen to twenty year transition period for mandatory profit sharing and ESOPs seems reasonable.

34. See, for example, Latta's excellent summary on contrasting unionism and profit-

sharing developments in Europe, supra note 23. See also Labich, supra note 14, and sources cited note 59 infra.

35. See, for example, Rosen, supra note 3, at 434; Kotkin, Taking Stock in Where You Work, Esquire, Feb. 1984; at 122; Morrison, When Employees Get a Slice of the Action, Nation's Bus. Dec. 1983, at 20; along with other sources cited. Surpa notes 1 and 14, infra note 59.

36. Latta's summary, supra note 23, emphasizes the differences in union background for most of Western Europe. See also R. Flanagan et al., Unionism, Economic Stabilization, and Incomes Policies (1983); Owen E. Smith, Trade Unions in the Developed Economies (1981); Adolf Sturmthal, Left of Center: European Trade Unionism since World War II (1983).

37. For extensive bibliography on Japanese economic development, see Lovett, Inflation and Politics, supra note 8, chap. 5, note 4; Lovett, Competitive Industrial Policies and the World Bazaar, supra note 8. In addition, see T. Hanami, Labour Law and Industrial Relations in Japan, Kluwer, Netherlands (1979); Mashimoto & Raisian, Employment Tenure and Earnings Profiles in Japan and the U.S., 75 Am. Econ. Rev. 721 (1985); Duff, Japanese and American Labor Law: Structural Similarities and Substantive Differences, 9 Employee Rel. J. 629 (1984); and Tsurumi, Labor Relations and Industrial Adjustment in Japan and the U.S.: A Comparative Analysis, 2 Yale L. & Pol. Rev. (1984).

38. See sources cited in Lovett, Inflation and Politics, supra note 8, notes 46, 47; Roy Hofheinz & Kent Calder, The East Asia Edge (1982).

39. See sources cited on Marxist systems, supra notes 6 and 7. In addition, see L. Lyontyev, Political Economy: A Condensed Course (1975); Tony Cliff, Lenin vols. 1– 3 (1975, 1965, 1978); John Reed, Ten Days That Shook the World (1918); Alec Nove, The Soviet Economy (2d rev. ed. 1961); Abram Bergson, The Economics of Soviet Planning (1964); Marshall Goldman, Soviet Marketing: Distribution in a Controlled Economy (1963); Leo Huberman & Paul Sweezy, Introduction to Socialism (1973); Morris Bornstein & Daniel Fusfield, The Soviet Economy: A Book of Readings (4th ed. 1974). For an excellent comparative economic systems text, see John Elliott, Comparative Economic Systems (1973), with sophisticated review of arguments. See also, more broadly, Albert Fried, Socialism in America: From the Shakers to the Third International (1970); Michael Harrington, Socialism (1970); David Memelstein, Economics: Mainstream Readings and Radical Critiques (1970); Erik P. Hoffman, ed., The Soviet Science, vol. 35 (1984); Blair Ruble, Soviet Trade Unions: Their Development (1981).

40. See review of criticisms in Elliott, supra note 39; with Milovan Djilas, The New Class (1957); Milovan Djilas, The Unperfect Society: Beyond the New Class (1969); Ota Sik, The Third Way: Marxist Leninist Theory and Modern Industrial Society (1976); Ronald J. Hill, Soviet Politics, Political Science, and Reform (1980). See also Ralf Dahrendorf, Class and Class Conflict in Industrial Society (Rev. ed. 1959); Paul Sweezy & Charles Bettelheim, On the Transition to Socialism (1971).

41. See Elliott, supra note 39, Oskar Lange & Fred Taylor, On the Economic Theory of Socialism (Lippincott ed. 1964); Albert Waterston, Planning in Yugoslavia (1962); World Bank Country Economic Report, Yugoslavia: Development with Decentralization, World Bank (1975); Branko Horvat, The Yugoslav Economic System (2d ed. 1976); E. G. Liberman, Economic Methods and the Effectiveness of Production: A Study of Soviet Economic Reforms (1971); Gyula Eorsi & Attila Harmathy, Law and Economic Reform in Socialist Countries (1971); H. H. Hohman, M. C. Kaser, & K. C. Thalheim,

eds., The New Economic Systems of Eastern Europe (1975); Branko Horvat, M. Mar-
kovic, & R. Supek, Self-Governing Socialism, A Reader vols. 1–2 (1975); Jaroslav
Vanek, The Labor Managed Economy (1977); and Gerry Junnius, G. D. Garson, & John
Case, Worker's Control: A Reader on Labor and Social Change (1973). See also, Georges
Lassere, Reformer l'enterprise en 1975: Des pouroirs les travailleurs (1975).

42. Awareness of the need to rejuvenate Western economies is widespread in the
early to mid–1980s. See, for example, Paul Erdman, Paul Erdman's Money Book (1984);
John Makin, The Global Debt Crisis: America's Growing Involvement (1984); A State-
ment by 26 Economists from 14 Countries, Promoting World Recovery (1982); John
Kendrick, ed., International Comparisons of Productivity and Causes of the Slowdown
(1984); Richard R. Nelson, High Technology Policies: A Five Nation Comparison (1984);
J. Grunwald and K. Flamm, The Global Factory (1985); Alice Rivlin, ed., Economic
Choices, 1984 (1984); Phillip Cagan, Essays in Contemporary Economic Problems, 1985:
The Economy in Deficit (1985); together with most of the other recent works cited supra
note 8 and President Reagan's Commission on Industrial Competitiveness, supra note
13.

43. See, for example, 1984 Foreign Trade Highlights, International Trade Adminis-
tration (March 1985); Culbertson, supra note 8; Culbertson, The Danger of "Free Trade"
(1985); C. Fred Bergsten, The U.S.-Japan Trade Imbroglio, Challenge, July-Aug. 1985;
Collision Course: Can the U.S. Avert a Trade War with Japan? Bus. Wk., April 8, 1985;
Mary Saso & Stuart Kirby, Japanese Industrial Competition to 1990 (1982); and Hofheinz
& Calder, The East Asia Edge (1982).

44. Many pollsters, journalists, educators, and other observers have noticed a more
conservative personalism and concern for individual and family economic success.

45. See, for example, Beyond Unions, Bus. Wk. July 8, 1985, which projects a
continued decline in the share of nonfarm work force that is unionized: from 32 percent
in 1953 (the peak year), 29 percent in 1975, 23 percent in 1980, and 19 percent in 1985,
to 17 percent in 1990, 15 percent in 1995, and less than 14 percent in 2000. A decline
in prestige for unionism is illustrated in recent literature, too, as explained by McElvaine,
Workers in Fiction: Locked Out, N.Y. Times Book Rev., Sept. 1, 1985, at 1. And yet
unions are trying to withstand these trends by updating their appeal. See, for example,
Greenhouse, Reshaping Labor to Woo the Young: Unions Are Making a Play for the
Under-35 Crowd, Shifting Goals to Attract a Job Hopping, Pro-Business Generation of
Workers, N.Y. Times, Sept. 1, 1985, at 1.

In addition, see Are the Unions Dead or Just Sleeping? Fortune, Sept. 20, 1982, at
98–100; Marth, The Sorry State of Unions, Nation's Bus., July 1982, at 50–52; Craver,
The Current and Future Status of Labor Organizations, 36 Lab. L. Jr. 210 (1985); Laude
& Zerbe, Reducing Unions' Monopoly Power: Costs & Benefits, 28 J. L. & Econ. 297
(1985); Craver, The Vitality of the American Labor Movement in the 21st Century, U.
Ill. L. Rev. 633 (1983); Rehmus, Labor and Politics in the 1980's, 473 Annals, 40 (1984);
Unions in Retreat, 31 World Press Rev. 47 (1984); English, Why Unions Are Running
Scared, 97 U.S. News & World Rep., Sept. 10, 1984; and Perlis, Organized Labor
Needs a Facelift, 50 Vital Speeches, Sept. 15, 1984.

46. See, especially, Culbertson, supra note 8, other sources cited, supra notes, 38,
39, together with William Lovett, World Trade Rivalry: Finance and Indusrial Policies
(forthcoming). See also Malcolm, U.S. Workers say Japanese Are Superior, N.Y. Times,
Sept. 1, 1985, at 1, for a thoughtful analysis of U.S. worker morale and productivity
problems.

47. Tax relief for the higher-income and wealthier families has been signficant in the Reagan years. And tax-sheltering opportunity has been extended modestly for IRAs, Keoghs, and some pension plans. Investment and tax-sheltering opportunities remain significant for real estate and a considerable range of international trading, investment, and financial service activities. (The Tax Reform bill of 1986 did seem to cut back on some tax sheltering, especially in the real estate area, but most experts were unsure about the durability of reforms in this direction). A desire of the middle class to share more broadly in these activities is natural and could be accommodated by more widespread profit sharing and ESOP availability (linked to significant tax sheltering of income and wealth accumulation). This trend has powerful political logic, as well as a spreading tendency and response to demands for more equal access and fairness.

48. See sources cited notes 1, 14, 35 supra, and note 59 infra.

49. Impelled by increased inflation rates, greater marriage, divorce and career risks, higher costs for home ownership, and desires among women for more fulfillment, independence, and economic well-being, the majority of younger families are becoming double earners. Typical strategies for building savings and investment include the purchase and renovation of homes (and summer cottages), other real estate investments, side-line businesses (for the wife or husband), and more systematic use of IRAs and Keoghs. In this climate more of the work force will regard profit sharing and ESOP opportunities favorably.

50. See, for example, Lovett, Banking and Financial Institutions Law chap. 6 (1984) (insurance industry developments). Many life insurance salespeople style themselves as investment counselors now, and they must compete for savings and investment allocations among families, higher-income earners, and business entrepreneurs.

51. The phase-in period for general or mandatory profit sharing and/or ESOPs should be somewhat shorter than the thirty to forty years allowed for full funding of defined pension benefits under ERISA. (Defined contribution pensions plans required no special funding regulation. Employees generally understood their rights under defined contribution arrangements and were not subject to being misled by overly generous defined benefit plans with unsufficient or negligible funding.) Many defined benefit pension plans had little funding previous to ERISA and had been designed for pay as you go current payments as retired obligations accrued. For these reasons, a long, nonburdensome thirty- to forty-year transitional phase-in for full funding was desirable. See Lovett, supra note 25; Munnell, supra note 31.

With respect to general or mandatory profit sharing or ESOPs, fifteen- to twenty-year phase-in requirements would allow relatively easy, gradual, and steady accumulation of major ownership interests in larger companies for their work forces. Neither real wages nor profits will be significantly diluted, and in most situations, expanded productivity earnings and profitability from improved teamwork and incentives would add significant net gains.

For convenient summaries of current law and regulation in this area, see Russell K. Osgood, The Law of Pensions and Profit Sharing (1984); Bachelder & Rizzo, supra note 14. See also A. H. Kroll, ed., 14th Annual Employee Benefits Institute, Course Handbook No. 200 (1984); J. P. Klein, Flexible Compensation Plans, 1984, Course Handbook No. 204 (1984).

52. Some elements of total compensation to executives are more in the nature of entrepreneurial or profit returns. Yet not all the real benefits actually received by executives or ownership interests are included in these total compensation data. Nor do the corporate

funds flow and profit data reported from tax returns represent a complete picture of business profits or entrepreneurial returns. But a rough estimate of residual profits by deducting wage and salaries can be achieved this way.

53. The strongest arguments for widespread profit sharing (and/or ESOPs) focus on improved productivity, more teamwork, stronger incentives, and improved morale. Better self-esteem for workers, greater mutual respect among workers and managers, and more stable, long-term commitments to successful enterprises are part of these benefits. But the worker share must be sizable enough to offer real incentives and should constitute a significant element (at least over the longer run) in the voting power of the corporation and major policy decisions. See, for example, the survey results reported by the National Center for Employee Ownership, published by Rosen & Klein, Job Creating Peformance of Employee-Owned Firms, Monthly Lab. Rev., Aug. 1983, at 15–19; and Rosen, Klein, & Young, supra note 1. Also, for the importance of stronger motivation, self-esteem, and employee dignity, see Studs Terkel, Working (1975); W. Baldamus, Efficiency and Effort: An Analysis of Industrial Administration (1961); Georges Friedman, Industrial Society: The Emergence of The Human Problems of Automation (1955); John Dunlop, Automation and Technical Change, The American Assembly (1962); Roger M. D'Aprix, Struggle for Identity: The Silent Revolution against Corporate Conformity (1972); Thomas Peters and R. Waterman, Jr., In Search of Excellence: Lessons from America's Best-Run Companies, (1982); and R. Levering, Milton Moskowitz, & Michael Katz, The 100 Best Companies to Work for in America (1984). In addition, for the enduring opportunity enjoyed by smaller companies, often led by creative entrepreneurship, see Small Is Beautiful, Bus. Wk., May 27, 1985. See also sources cited supra notes 14 and 35 supra and infra 59.

54. In large industrial organizations and smaller business enterprises, it would seem that greater productivity, incentives, collaboration, and teamwork should come from general profit sharing and/or ESOP arrangements. But the magnitude of these gains should be stronger in the bigger companies, which would justify imposing such plans first among them as a general policy. Also, supervising a transition process would be easier in starting from the top down (among large companies initially). And finally, the demonstration effects of success among more prestigious, well-known companies will facilitate the spread of these wage and stock ownership policies more broadly into smaller business.

55. Industrial relations systems where most workers fail to share in productivity gains or their company's success tend to lose momentum and develop morale problems. In the politics of many nations, their trade unions, when powerful and influential, tend to impose rigid wage, social welfare, and working condition demands, regardless of the real economic performance of their industry in world market competition. Such nations tend to suffer weakening productivity against the rising competition of new industrial countries, with continuing problems of stagflation (inflationary momentum and excessive unemployment on a chronic basis). See the major recent study by R. Flanagan, David Soskice, & Lloyd Ulman, Unionism, Economic Stabilization, and Incomes Policies: European Experience, Studies in Wage-Price Policy (1983).

56. Martin L. Weitzman, The Share Economy: Conquering Stagflation (1984), for example, makes these arguments. While conceding that productivity gains may be significant, Weitzman prefers to rely mainly upon the employment gains from wage flexibility in a share economy. See also Gottfried Haberler, The Problem of Stagflation (1985).

57. See, for example, Rosen & Klein, supra note 53, at 15–19. A particularly interesting finding is that employee-owned firms (where employees are majority owners) use

less new labor than employee-owner companies. But in their entire study sample of ESOP companies, overall economic growth was faster than conventional companies, with significantly greater new hiring. This study tends to confirm the foregoing analysis. See also Conte & Tannenbaum, Employee Owned Companies: Is the Difference Measurable? 101 Monthly Lab. Rev. 23, July 1978. Most of the literature cited supra notes 14 and 35 suggests considerable productivity enhancement potential from substantial profit sharing and/or appreciable employee ownership.

58. See, for example, the President's Commission on Industrial Competitiveness, supra note 9; Culbertson, supra note 8; and M. Kosters, Disinflation in the Labor Market, in Essays in Contemporary Economic Problems: Disinflation (1983–84 ed. 1984).

59. See, for example, Leopold, Iron Workers Forge a Buy-Out, Progressive, April 1984 at 16; Kotkin, The Steel Industry: Turning a Depressed Grant into a Small Wonder, Esquire, May 1984, at 192; English, When Employees Run Their Own Steel Mill, U.S. News & World Rep., May 7, 1984, at 77; Hoerr and Symonds, A Brash Bid to Keep Steel in the Mon Valley, Bus. Week, Feb. 11, 1985, at 30; Epstein, Reluctant Capitalists, Nat'l Rev., Feb. 22, 1985; Uphill in West Virginia, Forbes, Mar. 25, 1985; Goldstein The Weirton Buy-Out: Saving Jobs, But at What Price? Dec. 10, 1983, at 594; and A Steel Town's Fight for Life, Newsweek, March 28, 1983, at 49. In addition, see other sources cited supra notes 14, 35.

60. The industry potentials for widespread ESOP and profit-sharing potential (table 2) are based on employment levels and value-added in the major sectors of the economy, together with rough estimates for achievable percentages of employee coverage under mandatory ESOP and profit-sharing plans (for larger companies). Subsequent profit-sharing and/or ESOP participation percentages for employees could be significantly higher over the long run as these arrangements spread into smaller business enterprises.

61. In the public utility sector, cost of service ratemaking (as practiced traditionally) might not allow profit sharing or ESOPs in some jurisdictions. This would be a policy matter resolved by state legislatures, public service commissions, and/or state courts, together with Congress and federal courts for interstate ratemaking jurisdiction. The efficiency and productivity arguments could be justified in this sector (as highly capital-intensive industries, with somewhat lower worker shares), but explicit policy decisions would be needed to enable these practices in the highly regulated public utilities. Few ESOPs and general employee profit-sharing plans exist now in the public utility sector.

62. Because the bigger business sector tends to be more capital intensive and also comprises a large share of manufacturing and some other sectors, a sizable chunk of the value-added to national income is generated already in companies that could be more readily enrolled in profit-sharing and/or ESOP plans.

63. Some companies could experiment (as at present) with even larger shares of employee ownership or capitalization. But a goal of one-third of the outstanding equity in companies with low or moderate capital intensity seems reasonable, and one-quarter of outstanding equity is sensible for highly capital-intensive industries (where debt and other outside capital is naturally more important).

64. The most logical phase-in formula for general or mandatory employee stock ownership (or profit sharing) is fifteen to twenty years, with equal contributions from employees and their company (contributions pegged to annual earnings of each employee). In normal years, the contributions from the employer would amount to less than 10 percent of annual profits. (A waiver or deferral option should be allowed for employers,

so that shortages in bad or low-profit years could be amortized with appropriate borrowing.)

In Sweden, the Social Democratic government recently enacted, despite much business opposition, a harsher mandatory program of employee stock ownership. The new Swedish program finances the employee stock purchase through only a stiff tax on company profits, with no contribution or deduction from wages. By 1990 it was projected that 10 to 14 percent of corporate stock could be owned by workers through union-dominated trust funds. Such an unbalanced, lopsided approach would not be appropriate for the United States. See Feder, Swedes Split on Plan for Union Investments, N.Y. Times, sec. D, Nov. 14, 1983, at 1; Swedes Vote Stock Funds, N.Y. Times, sec. D., Dec. 22, 1983, at 9; Feder, Profit Now in Style in Sweden, N.Y. Times, April 21, 1984, at 27; Feder, Economic Freedom Is Swedish Issue, N.Y. Times, sec. D, Nov. 26, 1984, at 4. See also Himmelstrand, Sweden: Toward Economic Democracy: A Social Democratic Government Contemplates New Policies, Dissent, Summer 1983; and Lundberg, The Rise and Fall of the Swedish Model, 23 J. Econ. Literature 1–36 (March 1985).

65. Extensive tax sheltering is allowed already for most executive compensation, bonus, stock option, Keogh, and IRA contributions. It is natural, proper, and fair that general employee stock purchase and profit-sharing plan contributions (by both employees and employers) should be sheltered from income taxes too.

66. Flowing profit-sharing contributions directly into employee IRAs (with increased limits to allow for these increments) would yield immediate vesting of capital assets, which would build up nicely over the years. Full portability of such assets would be ensured for each employee's IRA, and current practices on allowing the employee to select fund management and account fiduciaries would continue. Some IRAs (normally smaller ones) would be invested in federally insured bank or thrift accounts, and others would be held as securities portfolios by fund managers (mutual-type funds or self-directed accounts).

67. Another approach would be company, labor union, or independent trusteeship and fund management. These fiduciaries are also government regulated, and such regulation may need to be strengthened substantially over time to protect employee-investor interests.

68. Greater choice is already popular with profit sharing and ESOP plan beneficiaries and seems the logical trend. Portfolio diversification can be more readily achieved this way too.

69. Even in plans now tied more or less substantially to the company's own stock, it may be desirable to allow reasonable diversification of these portfolios over time in line with the interests of most employee families for sound portfolio distribution. If most plans give this discretion to employee beneficiaries (or their trustees), the other employers could be forced by competitive pressures to follow the trend. This diversification pressure would also encourage company managements to maintain more reliable, sound, and marketable values for their securities and thereby be more prudent, responsible managers.

70. Competition in the marketplace for hiring employees will be transformed by the increasingly general availability of ESOPs and/or profit sharing. Once the larger companies use such plans (for the most part), higher-quality small business enterprise will be forced to offer equivalent treatment in getting good-quality labor. Generalization pressures will spread more rapidly. The same logic applies to more generous ESOP and profit-sharing plans, with easier vesting, more liberal portability, and greater freedom to select the best fund management for each families' interests.

71. Until recently, most corporate law developed on the assumption that stockholders

were the primary interest to be protected, with more or less stockholder democracy to be enforced. For a traditional corporate law treatise, see Harry G. Henn & John R. Alexander, Hornbook on Laws of Corporations (3d ed. 1983). Although employee relations people urged teamwork themes, corporate law, officers', and directors' liability emphasized paramount duties to stockholder interests. As employees become significant shareholders (under ESOP and profit-sharing plans), however, their overall interests should be better protected and receive more separate emphasis as members of the corporate team—with important stock ownership, pension and retirement security, wage and salary, and career interests at stake. For suggestive analysis, see Patterson, Legal Ethics: The Law of Professional Responsibility chap. 10 (2d ed. 1984). See also Comment, Employee Stock Ownership Plans and Corporate Takeovers: Restraints on the Use of ESOP's by Corporate Officers and Directors to Avert Hostile Takeovers, 10 Pepperdine L. Rev. 731 (1983); Miller & Lindsay, Mergers and Acquisitions: Labor Relations Considerations, 9 Employee Rel. L. J. 427 (Winter 1983–1984); and Reich, Bailout: A Comparative Study in Law and Industrial Structure, 2 Yale J. Reg. 163 (1985).

72. Ibid. Employee interests can be more effectively represented, with more legal clout, class action, and derivative suits, when employees become sizable shareholders, and enjoy significant profit-sharing benefits. In the long run, corporate law and decision making should evolve to represent employee interests more effectively. Nonunion employees will receive stronger legal leverage and representation this way, and unions will have better legal remedies and bargaining power when their workers become sizable stockholders and beneficiaries of stockholding. In the end, unions will become more effective, enlightened representatives of employee-owner-corporate-profit interests as a whole. Greater cohesion (and reduced conflicts of interest) will be the result of this transformation.

73. Excessive corporate raiding, questionable takeover and tender offers, greenmail (blackmail) payments, and bribes to protect existing managements, pressures to add undue corporate debt or excessive leverage, overly short-term perspectives for managers, with sufficient attention to long-run corporate viability and growth prospects, and neglect of sound labor-management teamwork are all problems of the corporate sector in recent years.

See, for example, Grunwald, Swallowing Up One Another, Time, Feb. 6, 1984, at 46; Reilly, Merger Madness, Fortune, May 13, 1985, at 101; Greenwald, The Great Takeover Debate, Time, April 22, 1985, at 44; Proxmire, Hostile Corporate Takeovers and Raids, Vital Speeches, April 15, 1985, at 388–95; Sloan, Why Is No One Safe? Forbes, Mar. 11, 1985, at 134; Irv the Liquidator, Time, Mar. 4, 1985, at 67; Eklund, The Dr. J. of the Wheeling and Dealing, Bus. Week, Feb. 4, 1985, at 33; An Outcry against Hostile Takeovers, Bus. Week, Aug. 27, 1984, at 16; Pauly, Why All the Mega-Mergers? Newsweek, Mar. 19, 1984, at 70; Corporate Raiders and Their Targets, Bus. Week, April 2, 1984, at 29; The Legal Masterminds behind Merger Mania, Bus. Week, Aug. 13, 1984, at 122; Bernstein, Taking on Takeovers, Fortune, Sept. 3, 1984, at 96; Gelman, Wang, & Pedersen, The Next Wave: Any Undervalued Company Can Be Raided, Newsweek, April 1, 1985, at 60; Haertzberg, Borrowing Time: Take-Over Targets Find Loading Up on Debt Can Fend Off Raiders, Wall St. J., Sept. 10, 1985, at 1; Demott, Three Who Watch, Wait, and Strike: A Trio of Gamblers Sends Shudders through Executive Corridors, Time, Mar. 4, 1985, at 65; Gelman & Pedersen, The Days of the Jackals, Newsweek, Mar. 18, 1985, at 53; and Do Mega-Mergers Drive Up Interest Rates? Business Wk., April 16, 1984, at 176.

Substantial employee stock ownership and profit-sharing interests will be a helpful constraint and corrective influence against such dangers, malpractices, and abuses of the current corporate marketplace.

74. Extensive branch plant and job relocation has already occurred in recent years, and this explains part of the decline in U.S. manufacturing and exports (along with a high dollar, high interest rates, and excessive U.S. budget deficits). See, for example, Anderson, America's Foreign Trade Crisis, AFL-CIO American Federationist, Oct. 13, 1984; United States Trade, Performance in 1984 and Outlook, Office of Trade and Investment Analysis, Int'l Trade Admin., U.S. Dept. Commerce (June, 1985); Phillip Cagan, Essays in Contemporary Economic Problems, The Economy in Deficit, 1985, American Enterprise Institute, cited note 42 supra; and Grunwald and Flamm, The Global Factory, 1984.

75. The case for greatly enlarged employee stock ownership and profit sharing is multidimensional. Increased incentives, productivity, teamwork, and cohesion are the core arguments. Improved equity and wealth distribution, enlarged national income, stronger competitiveness in world markets, greater prosperity, and more job opportunities are important too. Although some details will need to be adjusted over time (such as precise sharing formula, vesting, choice and selection of funds, and trustee representation), these problems can be solved pragmatically. Enough flexibility should be allowed for divergent plans, varied momentum already accumulated, and different industrial or business circumstances. Some litigation and test cases will be needed to straighten out problems, but these will come naturally as ESOPs and profit sharing become prevalent. But on the merits as a whole, the justification for greatly enlarged profit sharing and ESOPs already has been established. The time is ripe to go forward with national legislation more strongly encouraging these arrangements. In my judgment, we are ready for mandatory profit sharing and/or ESOPs (with some flexibility as to choice of plans) under federal law, for all larger companies (with a fifteen- to twenty-year phase-in period), following the earlier precedent and success with ERISA in 1974.

76. With growing public support and powerful economic arguments (improved incentives, productivity growth, equity, and cohesion), reinforced by strong teamwork themes in the American ideology, the idea of profit sharing and employee stock ownership is a natural winner in politics today. The concept has some appealing freshness, most employees will applaud, labor unions should offer support as a means to greater popularity and bargaining leverage, and business interests in the main should endorse measures that broaden their economic base and the popularity of capitalism (so long as they can see net advantages). A bandwagon momentum could get going quickly. A number of presidential candidates in 1988 should strongly urge profit sharing and ESOPs as part of their platforms.

SELECTED BIBLIOGRAPHY

This bibliography lists some of the books that deal with corporate social responsibility and with the economy as a system of power. No articles are listed; they may be found in the appropriate indexes for legal, economic, political science, business, and sociology periodicals. For technical discussions of corporation law, consult the relevant textbooks and legal encyclopedia. (In addition to this listing of books, each chapter in this book contains numerous references to other pertinent books and articles.)

Adams, Walter, ed. *The Structure of American Industry*. New York: Macmillan, 1977.

Allen, Frederick Lewis. *The Lords of Creation*. Reprint ed. Chicago: Quadrangle, 1966.

Allvine, Fred C., and Tarpley, Fred A., Jr. *The New State of the Economy*. Cambridge, Mass.: Winthrop Publishers, 1977.

Appleby, Joyce. *Capitalism and the New Social Order*. New York: New York University Press, 1984.

Arnold, Thurman. *The Folklore of Capitalism*. New Haven: Yale University Press, 1937.

Bain, Joe S. *Barriers to New Competition*. Cambridge: Harvard University Press, 1956.

————. *Industrial Organization*. 2nd ed. New York: John Wiley, 1968.

Bannock, Graham. *The Juggernauts*. London: Weidenfeld and Nicolson, 1977.

Baran, Paul A., and Sweezy, Paul M. *Monopoly Capitalism*. New York: Monthly Review Press, 1966.

Barber, Richard, *The American Corporation*. New York: E. P. Dutton, 1970.

Barnet, Richard, and Muller, Ronald. *Global Reach*. New York: Simon & Schuster, 1974.

Bell, Daniel, and Kristol, Irving. *Capitalism Today*. New York: Basic Books, 1971.

Berle, Adolf A. *Power without Property*. New York: Harcourt Brace, 1959.

————. *The Twentieth Century Capitalist Revolution*. New York: Harcourt Brace, 1954.

Berle, Adolf A., and Means, Gardiner C. *The Modern Corporation and Private Property*. Rev. ed. New York: Harcourt, Brace & World, 1968.

Beth, Loren. *The Development of the American Constitution, 1877–1917*. New York: Harper & Row, 1971.

Blair, John. *Economic Concentration*. New York: Harcourt Brace Jovanovich, 1972.

Bluestone, Barry, and Harrison, Bennett. *Capital and Communities*. Washington, D.C.:
    Progressive Alliance, 1980.
Boulding, Kenneth. *The Organizational Revolution*. New York: Harper & Bros., 1953.
Boulton, David. *The Lockheed Papers*. London: Jonathan Cape, 1978.
Brandes, Stuart D. *American Welfare Capitalism, 1880–1940*. Chicago: University of
    Chicago Press, 1976.
Braverman, Harry. *Labor and Monopoly Capital*. New York: Monthly Review Press, 1974.
Brodeur, Paul. *Expendable Americans*. New York: Viking, 1974.
Burch, Philip H., Jr. *The Managerial Revolution Reassessed*. Lexington, Mass.: Lex-
    ington Books, 1972.
Burns, Arthur R. *The Decline of Competition*. New York: McGraw-Hill, 1936.
Carnoy, Martin, and Derek Shearer and Russell Rumberger. *A New Social Contract*. New
    York: Harper & Row, 1983.
————. , and Shearer, Derek. *Economic Democracy*. White Plains, N.Y.: M. E. Sharpe,
    1980.
Chamberlain, Neil W. *The Place of Business in America's Future*. New York: Basic
    Books, 1973.
Chandler, Alfred D. *Strategy and Structure*. Cambridge: MIT Press, 1962.
————. *The Visible Hand*. Cambridge: Harvard University Press, 1977.
Childs, Marquis W., and Cater, Douglass. *Ethics in a Business Society*. New York:
    Harper & Bros., 1954.
Clinard, Marshall, and Yeager, Peter D. *Corporate Crime*: New York: Free Press, 1980.
Cochran, Thomas. *Business in American Life: A History*. New York: McGraw-Hill, 1972.
————. *Railroad Leaders, 1845–1890*. Cambridge: Harvard University Press, 1953.
Coleman, James S. *Power and the Structure of Society*. New York: Norton, 1974.
Commons, John R. *The Economics of Collective Action*. Madison: University of Wis-
    consin Press, 1950.
————. *Legal Foundations of Capitalism*. Madison: University of Wisconsin Press, 1924.
Curtiss, Ellen T., and Untersee, Philip A. *Corporate Responsibilities and Opportunities
    to 1990*. Lexington, Mass.: Lexington Books, 1979.
Dahl, Robert A. *Dilemmas of Pluralist Democracy*. New Haven: Yale University Press,
    1982.
————. *A Preface to Economic Democracy*. Berkeley: University of California Press,
    1985.
Dan-Cohen, Meir. *Rights, Persons, and Organizations*. Berkeley: University of California
    Press, 1986.
Davis, John P. *Corporations*. Edited by Abram Chayes. New York: Capricorn Books,
    1961.
Davis, Lance E., and North, Douglass C. *Institutional Change and American Economic
    Growth*. New York: Cambridge University Press, 1971.
Dewey, Donald. *Monopoly in Economics and Law*. Chicago: Rand-McNally, 1959.
Dickie, Robert B., and Rouner, Leroy S., eds. *Corporations and the Common Good*.
    Notre Dame: University of Notre Dame Press, 1986.
Domhoff, G. William. *The Higher Circles: The Governing Class in America*. New York:
    Random House, 1970.
Drucker, Peter F. *The Concept of the Corporation*. New York: Thomas Crowell, 1972.
————. *The Unseen Revolution*. New York: Harper & Row, 1977.
Edwards, Corwin. *Maintaining Competition*. New York: McGraw-Hill, 1949.

Eells, Richard. *The Political Crisis of the Enterprise System*. New York: Free Press, 1980.

Eisenberg, Melvin A. *The Structure of the Corporation*. Boston: Little, Brown, 1976.

Engler, Robert. *The Politics of Oil*. Chicago: University of Chicago Press, 1959.

Etzioni, Amitai. *Modern Organizations*. Englewood Cliffs, N.J.: Prentice-Hall, 1964.

Ewing, David W. *"Do It My Way or You're Fired": Employee Rights and the Changing Role of Management Prerogatives*. New York: John Wiley, 1983.

Farmer, Richard N., and Hogue, W. Dickerson. *Corporate Social Responsibility*. 2d ed. Lexington, Mass.: Lexington Books, 1985.

French, Peter A. *Collective and Corporate Responsibility*. New York: Columbia University Press, 1984.

Friedman, Lawrence M. *A History of American Law*. New York: Simon & Schuster, 1973.

Furlong, James. *Labor in the Boardroom*. Princeton, N.J.: Princeton University Press, 1977.

Galbraith, John Kenneth. *Economics and the Public Purpose*. Boston: Houghton Mifflin, 1973.

————. *The New Industrial State*. Boston: Houghton Mifflin, 1967.

Gilb, Corinne Lathrop. *Hidden Hierarchies*. New York: Harper & Row, 1966.

Goldschmidt, Harvey J., ed. *Business Disclosure*. New York: McGraw-Hill, 1979.

Gordon, Robert Aaron. *Business Leadership in the Large Corporation*. Berkeley: University of California Press, 1966.

Grant, Wyn., ed. *The Political Economy of Corporatism*. London: Macmillan Publishers Ltd., 1985.

Green, Mark, ed. *The Big Business Reader on Corporate America*. New York: Pilgrim, 1983.

Greenstone, J. David, ed. *Public Values and Private Power in American Politics*. Chicago: University of Chicago Press, 1982.

Hacker, Andrew, ed. *The Corporation Take-Over*. Garden City, N.Y.: Doubleday, 1965.

Hale, Robert L. *Freedom through Law*. New York: Columbia University Press, 1952.

Heilbroner, Robert L., et al. *In the Name of Profit*. New York: Doubleday, 1972.

Herman, Edward S. *Corporate Control, Corporate Power*. New York: Cambridge University Press, 1981.

Hessen, Robert. *In Defense of the Corporation*. Stanford: Hoover Institution Press, 1979.

Hirsch, Fred. *Social Limits to Growth*. Cambridge: Harvard University Press, 1976.

Horowitz, David., ed. *Corporations and the Cold War*. New York: Monthly Review Press, 1969.

Hurst, James Willard. *Law and the Conditions of Freedom in the Nineteenth Century United States*. Madison: University of Wisconsin Press, 1956.

————. *The Legitimacy of the Business Corporation in the United States, 1780–1970*. Charlottesville: University of Virginia Press, 1970.

Jacoby, Neil H. *Corporate Power and Social Responsibility*. New York: Free Press, 1977.

Jacquemin, A., and de Jong, H. W. *Corporate Behaviour and the State*. The Hague: Martinus Nijhoff, 1976.

Kapp, K. William. *The Social Costs of Private Enterprise*. New York: Schocken Books, 1971.

Katzenstein, Peter J. *Corporatism and Change*. Ithaca, N.Y.: Cornell University Press, 1984.

Kaysen, Carl, and Turner, Donald F. *Antitrust Policy*. Cambridge: Harvard University Press, 1959.

Keane, John. *Public Life and Late Capitalism*. New York: Cambridge University Press, 1984.

Kempner, Thomas; Macmillan, Keith; and Hawkins, Kevin. *Business and Society: Tradition and Change*. London: Allen Lane, 1974.

Kindleberger, Charles. *American Business Abroad*. New Haven: Yale University Press, 1969.

——, ed. *The International Corporation*. Cambridge: MIT Press, 1970.

Kolko, Gabriel. *Railroads and Regulation, 1877–1916*. Princeton, N.J.: Princeton University Press, 1965.

——. *The Triumph of Conservatism*. New York: Free Press, 1963.

Kotz, David M. *Bank Control of Large Corporations in the United States*. Berkeley: University of California Press, 1978.

Kristol, Irving. *Two Cheers for Capitalism*. New York: Basic Books, 1969.

Kwitny, Jonathan. *Endless Enemies*. New York: Congdon & Weed, 1984.

Lawrinsky, Michael. *Corporate Structure and Performance*. New York: St. Martin's Press, 1984.

Letwin, William. *Law and Economic Policy in America*. New York: Random House, 1965.

Lindblom, Charles. *Politics and Markets*. New York: Basic Books, 1977.

Lundberg, Ferdinand. *The Rich and the Super-Rich*. New York: Bantam, 1968.

Lustig, R. Jeffrey. *Corporate Liberalism*. Berkeley: University of California Press, 1982.

McCann, Thomas P. *An American Company: The Tragedy of United Fruit*. New York: Crown Publishers, 1976.

McConnell, Grant. *Private Power and American Democracy*. New York: Knopf, 1967.

McEachern, William A. *Managerial Control and Performance*. Lexington, Mass.: Lexington Books, 1975.

March, James F., and Simon, Herbert A. *Organizations*. New York: John Wiley, 1958.

Marris, Robin. *The Economic Theory of "Managerial Capitalism."* New York: Basic Books, 1964.

Martin, Roderick. *The Sociology of Power*. London: Routledge & Kegan Paul, 1977.

Mason, Edward S., ed. *The Corporation in Modern Society*. Cambridge: Harvard University Press, 1959.

Means, Gardiner C. *The Corporate Revolution in America*. New York: Crowell-Collier Press, 1962.

Miliband, Ralph. *The State in Capitalist Society*. New York: Basic Books, 1969.

Miller, Arthur Selwyn. *The Modern Corporate State*. Westport, Conn.: Greenwood Press, 1976.

——. *The Supreme Court and American Capitalism*. New York: Free Press, 1968.

Mintz, Morton. *At Any Cost: Corporate Greed, Women, and the Dalkon Shield*. New York: Pantheon, 1985.

——, and Cohen, Jerry S. *America, Inc.* New York: Dial Press, 1971.

Mizruchi, Mark S. *The American Corporate Network*. Los Angeles: Sage, 1982.

Moore, Wilbert E. *The Conduct of the Corporation*. New York: Random House, 1962.

Morgan, Dan. *Merchants of Grain*. New York: Viking, 1979.

Munkirs, John R. *The Transformation of American Capitalism*. Armonk, N.Y.: M. E. Sharpe, 1985.

Nadel, Mark V. *Corporations and Political Accountability*. Lexington, Mass.: Heath, 1976.

Nader, Ralph, and Green, Mark. *Corporate Power in America*. New York: Grossman, 1973.

Nader, Ralph; Green, Mark; and Seligman, Joel. *Taming the Giant Corporation*. New York: Norton, 1976.

Neston, J. Fred, and Ornstein, Stanley, eds. *The Impact of Large Firms on the United States Economy*. Lexington, Mass.: Lexington Books, 1973.

Noble, David F. *America by Design*. New York: Knopf, 1977.

————. *Forces of Production*. New York: Knopf, 1984.

Novak, Michael, and Cooper, John W., eds. *The Corporation: A Theological Inquiry*. Washington, D.C.: American Enterprise Institute, 1981.

Nutter, G. W. *The Extent of Enterprise Monopoly in the United States, 1899–1939*. Chicago: University of Chicago Press, 1951.

Offe, Claus. *Disorganized Capitalism*. Cambridge: MIT Press, 1985.

Owen, Bruce M., and Breautigam, A. *The Regulation Game*. Cambridge, Mass.: Ballinger, 1978.

Papandreou, Andreas G. *Paternalistic Capitalism*. Minneapolis: University of Minnesota Press, 1972.

Penrose, Edith T. *The Theory of the Growth of the Firm*. New York: John Wiley, 1959.

Posner, Richard. *The Economics of Justice*. Cambridge: Harvard University Press, 1983.

Quinn, T. K. *Giant Business: Threat to Democracy*. New York: Exposition Press, 1953.

Reagan, Michael D. *The Managed Economy*. New York: Oxford University Press, 1963.

Reisman, W. Michael. *Folded Lies: Bribery, Crusades and Reforms*. New York: Free Press, 1979.

Rowen, Hobart. *The Free Enterprisers*. New York: Putnam, 1964.

Sampson, Anthony. *The Money Lenders*. London: Hodder & Stoughton, 1981.

————. *The Seven Sisters*. London: Hodder & Stoughton, 1975.

————. *The Sovereign State: The Secret History of ITT*. London: Hodder & Stoughton, 1973.

Samuels, Warren J., ed. *The Economy as a System of Power*. New Brunswick, N.J.: Transaction, 1979.

Sawyer, George. *Business and Society*. Boston: Houghton Mifflin, 1979.

Seth, S. *Up against the Corporate Wall*. 4th ed. Englewood Cliffs, N.J.: Prentice-Hall, 1982.

Shepherd, William G. *Industrial Market Structure and Economic Welfare*. New York: Random House, 1970.

————. *Public Enterprise*. Lexington, Mass.: Lexington Books, 1976.

Shonfield, Andrew. *Modern Capitalism*. New York: Oxford University Press, 1965.

Silk, Leonard, and Vogel, David. *Ethics and Profits*. New York: Simon & Schuster, 1976.

Smith, Bruce L. R., ed. *The New Political Economy*. London: Macmillan, 1975.

Sobel, Robert. *The Age of Giant Corporations*. Westport, Conn.: Greenwood Press, 1974.

————. *The Rise and Fall of Conglomerate Kings*. New York: Stein & Day, 1984.

Stone, Christopher D. *Where the Law Ends*. New York: Harper & Row, 1975.

Sutton, Francis X. *The American Business Creed*. New York: Schocken, 1972.

Tannenbaum, Frank. *The Balance of Power in Society*. New York: Macmillan, 1969.

Thorelli, Hans B. *The Federal Antitrust Policy*. Baltimore: Johns Hopkins Press, 1955.

Vernon, Raymond, ed. *Big Business and the State*. Cambridge: Harvard University Press, 1974.

Vogel, David. *Lobbying the Corporation*. New York: Basic Books, 1979.

Votaw, Dow. *Modern Corporations*. Englewood Cliffs, N.J.: Prentice-Hall, 1965.

Walker, Robert H. *The Age of Enterprise*. New York: Putnam, 1967.

Walton, Clarence. *Corporate Social Responsibilities*. Belmont, Calif.: Wadsworth, 1967.

Watson, Thomas, Jr. *A Business and Its Beliefs*. New York: McGraw-Hill, 1963.

Weinstein, James. *The Corporate Ideal in the Liberal State*. Boston: Beacon Press, 1968.

Wiebe, Robert H. *Businessmen and Reform*. Cambridge: Harvard University Press, 1962.

———. *The Opening of American Society*. New York: Knopf, 1984.

Wilcox, Clair, and Shepherd, William G. *Public Policies toward Business*. Homewood, Ill.: Irwin, 1975.

Wolfson, Nicholas. *The Modern Corporation*. New York: Free Press, 1984.

Wolin, Sheldon. *Politics and Vision*. Boston: Little, Brown, 1960.

Zinn, Howard. *A People's History of the United States*. New York: Harper & Row, 1980.

INDEX

ABOUT THE CONTRIBUTORS

WALTER ADAMS is Distinguished University Professor (Economics) and Past President, Michigan State University. He was a member of Attorney General Herbert Brownell's National Committee to Study the Antitrust Laws (1953–1955) and has appeared frequently as an expert witness before congressional committees on such public policy issues as mergers, monopoly, antitrust revision, import restraints, price discrimination, and deregulation. His books include *Monopoly in America* (Macmillan, 1955), *The Brain Drain* (Macmillan, 1968), *The Structure of American Industry* (Macmillan, 7th ed., 1986), and *The Bigness Complex* (Pantheon, 1986). His articles have appeared in the *American Economic Review*, *Quarterly Journal of Economics*, *California Law Review*, *Columbia Law Review*, and *Yale Law Journal*. He has served as visiting professor at the University of Grenoble, the University of Paris, the Salzburg Seminar (Austria), and the Falkenstein Seminar (Germany). He is an honorary faculty member of the Industrial College of the Armed Forces.

MICHAEL BARZELAY is Assistant Professor of Public Policy at the John F. Kennedy School of Government, Harvard University. His research and teaching interests are in the analysis, comparison, design, and management of politico-economic institutions and systems. He is the author of *The Politicized Market Economy: Alcohol in Brazil's Energy Strategy* (1986) and coauthor of "Is Capitalism Necessary? A Critique of the Neoclassical Economics of Organization" (*Journal of Economic Behavior and Organization*, 1986).

MARTIN BENJAMIN teaches philosophy at Michigan State University, where he specializes in ethics and social and political philosophy. His articles include "Can Moral Responsibility Be Collective and Nondistributive?" (*Social Theory and Practice*), and he is coeditor of *Ethics at the Onset of Life* (Blackwell, forthcoming). He is working on the relationships between compromise and integrity in ethics.

JAMES W. BROCK is Associate Professor of Economics at Miami University (Ohio). His professional interests are in public policy toward business in general, antitrust policy in particular, and the structure of U.S. industry. He is coauthor of *The Bigness Complex* (1986) and author of "The 'New Learning' and the Euthanasia of Antitrust" (*California Law Review*, 1986) and "The Automobile Industry," in Walter Adams, ed., *The Structure of American Industry* (7th ed., 1986).

DANIEL A. BRONSTEIN, a lawyer, is a Professor at Michigan State University, teaching environmental law in the College of Agriculture and Natural Resources, and Law, Medicine and Public Health in the College of Human Medicine. His primary research area is government regulation of toxic substances. He is currently revising and updating Bronstein and Engelberg, *Legal Regulation of Toxic Substances: Cases and Readings* (1984).

JOHN J. FLYNN is Hugh B. Brown Professor of Law at the University of Utah and teaches and writes in the fields of antitrust, regulated industries, corporations, constitutional law, and legal philosophy. He is a coauthor of *Free Enterprise and Economic Organizational Antitrust* (6th ed.) and a companion volume, *Government Regulation*. He is a frequent contributor to law reviews and authored the chapter "Corporate Democracy: Nice Work If You Can Get It" in *Corporate Power in America* (Nader and Green, eds., 1973). He has also served as Special Counsel to the U.S. Senate Judiciary Committee and its former Subcommittee on Antitrust when it was under the direction of the late Senator Philip Hart of Michigan.

MORTON J. HORWITZ is Charles Warren Professor of the History of American Law at Harvard Law School. His *Transformation of American Law, 1780–1860* won the Bancroft Prize in American History.

SAMUEL M. LOESCHER is Professor of Economics at Indiana University. He is interested in the institutional reform of systems of economic incentives that encourage price competition within oligopoly, decentralized spinoffs within conglomerate giantism, and enhanced productivity within absentee corporate ownership. His writing stretches from *Imperfect Collusion in the Cement Industry* (1959) to "Bureaucratic Measurement, Shuttling Stock Shares, and Shortened Time Horizon: Implications for Economic Growth" (*Quarterly Review of Economics and Business*, 1984).

WILLIAM A. LOVETT is Professor of Law and Economics at Tulane Law School. He received the A.B. from Wabash, the J.D. from New York University, and the Ph.D. from Michigan State University. He has been trial attorney in the Antitrust Division of the U.S. Department of Justice and staff economist at the Federal Trade Commission. He has worked in the fields of economic regulation, antitrust, labor, and law and economics. He is the author of *Inflation and Politics* (Lexington Books, 1982) and *Banking and Financial Institutions Law* (West, 1984).

DAVID DALE MARTIN is Professor of Business Economics and Public Policy at Indiana University and has served as Chief Economist of the Senate Judicial Subcommittee on Antitrust and Monopoly and as a consultant on antitrust issues to the Antitrust Division of the Department of Justice, the Federal Trade Commission, the Council of Economic Advisers, and private law firms. His publications include *Mergers and the Clayton Act* (University of California Press, 1959) and "The Role of Antitrust in the Industrial Policies of the United States," in *Policies for Industrial Growth in a Competitive World* (Joint Economic Committee, April 27, 1984).

ARTHUR S. MILLER is Professor Emeritus of Constitutional Law, The George Washington University. He is the author of *The Supreme Court and American Capitalism* (Free Press, 1968) and *The Modern Corporate State: Private Governments and the American Constitution* (Greenwood Press, 1976). His most recent book is *Politics, Democracy, and the Supreme Court* (Greenwood Press, 1985). He is a frequent contributor to legal and political science periodicals.

WARREN J. SAMUELS is Professor of Economics at Michigan State University, specializing in the history of economic thought, law and economics, and public utility regulation. He is the author of *The Classical Theory of Economic Policy* (1966) and editor of *The Chicago School of Political Economy* (1976) and the annual *Research in the History of Economic Thought and Methodology*. He is writing a book on the concept of the invisible hand.

MARTIN J. SKLAR teaches U.S. history at Bucknell University, where he is MacArthur Chair Associate Professor. He is the author of *The Corporate Reconstruction of American Capitalism, 1890–1916: The Market, the Law, and Politics* (Cambridge University Press, forthcoming), and, with Carl P. Parrini, "New Thinking about the Market, 1896–1916: Some American Economists on Investment and the Theory of Surplus Capital" (*Journal of Economic History*, 1983). He and Parrini are collaborating on a book on U.S. objectives in China from the 1890s through 1914. He has a long-term interest in liberalism, capitalism, socialism, and democracy in twentieth-century United States, on which he has published essays and articles.

ROGERS M. SMITH is Associate Professor of Political Science at Yale University and the author of *Liberalism and American Constitutional Law* (1985) and coauthor of *Citizenship without Consent* (with Peter H. Schuck, 1985). His chief research interests are in U.S. constitutional law and political thought, as well as contemporary legal and political philosophy. He is completing a general study of citizenship in U.S. public law and political theory.

AVIAM SOIFER teaches U.S. legal history, constitutional law, and federal courts at Boston University School of Law. He recently published "Confronting Deep Strictures: Robinson, Rickey, and Racism" (*Cardozo Law Review*, 1985). His scholar-in-residence address at the University of Colorado School of Law, "Truisms That Never Will Be True: The 10th Amendment Tested, the Spending Power Squared," will appear in that school's law review. He is working on a book on the intellectual and social history of the Thirteenth Amendment.